Discourse on Civility
and Barbarity

Discourse on Civility and Barbarity

A Critical History of Religion and Related Categories

TIMOTHY FITZGERALD

OXFORD

UNIVERSITY PRESS

2007

OXFORD
UNIVERSITY PRESS

Oxford University Press, Inc., publishes works that further
Oxford University's objective of excellence
in research, scholarship, and education.

Oxford   New York
Auckland   Cape Town   Dar es Salaam   Hong Kong   Karachi
Kuala Lumpur   Madrid   Melbourne   Mexico City   Nairobi
New Delhi   Shanghai   Taipei   Toronto

With offices in
Argentina   Austria   Brazil   Chile   Czech Republic   France   Greece
Guatemala   Hungary   Italy   Japan   Poland   Portugal   Singapore
South Korea   Switzerland   Thailand   Turkey   Ukraine   Vietnam

Published by Oxford University Press, Inc.
198 Madison Avenue, New York, New York 10016

www.oup.com

Oxford is a registered trademark of Oxford University Press

Library of Congress Cataloging-in-Publication Data
Fitzgerald, Timothy, 1947–
Discourse on civility and barbarity : a critical history of religion
and related categories / by Timothy Fitzgerald.
   p. cm.
Includes bibliographical references.
ISBN 978-0-19-530009-3
1. Religion—Philosophy. I. Title.
BL51.F54 2007
200.71—dc22   2007003034

9 8 7 6 5 4 3 2 1

Printed in the United States of America
on acid-free paper

In loving memory of my father, Walter Fitzgerald [Bond] (1896–1976), whose acting career on the English stage during a period of nearly fifty years witnessed many magical transformations in the sacred space of the theatre, and who engendered in me some intensity about what one should do or be

Acknowledgments

The argument of this book, which is interdisciplinary, was developed over a period of years in papers read at conferences, symposia, research seminars, and invited lectures in many universities in several different countries. These are too numerous to list, but my thanks are due to the many colleagues with whom I discussed and debated issues closely related to the ones that appear here. The research for the book, and some of its writing, was done mainly on the holidays, weekends, and evenings when it was possible to momentarily escape the concentration-busting obligations of administration, marketing, funding applications, committee meetings, retraining courses, student counselling, along with the teaching, writing, revising, and submitting of lecture courses. In my fifth year at the University of Stirling I was granted a one-semester spring sabbatical leave (2006) during which I was able to bring the written and unwritten parts of the book together into what I believe and hope is a coherent structure. My application to the Arts and Humanities Research Council of the United Kingdom (AHRC) for funding for a second semester sabbatical in the autumn of 2006 was turned down by the Philosophy, Theology, and Religious Studies panel, despite a signed contract with Oxford University Press and a 2007 publication deadline ultimately determined by another U.K. government agency, the Research Assessment Exercise (RAE). This AHRC decision affected the final outcome in various concrete ways, one of which was to reduce the time for proofreading and pruning, and I can only apologise for some badly formed sentences, inappropriate expressions, and irritating repetitions and hope they do not distract the reader too badly.

Another, perhaps more serious, consequence of the failure to win a second semester sabbatical was that the possibility of a last-ditch period of consultation on a final draft with specialists in history, political theory, and other relevant areas, who might have helped me avoid the kind of mistakes which interdisciplinary nonspecialists such as myself are almost bound to make, was eliminated. I would therefore beg some indulgence, particularly from specialists in sixteenth-, seventeenth-, and eighteenth-century English and American history and political theory, who may feel that their highly complex areas have not been treated with the degree of discernment that they deserve. I am not a historian and do not have any original new historiography to add. My purpose is parasitic on the work of historians, and in that sense I approach it with respect for their specialist knowledge of a specific historical period and what their findings can teach me about the changing usages of categories in historical time. I marvel at the erudition of the authors and editors of the works that I have relied on and have not been motivated by a critical attitude towards their historiographical expertise itself, which would be inappropriate. My concern is methodological; I am interested in the way that modern categories such as 'religion' and 'politics' are reproduced in the organization of our view of the past, such that they take on an appearance of permanence, as though essentially in the nature of things. The paradox is that historians, like anthropologists in the study of contemporary non-European cultures, are usually more aware than their critics of the dangers of projecting modern ways of thinking into those worlds that had or have different forms of thought and spoke (or speak) a different language. Yet even in the texts of highly knowledgeable and methodologically sophisticated writers, such projections create conflations of meaning which I have argued can only amount to misrepresentation. It is presumably an occupational hazard for historians to describe and analyze a previous historical era with the categories of the contemporary one, and the same point can be made for anthropologists and their representations of contemporary non-Anglophone cultures. I can only hope that at least some aspects of my argument, which attempts to bring together common problems of interpretation and translation in areas such as politics, history, cultural anthropology, sociology, travel writing, and religious studies, will have some positive resonance in those fields. I owe a huge debt of gratitude to my colleagues in the study of religion at Stirling, and more widely the School of Languages, Cultures, and Religions, who shouldered so much of the administrative burden during those final weeks by cutting managerial slack for me to meet my deadline. I should in particular mention my close colleagues Fiona Darroch, Andrew Hass, Alison Jasper, Andrew Ginger, and Richard Roberts, who went out of their way to be supportive in countless ways, despite having their own research commitments and often their own heavy administrative and teaching obligations. It was due to their generosity of spirit, and at personal cost to themselves, that my teaching obligations did not overwhelm my book-writing.

I also wish to thank the outstanding team at Oxford University Press, New York, especially Cynthia Read, Meechal Hoffman, and Stacey Hamilton, for their patience and support, and their dedicated professionalism. But for them I would not have been able to meet the deadlines determined by the U.K. government-sponsored agencies and their representatives. I owe a debt of gratitude to Minako Takahashi that can hardly be repaid. I also want to thank my friends and neighbours in Alloa, Jairo Lugo and Corinne Fowler, for their emotional and intellectual support during a time of personal crisis that coincided with the writing of the book. Finally, thanks to my beloved children, James Taro and Elizabeth Mari, for patiently putting up with their dad during times of great pressure and stress, and for not losing faith in me.

Front Cover Image

I want to thank my friend and colleague Jairo Lugo for first showing me an image of the Bull of Wall Street, the powerful sculpture by Arturo Di Modica. I would like to explain to the reader its significance for the argument in this book. This may not be immediately obvious. The major focus of this book is on the historical process whereby 'religion' and 'politics' or 'the state' came to be imagined as essentially separated domains having problematical relations. I am concerned with the way that a modern notion of politics has been rhetorically constructed as a secular, 'nonreligious' arena of rational action. I have argued that to invent such a seemingly self-evident discourse, it has been historically necessary to invent the dichotomous discourse on 'religion' and 'religions'. Politics, as finally separated from the domain of religion, is the natural as against the supernatural, the commonsensical as against the supersensible, the empirical as against the speculations of metaphysics. 'Politics' is paradigmatic of modern rationality, as compared to the obfuscations of earlier forms of religious and traditional irrationality.

However, integral to this story is the emergence of a second, closely connected domain of modern rationality, the 'economic'. 'Economics', in the form of an autonomous science or discipline, has developed as a virtual theology of liberal capitalism, which is represented rhetorically and theoretically as a fundamental and virtually self-evident human practice, obscured for centuries by irrational 'religious' prohibitions but now emerging as the ground of human self-realisation. From a transitional notion of 'political economy' in the eighteenth century, politics and economics have emerged as the uneasily overlapping domains of modern rationality. I have argued that only by inventing an illusory and separated arena of 'religion' and 'religions', so assiduously pump-primed by the modern religion industry, could the rhetorical construction of 'politics' and 'economics' have been made to seem like inescapable commonplaces, as if they are inscribed into the nature of things.

It is in such a context that Arturo Di Modica's superb sculpture can be seen as emblematic of one strand of my argument, which is that many of the characteristics assumed by common sense to belong to 'religion' are simultaneously at the basis of that other great class of illusory arenas, the 'secular'. The Bull perfectly represents capital as a force of nature, inscribed into the real order of the world. But more than merely a force of nature, the Bull is virtually a supernatural beast with its own volition. This powerful sculpture conveys to us a mystical power, the aggressive life force of the Bull market. The fetishistic nature of this ferocious Beast is illustrated in other pictures available on the Internet in which tourist pilgrims gingerly touch and stroke its magnificent surfaces, as though some extraordinary but potentially dangerous energy might emanate from it and liberate them in a spasm of self-realisation from the sin of poverty and the crippling disease of permanent indebtedness.

One could say that this masculine bovine divinity belongs in the same general category as a female deity I once researched, Mariai, an unmarried goddess who, if neglected, periodically strikes down the villagers with vomit and stomach cramps. However, her dangerous anger can, as a result of the appropriate sacrificial and redemptive disciplines, be auspiciously transformed for married yet barren women into the gift of fertility.

Yet in another sense the goddess of stomach cramps and the god of capital couldn't be more different. For this Wall Street Leviathan is no sacred cow grazing the pastures of agricultural hierarchies. Looked at from the back view, you can see he has bronze balls the size of mystic gongs, and you wouldn't want to be tossed, mauled, and trampled in this arena. The Beast of Capital can normally be placated through the performance of the appropriate ritual proprieties, but he will fork you on his horns if you waver in your faith.

The Bull is in some ways similar to the Leviathan of the modern Nation-State with whom he is uneasily twinned—witness the New York Stock Exchange draped in the national flag of the United States, a draping that tastefully conceals their squabbles of jurisdiction. The Leviathan of the Nation-State and the Great Bull of Capital were both generated by the same historical processes that gave us Enlightenment Reason. Worship of capital, disguised as a science of economics, is an example of what anthropologists and religionists used to call animism— belief in the independent autonomy of the products of the collective imagination.

Our collective belief in ultimate economic virtues like the value of money and the price of commodities is a circular, self-validating rhetorical construct that alienates us from our own productive power by seeming to stand above and over us as a god that controls our destiny. Should we at any time falter in our belief, we engender the perils of inflation, deflation, or stagflation or, worst of all, another Great Depression. Then we must turn to the prognostications of the gurus—professional economists and the managerial functionaries, the politicians, whose *religio* is, like all priests, prophets, and liturgists, ultimately inspired by blind faith in the necessary existence of their gods.

Contents

Discourse on Civility and Barbarity

I

Introduction

The argument in this book is that the formation of a distinct subject area within the humanities and social sciences known as
religious studies, and the accompanying reification of the category
'religion', has produced and continues to reinforce a one-sided and
distorted discourse that has repercussions beyond its own de-
limited area. The degree to which, for example, the 'history of religion'
has sealed itself from the history of political theory, and thus from
any serious discussion of the importance of the state in the modern
construction of 'religion', is a flaw in the field's conceptualisation.
This academic separation may also account for distortions in the
understanding of 'religion' from the point of view of political theorists, with consequent repercussions for their understanding of
the state too. My arguments here will be more tentative in terms of
the critique of political theory, because I was not trained in that
discipline, and my explorations of the relevant literature from that
discipline are consequently less confident. Nevertheless, I have
here attempted to offer an interdisciplinary discussion of the category 'religion' in order to suggest the theoretical confusions and historical inaccuracies upon which religious studies as a discipline
has been founded, and to argue in favour of a theoretical reconnec-
tion of the study of the state and those areas of life that are now
known as 'politics' with religious studies.

I am by no means the first or only voice to challenge the viability
of the category for valid description and analysis, and many arguments on the topic have been put forward by other writers. However,
despite this critically reflexive literature, there is considerable

evidence that misleading and even mystifying discourses on religion persist both in the academy and in wider rhetoric. The discipline of religious studies has been historically constructed around a highly unstable and contested category 'religion'; yet despite the historical struggles over its meaning within Christian history, religion has come to be researched and described as though it is a transparent notion, based on commonsense observable reality, universally applicable, a word and an idea which unproblematically translate into any language of any culture at any time in human history. This assumption about the category 'religion' was historically invented by a number of theorists who were not necessarily conscious that they belonged to an academic discipline called religious studies or the science of religion, though some of the nineteenth-century ones were. Clearly, the movement known as the phenomenology of religion (if movement is the correct word for a fairly loose category of thinkers), which derived its theoretical principles from Husserl (see Cox, 2006), has been a major contribution to the notion that religion is a field of study in its own right. On the other hand, nineteenth-century scholars such as Max Muller (*Introduction to the Science of Religion*, 1873) and C. P. Tiele (*Elements of the Science of Religion*, 1897) had already done much to formulate a science of religion (Molendijk & Pels, 1998); and less directly and self-consciously, and perhaps unintentionally, anthropologists, sociologists, and psychologists, such as E. B. Tylor, James Frazer, William James, Emile Durkheim, Max Weber, and others, had contributed to the formation of a discipline. Most important, whether or not they saw themselves primarily as students of 'religion', these intellectuals from theology, philosophy, anthropology, philology, and various other disciplines have been brought together into a distinctive collection of discourses by themselves or by other writers, many of these in the twentieth century, and are now considered the ancestors or founding fathers of a distinct discipline with a distinct object of study. Through this complex but historically traceable process, or combination of processes, a theorised notion of generic 'religion' as something that in principle exists in all cultures and languages in all historical times, and indeed in prehistorical times, is now well established and permeates the humanities and social sciences.

It can also be noted that many of these same theorists by and large have had no doubts about the universal validity and applicability of other generic modern categories such as the state, politics, and economics. This turns out to be a key point, for I shall argue that it is precisely through the exclusion and separation of these other modern categories that generic religion has appeared as a distinct and autonomous reality. This process of separation and reification seems to begin—if one is to avoid an infinite regression—in the seventeenth century, in the English language at least.

There are, of course, big variations in the way that religion is explained and defined by different theorists, some of whom would not even agree that religion can be explained or defined. What holds the majority of this recognisable body of theorists together is the assumption of the universality of religion. Religion is there, in the nature of human experience and practice, an autonomous and self-evident dimension of the world. However much scholars may argue about the best way to describe, explain, and define religion, the ubiquity of religion itself is not doubted. On the contrary, as I shall show in this book, these intellectual exercises have had the effect of further embedding the reality of 'religion' into common sense. Not only are there religions in the world, but they can be described, classified, analysed, and compared. Though there are many different views about the correct definition of religion, there is little doubt that 'religion' is an important fact in human history, and that any attempt to describe or analyse a culture or a period of history without recourse to it would be deficient, strange, and perhaps even unthinkable. Departments of cultural or social anthropology teach courses on the anthropology of religion, sociology has a well-established branch of the sociology of religion, and psychology and philosophy have their perspectives. This view of the universality of religion as a real dimension of human existence essentially separate from, though contingently connected to, other domains such as the state also is widely disseminated by historians, that is to say, historians who do not see themselves as belonging to religious studies as a discipline, but who are happy to use 'religion' and other basic modern categories such as politics and economics as though they are universally valid. To question such constructions will be widely resisted, not least because they seem to have self-evident validity as universally descriptive and analytical notions. Yet, as we will see, some historians are aware of the methodological fallacy of describing and analysing premodern societies in these modern terms; and some anthropologists are wary of using the term to interpret non-European forms of life. But they are a critical minority.

There are two different senses in which the idea of critical thinking can be used in relation to religion, or indeed in relation to any academic subject.[1] One notion of critical thinking is that one criticises others' definition of religion, or their explanation of religion in general, or their description of a particular religion, or their classification of a religious belief, or their interpretation of a religious practice. The second notion of critical thinking is that one questions the idea that there is such a thing as 'religion' in general, or 'a religion', to be defined, explained, or described, or that there is such a thing as a religious belief as distinct from any other kind of belief; or one questions the very idea of a practice that is 'religious' as distinct, for example, from an economic, aesthetic, or political practice. My aim in this book is the latter, and I approach it by retelling the story of the modern category of generic religion in a way that changes our view of it. In searching for the basis of this persistent idea of generic religion, I want to reconnect it with categories such as the state with which it has been imbricated for most of Christian and European history, and in so doing throw doubt on modern uncritical reifications of religion as something that exists in and for itself, as something autonomous and essentially distinct from 'politics'. Rather than write a study of religion as something which is only disputed in the details of its definition or description or explanation, but which as some kind of autonomous object of inquiry is unquestioned, I have written a critical history of 'religion' as a category, in the hope of showing that far from being a kind of thing or an objective and observable domain around which an industry of scholarship can flourish, religion is a modern invention which authorises and naturalises a form of Euro-American secular rationality. In turn, this supposed position of secular rationality constructs and authorises *its* 'other', religion and religions.

The critical questioning in this book of the category religion and the assumption that religious practices can be distinguished from nonreligious or secular practices has as one of its purposes the subversion of a number of other dichotomies. The separation of religion from secular politics has historically derived some of its rhetorical force from the strategic substitution of a number of other dichotomies, such as supernature and nature, spirit and matter, mind and body, male and female, rational and nonrational or irrational. By rhetorically reintegrating 'religion' with the state or with the politics of everyday life, much else could be transformed. For example, it should be possible to trace an embedding of dominant gender constructions through the agency of the mind-body distinction invented by Descartes and other philosophers of the seventeenth century (Gatens, 1997; Lloyd, 1990). But this dichotomy also forms a basis for the distinctions between fact and value and between scientific knowledge and 'faith'. Through the reification of the distinction between material nature (the object of scientific knowledge) and immaterial or spiritual supernature (the object of faith), we can see how the modern idea of 'religion' as a special realm of inner experience separated from the rationality of the public space (the secular state and politics) has been so important. These binaries reinforce each other, though not necessarily in any obvious alignments. It is not that there is a clear and logical set of equivalences, but that, as with myth, categories and their opposites float in and out of discourses in unpredictable ways which strengthen other dichotomies. Arguably, the construction of competitive capitalism and the idea of self-interested individuals depend also on these categories.

The first notion of critical thinking mentioned earlier concerns itself with disputing certain kinds of scholarly representations of religion, and presents evidence to show that religion itself should be explained in this or that way, or that a specific religion, or religious belief or practice, should be interpreted in one way rather than in some alternative way. However, that idea of the critical study of religion is not really critical at all, and its effect is to protect the idea of religion in the first place from genuinely critical inquiry. The existence of religion in general and religions in particular is not seriously questioned in such scholarly productivity. Instead such debates about 'the nature of religion' have the effect of embedding it even further into the nature of things. For how could there be so much knowledgeable disputation about something that does not exist? The secular academic study of religion is made plausible by these activities, such that the production of data in books and journals about religion and religions, or about religious beliefs and practices in this or that society, or the studies of the relation between religion and society or religion and economics, has as their most important function the maintenance and reproduction of a myth.

The critiques of religion pursued in this book, then, will set up 'religion' in relation to the articulation of a number of other categories. I will argue that the construction of modern discourses on generic religion has been made possible and conceivable by the parallel construction of a number of overlapping discourses on nonreligious/secular science, politics, the nation-state, economics, law, and education. My working hypothesis is that it is only by looking at categories in relation, rather than assuming their discrete functionality, that the field of religion can be adequately analysed. The success of such an enterprise must also necessarily involve a critique of a range of historiographies which uncritically reembed religion into the order of things.

For example, the distinguished Canadian historian of religion Michel Despland says near the start of one of his essays on the early formation of the science of religion in France between 1830 and 1848:

> I would like in this paper to look at institutionalization as a complex historical process, not as a state of affairs. Instead of asking how institutions acted on an interest in what we call 'the study of religion' and how such study found a niche in the academic structures built and funded by the modern State, I wish to look at the rise in France of a general public interest in the subject of 'religion'. How was religion as an object constructed? How did it become the object of methodical study? In other words, rather than look at what people wish to do about religion as they find it in their cultural scenery, I would like to direct the reader's attention to the very construction of the scenery, and to the demarcation in it of a specifically religious area in need of study. The furniture in people's homes is not just looked at—or rearranged; it is made by humans to start with. (Despland, 1998:32)

While this is an admirable theoretical goal, consistent with the second meaning of 'critical' suggested above and stated by one of the most rightly respected historians in the field, the actual analysis that follows seems to bear little relationship to it. This is because Despland fails to notice that the modern state is also part of the furniture, or perhaps is the house itself in his metaphor, and it has also had to be constructed. One might therefore ask how the construction of religion as an object made the construction of the nonreligious modern state conceivable. But this is ignored.

If one is interested in how 'religion' as an object of study has been constructed, then it becomes the critically sensitive term, and it makes no sense to then go on to use it in a taken-for-granted way as though it is obvious what one is talking about. Or, to extend Despland's own analogy, you cannot simply sit in the chair and consider its different possible positions in the room if you are taking it to pieces to see how it has been constructed in the first place. Yet throughout the essay that follows Despland's introduction, we find key problematic terms such as 'religion', 'politics', and 'secular' used as though they are simply good for sitting in. For example, discussing such men as Fontenelle, Voltaire, and Montesquieu, he says, "all were interested in the social impact of religious beliefs and in the interface between religion and politics" (1998:32). But we are not told what counted as 'religious beliefs' for them, how 'religion' got separated from 'politics' in the first place, nor what kind of ideas are being conveyed in the expressions "social impact" and "interface between." Can 'religious beliefs' have a 'social impact', as though they are on the outside coming in? And we need to know to what extent these thinkers, consciously or unconsciously, were actually constructing new meanings for these terms. And when Despland mentions in passing that their "interest in travel reports remained high," this suggests that travel writing played an important role in the process of the construction of 'religion' as an object in the minds of the *philosophes* and as an object of study in the academy. This immediately raises to the reader's mind the degree to which France and the French language had power over colonial subjects. But there is no analysis of how these ideas were put together, how they differed from previous usages, the role of the French language in the classification of the non-European world, and what wider developments would throw light on the process of construction in which we had thought Despland was interested.

Throughout the essay, the author makes uncritical assumptions that fly in the face of his stated aim:

> Silvestre de Sacy was a strict Catholic. Although he was a towering
> expert in Arabic and Persian, he showed no interest in Islam as a
> religion . . . he was among those who saw only superstition or heresy
> in cultures other than the Christian one. (Despland, 1998:33)

But why should he have thought of Islam as 'a religion'? This is not to say that Islam was never described as a religion at this time, or indeed much earlier, but that if such a description were employed, it would have been problematic. At the time, 'religion' usually meant Christian Truth for most Europeans, not only for Silvestre de Sacy; and the idea of 'religions' in the world is precisely the idea that we thought was to be historically deconstructed, so that we could see what was entailed by it, what meanings it had, how it differed from the older idea of religion and its opposition to 'barbaric superstitions' and 'perverse infidelities' such as Islam, and why it would be at this particular historical juncture that these processes of constructing new categories were occurring. Those of us with less knowledge of the French Enlightenment than Despland might be forgiven for thinking that for almost everyone at that time, including many of the enlightened *philosophes*, non-Europeans were ignorant savages who did not have 'religion'. For example, their contemporary Thomas Jefferson imagined many religions in the world; there are "probably a thousand different systems of religion" of which "ours is but one of that thousand" (*Notes on the State of Virginia*, 1787:267). On the other hand, the indigenous Americans, Jefferson's own colonial others, to whom he referred as "Indians," "Aborigines," and "Savages," did not have either civil government or religion (1787:150). They have "never submitted themselves to any laws, any coercive power, any shadow of government" (1787:150). Yet in 1613, one hundred and fifty years earlier than Jefferson, an English vicar called Samuel Purchas had not only referred to the 'religions' of India, China, Japan, the Americas, and many other parts of the world, but had attempted to describe and analyse them (see chapter 6). His usage, however, was ironic, since in his understanding 'religion' meant Christian (or more precisely Protestant Christian) Truth, and when applied to others the term 'religions' really meant its opposite, superstitions, and thus pagan and irrational misunderstandings. Yet arguably we can see a wobble in his text between irony and straightforward generic usage.

Despland, referring to a contemporary writer, Champillon, says of him that he was "interested in the religious documents which his skills enabled him to read, and unlike Silvestre de Sacy, his deism enabled him to accept the idea that the ancient Egyptians had a religion" (1998:33). One can accept that in a short article there are limits to what can be said and explained. The reader must accept some density of prose. But if the furniture is to be deconstructed, rather than simply sat in, we want to know what it was about deism that made the idea of Egyptian religion possible, and in turn what constructed deism?[2] Furthermore, is Despland saying that the documents in which Champillon had an interest were religious, or that his deism enabled him to accept the idea that they were 'religious'? This is not a small distinction.

This confusion about what a critical approach to religion entails is not harmless; it has consequences. The main consequence is, as I suggested before, that 'religion' gets reinscribed into common sense. The category is further embedded into the natural order of things. I am of course not talking here about a conscious and intentional conspiracy, which would be absurd for various obvious reasons, not least because no one would believe in it. But I am talking about an illusion or a myth—collective, powerful, and so widely disseminated that to deny it is represented as an act of bad faith.[3] Religion as a distinct and substantive reality in the world or as a universal and autonomous domain of human experience and action is a myth, or a rhetorical discursive formation, and I conclude that religious studies is an agency for uncritically formulating and legitimating this myth and embedding it into the warp and

woof of our collective consciousness—a modern ideological category transformed by ritual repetition such that it seems as though it is in the nature of
things. It is the modernist equivalent of spinning prayer wheels, from which a
whole cosmology of meaning and social order is generated.

But this critique of religion also has implications for other categories,
especially the modern idea of the 'secular' state, which has been constructed,
for example, by constitutions, by the naturalisation of politics and economics
as the ubiquitous domains of normal human rational behaviour, and through
academic practices which represent themselves as nonreligious and objective.
In this sense, I want to suggest that universities can be thought of more as
ritual institutions in the economy of contemporary affairs, something analogous to the monastic chanters of medieval times. The difference is that the
rituals performed in the humanities and social sciences faculties of modern
universities are generating the myth of the religion-secular distinction as objective knowledge achieved through disinterested rational procedures, whereas
biblical exegesis in medieval monasteries would have been considered illegit-
imate if divorced from a more general commitment to the truth of the Bible
in confessional practices such as prayer. Today the most obvious challenge to
these Euro-American categories comes from Islam; however, arguably, many if
not most non-European cultures do not think in terms of 'religion' and 'religions' as objects of comparative knowledge, and only began to do so through
the processes of colonial power, which generated the need for anticolonial
national movements to reformulate their own collective representations in
terms of the dominant Western paradigms.

As a consequence of the reification of religion, most religious studies
scholars and many historians, anthropologists and other specialists, assume
and write as though religion and the state have always been two essentially
different domains of human endeavour, having some problematic but *external*
relationship. For example, a historian of medieval England such as R. N.
Swanson (discussed later in this chapter) will tell the reader that church and
state had problematic relations with each other in the late medieval period, and
might even suggest that one cannot distinguish between church and state, at
least not in anything like the modern sense, and that we should therefore talk
in terms of the church-state. Yet the historian will continue to write as though
'church' was synonymous with 'religion', but 'state' (or 'society' or 'politics')
with 'secular', and thus misrepresent medieval thought and practice. This is
not only a factual error about the medieval use of words; it is also the way a
modern essentialised distinction between two autonomous domains is inadvertently employed to organise the description and analysis of a society in
which these terms had profoundly different semantic relations. The effect of
this is not only to confuse our understanding of what medieval life was like.
Perhaps more important, such usage embeds a notion that 'church' and 'religion', on the one hand, and 'state' and 'secular', on the other, are all terms

with essentially unchanging meanings, then and now, and that what changes historically is merely the articulation of their external relations.

The assumption found implicitly in these and other discourses is that these essentially separate domains have sometimes become confused at different periods of history, but now that we have arrived at a nonreligious scientific understanding of the world, we can step aside from religion's powerful hold as committed faith or as outmoded belief and look at it from a methodologically neutral standpoint. This is the academic equivalent of the 'end of history'. Though there may be a few loose ends to clean up, we have finally arrived at reality. We now 'do' history; or we now study 'religion'. They were unable to do so then because they hadn't yet understood that what they confused is really distinct.

This belief in our own neutral and thus more exact and objective vision does not necessarily imply lack of empathy for 'religion'. Though some of the writers who are regularly claimed as founding fathers of the study of 'religion', such as David Hume or Edward Tylor, were explicit about the irrationality of religion, others like C. P. Tiele were Christian (especially Protestant) believers, and yet others such as Herbert Spencer were 'agnostic'. Today, the dominant virtue is one of empathetic neutrality, which is supposed to mean that we can put to one side our own personal beliefs in order to be objective and impartial. And here the very powerful dominant notion that religion is essentially about personal belief in some unseen supernatural power separated from the public rationality of the secular objective standpoint of scholarship, by being implicitly or explicitly assumed, is actually being constructed. This in my view is the crucial issue. But it is disguised by a relatively secondary methodological issue about whether we are theists, atheists, or agnostics, itself a debate which appears to be as old as the hills but is modern in the sense that it presupposes a modern epistemology. The term 'agnostic' was actually coined by T. H. Huxley in the middle of the nineteenth century in the context of the religion-science debates and also reflects his interest in Kantian epistemology.[4] The question of 'belief' as it is set up in much discourse on 'religion' is a red herring. It distracts attention from the crucial point, which is the assumption, usually unstated, that in modern knowledge the essential difference between religion and the nonreligious domains of life has been finally understood, making neutral and objective sciences possible for the first time. Religion has been naturalised as an autonomous, generic reality and embedded into the order of existence.

It needs to be noticed that the constitutional separation of church and state is reflected in, and quite probably served by, the academic separation of the history of the state and political theory, on the one hand, and the history of religion, on the other. A rhetorical and constitutional invention of privatised, essentially nonpolitical 'religions' separated from the public rationality of the secular state, an idea early and clearly stated (in English at least) by late seventeenth-century rhetoricians, such as William Penn (founder of the state of Pennsylvania and writer of its first constitution) and John Locke (secretary of the Board of Trade and Plantations and with colonial interests in Carolina),[5] is being actively even if unconsciously promoted by two disciplines, the students of which rarely read each other's books or journals. That religious studies scholars conceive their field as autonomous and separated from the study of politics and the state can easily be seen by looking at the contents of standard textbooks, at the organisation of standard degree courses within religious studies departments, and at standard reading lists and bibliographies. Arguably the most fundamental historical discourses on 'religion' have at the same time been discourses on the state and issues of sovereignty, yet these rarely appear in courses and publications in religious studies. Religion is taught as though it is an autonomous and separate area of life, albeit one which at certain points comes into collision with 'society' or 'politics'. Much the same can be said about studies of 'politics' and the state, which almost completely ignore the publications of religious studies. We today have the situation where academic fields such as 'religion' and 'politics' have structured a disciplinary divide that reflects a highly contentious aspect of modern ideology and rhetoric. No wonder there is miscommunication between Western and Muslim scholars and politicians.

In his paper on the importance of the concept of 'civil religion' for theories of the state since the seventeenth century, Mark Goldie remarks critically on

> the enormous intellectual investment that political science has in the notion of the disjunction between the civil and the religious. Secularism remains as much a boast as a fact. To discover the moment at which politics became 'autonomous' and 'rational' is a constant endeavour for a profession still deeply imbued with the Enlightenment presumption that the maturity of the species consists in its ability to conduct civil life without recourse to superstition . . . . The positivist mode in the history of political thought eagerly searches the era of human adolescence, and rewards philosophers for signs of 'science', the 'modern', the 'secular'. Machiavelli . . . and Hobbes are the pre-eminent bearers of this celebration of the struggle of science to emerge from the embrace of theology. (Goldie, 1987:198)

It could be noticed here that while Goldie's ironic commentary on the pervasive assumption among political theorists that the discovery of secular civil life and politics is the sign of a more rational mentality, his comment also implicitly notes the discovery of 'secularism' in a more general sense as the ground which underlies the superior rationality of political science. The construction of the modern concept of politics as separated from religion is not the only superior characteristic of modernity over earlier intellectual adolescence; the possibility of a more rational political science also seems to be implied.

Goldie is here tacitly noting how the field of political science constructs and legitimates itself by reference to an autonomous and rational concept of politics and civil society freed from the superstitions of religion. One implication of this insight is that the ground of academic political theory, the rational secular, is precisely the same ground as the object of its analysis, modern politics. Whereas in past centuries religion and politics were confused, and thus theories of the state were permeated by irrational 'religious' elements, today both modern politics and the modern study of politics occupy the higher rationality of the secular.

This is mirrored in the case of the study of religion. Religious studies since the nineteenth century has self-consciously helped to construct the idea of a secular and rational ground from which these putative reifications 'religions' and 'world religions' could be objectively studied. It did this by drawing on seventeenth- and eighteenth-century movements of thought such as 'deism' that constructed 'natural religion'. This consisted of various attempts by Christian thinkers, or thinkers who were sceptical about the implications of an exclusive Christian revelation but thought of 'religion' in theistic terms, to find a universal basis for analogous beliefs derived from a colonial context. David Hume, certainly a sceptic and arguably an atheist (though see Noxon, 1968:361–83; see also Segal, 1994), was especially important in his attempt to construct some generic concept of religion and religions as a distinct object of rational description and explanation. It has been by the technique of inventing these reified domains as objects of study that a nonreligious domain, the secular, has become thinkable. What have come to be thought of as undeniable features of the world, religions, have historically made possible the embedding of the rational secular into our everyday assumptions about the nature of the world. We can only retrieve a critical grasp of this process by determinedly straddling the institutionalised divide between the different disciplines. We can then, I shall claim, see that the idea that religion and politics are essentially distinct domains of human life is a recent ideology, and that when viewed in this light the academic disciplines look less like 'objective sciences' and more like spinning prayer wheels.

I hope the purposes and methodologies of this book will become apparent to the reader fairly quickly as I proceed. There is a story, or grand narrative, or call it myth if you will, or part myth and part history, which gives the specific textual analyses to be found in this book their overall coherence. In very general terms, the story is about the development of modernity as a new all-embracing paradigm underpinned by 'secularisation', the privatisation of religion, individualism, and the rise of capitalism in the context of colonialism. Colonialism, I believe, is a fundamentally important part of the context for understanding the birth and legacy of the Enlightenment and Euro-America generally, and in particular the separation of religion and politics. In that sense, my take on this grand narrative is critical and postcolonialist, and would surely be compatible not only with Edward Said's thesis on Orientalism but also with the debates that his work has generated among other critical scholars (Breckenridge & Van der Veer, 1993; King, 1999; Macfie, 2000). In this sense, my approach to the grand narrative of the rise of Euro-American modernity is the opposite of the position ironically indicated by the political scientist Goldie in the earlier quotation: "The positivist mode in the history of political thought eagerly searches the era of human adolescence, and rewards philosophers for signs of 'science', the 'modern', the 'secular'" (Goldie, 1987:198). I am investigating the emergence of different discourses on science, the modern, and the secular, but with a view to challenging the essentialisation of these categories and the ideological role that academic departments and subject areas play in the representation of these constructs as though they are universal and 'in the nature of things'. Rather than taking for granted the grand narrative of the rise of a superior, triumphant, and scientifically rational Euro-America, and thereby tacitly endorsing the objectivity of our Anglophone categories in our descriptions of the world, my aim is to question them and thus to invite a reanalysis of the assumed objectivity of the disciplines.

In this sense, my position runs close to that of Richard Roberts and J. M. M. Good in *The Recovery of Rhetoric: Persuasive Discourse and Disciplinarity in the Human Sciences* (1993) when they argue:

> [R]hetoric has played a central part in the formation, development and legitimation of the emerging human sciences.... If we are to understand the present-day classifications and hierarchies of the various disciplines in the human sciences, then it is essential to understand their rhetorical constitution. (1993:4)

The argument of this book is very much concerned with "the processes by which disciplines establish themselves and assert their credibility through the generation of 'commonplaces'" and the way in which "the discourses and practices of the human sciences both enact and *conceal* the persuasive strategies essential to the establishment of knowledge about the human world" (Roberts & Good, 1993:1–2; my italics). The discourses on religion and religions are inseparable from discourses on politics and the state, for example, yet religion as a category and religious studies as a discipline thrive by suppressing these connections from view and making them appear merely external. But the same could be said about political theory, so long as it imagines itself as a discipline essentially separated from discourses on religion, which are represented as having only a contingent and nonessential relationship to 'politics'. Roberts and Good encapsulate this point when they say, "Whilst rhetoric is essential to the constitution of disciplines in the human sciences it also tends to foster a false sense of disciplinary self-sufficiency" (1993:9). By recovering discourses on religion, the state, and other connected categories, I hope to show how the rhetorical constructions of individual writers, official representations, constitutions, and other forms of discourse have not only constituted the modern field of religious studies but also have concealed those rhetorical constructions by a form of language that inscribes religions as objective realities or aspects of all human societies at all times.

Inevitably though, I am entangled in this narrative, or in some of its tropes, and one problem of any such attempt at a critical deconstruction is that the writer inadvertently reconstructs the story that is being questioned. I am like Lévi-Strauss's *bricoleur*, who employs the bits and pieces of our discourses, the bric-a-brac of our common story telling, to put together my own version of a rhetorical machine, and use it for my own purposes. I am after all hoping to persuade the reader that we need a different standpoint from which to view our own conceptual productions in a dangerously volatile world in which material satisfaction through processes of globalisation and consumerism can only be challenged by non-Western forms of life such as Islam. It is the story of the modern invention of 'religion' and 'religions' and the globalisation of these concepts through the processes of colonial and neocolonial domination of the world by Euro-American values of economic rationality, materialism, and consumerism.

It seems to be generally accepted by historians that a major shift of paradigm, already inscribed into our own ideology by countless other writers, indeed took place during the seventeenth century in the period often referred to as the Enlightenment. The earlier historical roots of this paradigm shift are usually believed to have occurred as a result of such historical contingencies as greater contact with more technologically advanced Muslim cultures, the Renaissance rediscovery of classical philosophy and science, and the challenge posed by the Reformation to the authority of the Catholic Church, which upheld the older paradigm of Christian civility. More recently, most critically alert scholars would be well aware of the importance in this story of colonialism, slavery, and the invention by Scottish Enlightenment thinkers of modern economics. Today, liberal economists seem to take it as a given fact that markets and rational, self-interested individuals are natural rather than ideological, and that modern liberal capitalist democracies represent a final evolutionary emergence of rational humanity from its mystified past. And Marxists might agree that this shift of paradigm was required for, or at least made possible, the development of new means and relations of production, the development of the empirical sciences, capitalism (and hence colonialism), a new concept of the nation-state and thus of collective identity, the development of a language of democracy and human rights and thus the sanctification of the individual, and the development of the ideal of the secular state and civil society.

I want to show the important role that the conceptual separation of 'religion' and 'politics', along with various other examples such as 'religion' and 'society' or 'religion' and 'economics', has had in the creation of this modern ideological configuration. Or, to put it more stringently and therefore more accurately, rather than claiming that religion and politics became separated, as though they were essentially separate but confused domains, I will attempt to show how they were both invented as part of the same rhetorical movement, and that their imagined separation has made possible many other basic features of the modern landscape. One of the implications of this view is that a major historical rift in the way Europeans represent themselves and the world makes it difficult for us to imagine a premodern world, such that developing a historical *imaginaire*[6] appropriate for late medieval or early modern Europe is analogous to the problems for anthropologists of entering the world of non-European cultures.

When I use the expression 'premodern world', I do not wish to imply any value judgment about relatively greater or lesser degrees of rationality. After all, it is perfectly conceivable that the American philosopher Whitehead was right when he argued that Western philosophy has consisted of a series of footnotes to Plato (Whitehead, 1979:39), or that the literary critic Harold Bloom was right to claim that anything interesting in Freudian psychology was already more effectively expressed and comprehended in Shakespeare (Bloom, 1994). In both cases, greater understanding is being attributed to an earlier age; rather than assuming that our paradigms of knowledge and rationality are the result of progress, these positions imply that we can only unpack what others have already known. I am not claiming that these specific claims are necessarily correct, only that these are examples that go against the assumptions of inevitable progress in understanding. My own methodological assumption is neither that the past is more rational than the present, nor that the past is less rational than the present, but that the past is different and 'other'. An imaginative grasp of the past's otherness allows us to see that what we today assume as given in the nature of things is actually a rhetorical construction. This in turn reflects my understanding of the postcolonial position, which is that the categories of the Enlightenment, in this case particularly 'religion' and what it helps to construct as 'secular politics' and the nonreligious state, have lost their rhetorical validity or persuasiveness, and that they now confuse rather than clarify meanings.

This book is concerned with the changes of meaning of a number of connected English-language categories, focuses on the way the major shift at the level of Anglophone rhetoric and ideology since the late seventeenth century has come to appear to be in the nature of things, such that highly contentious notions like religion, politics, the secular, and economics have taken on the appearance of inescapability, of inevitable ways of describing and analysing our collective realities. To refer back to Roberts and Good, rhetoric not only constructs fields of discourse but conceals their origins, and thus inscribes them into an unalterable essentialisation. These categories still inform the structures of the academy in significant ways. This structure has become a myth that distorts our perceptions of the world, and consequently it needs to be challenged.

Let me indicate some of the problems in understanding the meaning of terms such as religion and the state. The historian R. W. Southern, in *Western Society and the Church in the Middle Ages* (1970), clearly wishes—despite the implications of separation in his title—to stress that Religion, meaning Christian Truth, encompassed both church and state and the whole of what we today call 'society' when he says:

> [T]he medieval church was a state. It had all the apparatus of the state: laws and law courts, taxes and tax-collectors, a great adminis-trative machine, power of life and death over the citizens of Chris-tendom and their enemies within and without. (1970:18)

> When we speak of a church-state ... we say too much, for the church was weak in the means of coercion .... But in another sense it was much more than a state. In the first place it was not, and could never be simply, *a* state among many: it had to be *the* state or none at all. As soon as there were other states similarly equipped to rule, the church was on its way to becoming a voluntary association for religious purposes. Until this happened, there were several ways in which the unique state-like character of the church could be con-ceived. It could be envisaged as a universal society directed by a Christian Emperor, or by the pope, or by the two of them together, or by the Christian community as a whole. All these are medieval ideas, but undoubtedly the idea that came nearest to practical success ... is the theory of papal monarchy.... though men differed about the instruments to be employed, they all agreed that a universal coercive power resided in the church. Whether in the hands of pope, emperor, king or community, the purpose of human government was to direct men into a single Christian path .... In directing men along this road the church was the sole legitimate source of coercive power. (1970:21–22)

> But of course the church was much more than the source of coer-cive power. It was not just a government .... It was the whole of human society subject to the will of God. It was the ark of salvation in a sea of destruction. How far there could be any rational social order outside the ark of the church was a disputed question, but at the best it could only be very limited. It was membership of the church that gave men a thoroughly intelligible purpose and place in God's universe. So the church was not only *a* state, but *the* state; it was not only *a* society but *the* society—the human *societas perfecta*. Not only all political activity, but all learning and thought were functions of the church. (1970:22)

This is what I shall refer to as a discourse on encompassing Religion in this book. More strictly, it is a discourse about a discourse, a rhetorical construction of a past by someone who has been able to deeply appropriate the historical discourses and thus translate them into our contemporary language. Religion means Christian Truth,[7] and it is Truth that is supervised by the power of the church and that encompasses what we have today separated out as secular politics. One of the many implications of this situation is that relationships between terms whose meanings we take for granted and project onto the world, such as natural and supernatural, or religious and secular, or church and state, do not have any clear and easy semantic continuity even in English history.

Several years after Southern published his book, another distinguished medieval historian, R. N. Swanson, published *Church and Society in Late Medieval England* (1989). Again we have in the title the same separation of church and society which can be found in Southern's. However, I want to show that, compared to Southern's discourse on a medieval discourse, Swanson's is far looser and less exacting, because it is less guarded against the dangers of projecting back our own meanings of these terms, and thus tends to invite a modern dichotomy between religion and the nonreligious/secular as though the late medieval *imaginaire* is essentially the same as the one we inhabit, and different only in its secondary qualities, a rearrangement of the furniture. Throughout, there is ambiguity of language, such that the author seems both to want to use modern terminology to convey a similar distinction, while also from time to time urging the reader to understand that things were not really like that. For example, the title of chapter 3, "The Church and the Political Order," does not successfully exemplify or synchronise with this important point, but rather tends to confuse it. The confusion arises from recycling the problematic terms as though they are useful analytical and descriptive categories at the very moment that one is attempting to problematise them. The title of the chapter (like the title of the book) separates them in order to join them with the conjunction 'and'. In his interesting description of the fourteenth-century "divine ordination of government" established by the coronation ceremony (1989:95–96), Swanson says, "The ceremony was essentially religious—after all it was inserted into the Mass—but it also produced a fervent political statement, summarizing the theoretical relations between king and God, king and church, king and people" (96). This sentence and others like it identify 'religion' with 'the Mass' and the church, and 'politics' or the 'political order' with the king and his rule of the people. This reading is reinforced in other examples:

> The religious sanction to the political order was highly ambiguous in theory and practice. Religion, or the church, intervened not merely figuratively or theoretically, but to practical effect. Religious asso-

ciations could glorify the crown, or justify a rebellion. (Swanson, 1989:99)

Again, 'the religious' is associated with the church; in contrast the Crown is tacitly associated with the political order, and rebellion as a (political) challenge to it. Section 3-2 of the same chapter is titled "The Church in the State" (103), which heralds a different kind of relationship—not church *and* state but church *in* state—and contains ambiguous statements such as "it was only natural that the church and its personnel should be firmly integrated in the political structure." But how are we supposed to read "firmly integrated into" here?[8]

Yet in the preface, Swanson apologises for the implication in his title that church and society were two different things in the thinking of the medieval period, and he lucidly expresses and emphasises the point that "the church *was* society" (1989:ix; my italics). Perhaps Swanson was writing the preface as a result of rereading his text and regretting some of his ambiguous or even contradictory uses of language. On the other hand, he still published the book. It is difficult to know how his students could get a clear sense of the medieval polity. Terms such as church, religion, state, politics, and secular frequently follow the semantic contours of the modern discourse of religion and politics as essentially separated but coming into problematic relationship with each other; but then at other times he says or implies that the relationship was significantly different.

It is anyhow questionable whether the English word 'politics' or the expression 'the state' even existed at this time. Quentin Skinner holds that Bodin in *The Six Books of the Commonwealth* (1576) was the first to conceive of the state as an abstraction separated from the person of the sovereign prince (Skinner, 1978:352–53). I will argue in chapter 5 that to achieve this change in the nuance of 'the state', it would be reasonable to suppose that the meaning of 'religion' was also in process of transformation, because their semantic fields were linked in specific ways. But in Skinner's text we do not know from his translation of Bodin what the nuance of 'matters of religion' should be taken to be. Skinner's own use of words such as religion, religions, secular, politics, and political seems uncritical and confusing in some sections of the same work (see also Skinner, 1978:248).

The historian John Bossy has pointed out how, between the sixteenth and eighteenth centuries, words such as communion, charity, conversation, friend, penance, property, the state, society, and religion all quite radically changed in nuance, such that

[w]e are surely bound to try to envisage such individual migrations as instances of a larger process: as, for example, symptoms of Foucault's archaeological shift in the ways of the mind, or of what has been called the process of civilization. (Bossy, 1985:167–71)

On this logic, how then can we grasp the changed meanings of the English words 'state' or 'politics' without knowing how the nuance of 'religion' and 'religions' was also changing? This becomes clearer when we look at the process in the formation of the eighteenth-century American charters, bills of rights, and constitutions, where arguably the most powerful institutionalisation of these changes became fixed in writing and law. While the meanings of the First Amendment and Article VI of the U.S. Constitution are debated and contested, I will argue in chapter 9 that these debates would make no sense if there had not already developed historically a conceptual separation between what is 'religious' and what is not religious, a distinction which cannot be assumed ahistorically as an eternal feature Christian Europe, and certainly not of all cultures everywhere.

Though the ideological unity of Christendom was seriously undermined by the Protestant Reformation and the very early beginnings of the independent nation-state, a holistic and hierarchical vision of the order of things was deeply embedded in the collective consciousness of the male elite in England well into the eighteenth century. The idea of the commonweal as God's order on earth was hegemonic, even though its hierarchical features were challenged by levelling dissident groups. The commonweal was thought of on analogy with the body. Just as the proper functioning of each limb is necessary for the healthy body, so analogously each status and degree implied the dutiful performance of services and functions appropriate to one's station in life. All vocations or God-given duties were ultimately to be performed as services to God. To us today, this view may look retrospectively like a mask for inequality and the legitimation of power. But perhaps to many people in England and other parts of Europe at the time it seemed as natural and commonsensical (what, in *The Recovery of Rhetoric*, Roberts and Good indicate by the term "commonplaces") as capitalist markets, globalisation, and selfish individualism seem to us now.

The hierarchical model of human existence was also explicitly patriarchal. Filmer, for example, argued in *Patriarcha* (1991 [1680?]) that it was virtually self-evident that the father is the lord of the family, just as the prince is the lord of the realm, and God is the Lord of the universe. This was another way of affirming the commonweal and also the divine right of kings.

It was against this holistic vision that John Locke, in *A Letter concerning Toleration* (1689), sought to persuade his readers that we should think differently. His ideas about the world, about knowledge, rationality, and civility, seem radically and fundamentally different:

> I esteem it above all things necessary to distinguish exactly the
> Business of Civil Government from that of Religion, and to settle the
> just Bounds that lie between the one and the other. If this be not

done, there can be no end put to the Controversies that will be always
arising, between those that have, or at least pretend to have, on
the one side, a Concernment for the Interest of Mens Souls, and on
the other side, a Care of the Commonwealth. (Locke, 1689:8)

The Commonwealth seems to me to be a Society of Men constituted
only for the procuring, preserving, and advancing of their own *Civil
Interests. Civil Interests* I call Life, Liberty, Health, and Indolency of
Body; and the possession of outward things, such as Money, Lands,
Houses, Furniture, and the like. (9)

The duty of the civil magistrate "by the impartial Execution of equal Laws"
is to defend through the fear of punishment and the possession of force the
civil interests of his subjects. It seems clear to Locke that "the whole Jurisdiction of the Magistrate reaches only to these civil Concernments... and
that it neither can nor ought in any manner to be extended to the Salvation of
Souls" (1689:9). He gives a number of reasons for this. The second one is "The
care of Souls cannot belong to the Civil Magistrate because his power consists
only in outward force: But true and saving Religion consists in the inward
persuasion of the Mind, without which nothing can be acceptable to God"
(1689:10).

Are we to suppose that Bodin was already articulating this clear distinction
between two essentially different domains, privatised religion and 'outward'
politics, in the sixteenth century? Or should we make the rather different claim
that Bodin was an important forerunner of what only really becomes explicit
in the seventeenth-century context? It has been argued that there is another
reading of Locke, and that he had a concept of 'civil religion' which derived
from the Lutheran idea of the state and which has been exemplified in various
theories of the state by such writers as Harrington, Hobbes, and Hegel:

> The concept of the Christian Prince, whether in the form of the
> Divine Right of Kings, or translated into the corporate body of the
> republic, was integral to the development of the idea of the self-
> sufficiency of the secular commonwealth. The considerable stress in
> modern scholarship of the emergence of the rights of private reli-
> gious experience and of toleration in the Reformed tradition obscures
> the degree to which Reformed thought remains Erastian, and con-
> tinued to be a theory about the civil state's embodiment of 'true
> religion'. (Goldie, 1987:201)

It seems to me that there may not be an essentially correct reading of
Locke, since he was himself struggling to give expression to new ideas in the
context in which he found himself, one that included Dissent and colonial
interests, and we have to pay attention to the ways in which others have found

it possible to read his work. The quotations given above at least make it likely that he and Penn both had a significant influence on American constitutionalism. The important point to notice in my view is that it is not only 'religion' which has been redefined as a purely private matter; the meanings of 'civil' and 'commonwealth' are also being transformed in Locke's rhetoric. Locke's purpose seems to be to subvert the dominant and orthodox understanding of civil government as a *relatively* distinct branch of God's providence within the overall encompassment of Christian Truth, and to persuade his readers to imagine it as different *in kind*, that is, as *essentially* different, as a different ontology. His ability to persuade his readers depended on there already existing a class of literate men, most of them Dissenters and many of them gentry and nobility, many with trade interests reflecting the growth of markets internally and externally in plantations and colonies. The religion-civil society dichotomy has here been essentialised, the civil being essentially public and outward, on analogy with the body, and religion being essentially private and inward, on analogy with the mind. But this analogy both presupposes and reinforces a mind-body dualism which was itself a new philosophical formulation owing much to Descartes. And this dualism in turn presupposes new epistemologies and concepts of rationality, either Cartesian or the kind of empiricism advocated by Locke. One makes an "inward judgement" about Truth and salvation, and on such matters one cannot be compelled to believe by outward force. There is this assumption of the inner mind as distinct from the outer body, Religion being aligned with the inner working of the mind, and civil society with the outer, the body: "the Magistrate's power extends not to the establishing of any Articles of Faith, or Forms of Worship, by the force of his Laws" (Locke, 1689:11).

Religion is confined to the salvation of the soul. That is its essential definition. Religion has been rhetorically privatised and religious associations such as churches are merely voluntary organisations and have nothing essentially to do with the state or civil society. Religion has also been disassociated from 'force' or power, which is now the province of the magistrate alone. But it is just as important to notice that the concepts of civil society and political authority have changed. A reader who only follows the term 'religion' will miss the significant connection between the changes in the meaning of 'religion' and in those other terms which help to define it. Note, for example, that the above distinction equates the 'commonwealth' with 'civil government' and distinguishes it from Religion. Yet the English term commonweal or commonwealth was a formulation of the great chain of being, the universal hierarchical structure which invested God's purpose in every condition and degree. The commonweal was Religion seen from the point of view of what we moderns call the social order. Religion and social order were not separated. Locke is redefining the meanings of the commonwealth, of civil society, and of politics as *neutral* with regard to religion and therefore as nonreligious.

I do not wish to claim that in other writings of Locke the distinction be-tween private, nonpolitical religion and the public, nonreligious civil society is necessarily as clearly expressed as it is here. Locke, along with other writers, was attempting to conceive of this distinction partly as a result of the problems of Dissent and nonconformity, and so there is almost bound to be ambiguity. This same point applies to those who might have wished to interpret Locke to suit their own agendas by emphasising different aspects of his thought. What I think it would be difficult to deny is that, despite continual ambiguity about where the line should be drawn, this imagined distinction became im-portant for the whole church-state controversy, and it has been incorporated into the written or unwritten constitutions of modernity. The problem today, as I see it, derives from this radical redescription of the meaning, not only of religion, but of the commonwealth and the civil authority. For now the dom-inant trope is not Religion as encompassing Christian Truth; it concerns re-ligion as it stands in various binary oppositions: religion and the state, religion and politics, religion and economics, religion and civil society, and religion and science. These binary oppositions are fundamental to the modern construction of discourses on 'religion'. Of course, the definitions of all these domains are highly contested, yet in the ease with which these terms are used there lies a tacit assumption that we all know what they mean even if we can't quite define them exactly. My argument will be that none of these categories has fixed meanings and that they are fundamentally rhetorical and strategic. Yet un-derlying all these binaries there is one fundamental binary, which can be re-ferred to as the religion-secular[9] dichotomy, but which is at its most basic a distinction between religion and nonreligion. I will try to justify this in the chapters that follow by arguing that it is virtually impossible to understand many texts without this implicit or explicit conceptual separation.

The usage of 'religions' in the plural as an apparently objective, neutral, descriptive term for other people's beliefs and practices became systematically institutionalised in the nineteenth century with the development of the so-called science of religion and comparative religion. However, some of the most influential founders of this so-called science, such as Max Muller and C. P. Tiele (1890), were not so far from being liberal Protestant theologians. And some of these ancestral spirits to our secular field were still reproducing the discourse of barbarians, savages, and primitive prelogical mentalities, even while they were claiming to be neutral and objective.[10]

The historical perspective, when categories are properly contextualised, suggests that the idea that we can study 'religion' as though it is only exter-nally and contingently connected to those spheres of human activity such as politics and economics, which we imagine as nonreligious, is an illusion which our academic practices sustain and authorise. But the binaries are not merely static structural oppositions, but dynamic in the service of the legiti-mation of a hegemonic world construction.

The nonreligious sometimes takes the form of a positive commitment to a moral view of the world, as in some forms of humanism which construct 'religion' in a specific way and then declare themselves to be 'nonreligious' in opposition to that view. (On the other hand, of course, some humanists construct themselves as religious humanists, and humanism is sometimes described as a religion or as a pseudoreligion.) But the nonreligious standpoint, for example that of the U.S. Constitution, the modern nation-state, or the state education system, is more generally thought of as a position of neutrality and objectivity characteristic of 'modern' rational societies as distinguished tacitly from traditional irrational (religious or mythical) ones.

Behind this binary opposition (as argued earlier) lies a series of other oppositions, such as nature and supernature, reason and faith, this world and the other world, the material and the spiritual, the inner and the outer, mind and matter, male and female, which constantly displace each other in a never-ending deferral of meaning. None of these pairs of terms has an essential or even uncontested meaning and yet the way they have been set up tends to disguise the degree to which the boundaries between them are porous and constantly shifting. This flexibility gives them their power in the service of interests which can remain largely hidden. By essentialising and marginalising 'religion' as 'spiritual' and therefore as something distinct and separate from these other fields, such as 'society' or 'politics' or the natural material world, the idea of the 'nonreligious' becomes possible, and I argue in this book that both sides of this dichotomy are parasitic on each other. The assumption, prevalent throughout the humanities, that the referent of religion is intuitively obvious even though we may have a problem defining it, hides the sense in which the category makes possible the discourses on other, nonreligious domains such as politics, economics, and the state. Without paying attention to these binary oppositions, we cannot understand how 'religion' operates to construct what we now experience as the natural, the matter of fact, the common sense in modern rhetoric.

One of the implications of this approach is that 'religion' and other categories are not neutral descriptive and analytical terms but are on the contrary prescriptive and normative. They are rhetorical constructions, but they are widely used as though they are objective and factual, and thus conceal their own origins. Despite the appearance of common sense, a term such as 'religion' does not tell us what is in the world, but what we collectively think ought to be in the world. It is a classificatory device, a function of Euro-American world making, but it has acquired an appearance of being immutably in the nature of things. I wish to draw the reader's attention to the way our uncritical academic practices embed these categorical structures into the nature of things and render them difficult to see for what they are: collective affirmations about what kind of world we want to experience. Our incessant activity in the description and analysis of world religions could perhaps be imagined as a mirror image of those ritual performances that, as colonial masters, we have represented in ethnography: the irrational practices of natives in their world making. And just as ritual specialists in non-European cultures are held to be advertently or inadvertently embedding and legitimating gender and status inequalities, and rendering hierarchical distribution systems into immutable laws, historical evidence suggests that specific interests and classes in Euro-America have been served by this persuasive language.

This poses a considerable dilemma because in order to get a critical hold on the term 'religion' and its supposedly 'nonreligious' binaries, we need to find some different terminology, words which have *relatively* stable meanings and which provide at least a temporary ground from which to view our own more ideologically weighted discourses. We may be trapped in our own language games, but we can strategically deploy alternative conceptualisations which shift our perception of ourselves and render insights into the human heart. It is in this context that I hope that discourses on civility and barbarity, from Aristotle to George W. Bush's 'failed states' and 'axis of evil', may help us to view the language games of religion from a different perspective. I have also proposed in chapter 3 a different view of the sacred-profane distinction in this light.

It seems obvious that, historically, the whole semantic context for the one word 'religion' has changed significantly, and yet the illusion is created that religion is always here, and indeed always there. Though the change of historical context is well known, it is known in the sense that we know there is an elephant in the room but cannot see it. The discourse on religion and religions, or 'faiths' and 'spiritualities', institutionalised in universities and schools as religious studies (the secular study of religions), is an extension of this rhetoric, and constitutes a further embedding of the notion that these categories are not acts of rhetorical persuasion but are in the nature of things.

The only way we can see the implications of these historical changes is to take cognizance of the connections *between* categories, since they do not operate in isolation nor as singular entities, but in networks or in what Louis Dumont called 'configurations' (1986:11).[11] Though the history of the emergence of modernity is well known through the writings of historians, the changing ideological functions of 'religion' as a category in relation to the emergence of 'politics' and 'economics' conceived as separate domains tends to get buried from view. There are countless studies of the relation between religion and capitalism, or religion and society, or religion and science, or religion and politics. But these are not studies of the formation and function of categories in rhetorical discursive constructions. They are studies between something called religion and something called society, or something called politics. Today, it is widely assumed that religion and religions are and have existed universally at all times and in all places. That is to say, they are a constituent of human nature and in the order of things. As such they can be studied as special objects of scientific investigation. But my point is that this set of assumptions *is* modernity. The categories 'religion' and 'religions', which are being constantly regenerated by the subject area of religious studies, are an important constituent part of modernity. The ideology of religious studies defines both modernity and colonial consciousness. We are not studying what exists in the world, but by reproducing religion and religions we are tacitly reproducing the whole rhetorical configuration.

One feature of the naturalisation of religion, and its embeddedness in the ordinary assumptions of every day life, is the comfortable, uncritically assumed normality of the neutral, rational, natural, nonreligious, secular voice that makes authoritative statements about religion. Academics, politicians, and educators gain their professional credentials through the cultivation of this voice. An example of the latter is Joyce Miller, who is chair of the Association of Religious Education Inspectors, Advisors and Consultants in the United Kingdom. In a short article called "Let's Talk about Religion and Keep Teaching It," published in *The Edge*, the magazine published by the Economic and Social Research Council (ESRC), she says:

> The view taken by education law makers has been unequivocal:
> religion matters and pupils need to learn about them [*sic*] (and from
> them). For the first time, in 1988, the law required pupils to learn
> about the principal faiths in Britain, and common educational prac-
> tice since then has included teaching about the world's six major
> faiths.... Religion is in the world, it is a formative influence in every
> society, found in every culture in human history. (*The Edge* 22, July
> 2006, http://www.esrcsocietytoday.ac.uk/ESRCInfoCentre/about/
> CI/CP/the_edge/issue22/)

The elements of recycled discourse in Miller's short article to which I wish to draw attention are the following: (a) the simultaneous distinction between "religion" ("religion matters," "[r]eligion is in the world") and "religions" ("the world's six major faiths"). What is the relationship between religion in general and the individual world religions to which she claims to refer? (b) The reification of religions and world faiths as things that exist in the world, which follows from point (a), a relationship which appears to be incarnational, that is, that religions appear as incarnations of religion itself, most potently suggested by the expressions "religion is in the world," and it "is found in every culture throughout human history." The assumption that 'religion', which nobody has ever actually observed, is an existing ideal object, perhaps a Platonic Form, is a vast claim for an invisible essence that manifests itself in a variety of different cultural symbolic representations. And (c) the unexamined assumption that our English-language word 'religion' is instantly and obviously translatable into all the languages of the world, an assumption that seems to be entailed by the grandiose claim that religion is found in every culture in human history. How could anybody know this?

There are several tropes which the author deploys in this short piece which are part of a discourse on religion and world religions widely disseminated in the United Kingdom by the SHAP working party on religious studies since the late 1960s, and embedded in UK school education as a result of their influence. I'Anson and Jasper (2006) have described this as the Official Account of Religious Studies (OARS). Well-known religionists such as Ninian Smart, W. Owen Cole, John Hinnells, Clive Erriker, and many others have contributed to this movement.

The style of SHAP intervention in the educational thinking of Britain's school inspectors is well illustrated by *Photopak 3: Discovering Religion in Festivals*, compiled by P. Longley and S. Kronenberg, and "designed for use with the secondary age range of 13 plus" (1973, page unnumbered). I give this example because, as I will show as I proceed, the thinking behind it is still essentially unchanged in the minds of at least some important people in education today, for example Joyce Miller, mentioned on the previous page. This Photopak "contains photographs, illustrative material and a series of work units to encourage young people to discover for themselves the nature of religion." This assumption that religion has a nature is organized under such headings as the "Way of personal awareness of the holy"; "The Way of sacred action—ritual and sacraments"; and "The Way of Spiritual Insight." The tacit understanding is that these are all ways to the same one sacred unseen Holy which manifests itself in different forms in different cultures.

The first section after the short introduction is "Way of personal awareness of the holy." The authors explain how the various photos could be interpreted. It tells the teacher and her or his students what 'religion' is. It bases itself explicitly on Rudolf Otto's *The Idea of the Holy*; Ninian Smart's *Religious Experience of Mankind*; and F. J. Streng's *Understanding Religious Man*, the essential idea of religion—its "heart"—being "religious experience." Talking of Otto, the teachers and their students are told, "He concluded that religion springs from an awareness and experience of the holy or sacred . . . . An encounter with the Holy is . . . an awareness of unseen presences in human consciousness . . . . Otto drew attention to certain basic elements in man's experience of the holy that occur in the history of religions" (page unnumbered). This generates feelings of awe, dependence, wonder, fascination, mystery, a sense of the wholly other, and "the smallness of man." Examples given are Mohammed experiencing the presence of Allah, and Isaiah in the Temple of Jerusalem before the Majesty of God. We are told that the mysterious power, the unseen presences, can be both personal and impersonal, the latter making space for 'religions' such as Hinduism and Buddhism.

In "The Way of sacred action—ritual and sacraments" the authors tell the reader that the "sacred invisible world" is made known through myth and

ritual: "Man responds to religion by participating in the sacred action of rituals, festivals and sacraments" (page unnumbered), and they go on to inform
us that "since a religious man believes that through sacred action and sacraments the unseen world is revealed and its creative power made available,
those places and times when this are thought to occur are especially important." They give as examples the Exodus in the Old Testament; "primitive
religious societies"; the Passover, the birth of Jesus, Easter, the "call of Mohammed," Jerusalem, Kab'ah, and Holy Communion.

In "The Way of Spiritual Insight" the authors instruct us that "Moments
of realisation . . . are at the heart of religion. Words in religion like 'conversion',
'enlightenment' and 'a sense of presence' indicate the believer's experience of
the unseen world in his personal life. The living heart of religion is the claim
that its followers have an inner experience of God, or whatever else is the focus
of their belief, such as attaining higher states of consciousness, or the con-
templative peace of Nirvana." Yoga, the enlightenment of the Buddha, and
"the Christian experience of conversion" are given as examples.

The photographs included in the pack are all described as "Responses to
the numinous" and include Stonehenge, the Easter Island statues, and an
Indian Totem from Canada. Photographs of "sacred time and place" include
New Year's Eve in Trafalgar Square, London; the Western Wall, Jerusalem; the
Ka'bah in Mecca; Benares in India; the shrine of the Footprints of the Buddha
at Bodh Gaya; Saturday evening prayers at a Jewish Synagogue; and Harvest
Festival. Photographs of "Moments of Insight and Response" are hands in
prayer; Buddhist monks at prayer; a nun teaching children; a Salvation Army
meeting; and Martin Luther King, Jr., on a civil rights march.

In this school educational aid, the essentialisation of religion is expressed
in the idea that religion has a living heart, which is experience of an unseen ultimate reality that manifests itself in these eclectic forms in different times
and places. The impression given, as much by what is omitted and edited out
as by what is included, is of essentialised and free-floating 'phenomena' detached from historical contextualization, from the power of the state, or from
any other kind of discursive domain. The tacit model is 'essence and manifestation'. I suggest that the purpose of this pack is to persuade young people and
their teachers to believe in some modern, ahistorical, theological invention, an
unseen essence that manifests itself in the various media of different 'religions',
which are tacitly voluntary acts of individuals essentially divorced from power
and the modern nonreligious state. Yet it is of course itself an act of power,
an ideological rhetoric designed to influence "young people," their school teachers, the school inspectors who as agents of the state monitor and validate the
schools' curricula, and quite probably the writers themselves. I hope, with my
own counter-rhetoric, to show in this book some of the unintended consequences of this decontextualised and ahistorical ideology of uncritical liberalism.

The prevalence of this modern liberal theology of essentialised religion whose heart lies in individual private experiences of the numinous is well if uncritically described by Glyn Richards in his essay "Religion and Religions" in a book entitled, without any apparent sense of irony, *The Future of Religion: Postmodern Perspectives: Essays in Honour of Ninian Smart* (Richards in Lamb and Cohn-Sherbok, 1999:16–25). Richards says his own paper examines "the manner in which the One finds embodiment in the many—which in Smart's view exhibit at least seven features or dimensions" (17). Richards actually offers a description of two different modern attitudes toward religion, that of those he describes as the relativists exemplified by Troeltsch, and the essentialists such as Schleiermacher, Otto, W. E. Hocking, Vivekananda, and Radhakrishnan.

Troeltsch for Richards is a paradigmatic relativist. He argued against those theological works which "elevate the concept of an essence to religion to the status of a norm" while giving an inferior status to historical knowledge. Richards's articulation of the essentialist position contextualises the SHAP educational material in relation to a number of influential modern thinkers, giving us some historical idea from whence originated the religious and theological phenomenology of the members of the SHAP working party on religious education. The Protestant theologian Schleiermacher is exemplary; talking of "the true nature of religion," he "conceives of religion as a transcendental entity pre-existing all individual, historical manifestations." Historical religions "may be regarded as concrete expressions of the primordial form . . . . The multiplicity of historical or 'positive' religions in Schleiermacher's view is the direct result of the work of the spirit" (18/19). Rudolf Otto followed Schleiermacher and "openly acknowledged his admiration for Schleiermacher's rediscovery of the true nature of religion." The Holy is "the common ground and essence of religion" (20). For Hocking also, different religions share the same ultimate essence, an insight which will eventually lead to "the possible establishment of a world faith" (21). For Vivekananda "religion is one in essence but diverse in manifestation" (21). Form and image are "external symbols manifesting men's endeavour to apprehend the eternal" (22). Radhakrishnan has a similar neo-Vedantist view of the various manifestations of the One. Richards holds that from this essentialist viewpoint shared by Schleiermacher, Otto, Radhakrishnan, and Vivekananda, it follows that "[t]he aim of religious education should be to seek to comprehend the basic principles of all the great religions of the world to promote mutual understanding" (23).

Richards is a little ambiguous on which view he himself takes, but his summary of the essentialists points to a central strand in the construction of the ideology of religious studies and the modern liberal ecumenical theology. The importance of these apparently harmless ideas is that they are the elephant in the room of the modern academy. Many historians, anthropologists, sociologists, and area studies specialists seem not to realize that each time they claim to be discussing the religion or religions of this or that culture or period of history they are riding partly on this modern theological essentialist construct. Many scholars uncritically recycle the rhetoric of 'religion' and 'religions' as though these are neutral and innocent categories with which to describe and analyse our own past or the practices of those who speak and think in non-European languages. This language game of religion and religions, I shall argue in this book, has further ideological consequences, beyond its own explicit limitations, in the rhetorical promotion of powerful discourses on the 'secular' as nonreligious: the religionless state which is neutral toward religion, positivistic science, and technology, the natural rationality of self-interest, and the objectivity and superiority of secular academic writing. Therefore the rather jaunty ease and familiarity of the article "Let's Talk about Religion and Keep Teaching It," written by Joyce Miller, the education inspector mentioned on a previous page, and published in a magazine funded by a State Agency, seems inappropriate to say the least.

In an article published in 1990, "Hinduism and the World Religion Fallacy" (*Religion*), I criticised in detail the construction of Hinduism as a world religion, and also the contributions of the members of the SHAP working party on religious education who were so deeply involved in it.[12] If I were writing about it today, I would draw out more strongly the colonial context for the invention of world religions (see, for example, King, 1999), and also the part played by the concept of Hinduism in the nationalism of Hindutva (see, for example, Searle-Chatterjee, 2000). The discourse on Hinduism and on world religions more generally has a history going back to the founding of the scientific study of religion in the nineteenth century, as Despland's article and other essays in the same volume testify; much of it derives from Christian theological traditions, substantively though not exclusively Protestant incarnational theology. "Religion is in the world, it is a formative influence in every society, found in every culture in human history," writes Miller. One could trace this idea back to the early seventeenth-century writing of the Protestant English vicar and nationalist Samuel Purchas, discussed in chapter 6, for whom there was one Truth (true Religion) which was Protestant Christianity, and there were many religions, which were really irrational superstitions because they were either at best merely dim memories of the revelation of God which had been lost from view for much of humanity by the Fall, the Flood, and the Tower of Babel; or at worst they were diabolical inventions.

The attitudes may appear to have changed in the neutral, objective, 'secular' world of government educational bureaucracy, but the structures may be deeply embedded. Religions are tacitly (and sometimes quite explicitly) depicted as incarnations of, or at least forms of, Religion itself. Though the educated elites of non-European countries have contributed to this construction and helped to give it an ecumenical plausibility (one thinks for example how well the ideal of the Brahman avatar fits this metaphysical speculative form, and the role played by the ecumenical concept of religious experience has allowed Christian contemplation, Zen, yoga, and shamanism to be collected into the ecumenical egg basket), it seems difficult not to see the personal God of Judaeo-Christian monotheism incarnating in Jesus Christ as a major trope. Even evolutionary atheists such as Tylor and the agnostic Spencer adopted many of the conceptualisations of 'religion' embedded in their own Protestant culture. Unknowingly, Miller, or the "education law makers" for whom she speaks, is turning the wheel of a theology constructed mainly by elite literate men imagining that this is objective knowledge and therefore fit for educational policy making. This seemingly innocent construction has been criticised by a growing body of studies in the history and ethnography of religion, which has analysed various contexts—not least the colonial context—for this modern invention (see Chidester, 1996, 2007; Asad, 1993, 2003). Yet the chair of the UK Association of Religious Education Inspectors, Advisors and Consultants displays no interest in them at all. It can of course be pointed out that this was a very short article and that it did not require a scholarly format. But nevertheless this is what she chose to say in the small space provided by the editors, and this is her viewpoint. There is not the slightest hint of embarrassment at recycling this contentious language in service to the state. And who can blame her, when so many historians of religion pay only lip service to the critique of their own discipline?

There is another point (d) that should be noticed here as well, and I think in a sense this is the most important one. The language Miller uses to talk about religion embeds into the discussion the unexamined but irresistible assumption that what she is doing is not religion or religious. She occupies an assumed nonreligious place of special authority from where she can make pronouncements which none of the 'religions' themselves would be qualified to make: pronouncements that religions exist in the world alongside each other; that they always have existed in all cultures everywhere; that they can be studied and learnt from; that six (not five or seven) of them qualify as "major faiths"; and that they can be treated as items in a healthy school curriculum that is itself neutral and without any 'religious' commitments of its own. This in my view is the most important function of the discourse on religion and religions—to embed the superior nonreligious space of objective neutrality deeper into our working and largely unquestioned assumptions about the world. We feel we are in touch with natural rationality, with ordinary reasonableness with which any normal person would agree. I argue that this invention of religions is what makes the secular discourse—by which I mean the neutral, objective, nonreligious discourse—operational, disguising its persuasive role as rhetoric, and also concealing the origins of this rhetoric.

Having embedded her own secularity as the nonreligious ground from which she can observe and comment authoritatively upon religion and the religions, the implication inevitably flows that what Miller means by religion and religions is something that is essentially different from the neutral, objective, tolerant, nonreligious space that today we call the secular. It is not stated explicitly. By being embedded into the discourse, it slips unnoticed below the radar screen and in this way acts far more powerfully as a tacit organiser of the rhetorical flows which we inhale in our day-to-day intercourse. I doubt if Miller was conscious of this herself. It is a feature of the dominant ideology of the Anglophone West today that it camouflages itself and merges into the natural environment, as though it is simply there, the place we have arrived at. Our language simply reflects what is there, and anyone who cannot see it is unreasonable. It is in the nature of religions that they can be studied by nonreligious people, or by people who in their private life are religious but who adopt a nonreligious educational standpoint. This dichotomy is thus built into the concept of religion which she is deploying. The embedded assumption is that religions, which have always existed in all cultures, are partly defined by their distinction from the secular, from what is not religion. The secular is not itself a constructed arena of values, an expression of collective commitments. The secular is that neutral, natural, given, commonsense reality that we all (especially highly qualified professionals) inhabit (unless we are mavericks, eccentrics, trouble makers, or subversives). If religions have always existed, then it tacitly follows that the most rational and objective ground has always existed as well. It follows that the secular—understood as the neutral, objective, nonreligious—is also an eternal feature of all societies everywhere.

It seems important to notice that in the same issue of the magazine, Muhammad Abdul Bari, secretary general of the Muslim Council of Britain, opens his short piece with the observation, "It is often said that Islam is not *merely* a religion but a way of life" (*The Edge*, 18; my italics). If the implications of this statement are thought about at all, then they could be very great indeed. What is a 'mere' religion, and what is the implication of saying that Islam is in contrast a 'way of life'? Muhammad Abdul Bari goes on to say that the purpose of Islam "is not *simply* to provide individuals that believe in a God with a mode of communication between the Divine and His devotees, but to provide those devotees with a framework through which their lives may be lead [*sic*]" (my italics). The implication of this seems to be that the English-language word 'religion', as commonly understood, is defined by a personal belief in God.[13] If by 'religion' is meant "merely" and "simply" a private faith separated from the secular state and society, as Muhammad Abdul Bari seems to be saying, then in this sense Islam is *not* a religion. Islam is a way of life. Islam is something more total, something more analogous perhaps to what Religion understood as Christian Truth was before the Enlightenment, a framework specifying the order of things and persons which, by its very nature as revealed Truth, encompasses and judges all valid human practices.[14]

There is an uncomfortable agreement in the syntax of religion in these two articles, which hardly disguises the chasm of their different implications. These word uses suggest that even between English speakers, such as the secretary to the general council of British Muslims and the chief school inspector, there is plenty of scope for mistranslation and misunderstanding about the nuances of the key term religion. Who is using the term in which sense or senses? Miller seems to be using the idea of 'religions' in the way that Bari also tacitly understands it, as private faiths or beliefs in God represented in autonomous, voluntary associations of believers and separated from the secular state and its education system. Yet it is in this sense of religion that Bari is suggesting that Islam is *not* "merely" or "simply" a religion. What kind of a dialogue can we expect between the discourse on world religions represented by the school inspector and the discourse on Islam represented by the secretary general of the Muslim Council of Britain?

Think how much more problematic this issue might become when pundits attempt to translate our English term 'religion', its implied incarnations in the 'religions', and their eternal separation from, but dichotomous connection to, the 'secular'—a web of English-language categories already carrying its own historical load of contention—into Yoruba, Arabic, Urdu, Persian, Marathi, Tamil, Chinese, Zapotec (a Mexican Indian language), and many other complex and ancient languages.

At some points in her short piece, Miller uses the terms "criticism" and "critically engage." "Criticism" is used in relation to the secular, viz., how can the teaching of religion be justified in a secular age? That 'secular' means 'nonreligious' is also implied when she says that pupils need to "critically engage with *that* aspect of the world," meaning the religious aspect (my italics). Referring to religion as that 'aspect of the world' has the effect of inscribing religion as one specifiable part of the natural order. The religion-secular dichotomy, then, is natural. It is embedded in the natural rationality of the world, and not something which domestic and colonial law makers, the writers of bills of rights and constitutions, missionaries, colonial civil servants, and academics have struggled and are still struggling to imagine, enact, authorise, and legitimate.

Of the various short articles in this edition of a magazine funded by the ESRC, I could not find any that approached the issue from a critical and historical analysis of the categories. And this is not surprising, for the ESRC is itself a 'secular' funding agent, which receives its funds from the secular state, and which is uncritically concerned with the content of secular education. It is by self-definition 'nonreligious' and has a vested interest in disguising the fact that nonreligious is an ideological position, one which is contested by many others, not only Muslims, a set of values which specific groups of people and individuals have historically struggled to bring into existence.

Another example of this confusion of meanings can be found in a full-page newspaper article written by Ellen Knickermeyer of the *Washington Post*'s Foreign Service and published as a special report in the *Daily Yomiuri Shinbun* (an English-language newspaper published in Japan) under the banner of the *Washington Post* (*Yomiuri Shinbun*, 25 August 2006:12).[15] The article, under the title "In Iraq, Sadr-Aligned Movement Signals Its Strength," analyses for English-language readers the growth in power of the Shiite movement and particularly of its Madhi Army. The report analyses the Sadr organisation under four headings: Madhi Army, political, religious, and social. As with all uses of such terminology, the report does not say if these are supposed to be English-language equivalents of Arabic words, or just the guesswork of the reporters. Those of us who do not know Arabic are therefore left to guess whether or not the Iraqi-language categories are being faithfully and accurately represented here. Generally, the assumptions embedded in the English-language categories assume a basic distinction between the religious and the nonreligious (the political, the social, the military), even though reading between the lines one cannot help suspecting that in the minds of the Muslim participants there is a radically different assumption operating, one closer to that which I found in the discourse of the UK Muslim Council's head representative. Moqtada al-Sadr is described several times as "the movement's central religious figure" or more generally as "the religious leadership." The 'religious' aspect of the movement is distinguished from the political, military, and social aspects. For example, the report says:

Sadr's followers answer as one when his movement calls them, and his organization of social, religious, political and military programs—as well as the young clerics, politicians and fighters around him—has become the most pivotal force in Iraq after the United States.

The distinctiveness of the religious, as distinct from the political and so on, is reinforced and reembedded time and again by the use of these English-language phrases: "Shiite religious authorities," attributed to Riyadh al-Nouri, a brother-in-law of Sadr; "Sayyid Moqtada," described as "a religious honorific of Sadr"; "religious law," which is tacitly equated with an "Islamic code"; and "the governing Shiite religious parties."

On the other hand, Moqtada al-Sadr is reportedly described by Joost Hilterman, Middle East project director for the Brussels-based International Crisis Group, as "clearly ... the most potent political figure," which renders the relationships between religion and politics as descriptors inherently unclear in their nuances. The "religious law" has under its jurisdiction the permitted dress of Muslim women; the arbitration of divorces, inheritances, and "other social matters"; a "United Islamic State," a "State within a State"; the provision of social services such as public schools, hospitals, and clinics; inexpensive burials; the God's Martyr Foundation, supporting veterans and their families;

and the rebuilding of shrines. In these cases, it seems difficult to know in what sense the political, social, and military can be separated from the religious in the way that Americans assume. And this point puts in doubt the expression "extra-judicial Islamic courts": does this mean that the Islamic courts are 'extra' to the American concept of the judiciary or to the indigenous concept? In this reportage anything associated with the Madhi Army—authority, law, polite language (honorifics), dress code, 'parties', the state, and social services—is 'religious' and thus, in terms of what Americans would often tacitly take to be normal, conveys a nuance of a voluntary, private category which is both a personal right guaranteed by the state, but also something from which the secular state needs protection in order to guard its secular neutrality.

Given the lack of clarity of this English-language terminology, it seems unsurprising that the Americans are "unable to figure out Sadr's militia or approach him on political terms," for the reporters and their readers do not know what the key terms mean. On the one hand, the report uses language that presumably reflects the Anglophone thinking behind the new Iraqi constitution, which the Americans desire to have implemented in Iraq.[16] On the other hand, there is a tacit undercurrent of meanings, presumably the meanings that Arabic speakers intend by their own speech acts, which point to Islam not as a religion separated from secular (nonreligious) politics, law, and economics but as an encompassing polity which is, contrary to our modernist terms, neither a religion nor a nonreligion, though nevertheless sacred.

This confusion of language is also being generated from within academia by Anglophone specialist scholars who generally see themselves as occupying roughly the same objective, neutral, nonreligious ground as the school's inspector and the *Washington Post* reporters. "A Matter of Power, Not Religion" is the title of a two-page interview with Fred Halliday in a recently published article in *LSE Magazine* (London School of Economics, Winter 2005:6–7). Halliday, who is Montague Burton Professor of International Relations at the London School of Economics, a fellow of the British Academy, and the author of books on Islam, was interviewed about the "war against terrorism" by Adam Holm of the Danish weekly political magazine *Opinion*. Halliday is an interesting writer but here I draw attention to the implications of the article's title, that religion and power are distinct and separate alternatives: a matter of power, not religion.

The logic of "a matter of power, not religion" allows in principle for the reverse: a matter of religion, not power. Whatever anyone thinks religion may be, the idea that it is not a matter of power seems counterintuitive. Yet this follows the same logic as the ideological separation of religion and politics.

In his second question to Halliday, Holm asks, "What is required to stop, or minimise, the religiously motivated terrorism that we are now witnessing in parts of the west and in many places in the Arab world?" In this question, the idea of a distinct form of terrorism—*religious* terrorism—is introduced effortlessly into the discussion. This usage, which is widely dispersed through-out the general media and academic publications, implies that some terrorism is religious but some is nonreligious or secular. In part of his reply, Halliday underwrites this when he says, "I would not say 'religiously motivated' because the main issues are nationalist and anti-imperialist ones if you read the statements of Al Qaida. . . . the main issues are eminently understandable, even conventional, political ones." For Halliday, "religion provides a means of ex-pressing" these conventional political motives. And in his answer to Holm's third question about Islamic terrorists, Halliday at one point says, "it is not the religion that determines the political means . . . it is the political groups of today who select and use religion."

The essential distinction between religion and politics is embedded in this interview by both scholars. Politics is secular, not religious: "terrorism . . . is a product of modern, secular, politics," Halliday asserts. "It has long had no re-lation to religion at all."

An interview is not the same as an academic paper. Yet these published usages are unsurprising, since they are part of our common discourse and trip off the tongue effortlessly. They seem entirely natural to us. The assumption that religion is not about power or politics, and when it becomes so then something is wrong, reflects a wider media and academic discourse about religion in which it is defined as essentially distinct from the secular, and thus as having a problematic relationship to it. The implication is that religion is essentially nonpolitical, and politics is essentially nonreligious.

I suggested earlier that William Penn and John Locke both pursued what in their day and age was the dangerously heterodox position that religion *ought* to be understood as essentially private and distinct from the magistrate, with different ends and purposes, against the prevailing view of the meaning of Religion at the time (Penn, 1680; Locke, 1689). One of the implications is that they were not appealing to ready-made concepts of church and state and merely demanding a reshuffle of the relations between two distinct compo-nents, as though reconceiving a relationship between essentially static ele-ments. As I argue in future chapters, neither Luther, nor Calvin, nor the Anabaptists, nor the papacy and the Catholic churchmen, nor the founders of the Church of England, nor John Bunyan imagined the idea of a neutral, nonreligious state separated from 'religion', as the idea came to be expressed much later, for example as formulated in the American Constitution. It is doubtful whether even the French revolutionaries thought of the republic as 'nonreligious'. The principles of the French Revolution seem especially signif-icant, because many of the principles upon which our secular societies are based, and by which they are legitimated, were most clearly articulated by the French revolutionaries, and before them the English and the American. In *Holy Terrors*, Bruce Lincoln points out that the chief actors in these revolu-tions "saw such doctrines as the rights of man, popular sovereignty, and the social contract as no less sacred—in fact, much more so—than the divine right of kings," and he goes on to quote Christopher Dawson that the revolutionaries in France "dreamt of a spiritual republic based on moral foundations" (Lincoln, 2003:87).[17] The great Indian constitutionalist B. R. Ambedkar, the chief architect of the modern Indian republican constitution, favourably described the French revolutionary principles of equality, liberty, and fraternity as "the religion of principles." He was contrasting such religion with the "religion of rules" (Ambedkar, 1982 [1936]:124, 126), referring to the Brahmanic dharma shastras such as the Manu Smriti.

Locke, Penn, Benjamin Hoadly, and the Americans of the Enlightenment such as Jefferson were attempting to construct new imaginings, what amounted to a new paradigm. They persuaded some people that it was as old as the hills, citing Jesus's saying about the things of this world belonging to Caesar and the things of heaven belonging to God. Up until that point the majority of Christians had assumed that the world also belongs to God, but had been usurped by ungodly princes, since he created it and since the contingency of the world is dependent on God's real causation. Of course, the idea that the sacred had been profaned by the Fall was not new as such.[18] What was new was the way this came to be formulated. Through complex processes, Religion became religions, religions became churches, and the profane became the modern secular. A profoundly different set of meanings came to be tied to old words in a configuration which constitutes modernity. This ideological reformulation was highly contentious at the time, went against the grain of established thinking, and made only marginal and much exaggerated progress in European church-states. But it fit the interests of a growing number of Dissenting and nonconformist men and women who conceived of their salvation in new Calvinistic ways, many of them in escape to America, and whose prosperity depended on success in colonial trade and the need for cheap labour and markets. What *ought* to be, in the minds of a few seventeenth-century radicals who were struggling against the encompassing Christian church-state in which church and state were hardly distinguishable, has become the dominant (even if still ambiguous) ideology. Religions, rather than being one or another conflicting sectarian interpretation of Christian Truth, or ironic references to barbaric, superstitious misunderstandings of Truth, have become imbued with misplaced concreteness, which suggests they are ontologically multiple; religions have become in the world generic things having some problematic relationship with a distinct sphere of nonreligious power, called 'politics'. They have been animated and fetishised in a way that now makes them appear like commodities (Carrette & King, 2004).

Arguably, the construction of our own modern practices as rational developed historically in the first place from the Protestant critique of Catholic superstitious ritualism. Christian representations of the other as irrational and barbaric were transformed in Protestant discourses to include Catholics. These were the internal pagans. Those Protestant representations of the superstitious Catholic 'other', along with the more general constructions of pagan incivility, in turn fed into Enlightenment and nineteenth-century evolutionary representations of colonised peoples. It is surely for such reasons that in the still-recent era of structural functionalism in anthropology, the distinction between the rituals of 'traditional' societies and the 'ceremonial' practices of Europeans might have seemed legitimate even to great anthropologists such as Raymond Firth, who could hardly be accused of colonial condescension. In anthropology, ritual, along with 'belief in gods', was frequently the working definition of religion.

But from our own postcolonial standpoint, it should be easier for us to question the idea that, whereas other, less-advanced peoples are permeated with ritualism and therefore with a 'religious' world view, we in Anglophone cultures do not 'do' ritual, except minimally in church. I ask, rhetorically but with serious theoretical intent, why should the legal procedures and taboos surrounding our courts and ideals of justice, our separation of the branches of government, our concept of private property, the practices of the stock exchange and the capital markets, the traditions of the civil services, be considered 'nonreligious', but the practices of divination, or the Islamic sharia, or the generic potlatch of various indigenous American peoples, or Buddhist meditation be assigned to the 'religion' basket? Why are transcendental values such as the belief in progress, or individualism, or nationalism, or the democratic virtues of 'freedom' and 'equality', the practice of secret ballots and elections of governments, which many millions of people died to establish and institutionalise, not included in books on 'religion'? Why should state institutions that defend the freedom of Americans such as the Pentagon, the White House, and the Congress be treated as nonreligious rather than 'religious' or ritual institutions? Is the queen of England, who is supposedly head of a secular state, but who is also head of a national religion, to be treated as a religious or a secular functionary? Is the raising and lowering of a national flag of religious or secular significance? It seems we are trapped by language when we consider these issues. For, arguably, they are all both religious and secular, and in that sense neither, for they undercut this grand dichotomy. We need to dissolve these reified binaries if a new paradigm is to have a chance to get articulated in public discourse.

Yet in our own Euro-American discourses we do not have such inhibitions in referring to many ostensibly 'secular' principles and institutions as 'sacred', not least our national identification with freedom and democracy. The Magna Carta, the Declaration of Independence, the United Nations Charter of Human Rights, constitutions, and other documents, principles, and procedures are surely treated as though they are sacred within secular polities. The sacredness of sovereignty has always been a feature of European Christian thinking and practice, and though concepts of sovereignty have changed, power is still legitimated through procedures and principles which are defended against profanation. For these reasons I argue in chapter 3 for a strategic distinction between the religion-secular binary, on the one hand, and the sacred-profane binary, on the other. What these examples point to is that the world, including Euro-America, is not divided into two great baskets, the religious basket and the secular basket. This distinction itself is an ideological discourse which historically has served specific ends. Yet we use these categories as though they are neutral descriptions of what there is in the world, and we base social scientific knowledge on them. In this book I want to look at the way that terms which have changed their dominant meanings through historical contestation have become naturalised as though they are part of human nature and as though they exist in the objective order of things.

Nor will it do, in a move to de-reify the category, to say that the term 'religion' is merely a heuristic device which we can use at our leisure to make our own meanings. In a famous passage in the preface to his seminal book *Imagining Religion: From Babylon to Jonestown* (1982), Jonathan Z. Smith made an influential claim about 'religion' as a category, which has been quoted many times by those who have sought to bring greater critical self-reflectivity into the discipline of religious studies. It bears quoting again here because, in the light of the arguments in this book, it seems problematic for a number of reasons:

> If we have understood the archaeological and textual record cor-
> rectly, man has had his entire history in which to imagine deities and
> modes of interaction with them. But man, more precisely western
> man, has had only the last few centuries in which to imagine religion.
> It is this act of second order, reflective imagination which must
> be the central preoccupation of any student of religion. That is to say,
> while there is a staggering amount of data, of phenomena, of human
> experiences and expressions that might be characterized in one
> culture or another, by one criterion or another, as religious—there
> is [sic] no data for religion. Religion is solely the creation of the
> scholar's study. It is created for the scholar's analytical purposes by
> his imaginative acts of comparison and generalization. Religion
> has no independent existence apart from the academy. For this rea-
> son, the student of religion, and most particularly the historian of
> religion, must be relentlessly self-conscious. Indeed this self-
> consciousness constitutes his primary expertise, his foremost object
> of study. (1982:xi; see also Smith, 1998:281–82)

Smith might mean by this that Anglophone discourses on 'religion' tell us more about Anglo-American collective representations than they do about any putative historical or ethnographic data, in which case his appeal to the student of 'religion' to be "relentlessly self-conscious" seems like good advice. What appears like an object to the secular scholar turns out to be a value-laden term which has been projected onto non-European peoples throughout the period of imperialism since the Spanish debated whether or not the Amerindians, who were patently without true Religion, could be considered as fully human or not. But he also adds that "there is a staggering amount of data . . . that might be characterized . . . as religious." If religion can in principle be used, and in fact is used, to refer to such a staggering amount of data, then it appears to become empty of any specific content. This would be a good reason for analysing the historical usages of the English word and the problems of translation into non-European languages. What appears to be an empty taxon reveals itself as an instrument of power. As Smith seems to recognise, there are certain hegemonic presumptions about what 'religions' are that derive from centuries of references to Christian Truth or Faith, and also from the religion-secular dichotomy which is far from universal. While pointing out that 'religion' has no essential content, Smith has a good idea what religion often means: "deities and modes of interaction with them." But this surely pushes the problem one stage back, since we now have the problem of understanding to what the English-language term 'deities' refers. As Smith has pointed out, the meaning of religion has been highly contested historically and anthropologically. Furthermore, the meaning of 'religion' has always had legal and constitutional implications. Discourses on religion have been controlled by various powerful agencies, and the sanctions on its correct understanding have been matters of life and death. The evidence that Smith produces in his article "Religion, Religions, Religious" is that for centuries 'religion' mainly referred to barbaric superstitions that have some superficial resemblance to Religion. Today, what counts as 'religion' and what does not count is controlled by secular (nonreligious) government agencies for tax and other purposes under a general category such as 'religious charity'. This reminds us that what counts as religion (rather than, say, a business or a political party) is policed by forces beyond the academy. For these reasons 'religion', rather than being a kind of neutral category which can be created by the scholar for his or her own purposes, is laden with cultural and ideological assumptions and interests. Perhaps it is these that Smith believes we should be studying. If so, I agree with him.

The examples given above, and the many more to come in this book, show that these discourses operate beyond our individual intentions, and convey confused meanings which are dangerous unless critically dissolved. We are not really engaged in 'secular' neutral research and description of things that exist in the world, but are engaged in acts of rhetoric whereby we try to persuade others to see the world in this particular way. The discourse on religion and world religions is ostensibly about one domain, for example, the 'supernatural' (another unstable and unclear term), whereas it is just as much about constructing another domain, the 'natural'. It is about 'faith', but it is also constructing and authorising 'knowledge'. It is about 'deities', but it is also about what constitutes fully rational (scientific and political) humanity. It is about the inner recesses of individual special experiences that go beyond reason, but it is also about legitimating the nonreligious state whose rationality is embedded in natural reason. It is ostensibly about 'faith communities' but it is also about naturalising the secular 'discursive space' from which these religions become objects of knowledge. Muhammad Abdul Bari helps us to see this more clearly, when he points out that Islam is not *merely* a religion but is a total way of life.[19] My argument here will be that the idea of Religion as Christian Truth, as it was policed by theologians and lawyers for many centuries, has become so progressively stripped down over the last two or three centuries in the ever-expanding process of Anglophone world domination that there is one remaining basic binary operating, which is the bottom-line distinction between religion and nonreligion. The borders between them are highly porous, and shift for strategic necessities in different rhetorical contexts. What ends up being classified as religious or nonreligious, or as natural or supernatural, is quite arbitrary, and now has significance not so much in terms of any positive conceptual content (note the impossibility of defining 'religion' satisfactorily) but as an ideological operator that destabilises any practices that seem to challenge the interests of American power.

2

Methodology 1

The Critical Study of Religion

My main focus in this book is on the modern development of 'religion' and 'religions' as English-language concepts, in relation to those other categories with which religion is represented in modern discourses as externally connected, such as politics, economics, and the secular. By externally connected, I mean that they are explicitly distinguished and separated, a distinction and separation which in turn generates discourses on religion and society, religion and politics, religion and economics, religion and law, religion and the state, and so forth. One aspect that becomes apparent when one traces the different Anglophone usages of terms such as religion, secular, sacred, hallowed, profane, supernatural and natural, politic or political, economical and economics, and so on is that, though those terms never have had essential meanings, it can be claimed perhaps unsurprisingly that some meanings have been significantly more stable in some historical contexts than in others.

The argument is primarily based on English-language historical texts and their interpretation, but it is interdisciplinary in its intentions and is therefore concerned with the problem of 'religion' from the viewpoint of sociologists, anthropologists, and religionists as well as historians. I use the term 'interdisciplinary' rather than 'multidisciplinary' along the lines well expressed by John I'Anson and Alison Jasper:

> [W]hereas multidisciplinary approaches take a given theme
> or subject and then explore how each of several disci-
> plines approach this differently, interdisciplinary approaches

take a very different tack in that a new object of enquiry is created 'that belongs to no one' (Bal, 2003:7) i.e., it is not owned or
controlled by any one disciplinary field. Another way of putting this is
to say that the object is constituted in and through the interplay of
diverse social and symbolic forces that need to be approached
through *interstanding* (Taylor, 1995) since there is no one specific
underlying discipline to which appeal can be made (as is implied by
understanding). (I'Anson & Jasper, 2006:81)

The object of enquiry here is not 'religion' either as a thing or things
assumed to exist in the world, nor as a lone category picking out some discrete
aspect of the world, nor as a heuristic device which we can choose to use or not
use for organising our data. I am concerned with the category 'religion' as it
operates *in relation* to other categories. The relationship, as I see it, is one of
mutual definition by mutual exclusion. By seeing religion, politics, economics,
and other disciplines as configured in overlapping discourses, the boundaries
between disciplines which are at present defined by a paradigmatic category
are inevitably questioned. For example, a methodological assumption of this
book is that we cannot understand what religion means at any given historical
point without taking account of what is conventionally termed political philosophy, for the relationship with 'politics' is inextricably bound with it. The
same can be said about 'economics' as a discourse. But the reverse is also true,
and this same methodological point holds for the other humanities disciplines,
for example, anthropology and its definitive object 'culture' or 'society'.

However, various criticisms of my methodology can easily be made, and
anthropology is one way of founding this criticism. Anthropology rightly takes
the oral and literate traditions of the non-elite, 'the people without a history', as
being as important as those of the elite.[1] A drawback of this work is that a review of historical documents necessarily excludes the ordinary language of
generations of people whose words have rarely been documented. The texts
represent mainly the thinking of male literate elites, and one could justly argue
that, insofar as modern academics belong to a literate elite, so does this writer.
I am therefore trying to identify dominant paradigms of the powerful, while
striving to remain aware of my own positionality, which is also inevitably an act
of rhetoric which attempts to persuade. The extent to which non-elites and
women in the historical past did or did not acquiesce and internalise such a
view of the world is difficult to judge, and I have had to rely on the work of professional historians. It is always open to other scholars to find counterevidence.

A further methodological point is that confining the focus to English-
language documents as I have done is an artificial procedure because the Latin
root of 'religion' and its co-opting by the Catholic church means that the
problem I am investigating is equally fundamental in all European languages
that have significant descent from Latin. However, it is also surely true that the

same methodological principles and approaches can be followed equally in other European languages.

One of the most important ways in which the separation, and therefore externalised connection, between 'religion' as a category and other 'nonreligious' categories such as politics and the state, has been institutionalised in the Anglophone world is to be found in North American constitutionalism (to which I will refer in more detail in chapter 9) and in the ways in which the American national and state constitutions generated nationalist manifestos and constitutions in other places, especially colonies or ex-colonies striving for independence and virtually forced to 'modernise' and thus, in a sense, to Americanize. North American constitutionalism is arguably one of the most important institutionalisations of the modern idea of religions as essentially private and nonpolitical, in English at any rate.

David Chidester, in his pioneering work *Savage Systems* (1996), has shown how 'religion' as a generic modern category and the field of religious studies, which claims to specialise in it, were at least partly constructed on the frontiers of colonised Africa and in the context of the power relations that existed there. My own work aspires to be critical in the sense that I take his to be so: he disembeds the category from the discourses which disguise its role in colonial power relations, and thus questions the whole construction of 'religion' as though it is in the nature of things. The originality of his work is partly that it begins at the subordinated end of the colonial relationship. This is another context in which the importance of relationships, and of the power differentials embedded in relationships, comes into view. That I am dealing mainly with the metropolitan end (except in the sense that white North Americans were themselves colonised, albeit in a very different way from their own colonisation of the indigenous peoples) is, I believe, methodologically justified because of the importance which I attribute to the colonial context in general.

The formation of a modern discourse on 'politics' and the parallel transformations of the meaning of 'religion' as a category need to be placed in the wider colonial context to be properly comprehended. The word 'religion' with all its inherent ambiguities has passed into general worldwide currency in English and has been problematically 'translated' into many non-European languages and constitutions. As many writers have shown, Anglophone 'religion' or some approximation to it has been adopted by historically colonized peoples in the assertion of their rights and national self-identity—peoples in situations as different as the indigenous American Pueblo (see Wenger, 2005; and the discussion on pp. 91–95) or the Hindutva nationalist movement in India (Searle-Chatterjee, 2000; Zavos, 2007, 2000). One basic issue is the translation problem. Translating the word 'religion' into non-European languages which have no obviously equivalent term requires that those things from which religion is separated in modern Anglophone discourse, such as the 'secular state' or politics, also be translated, as must other dominant categories such as 'economics' or 'written constitution' (see Isomae, 2007, on the debates about 'religion' in Meiji Japan). The introduction or imposition of Euro-American categories turns out to require a major reinvention of the traditional institutions and forms of thought of non-Western peoples. Yet many academics in history, anthropology, or religious studies use the term generically as though 'religion' is universal in time and place, and school and college syllabi glibly recycle a rhetorical construction as though it is natural.

This important problem of colonial and postcolonial translation must be one essential approach to understanding how 'religion' as a category operates in Orientalist and colonial rhetoric and the power interests that fuel it. Obviously my own limited abilities as a linguist and a scholar, the limits of a book, and the sheer volume of possible contexts demand some kind of boundary. Other scholars and I have claimed in another book, *Religion and the Secular: Historical and Colonial Formations* (Fitzgerald, 2007), that the visibility of the colonial end of the relationship is essential for the proper working out of the metropolitan end. We cannot for example understand British history except in the context of the colonial and postcolonial relationships.

Though I have not explicitly discussed Orientalism very much in this book, the theme runs subterraneously throughout, and Edward Said's thesis is, in general theoretical terms, an essential background to my own argument. Said has been criticised for the degree to which his seminal work *Orientalism* (1991 [1978]) concentrated on the Euro-American discourses which have constructed the Orient, but left out of his account the agency and strategies of the dominated 'other' in the making of their own history, a debate which has been well summarised by Richard King (1999:82–95; see also the useful reader by McFie, 2000). Yet it is difficult to doubt that Said's thesis has added hugely to our understanding of the ideological mechanisms, under the guise of neutral and disinterested scholarship or fiction, whereby European discourses have both constructed and dominated other peoples (see also the collection of essays in and the introduction to Breckenridge & Van der Veer, 1993; also Inden, 1990:36–37).

I have at all times attempted to place the historical analysis and interpretation of English-language texts, produced mainly in England and with special focus on categories such as religion, secular, sacred, profane, state, politics, and economics, in the context of the early growth of colonial power. Thus, for example, the radical redefinition of the meaning of 'religion' and 'civil magistracy' by writers such as William Penn and John Locke in the 1680s can in my view only be understood in connection with their various interests in the American colonies. Equally, their importance as what we would today call political theorists cannot be comprehended without understanding their importance in the development (directly or indirectly) of modern American constitutionalism. What I argue in this book is that Penn and Locke were themselves (along with other important writers and in a European context) rhetorically constructing what was only then beginning to be referred to as 'politics' in the modern sense of a practice distinguished from a practice called 'religion'. They were not the recipients of already formulated and distinct institutions, the 'religious' and the 'political'. They were, if you like, the inventors whose rhetorical constructions suited, through a process of elective affinity, some powerful interests of early colonialism.

The relationship between the colonising power and the dominated or colonised peoples must be constructed from both ends in order to understand both ends. This is because both ends have constructed each other, albeit in the crucial context of unequal power. This therefore justifies a study of the emergence of hegemonic ideology in the language of the metropolitan end of the relationship, as well as the equal need to critically investigate the site of the colonial encounter itself. The historian David Cannadine says of one of his works:

> [T]his book is concerned with recovering the world-view and social
> presuppositions of those who dominated and ruled the empire ... as
> well as with the imperial mechanisms and structures through which
> they dominated, ruled, supported and went along with it. This is
> not because I consider the victims and critics of empire to be un-
> important, but because the outlook of the dominators and rulers and
> fellow travelers ... is one major element of the British imperial ex-
> perience .... This book lends support to the increasingly insistent
> argument that there can be no satisfactory history of Britain without
> empire, and no satisfactory history of empire without Britain.
> (2001:xx)

The present book is admittedly a different kind of book from Cannadine's. It is not so much a history of empire, and anyhow I am concerned here more with the historical period of the sixteenth, seventeenth, and eighteenth centuries before Britain, France, or America had reached the peak of their imperial ambitions in the nineteenth and twentieth centuries. My own book is a more limited analysis of discourses on religion and other categories and the way their meanings and usages have changed in relation to processes such as the early formation of the nation-state, the early growth of trade and plantations, and the institutionalisation of rhetoric on 'religion' and 'the state' in eighteenth-century American constitutionalism.

Nor is this a history of ideas in the conventional sense. The main focus of my book is the way that religion has become essentialised as a generic category and used descriptively and analytically as though religion is something that unproblematically exists in the world, or alternatively as a heuristic category, as though it is merely available for the scholar's personal decision as to what it will mean. In this sense, I view the conventional history of ideas more as a rhetorical technique for reembedding a category such as 'religion' into the nature of things, and investing it with an aura of inevitability. A conventional text in the history of ideas genre may be superlatively researched and contain much significant information. But at the same time it is likely to leave the key problematic categories untouched by recycling them as though they are neutral for analysis and description. In this sense, the genre of the history of ideas employs rhetorical techniques which actually reproduce the discursive domain and embed it into the natural order of things, while at the same time concealing its origins and the ideological interests which the dominant organising category embodies.

A significant aspect of the modern myth of religion, extensively and effectively analyzed by Russell McCutcheon in a number of publications (e.g., 1997, 2001), is its rhetorical representation as sui generis in the institutionalisation of religious studies as a discipline. There are a number of books and specialist papers that trace the historical vicissitudes of 'religion' as a category—though some are doing a great deal more than that as well—such as those by Wilfred Cantwell Smith (1978 [1962]), Jonathan Z. Smith (1982, 1998), John Bossy (1982, 1985), Peter Biller (1985), Daniel Dubuisson (1998), Danièle Hervieu-Léger (2000), Derek Peterson and Darren Walhof (2002), Peter Harrison (1990), the contributors to the Despland and Vallée collection (1992), Richard King (1999), Talal Asad (1993, 2003), Gavin Flood (1999), Tomoko Masuzawa (2005), and James Cox (2006). Which of these writers are engaged in 'critical' analysis is open to argument; and I cannot do justice to the rich and varied approaches to the study of 'religion' represented by all of these books. Talal Asad's work is widely and rightly recognised for its theoretical and historiographical significance. Perhaps the best short introduction to the history of the category 'religion' per se is by Jonathan Z. Smith, in his article "Religion, Religions, Religious" (1998), to which I referred in the introduction. This is a masterpiece of compression and clarity. Smith's outstanding scholarship is evident here, and his tracing of usages since the sixteenth century in several languages establishes a pattern of usage with which my own readings largely fit. But we seem to draw different conclusions (see a further discussion in chapter 6). One difference between our approaches is that, while Smith focuses exclusively in his article on the category 'religion', this book is concerned with religion and its changing usages in relation to changes in the rhetorical deployment of other categories such as 'politics', the 'state', and the 'secular'.

Peter Harrison (1990) and Tomoko Masuzawa (2005) have each written deeply researched yet conventional 'histories of ideas', or rather, histories of an idea, focused on 'religion'. Their research is comprehensive and valuable, but nevertheless ambiguous in relation to critical practice. While the history of the category of 'religion' is exhaustively traced, at the same time their work often seems only incidentally connected to other categories and the fields they construct. We do not see, for example, that there is a profound difference between Religion understood as Christian Truth encompassing all institutions in a world in which the 'state' and 'politics' did not exist in the modern sense, and 'religions' understood as private, nonpolitical, voluntary associations constitutionally separated from the secular state. Nor do they bring into theoretical focus the power games behind the control of meanings, and the ways in which 'religion' has been invented and reinvented. This is not merely a matter of emphasis, but an index of much deeper and broader shifts in the construction of modern consciousness which has repercussions in many other areas. In my view, the conventional history of ideas approach of Harrison and Masuzawa tends to naturalise the term without disembedding it from the rhetorical fields that are actually constructing it.

The histories of the category of religion executed by Harrison and Masuzawa, probably for reasons related to the production of a readable book, tend to consider a large number of texts briefly and summarily. One valuable part of their work is their bibliographies. My own method in some of these chapters is to subject a much smaller number of texts to greater analysis. I am interested in the general usages and discourses that form the warp and woof of our collective consciousness, but which can usually only be pinned down in specific texts of specific genres by specific authors. It is the particularity of usage that interests me, but by particularity I do not refer to one-off uniqueness. Any specific author exemplifies (usually in an authoritative way, and therefore in a way that will be imitated and influential) certain usages that seem to conform to the commonsense understandings current at the time. Thus, for example, while the bibliographies of J. Z. Smith, Peter Harrison, and Tomoko Masuzawa list several books published in the seventeenth century with expressions such as 'religions of the world' in their titles—all of them relevant and worthy of attention—I have chosen to spend a whole chapter looking at one of these, by Samuel Purchas (1626 [1613]; see chapter 7).

Readers who have expertise in a specific period may challenge the texts I have chosen as unrepresentative or only partially representative of that period. But this is an open-ended enquiry; the number of texts one could subject to this kind of investigation is very large indeed, as the bibliographies of Smith, Harrison, and Masuzawa attest. Thus while my method of reading a comparatively limited number of texts can be criticised on grounds of selectivity, one can at least subject the text to a wider and deeper search. For I am not looking only at 'religion'; I am interested in other things that are going on in a text that do not seem to be connected at first to 'religion', or not in any immediate and direct way, such as an ironic usage that carries another meaning, like superstition or deceit or barbarity, or the appearance in relation to 'religion' of a discourse on politics or economics. When a text begins to configure in new ways these other terms—for example, 'state'—then it is likely that 'religion' is being reconfigured too. Most authors take the meaning of 'religion' for granted. If not, they may attempt to define the term. I am not interested in that project, since definition assumes that there is something to define, and it is this assumption that I am questioning. The way that people define is important. The method for defining Christian Truth was entirely different from the modern method for defining religions, and yet the older meanings are not dead. For one thing, there are a number of other dichotomies that come up in texts ostensibly about religion which may be equally as important or even more so. When writers like John Locke in the late seventeenth century, or Benjamin Hoadly in the early eighteenth century, or William Warburton in the mid-eighteenth century, or Tiele in the late nineteenth century, are all ostensibly talking about the relation between religion and society, or religion and politics, or church and state, they are often also talking by analogy about the relation between mind and matter, or the body and the soul, or the public and the private, and possibly about male and female. These, and other pairs, are often standing in for each other, and they form chains of deferred meanings. Their discourses therefore come to be seen as rhetorically constitutive of modernity, rather than simply the works of people who had interesting things to say about religion.

This is connected to a further point. A late seventeenth-century Quaker Dissenter such as William Penn was not only concerned with 'belief' in the sense of abstract doctrinal issues or even only with 'toleration' as a highly contentious matter affecting personal lives. He and other Dissenters, like the status quo which they wished to change, were also concerned with 'hat etiquette' and usages of language which inscribe status differentials such as 'thee and thou', and thus with rank and status, hierarchy and equality. They were concerned with the presentation of self in everyday life. They were concerned with attitudes to individual bodies and to representations of the politic body in general. Research on religion, it seems to me, must be concerned with ritual performance in a wider sense than church ceremonies. As the Phythian-Adams (1972) historiography discussed in chapter 3 suggests, medieval and early modern social relations were permeated with ritual practices and public performances to such a degree that it was taken for granted by contemporaries and thus rarely brought into explicit discussion. The later seventeenth-century concern of the Quakers with hat etiquette, their parallel concern with the respect implied in the language of thee and thou, and the extreme violence of the reaction against them on these issues tend to suggest that such everyday practices were the warp and woof of the hierarchical construction of the world which they were challenging. Thus while Religion almost always referred at that time and for long after to Christian Truth, the antithesis of which was not 'the secular' but superstition and paganism, they were not merely talking about 'beliefs' as though these were abstract propositions about God; they were talking about the presentation of self in everyday life, and the way that dress codes, forms of language, and shared public performances can determine a vision of the good life. They were talking about the disciplines of civility and how they should be reformed, which will be discussed also in chapter 4.

This understanding of the significance of the threat posed by Dissenting nonconformity to the dominant dress codes and forms of polite speech opens up a range of opportunities for reassessing the changing meanings of 'religion' in other contexts. For example, I have argued that 'religion' was for centuries in England virtually impossible to separate from the sacred hierarchy idealised in the 'commonweal'; and that this in turn can be connected with a European tradition of what has been called 'civility' as distinct from 'barbarity' going back to Aristotle and the ancient Greeks. To get beyond modern ideological constructions of 'religion' as private and nonpolitical assent to a doctrine of salvation, or as voluntary organisations with problematic relations to civil society and the state, we need to look at ritual practices—the disciplines of civility—in a much wider sense, not merely symbolic of power relations but as constitutive too. The court rituals of the Tudors and subsequent monarchs, including the contemporary British monarch, Queen Elizabeth II, the dress codes of the aristocracy, the sumptuary laws of the first Elizabethan period, the rituals of chivalry, the transformation of the value of sumptuous display, still clearly observable in the court of the prince regent in the early nineteenth century, into the sober three-piece suit of Victorian bourgeoisie (Kutcha, 2002), the rituals of contemporary political party conventions and their public declarations of undying loyalty—all need to be charted in relation to the construction and reconstruction of what it means to be 'religious' or 'secular' or 'political'.

These issues are, of course, very much about the status of women, and the sense of what is proper and ritually correct is also a coded grammar of gender. For example, Christopher Hill, while dissolving the illusion that 'religion' was somehow distinct from the hierarchical state and commonwealth in the early modern period, implies that gender equality did exist in some contexts: "Parish officials were local government officials, responsible for poor relief and the poor rate, and for flogging vagrants 'until his or her body be bloody'" (Hill, 1980:75). On the other hand, women were the special targets of male authorities in relation to dress codes:

> The pulpit was used for making government announcements, and
> ministers were frequently instructed by the government to preach
> sermons slanted in a particular way. Thus in 1620 James I ordered
> the Bishop of London to instruct his clergy to preach against 'the
> insolency of our women and their wearing of broad-brimmed hats,
> pointed doublets, their hair cut short or shorn.' A fortnight later
> a news-letter records, 'Our pulpits ring continually of the insolency
> and impudency of women.' (1980:75)

Given that women were until quite recently conceived to have undeveloped rationality, like that of a child—a view sanctified by Aristotle, Aquinas, and Protestant writers—then in principle matters of gender and status and the ritual behaviours that make and mark such distinctions were all part of the subject matter of 'religion'.

Corinne Fowler (2007) in a prize-winning essay has shown how the burqua worn by Afghan women has been used by the British media to portray Islam as an essentially oppressive 'religion' for women, with the implied comparison with Western freedom. They do this by constructing an essentialised 'Islam' around the trope of women forced to cover their faces. Her analysis offers a more nuanced picture which questions both the construction of a static Islam and the construction of women by the media, whose depictions

> may be criticised on two fronts. Firstly, it peddles what Nirmal Puwar has called 'homogenised, static readings' of the garment . . . and, secondly, it implies that Islam is, in the words of Nadia Wassef, the ultimate 'explanatory force behind women's lives' . . . . One means of combating 'homogenized' readings of the garment is to historicize the *burqua*'s origins and to catalogue its changing significance at different historical junctures. The *burqua* made its first appearance in the Ottoman Empire, where it was used as a curtained sedanchair by upper-class Christian women to denote status and as protection from thieves and dust. From this period, the head-to-toe *burqua* evolved within a Christian context . . . . Moreover, the garment has a more complicated relationship to political patriarchy than news media coverage generally allows. As Christine Aziz notes, during the twentieth century, Afghan women have 'slipped in and out' of the *burqua* 'according to the male dictates of the day'. Although Amanullah's rule between 1919 and 1929 was in many ways an emancipatory time for Afghan women, they had to adhere to a strict policy of forcible unveiling . . . . Neither has the *burqua* been a classless garment. (Fowler, 2007)

Today, 'religion' is a powerful ideological term because it combines a number of analytically separable meanings which, when merged in the flow of unanalyzed discourse and rhetoric, render the term inherently unstable. Connected categories such as politics, economics, the state, and science have necessarily changed in meaning (or in the case of 'politics' and 'economics' virtually have been invented since the late seventeenth century) and, to the extent that they are framed implicitly or explicitly as 'nonreligious' instead of 'religious', as natural in distinction from supernatural, and therefore as rational as distinct from irrational or nonrational, they together form inseparable links to what they are held to be separate from. We cannot understand what we mean by religion unless we put it into relation with what we mean by nonreligion; but then the reverse is also true. They are semantically parasitic categories.

In this sense, my argument should be distinguished from some of the historical approaches mentioned above. While these all make important contributions to the field, the tendency of many to focus exclusively on 'religion' and 'religious studies' is precisely their danger as well as their benefit (though clearly Talal Asad, 2003, does not fall into this category, and Asad is surely one of the first scholars to focus on critical constructions of the secular). By tending to concentrate on 'religion' as a lone ranger, as a category in and for itself, such authors tend to represent politics, economics, and science as externally and contingently related to religion. In this way, they construct the field even as they describe and analyze it. In a sense, they are turning the very prayer wheels that generate the cosmology which they claim to describe. This deepens the reification of 'religion' discourse by excluding or marginalising perceptions of its wider role in the ideological economy of modernity.

My focus, then, is partly on the historical emergence of the oppositional relation between 'religion' and 'nonreligion', and the significance that this configuration holds for a modern idea of privatised religions which are countable and which are preeminently defined by modern secular (in the sense of nonreligious) and yet sacred constitutions. This is fundamentally different from the older meaning, what I am calling encompassing Religion, that is Christendom, or Religion as Christian Truth. Christian Truth defined the profane as well as the sacred. The word 'sacred' seems to have been used most frequently for the king or queen in English in the sixteenth, seventeenth, and eighteenth centuries. It was therefore also used for the civil government, which in England has been called the 'king-in-parliament'.[2] The 'profane' was not a realm set apart but a relative absence of sacredness. The modern concept of the secular is different from the profane. The specifically modern idea of privatised religions is required to define the nonreligious secular space; 'politics', which is centrally occupied *by* constitutions; and its historical offspring 'economics'.

For centuries, the English word Religion stood for Christian Truth,[3] and Truth was in opposition to superstition. The binary opposition between Christian Truth and superstition is also expressed in the thirteenth-century Aristotelian-Thomist paradigm as an opposition between rationality (natural reason) and irrationality. But these ideas are also strongly connected in the literature to the distinction between civility and barbarity. I will suggest in chapter 4 that if Religion meant Truth in opposition to superstition, it also meant civility as contrasted with barbarity. Throughout Christian history, there has been a significant overlap between discourses on Religion and superstition, on rationality and irrationality, and on civility and barbarity. Indeed, so closely do these discourses stand in for each other in pre-Enlightenment rhetoric that it is difficult to drive a conceptual wedge between them. The paradigm shift that occurred as a result of the Enlightenment, or rather the paradigm shift that defines the Enlightenment, established scientific method as the dominant criterion of rationality. There was a simultaneous change from the Religion-superstition binary to a binary opposition between Protestant-derived concepts of religion, defined mainly by private belief, and the public rationality of science. We tend to read back into Christian history our own Protestant and post-Protestant epistemological legacy, which has until relatively recently been dominated by a concern with doctrines modelled on naïve forms of propositional truth and belief, in the sense that the existence of God might be thought to be proved on the basis of empirical evidence, for example, the argument that design requires a cosmic designer. 'Deist' writers, for example, who reified God as a possible object of knowledge as the First Cause, tended to construct knowledge of God as analogous to scientific knowledge of the material world, exemplified in arguments from design. I suggest that deism should be seen as a transitional discourse bridging the different meanings of the world as 'profane' and as 'secular' (see chapter 3).

Yet despite the transition mentioned above, the rhetoric of civility-barbarity continued well into the nineteenth-century colonial era, and arguably until today, its defining character transformed by European Enlightenment, underpinned by evolutionary models of higher civility and rationality. Today, our postcolonial ideas are increasingly concerned with reembedding knowledge into practice, in which case we can reassess what it means to say that Christianity was concerned centrally with orthodoxy (correct belief) in contrast to orthopraxy (correct practice). This is because civility was often as much about correct dress code or diet as about belief as a propositional statement in the form of a doctrine.

Since the seventeenth century, the immanence of God in the everyday workings of the world has been increasingly replaced by scientific explanations which incorporate the assumption that the world is a self-subsistent material system or system of systems that contains the explanation for itself within itself. This point is exemplified by evolutionary theory as evangelised by Richard Dawkins, for example, which derives much of its power from its account of the development of all consciousness from increasing evolutionary complexity. His identification of 'religion' with 'God' and the 'supernatural' in *The God Delusion* (2006) derives from the post-Reformation and Enlightenment tradition of redefining and reconceiving the supernatural as essentially external to the real world of common sense described by science. For many writers who believe they occupy the obvious ground of secular rationality and common sense, 'religion' means 'belief in God or gods', and is unreal, a fantasy requiring explanation according to psychological or sociological realities.[4] On the other hand, Dawkins's belief in the scientific paradigm and in evolutionary theory has a zealous certitude which is not unlike the fanaticism often attributed to 'religious faith' (McGrath, 2005).

I am concerned with the essentialising process of modern discourses which has produced binaries such as 'religion' and the 'secular', 'supernatural' and 'natural', 'God' and 'world'—all of which are contested concepts and yet are policed on both sides by zealots as though it is clear what is meant by these multivalent and unstable terms. The emergence of a new conceptualisation of the supernatural has a significant function in making the secular world of politics and economics thinkable; it is what they are not. Until the seventeenth century approximately, the supernatural was not the same as irrationality; it was distinguished from superstition and irrationality. In a sense, the whole relationship between nature and supernature has been reversed. The supernatural was best exemplified by the central and fundamental ideology of the real presence; the term 'real' here indicating an entirely different ontology from the modern one. The relationship between the categories 'nature' and 'supernature' today has a similar binary form as the distinction between 're-ligion' and the nonreligious 'secular'. They are each defined negatively by what the other is not. The older distinction was more closely similar to the form of the sacred-profane distinction. In its more neutral form, as discussed in the next chapter, the profane was a relative absence of sacrality, a relative distance from the symbolics of Christ, though ultimately Christ encompasses every-thing. It was not only the church and the priesthood that were sacred; the sov-ereignty of the prince was sacred, as was the whole hierarchical order of human life. In its association with evil, as when sacred things are profaned by barbarity and perversity, it is still in a sense a positive relationship. The devil is a fallen angel, and the profane world as the fallen world is defined by its inversion of the sacred.

This distinction between the supernatural and the natural was (and, in-sofar as it still persists in Catholic practice, is) a quite different distinction from the modern one between the natural, which is considered as the 'real world' and the province of rationality, and the supernatural, which is a fantastic arena hived off, and either irrational or nonrational. Here, the world has been split asunder into two distinct ontological domains. One has been constructed as 'nature' and the material world, which is somehow inhabited by conscious individuals who are part of it and yet look out onto it as observers. This is as much a metaphysical invention as the earlier one, but it seems obviously true because we are conditioned from birth to perceive the world and ourselves within conceptual frames which none of us invented. The other domain, re-ligion, is the arena of 'spirituality' or 'faith', constituted by a marginalised basket of private fantasies, those idealised visions and unreachable goals of mystical yearnings and strivings. Psychologists have tried to classify them in terms of mental or experiential types, and sociologists in terms of organisa-tional types. But both these approaches assume the natural, secular rationality of the observer operating with a set of static assumptions and without much awareness of the point that the observer's own 'nonreligious' scientific stand-point is actually made possible by the construction of this alienated 'religious' sphere.

There is now a rampant commodification of 'religions' and the category has progressively extended its distance from its emic origins in a concept of Christian Truth and become transformed into a catchall term for a vast range of commodities which usually only have in common that they are categorised as privatised rights which pose or ought to pose no threat to the secular order. When a set of representations seems to demand power and challenges the state, then it becomes 'politics' masquerading as 'religion'. Yet the groundwork for this process of commodification lies to some extent with Christian missionaries, especially but not only Protestant missionaries who directly or indirectly, consciously or unconsciously, linked the idea of salvation to the increased circulation of goods and Western commercial civilisation;[5] with theologians who founded comparative religions and invented world religions; with colonial administrators who used 'religion' as a generic classification for the 'traditions' of the colonised people over whom they had power; with academics who have stroked the terminology into competing ritual refinements and contested magical efficacy, performing ceremonial dances at conferences and in symposia to summon up the perfectly efficacious definition and exemplary flora and fauna; and with politicians, newspaper editors, and journalists who have amplified the rhetoric. I will suggest in this book that all of these people helped to invent, and continue to invent, not only religions but also the idea of the nonreligious, the secular, the neutral and objective standpoint, the rational arenas of political and economic activity, or the world of our everyday, banal consciousness.

Contemporary religious studies is parasitic on these processes, was formulated in terms of them, and continues to reproduce them. There is a vast publishing industry on world religions, religions of the world, new religious movements, spiritualities, and the religious experiences of humankind. Authors who believe they are merely reporting what they find in the world continue to construct the field by the uncritical assumptions embedded in their reporting. But for the present I want to direct the reader's attention to encompassing Religion and privatised religions, for both of these entirely different but fundamentally important nuances of 'religion' cohabit in a large range of scholarly texts, politicians' rhetoric, and media frenzy.

The historiographical problem addressed here may to some extent be clarified by looking at an analogous problem in anthropology in the interpretation of other cultures. There are similarities in the problems that arise when modern English-language categories are employed to describe and analyse the constructed past of one's own culture and the constructed present of others' cultures. One area of modern discourse that has been imagined as 'secular' (in the sense of 'nonreligious') in contradistinction to 'religion' is 'economics', which historically first emerged as 'political economy' in the late eighteenth century.[6] In his introduction to *Economic Anthropology* (1989), the anthropologist Stuart Plattner has put the anthropological problem like this:

> Economics grew up as a field of study in rapidly developing capitalist societies. Although the basic terms of economics are defined ab-

stractly, they fit best the capitalist, industrialized economy in which they were developed. The attempt to transfer them to the analysis of noncapitalist societies has created problems. Trying to comprehend the economic activity of an economy organised on the basis of corporate kinship groups, for example, is as difficult as it is for a speaker of English to understand the importance of tones in Chinese or Zapotec (a Mexican Indian language). The main problem is the 'embeddedness' of economic activities.... The social and cultural matrix of our own economic behaviour is transparent to us so that, for example, heightened retail sales at Christmas seem 'just' economic, not religious. But the cultural context of economic behaviour in exotic societies is blatantly obvious. For example, *production* implies a discrete activity, a creation of economic value by changing the characteristics of a good. This activity is conceptually separate from *religion*, because in Western society, religious actors do not create economic production while they are doing religious acts. The closest we get occurs when religious leaders bless or certify the tools of production (for example, the priest blessing the fishing boats or the rabbi certifying that the food factory is kosher). This separation of spheres of behaviour creates a problem for the 'economic' anthropologist, who analyses something that looks like economic production but that is also clearly 'religious'. (1989:10–11)

I take modern economic theory to be persuasive rhetoric based on myths such as progress and autonomous individuals whose rationality lies in the maximisation of personal profit, not as a theory that represents real processes that objectively exist in nature (see Wolf, 1997 [1982]; Dowd, 2000). However, unless we are going to assume that only Euro-Americans and European-language speakers can be in touch with these putative natural realities, then we have to take the problem of translation seriously.

Hiroshi Mizuta, in his essay "Adam Smith in Japan" (2003:195), tells us about the problem of translating the basic categories of liberal capitalism into Japanese during the early Meiji period:

As another example of the difficulty of transplanting western liberalism... J. S. Mill's *On Liberty* was translated into Japanese in 1872.... The translator could not understand what was meant by the word 'society', which did not exist in Japan then in the strict sense of Mill's terminology. It was translated as government or village elders and thus completely missed Mill's idea of the tyranny of the majority.

The historian Jun'ichi Isomae has shown the problem that the Japanese ruling elite experienced in trying to render the English-language word 'religion' into Japanese (Isomae, 2000, 2007). Isomae says that the Western powers divided the non-Western parts of the world into three categories: (a) civilised nations; (b) savage or semi-civilised; and (c) primitive or underdeveloped. The latter, which included vast areas of Asia, Africa, and America, were deemed to be virtually uninhabited and therefore the peoples living there, often nonliterate, were hardly deemed to exist as human societies. In the middle category were placed ancient literate cultures such as Japan, China, and India. Japan had a desire to be elevated to the "civilised" category (e.g., equal with Euro-Americans) and thus to avoid either direct colonisation or, marginally better, unequal trade treaties, bullying, and the generally condescending attitude of the West. One of the conditions for inclusion in this elevated group was a Western-style constitution that included the separation of 'religion' and 'politics' and the principle of freedom of worship. The English-language word 'religion' was associated in the minds of educated Japanese with Christianity. It was therefore from the beginning something foreign which was being imposed from the outside. Eventually the word *shûkyô* was chosen. After a great deal of debate, the Meiji elite obliged with the 1889 Constitution, which in turn led to the invention of state Shinto and the divinisation of the emperor.

What I want to press here is that, when we apply modern concepts of 'religion', 'politics', or 'economics' to virtually any culture at any time in history, we are importing into the analytical situation a distorting medium. What we have constructed as the domains of 'politics' or 'economics', part of that modern 'nonreligious' secular domain which has been separated from something we call 'religion', were in sixteenth- and seventeenth-century England, and for much of the eighteenth, embedded in Christian Truth. Insofar as anything like a concept of 'the economy' existed, it was not in opposition to Religion but encompassed by it. To use twentieth-century anthropological jargon, the economy was embedded in the total order of human relations, and not imagined as a distinct domain or 'discursive space'. For example Tyndale, in *The Parable of the Wicked Mammon*, said: "Let him buy and sell truly . . . . And let your superfluities succour the poor, of which sort shall ever be some in all towns, and cities, and villages" (quoted in Williams, 1967:293). Rather than seeing the reinvestment of personal profit as a sound economic principle, Tyndale refers to "superfluities" which should be offered to the poor as charity and as service to the harmony of the commonweal. The capitalist motive of private investment which Weber identified as partly a consequence of Calvinist doctrine concerning the transformed meaning of Christian Truth had not yet been established as a dominant discourse.

The historical process whereby domains such as politics and economics came to be disembedded from encompassing Religion is not meant to suggest the recovery of something already there but waiting for a superior intelligence to find it. By 'disembed' in this context, I mean to 'invent', in a way rather similar to Gellner's meaning when he said of nationalism, "Nationalism is not the awakening of nations to self-consciousness: it invents nations where they do not exist" (quoted in Anderson, 1991:5).[7] So we find 'religions' and 'economies' where they did not exist before. I will here be making that point about a number of our taken-for-granted categories.

The usual use of 'œconomy' was for the household. In the model of the commonweal developed by Starkey in "A Dialogue between Pole and Lupset,"[8] what we think of as the economic domain is here thought of as an encompassed part of the politic body working efficiently or inefficiently. The tendency in Starkey's version to greater theoretical explicitness, and the wider range of worldly experience through travel and overseas study, allows him to compare and thus to some degree to relativise scarcity, want, and high prices. He argues that these are caused by lack of productivity. However, this is not a natural state of affairs, but unnatural. It is explained in moral terms, by vices such as gluttony and idleness:

> [T]hose many and great waste grounds here in our country, the great
> lack of victual and the scarceness thereof, and dearth of all things
> worked by man's hand, do not only show the great negligence of the
> rest of our people, but . . . doth argue and declare manifest lack of
> diligence . . . . If our artificers applied themselves to labour as dili-
> gently as they do in other countries [he mentions France, Italy,
> and Spain] we should not have things . . . so scarce and so dear. (quoted
> in Williams, 1967:299–300)

The idea of economics as a domain of rational activity rooted in 'nature' and having nothing essentially to do with Religion is hardly present here, even though one might claim retrospectively to see it emerging. Jumping forward two hundred years or so to the time of Adam Smith's *Wealth of Nations* (1776), Kathryn Sutherland, in her explanatory notes and commentary to her edition of that work, says about the idea of "political œconomy":

> The modern term 'economics' did not exist in Smith's time . . . .
> Throughout the eighteenth century, the . . . term 'œconomy' (subse-
> quently 'economy', from the Greek oikonomia) retained as its pri-
> mary significance 'the management of a house' or 'domestic
> regulation' . . . 'Political œconomy', cited in the OED from 1767,
> though it can be found in English in the late seventeenth century, is
> an extension from the domestic context, referring to arguments
> concerning the laws and management of a national economy as an
> aspect of the state. (Sutherland, 1993:466)

This is borne out by checking the first edition of the *Encyclopaedia Britannica* of 1773 where the entry for *œconomics* has not constructed it as a science or as a discrete field but as an activity or status:

the art of managing the affairs of a family, or community; and hence the person who takes care of the revenues and other affairs of churches, monasteries, and the like, is termed œconomus.

Œconomy denotes the prudent conduct, or discreet and frugal management, whether of a man's own estate, or that of another. (3:410)

This entry is immediately followed by:

Animal Œconomy, comprehends the various operations of nature in the generation, nutrition, and preservation of animals. SEE GENERATION, NUTRITION, Etc.

The doctrine of the animal œconomy is nearly connected with physiology, which explains the several parts of the human body, their structure, use, etc. SEE ANATOMY.

There is no entry precisely for *political œconomy* in the 1773 edition, but the entry under *politics* links the two:

POLITICS, the first part of œconomy, consisting in the well governing and regulating the affairs of a state, for the maintenance of the public safety, order, tranquillity, and morals.

What seems to me to be an interesting point here is that, three years before the American War of Independence, the new *Dictionary of Arts and Sciences* published in Edinburgh, the city of David Hume and Adam Smith, does not record entries for either economy or politics as separate discrete fields. Political economy is here, but is generally concerned with public safety, order, and morals. The nearest the encyclopaedia comes to what we might think of as politics is under "POLITY, or Policy," viz.:

POLITY, or Policy, denotes the peculiar form and constitution of the government of any state or nation; or the laws, orders, and regulations, relating thereto.

Polity differs only from politics, as the theory from the practice of any art.

By the edition of 1815, the entry for *economics* makes it part of 'political economy', which may reflect the growing influence of Adam Smith and others, such as Ricardo and Bentham. Douglas Dowd argues that Ricardo's arguments for free trade against mercantilism in Ricardo's *Principles of Political Economy and Taxation*, published in 1817, "triumphed in Britain in the 1840's, after a bitter struggle over 'The Corn Laws'," and that his underlying theory remains "virtually intact today, both in form and content" (Dowd, 2000:31). Bentham published his theory of human nature and utilitarianism in *An Introduction to the Principles of Morals and Legislation* in 1780. Dowd notes that in his case as well the effects of the theory took time to become influential, and "first emerged in the 1850's, a full generation after [his] death" (2000:38). Perhaps this delay explains why there is no entry for economics as a science in the 1815 edition of the encyclopaedia. Presumably this idea existed by that time, but only in narrow advanced circles.

Many of the words we use today as nouns, such as 'society' in the singular and 'societies' in the plural, existed in the sixteenth and even the seventeenth century only as adjectives, or as attributes of specific human relations (see Bossy, 1982). This is not merely of historical interest; it concerns the methodology of historiography itself. If, as the anthropologist Plattner has argued above, we cannot understand noncapitalist economies by importing a theory-laden, modern English-language category such as 'economics' into the situation, then arguably the same principle applies in the case of our own Euro-American past.

Some readers might feel that the two analytical situations are not perfectly comparable, and they would be right, because whereas in the case of Zapotec the languages are entirely different, in the case of the English and close European languages there is not the same problem of translation. It is true that the problem of translation is not identical, but in some ways it is even more complex in the English case. This is because the historian can easily assume that when she talks about economics or politics or the secular in English, the word and the concept have always been there in some essential form, even though they may have changed their nuances. Another way of putting this would be to say that the idea was there tacitly, but had not been brought fully into consciousness yet through a process of historical development and the growth in rationality. This would be a variation on the illusion that what we now call religion, economics, politics, or the state are essentially ubiquitous in all societies throughout history, and that any lack of reference to what we now know to be the fundamentals of all societies is merely a sign that these domains had not been properly discovered or articulated, as though the fully rational categorisation of the Enlightenment and modernity had not fully reached consciousness, with the possible added implication that they were not quite intelligent enough to have realised the truth about their own social processes which we now, in retrospect, have finally come to realise.

In "Theses on Method" (1996), Bruce Lincoln has tried to establish an essential difference between 'religion' as an object of investigation, and 'the study of religion' as a secular (nonreligious) practice of neutrality and objectivity. The value of this attempt is that it makes very explicit what is usually only implicit in religious studies and anthropology. In making the distinction between the religious and the secular clear and explicit, we can also see why it is really a rhetorical distinction, an attempt to persuade us to view the world in a particular way. In Lincoln's book *Holy Terrors* (2003), the distinction between secular scholarship as a nonreligious activity and religion as a distinct domain of human practice and an object of research is implicit throughout. In chapters 4–6, Lincoln is concerned with the relation between the category 'religion' and the hegemonic aspects of capitalism and colonialism, and he has many valid and interesting things to say about the colonial context. In some places, he indicates the difficulty of distinguishing between 'secular' and 'religious' ideologies in potentially interesting ways, for example in an extended footnote where he discusses the difficulty of distinguishing between religions and so-called secular ideologies such as Marxism, Freudianism, nationalism, and anarchism (2003:129n10).

However, as I have argued in my own response (Fitzgerald, 2006), his treatment on the whole essentialises and universalises English-language categories as though they are fixed in the nature of things. His potentially useful distinction between "Maximalist" and "Minimalist" models of culture (2003: 59), like the distinction between religion and the secular that it implies, tends towards a static and essentialist model of alternating phenomena, like an eternal duo fox-trotting together through the whole of human history. Lincoln assumes, without critically reflective comment, to represent *generic* religion, and his model building is designed to throw a very wide net, and to gather within one 'religion' basket a whole range of different movements, ideologies, and practices which are themselves all distinguished from 'secular' ideologies and practices.

That Lincoln's intention, while at times apparently critical, is more in the direction of essentialising and naturalising the religion-secular dichotomy can be seen from something he says in the preface, where he indicates that he is still searching for "the nature of religion," as though religion has a nature:

> This book represents my attempt to think through the nature of
> religion, to identify its core components (discourse, practice, com-
> munity, institution), and to specify its historically changing relation
> to other aspects of culture (particularly the ethical, aesthetic, and
> political). (Lincoln, 2003:ix)

But it is not clear why we should assume that religion has a nature distinct from the aesthetic, the ethical, or the political. The implication is that all these categories refer to things with natures. This is surely to embed these contingent and arbitrary rhetorical constructions into the natural order of things. If discourse, practice, community, and institution are what constitute the core components of the nature of religion (its essence), it is difficult to see how religion differs from secular history, or from secular politics, or from secular anything. Presumably, ethics, aesthetics, and politics can all be analyzed and described in terms of discourse, practice, community, and institution. My point is that he is not doing anything essentially nonreligious himself. We only think he is because, well, because we keep telling ourselves that there is this essential difference between what Western[9] scholars do and what 'the religious' (such as vicars, brahmins, and imams) do. In an extended footnote, he says:

> To my mind, one of the most difficult of all questions is assessing the extent to which 'secular' ideologies of the nineteenth and twentieth centuries—Marxism, anarchism, psycho-analysis, and the like—are significantly different from religious ideologies, and to what extent the undeniable differences between these two modes of ideology are more superficial than substantive. What can be observed is that until relatively recently in human history, all ideologies were explicitly religious. Within the last two centuries, however, such developments as the emergence of the modern nation-state, mass communications, and industrial production have created situations in which ostensibly nonreligious ideologies have come into being and flourish alongside of religious ideologies. One must note, however, that these new ideologies still possess powerful mythic, ritual, and soteriological dimensions, whatever their position towards 'religion' per se. At the very least, we may thus be justified in calling them 'para-religious'. (2003:129n10)

It is useful to take note of the actual usages in Lincoln's paragraph here, such as "religion per se." Why does he put the first 'secular' and the final 'religion' in quotation marks, as though to sensitively separate them and indicate them as problems, when he is using these terms uncritically as fundamental and universal organising categories throughout his book? If these 'secular' ideologies are so similar in so many important ways to 'religions', then what are the "undeniable differences" between them that he asserts in passing? How far does the term "para-religious" differ from the widely used terms quasi-religious, pseudoreligious, religious-like phenomena?[10] He says that "until relatively recently in human history, all ideologies were explicitly religious." How does he know that? This is not a hypothesis based on observations, but a rhetorical promulgation. How were they explicated as "religious," in for example, Chinese, Japanese, Arabic, different African languages, or even in English? For even in English, until quite recently, nobody would have described Christianity as a 'religious ideology'. It is a striking example of the way in which modern English terminology, one is tempted to say triumphalist English terminology, is simply proclaimed as having universal validity.

We can get a taste of the ubiquity of 'religions' and its hypostatised forms from his distinction between 'religion of the status quo' and 'religions of resistance':

Whereas there will as a rule be only one religion of the status quo
within a given society at any given time, the variety of religions
of resistance that may thrive simultaneously is well-nigh endless, and
history attests to a rich variety of exemplars. They may be ascetic,
libertarian, or orgiastic; impassioned, cathartic, or quietistic; uto-
pian or nihilistic; esoteric, mystical; militant or pacifist; authoritarian, egalitarian, or anarchist; and so on ad infinitum. (Lincoln,
2003:83)

Is it a fact-based generalisation that, as a rule there will only be one "religion of the status quo" in any given society at any given time, but a wide
variety of possible "religions of resistance"? Does history attest to this as he
claims? I would argue that this is merely the uncritical imposition of parochial
English-language rhetoric, a sweeping act of the imagination which serves purposes other than objective or neutral scholarship. Yet it is apparently obvious
to Lincoln that some of the following at least are "religions of resistance":

The most obvious religions of resistance are those movements that
have been labelled 'heterodox' by religions of the status quo: Buddhists and Taoists in China; Jains and Buddhists in India; Hugue-
nots, Lollards, Hussites, Anabaptists, and countless 'heretic' groups
throughout European history, not to mention Jews and Freema-
sons; Baha'is and Isma'ilis in Iran; and Shi'ites in Arab nations, to
name but a few. (Lincoln, 2003:83)

Lincoln does not worry about the fit of the English-language category 'religion' to incorporate such a diverse set of essentialised human groups under
the same label. Nor does he hesitate to fix on them the labels of 'resistance',
'heterodox', and 'heretic'. After all, we all know what we mean. But this is not
sufficient for his purposes, for he has yet more religions to list and categorise:

Beyond these, one must also include the numerous independent churches and spirit possession cults of Africa; most of the
Melanesian Cargo Cults in their early phases; the Peyote and
Sun Dance Amerindian religions; such Afro-American movements as Candomblé, Umbanda, Santeria, Shango, Vodun, and
Ras Tafari; not to mention the rich variety of black churches, Pen-
tecostal groups, and new religions in the United States. (Lincoln,
2003:83)

The insertion of "in their early phases" to qualify "Melanesian Cargo Cults"
could be taken as a sign of a scholar concerned with great precision in the
attribution of technical terminology to his subject. But it is difficult to see these
vast generalisations about the religions of the world as the product of careful
historiography. Lists of names alone give us nothing of historical interest, and

we find out nothing either about the humans involved or about why anyone should have assumed that they all have something important in common—what is it that makes the complexities concealed behind Anglicised labels such as Shiites, Jains, and Melanesian cargo cults all essentially the same kind of thing? And what is it that makes them all essentially different in kind from Marxism or nationalism or, indeed, Bruce Lincolnism? His answer to my rhetorical questions, given in his "Theses on Method," is itself a rhetorical flourish structured by putative distinctions: transcendent and eternal as against temporal and terrestrial; tacitly infallible and god-like in contrast to the "human and fallible voice" of the humble historian:

> Thesis 2: Religion, I submit, is that discourse whose defining characteristic is its desire to speak of things eternal and transcendent with an authority equally transcendent and eternal. History, in the sharpest possible contrast, is that discourse which speaks of things temporal and terrestrial in a human and fallible voice, while staking its claim to authority on rigorous critical practice.

But this is itself a god-like proclamation. What we have here in the "theses" is Religion in the singular, a kind of mystical essence that speaks, and which in *Holy Terrors* manifests itself in all the different "religions of resistance" and "religions of the status quo" assumed to exist or to have existed in apparently every culture at all times. I question this idea of historiography, and suggest that it is far from being a "rigorous critical practice." It is itself a kind of prophetic utterance, or just wild guesswork.

In a footnote, Lincoln considers the idea that a whole range of ideologies such as Marxism and nationalism, which are usually categorised as secular, themselves look suspiciously like what in other contexts we prefer to call religions. If he had taken this observation to its logical conclusion, he would have rendered the distinction between the religious and the secular dubious from any presumed point of objective analysis or description, and usefully clarified it as 'ideological rhetoric'. But this insight would have required him, as a self-proclaimed secular scholar, to ask questions about his own power position in his assignment of vast swaths of human practices into their proper places. Sometimes he seems to be saying something like that too, especially in the context of his discussion of European and American colonialism (2003:82). But Lincoln does not allow these observations to distract him from his more fundamental determination to construct generic religion and its distinction from the secular as sound descriptive categories for the objective model building of all societies at all times (see his models, 2003:66–72). I would argue that without reified 'religion', his own myth of scholarly rationality, of the essential difference between doing history and being religious, his own intention of bringing us objective Enlightenment through the building of increasingly elaborate and comprehensive models,[11] would be impossible.

This kind of essentialisation of religion and religions, on the one hand, and society, state, or politics, on the other hand, encourages us to imagine that these words refer to things or domains with essential differences and substantive characteristics which persist through time, perhaps taking on different appearances, at one time being suppressed from view, marginalised, covered up, then emerging or reemerging but remaining essentially the same nevertheless. At one period of history in this part of the world, religion is dominant and the secular aspects of culture are subordinated; but then at another point of time or in another place, the secular can reassert itself and marginalise religion. It doesn't matter whether we are talking about ancient China, colonised Africa in the nineteenth century, the indigenous people of North America, or the English civil wars of the seventeenth century—the terms remain essentially the same. And we know what they mean even if we can't precisely define them.

There are any number of books with titles like 'religion and society in Edo Japan', or 'religion and society in contemporary America', or 'religion and society in medieval France'. One could add the various other equally dubious and uncritical conjunctions that proliferate of the kind religion and economics, religion and politics, or religion and the state, which imply, often unconsciously, essentially contingent combinations of distinct domains in different historical situations. I have extensively criticised in other publications this conjunction of reified discourses, arguing that the idea that religion might in principle be separate from society, though joined with it at certain points, is profoundly incoherent, which makes the popularity of its usage all the more intriguing. However, whenever one considers the complexity of actual historical usage in English alone—putting aside the difficulty of translation into all the languages involved—in such wide sweeps of human history, and adding the problem of defining in any substantive sense the meaning of these general categories, it becomes clearer that, underlying a discourse such as 'religion and society' lies the same binary between 'religion' and 'nonreligion' as the one that underlies the religion-secular dichotomy. This idea is itself part of our modern ideology, and allows us to construct the categories of modernity as though they are themselves ubiquitous in space and time.

The argument in this book does not assume that 'religion' and the 'secular' correspond to two essentially different domains of human experience, providing us with authentic ways of thinking about different kinds of experience, different kinds of practice, or different kinds of institution. It makes more sense to understand these as rhetorical categories which have proved useful for certain groups of people with particular objectives and values at specific points in history, and to conclude that they therefore do not provide an 'objective' account of what is in the world. Nor can they act as neutral heuristic devices, as though they are merely one useful way of organising scholarly data, an idea which is a secondary fallacy that comes into operation when the primary essentialist fallacy is effectively questioned.

Once the ideologically constructed 'history of religion' has been grasped—or rather regrasped and reappropriated, because once we have remembered the contested character of our Anglophone past which gave birth to these categories, the point becomes more obvious—then it will be appropriate for us to ask whether or not this modern ideological formation any longer serves a valid purpose for us. For, undoubtedly, the distinction between private religious conscience and public duty to the state, or between inner religious experience and secular rationality, which lies at the origin of this dichotomy, was partly the result of genuine struggles against tyranny. It was partly the suffering of minorities in seventeenth-century England and eighteenth-century France, North America, and elsewhere which led to the establishment of rights, such as freedom of assembly, speech, and conscience, and the limitation of the encroachments of the church-state. Arguably, it was the struggles and sacrifices of many individuals and groups such as the Quakers and others that gave birth to the constitutional protection of the rights of the individual and thus to modern democracy. One could add another motive, which was to open up a conceptual and epistemological space not controlled by the church-state, and thus to allow alternative forms of thought and expression to develop. The development of scientific method and the consequent advances in useful technologies such as medicine are one part of the complex historical result. But these struggles were not the only sources of the dichotomy, nor was it only democratic values that were being asserted. Nor can we take it for granted in today's world that this form of dichotomous representation still serves the interests of human rights and democracy, or even of freedom of thought and expression. For it might be plausibly argued that the distinction between religion and secular politics or economics, as it is embedded in current discourses both inside and outside of the academy, serves interests which are in conflict with advances in democratic practice.

It is not my purpose in this book to directly argue for or against a defence of the separation of religion and the secular, but to show that both words 'religion' and 'secular' were reinvented and had profoundly different meanings attached to them, meanings that are rooted in a complete paradigmatic reconstruction of the world and its ontology which today is being challenged from many other directions. When I say that they had profoundly different meanings attached to them, I mean that they began to be used in profoundly different ways, within the context of different categorical systems, not that they had one essential meaning but then developed another essential meaning. It would therefore be a misreading of my intention to think I am claiming that some preexisting entity called Religion was simply marginalised, as though it were rolled back to reveal a preexisting domain of secular activity that had been covered over, dominated, or made to occupy a subordinate role, the secular state at last emerging fully into view after being mystified by a dominant institutionalised spirituality. On the contrary, I am arguing that something new was invented or imagined. The secular as the modern 'nonreligious' was not a preexisting domain that, having been under the control of the church, now in modernity has changed position and become dominant.

In modern discourse, an illusion has been created that these terms refer fairly unproblematically to eternally existing verities, that there has always and everywhere been religion, and that we can talk about the politics and economics of any human group at any time and in any place in history. When one looks at the actual use of language, at least in a mass of modern English texts about 'religion' and 'society', or 'religion' and 'politics', there is an unstated assumption that these words refer to domains of human action, discourses, and kinds of things that exist in the world and always have done so, that while 'politics' in 'democratic' Athens may in some respects have been articulated differently, we know what we mean intuitively and that between ancient Athenian politics and those of the modern state there is no essential difference, only differences of form, degree, and organisation. Politics after all is politics, as the English translation of Aristotle's famous text proves. If pushed, we might then say, well, politics is about power, or even the legitimation of power. That would be difficult to disagree with, but how much has been said? To make a general category like politics seem universally valid, it needs to be stripped of much specificity. And beneath this illusion is the idea that politics in ancient Athens or contemporary Britain or Iran are *essentially* nonreligious, and distinct from religion, though at times having a problematic relationship to religion, and even threatening to become confused with it. Thus, in Iran, it might be said in English that many essentially political functions are under the control of religious mullahs, a form of words that subtly embeds the religion-secular dichotomy into a representation of a culture which may, in its own terms, fundamentally contest such a dichotomy. Whereas I am suggesting that words create worlds, especially those categories that order dominant discourses. In this case, Iran has been encompassed or colonised by hegemonic English-language categories, and this could have implications for foreign policy and even military action.

There is a significant implication that follows from seeing that these kinds of speech acts, whatever the appearance of commonsense factuality, are really authoritative reassertions of a dominant ideological trope. It is the realisation that 'religion' is not a preexisting, perennial domain of human culture that has always somehow been there in one form or another, having had some problematic relationship to some other preexisting nonreligious domain like 'politics', the relationship undergoing various vicissitudes. On the contrary, I believe that this assumption is itself an aspect of our modern ideology, our supposed enlightenment, which appears to us as a natural description of the way things are.

Today, we have discourses on secular law, secular politics, secular economics, secular education, but we do not need to use the term 'secular' at all except to distinguish it from the 'nonsecular', and what is the nonsecular other than religion? Thus the only genuinely essential characteristic of the secular is that it means the nonreligious, and thus it exists purely as a categorical opposition to what it is not. It has no essential positive content.[12] To project that meaning of the 'secular' as the 'nonreligious' into our reconstruction of medieval or early modern Europe is to profoundly misrepresent and misunderstand it. To project an essential distinction between religious experiences and nonreligious ones into Chinese or African history, which is quite normal in our publishing industry, seems even more questionable when we cannot explain even which words were being used to formulate such a discourse.

But we are not only constructing our own imaginary object and clothing it with verisimilitude. We are doing far more than that, usually without realising it. We are naturalising and universalising our own meanings and therefore putting ourselves in touch with a presumed reality in a way which validates our own practices, our own sense of who we are as enlightened moderns. This may be the most important part of our knowledge industry, not to achieve enlightenment through its accumulation, but to construct a world where it seems normal to think that private property or the accumulation of corporate capital are parts of the immutable rational order of things. At last, rationality is breaking out and we can start to contemplate self-realisation and the end of history. We are subordinating the whole history of humankind to our own presuppositions. To talk about the religion, society, politics, or economics of medieval society is to construct imaginary objects which do not really give us understanding of them but rather it validates our present ideological categories, including the illusion of scholarly progress and objectivity, that knowledge is about truth, which is an inherently worthwhile thing to have. In this way our scholarship, for example, is clothed with an aura of factuality and common sense that assures us that, even if we disagree about the details, we are living in the real world of rational discussion and objective analysis in a way that those medieval people were striving for but had not yet quite achieved, or from which Osama Bin Laden, Pat Robertson, and Jerry Falwell are barred by their irrational fanaticisms.

3

Methodology 2

Religion and Secular, Sacred and Profane

It is often assumed without question that the sacred and the religious are coterminous, and that the profane and the secular are also coterminous. Thus, according to this way of thinking, the activity of digging a ditch is and always has been profane or secular in the sense of being technical, an example of instrumental rationality understood as 'nonreligious'. It might be conceded by the scholar holding this assumption that this profane activity sometimes has 'religious' meanings as well, as in digging a grave to bury someone while performing rituals because the dead person is believed to have a soul which is then destined to go to heaven or hell or perhaps to become an ancestor. This then leads to the problem of deciding which parts of the digging operation are merely the profane, the secular, the purely technical, and which parts are the religious or ritual aspects.[1] But this problem is generated, I suggest, by our ideological attachment for other reasons to the reifying idea that the world has these two distinct domains, one the religious, sometimes referred to by anthropologists as ritual,[2] and usually further associated with the 'supernatural', and the other the profane, secular, or merely technical, associated with the 'natural'. One can see behind this dichotomy a number of others, such as mind and body, spirit and matter, otherworldly and this-worldly, and rational and irrational (or nonrational). These dichotomous pairs are normally represented as though they have stable, self-evident meanings, are in the nature of things, and do not require historical critical contextualisation. It is on the basis of this assumption that they are used as fundamental organising principles not only in religious studies but in academic disciplines across the spectrum. But I am arguing that these dichotomies have become transformed into modern ideological constructs, that their meanings have changed because the world views or paradigms within which they are embedded have changed, and that rather than objectively describing features of the world, or acting as neutral organising principles validated by common-sense observation, they construct the world and our perceptions of the world in conformity with Euro-American colonial and neocolonial interests.

Here, I will make a methodological proposal which will help to clarify the argument and the analysis of texts and contexts. I propose to make an analytical distinction between two conceptual dichotomies that have become confused in religious studies and the humanities more widely. It is frequently assumed that 'religion' is the province of the 'sacred'. This domain is then taken to be in contrast to, or in opposition to, the 'secular', which is further identified with the profane. Religion and the sacred are further identified with the 'church' and with 'ritual', whereas the secular and profane are identified with the state or politics, and with technical practices.[3] In this way, two great binaries are assumed. These pairs are often further reinforced by identifying the sacred and the religious with 'things set apart', with 'the other world', or with the 'supernatural'. This is typically constructed in opposition to the secular and profane as the ordinary things of 'this world' or the 'natural'.[4]

This dichotomisation is not necessarily consistent, and indeed a salient feature of much writing on religion is how the meaning of these terms shifts in relation to context, often in the same scholarly text.[5] Nevertheless, this is a broadly assumed dichotomy which can be found in texts throughout the humanities. It is usually unconscious and has been influenced greatly by Eliade and Durkheim. For example, Durkheim defines 'religion' like this:

> All known religious beliefs, whether simple or complex, present a common quality: they presuppose a classification of things—real or ideal things that men represent for themselves—into two classes, two opposite kinds, generally designated by two distinct terms effectively translated by the worlds *profane* and *sacred*. The division of the world into two comprehensive domains, one sacred, the other profane, is the hallmark of religious thought. (Durkheim, 2001:36)

Durkheim's ideas about classification and systems of representation have proved seminal. However, had he delinked the sacred from 'religion', and the profane from the secular, I believe his arguments would have gained in clarity and power. I want here to argue that there are good historical, as well as analytical, reasons for distinguishing between these dichotomies. In succeeding chapters, I will attempt to substantiate what I here merely attempt to sketch out broadly.

I have placed this chapter early because I am trying to formulate some relatively less-problematic conceptual ground from which to view 'religion' in the context of what I take to be one of the fundamental binaries of modern ideology. My purpose, however, is not to construct an alternative authoritative ground from which to judge and classify others, but to subvert what I see as a major element of our colonial inheritance, which for convenient brevity I refer to as the religion-secular dichotomy. On the face of it, shifting the analytical weight to a concept of 'sacred-profane' will seem to many readers as implausible and perhaps even reactionary, as the simplistic substitution of one uncritical Anglophone category for another.[6]

In a sense, it may be inevitable that any attempt to develop a standpoint in the English language about other people's meanings, that is the meanings of people who think in non-European languages, will distort what it is claiming to represent. This will surely be true whether we talk about the religious or the sacred, the secular or the profane, or the application of any other powerful Anglophone category to the analysis or classification of what have been constructed as 'other cultures'—itself a problematic term. The problem does not only rise from the simple fact that different groups of people have historically produced different systems of representations, and that there is an inherent problem of translating one set of representations into the terms of another. For that problem, which is a very real one, is also a matter of power. British colonial policy seems to have encouraged not merely the elevation of English as a useful universal medium for the promotion of international understanding, but also the active suppression of indigenous languages. Let us just consider one witness to this language policy of the British Empire. The Kenyan writer Ngugi wa Thiong'o, author of seven novels, whose native language is Gikuyu and who is now a professor of English and comparative literature at the University of California at Irvine, remembers his education at a British colonial school. Lynne Duke of the *Washington Post* reports:

> Ngugi wa Thiong'o was 12 when he witnessed the beating. Teachers at his British colonial school in the 'white highlands' of Kenya caught one of his school chums speaking Gikuyu. The indigenous language wasn't allowed at school. Only English was to be spoken. In front of a student assembly, two teachers held the boy down. They called him 'monkey' while another teacher lashed him. The whip cut his skin. Blood appeared. Ngugi registered, even then, that Gikuyu was not only a forbidden thing but a thing that brought pain and humiliation. Only much later, he says, did he realize how the boy's screams and the shouts of 'monkey' were the building blocks of the 'linguistic prison' into which generations of colonized Africans were thrust. ("Rebuilding the Cultural Base: The Voice of Kenya Practises the 'Aesthetics of Resistance' in His Mother Tongue," *Weekly Guardian*, 6–12 October 2006:12)

Today, in the postcolonial era of supreme American power, English is a language which the whole world is expected to speak if they want to be heard and taken seriously in any major organisation or site of negotiation. Non-European scholars who want their views to be heard have no choice but to publish in English-language journals, and thus to organise their ideas in terms of English-language categories. Subaltern peoples are compelled to defend their traditional customs by renaming them as 'religion' and then lobbying for the right of religious freedom under Western-style constitutions.[7] This is the reality and there is not a lot that anybody can do about it, until some alternative dominant power such as China arises, with all the consequences that would ensue. Of course, many readers will rush to protest that without a universal language there could be no world communication, in which case the dangers of misunderstanding between peoples and nations would be increased. However, apart from the incontestable fact that misunderstandings in international communications proliferate in the contemporary world, it is also surely true that those people who are not European but have some other native language are constantly faced with the problem of rendering their own indigenous ideas and the formulation of their own interests and values in a language which does not fit at many key points. Most American and British spokespersons, and many scholars, seem to assume that their own English-language meanings are instantly and obviously translatable into Urdu, Japanese, Arabic, Marathi, Korean, Gikuyu, and any other language. If they are not translatable, then there is sometimes a tacit assumption that there must be a problem or deficiency with the other language. Yet, as we will see, there is no clearly identifiable meaning to words like 'religion' or 'secular' even in the context of English itself! But this is disguised by 'official' narratives about religion, authored by religious studies scholars and institutionalised in school curricula and a vast number of textbooks and readers, by displacing attention from the primary to a number of logically secondary problems. The primary problem is the lack of semantic clarity of the category, its transformations of meaning, and its function in the birth of modern ideology, for example, in the definition of national constitutions and the secular state. Attention is deflected from these fundamental issues of power to secondary problems such as the *definition* of 'religion'; or whether 'religion' is best explained in psychological or sociological terms; or whether 'religion' has an essence in emotion or morality or the feeling of dependence; or whether it gets its meaning from a context of family resemblances; or how it should be distinguished from magic or witchcraft; or what kind of relation 'religious' rituals have to political or economic practices. Not only do these discourses not lead to doubts about the reality of 'religion itself'; on the contrary, by displacing attention to questions about the best way to explain or describe it, they further inscribe the uncritically constructed object into the order of things. What all of these vigorously pursued activities do is to further embed the term 'religion' and its implicit or explicit distinction from the 'secular' into our ideological construction of the world, as though they represent two great classes of objects, or two distinct domains.

In a paper on the medieval city of Coventry, the historian Charles Phythian-Adams gives us some interesting insights into the world of the late middle ages in England (Phythian-Adams, 1972:57–85). By focusing on the city of Coventry, we get not only knowledge of one unique city and its organisation and public life. We get an imaginative insight into a period of our own Anglophone history, before a whole number of our modern assumptions had been formulated or thought about, and for which there existed no language.

Phythian-Adams is explicitly interested in using a social anthropological approach to describe Coventry (see his note 1), and seems to suggest that England at that time, with its small, largely peasant population, might be amenable to a similar kind of analysis as those provided by many twentieth-century anthropological studies of small-scale societies of the 'holistic' kind. He offers a structural functional account of the ritual process of Coventry (this book was published in 1972), its symbolism, expressiveness, and tension-releasing functionality. He suggests an organic model of community in which the separate functions, occupations, degrees, and guilds are reaffirmed and reconstituted through various ritual techniques. He uses the terminology of 'class' and class interests to some extent, but does not push for a Marxist interpretation in any full-blown degree. Indeed, he suggests (80) that the emphasis on community and integration disappeared after the Reformation and was *then* replaced by class concerns. This implies a change of paradigm that produced a transition from medieval hierarchy and the integrated conception of the commonweal to the privatisation of interests and the emergence of class economics.[8]

One of the interests of this article for the purpose of my present book is the way that Phythian-Adams uses terms such as religious (often interchangeable in his paper with 'ritual') and secular to describe and analyze his topic in ways which tend to confuse modern meanings with the meanings that were regnant at the time, which he has—in other ways—so brilliantly described. By looking at public ceremonies in Coventry, we can see much about how participants imagined their own collective identity. One thing that becomes apparent is that the society was imagined as a commonweal unified in Christ, and therefore as a structural totality. The historian's representation of this medieval holism— which I refer to as encompassing Religion or Christian Truth—may be partly indebted to an anthropological viewpoint deriving from Durkheim and the structural functionalists. However, the representations of late medieval and early modern society in England given by its contemporary literate elite[9]—and the idea seems to have been hegemonic and shared widely even among the nonliterate—lend themselves well to a structural functional model and may well themselves have been the origin of the *anthropologists'* ideas in the first place. The commonweal, or politic body, was not a modern secular state or civil society separated from religion in the way of modern constitutions and secular sociology or ideology. It was a holistic concept of a divinely ordered world in which everything and every person had its proper place and function. I say 'holistic' in the sense that, in the ideological representation, the parts are subservient to the whole, conceived on analogy with a body and its various limbs. If the king is the heart, his advisors the head, and the labouring peasants the feet (on one of various rhetorical versions), then each part has a preordained function or 'vocation', and the health of the whole organism depends on the proper functioning of the various parts. I have argued in this book in various places that the commonweal *is* Religion (Christian Truth) seen from the point of view of what we would call 'social relations'.

The anthropological model of the integrated whole, often applied to small-scale nonmodern societies by anthropologists, and also to whole continents such as India, may have also been inspired by the colonial encounter with other peoples and their 'societies', which also gave rise to the extension of the term 'religion' from a very specific meaning located in Christian revealed Truth to a generic concept with universal applicability. Whether or not we are explaining anything causally or just observing correlations, surely John Bossy's problem about whether the changes in ideas and values can be attached to any material events can be partly solved by reference to the acquisition of colonies and the need for description, explanation, and domination when confronted with 'the other' in many locations around the world (Bossy, 1985:169–70).

A holistic cosmology does not lend itself well to the modern idea of a religion-secular dichotomy, but it does lend itself well to the idea that there are degrees of sacredness and profanity which are relative to context. Phythian-Adams, in this study of medieval Coventry, distinguishes between 'ritual' and 'secular' practices and the 'ritual' and 'secular' halves of the year. I am going to suggest that a distinction between sacred and profane, understood not as essentially different domains in the modern formulation, but in the sense of relative degrees of sacredness, is less misleading when applied to a totalising cosmology and ideology such as the commonweal. Phythian-Adams says he

> will seek first to demonstrate some simple congruities between
> Coventry's late medieval social structure (that relatively enduring but
> acceptable framework of institutionalized positions and connective
> relationships) and its ceremonial or ritualized expressions in action,
> in time—with regard to the local calendar—and on the ground.
> (1972:57)

He describes this as "a coherent ceremonial pattern" which began to disintegrate in the middle and later years of the sixteenth century: "When all masters and journeymen annually processed in their respective companies at Corpus Christi-tide and on the eves of Midsummer and St. Peter . . . the community in its entirety was literally defining itself for all to see" (Phythian-Adams, 1972:58).

According to Phythian-Adams, these processions were dominated by the craft fellowships which thereby represented the main body of the community. They excluded 20 percent of adult males, such as common labourers and servants, and all single females under forty. Only women married to members of these guilds could be involved in the processions, and even these women were excluded from key rites of passage such as oath-taking ceremonies and had to dine apart from the men, presumably meaning at separate tables:

> To all those outside or on the edge of the community, therefore, ceremonies must have been a constant reminder of its discrete and predominantly masculine identity. For those inside it, on the other hand, they were the visible means of relating individuals to the social structure. The sequence of oath-taking ceremonies, in particular, regularly punctuated the life cycle of the successful citizen from the moment he pledged himself to his city, his craft or his guild, to that later period in life when similar rites de passage admitted him to the authority which was the reward of advanced years. (1972:59)

As well as gender exclusion, there was a strong seniority system based on age, length of service, the type of craft or guild, and property.

If by 'religion' we mean some integral domain separated from a different domain called 'the secular' then it did not exist in medieval Coventry. The church permeated all aspects of these 'social' rituals. For example:

> A corporate act of worship by all the participants ... seems to have been the normal custom at both craft and civil levels. In the early 15th century, the Tilers were accustomed to offer at High Mass in the White Friars before their election. The Mercers, on the other hand, were 'after election to bringe the new Maister to churche' in Elizabeth's reign. The Mayoral oath-taking ceremony, by the 17th century, was actually sandwiched between the first lesson and the sermon during morning prayers at the adjacent parish church of St. Michael. (Phythian-Adams, 1972:61)

Not only were these occupational structures highly ritualised and bound up with the church, but "office was hedged with taboos" (61), for example, relating to usury and adultery.

The ceremony of installing a new mayor and his officers gives some indication of the status etiquette in relation to the hierarchy:

> The incoming officers processed into St. Mary's Hall where the retiring officers and aldermen were already symbolically in possession. At the culmination of the ceremony the new mayor was obliged to doff his hat, in the presence of the people, as a public gesture of deference to the old mayor and aldermen, 'intreating their loves and

assistances.' Of the sheriffs and the coroner on the other hand, he simply entreated assistance, while the junior civic officers and the rest were more tersely 'required' to do their duties. (Phythian-Adams, 1972:61)

So the 'civic' life of York was, at crucially important points, a ritual process of crafts, guilds, and office hierarchies that had wide social meaning:

> In magnifying and publicising the importance of annually held offices, ceremony completed the transformation of wealth ownership into class standing for the upper levels of society. (Phythian-Adams, 1972:63)

> [C]eremony obviously helped to transform the formal constitution of the city into some sort of social reality [but] conversely it was also a valued instrument through which the basic divisions of humanity, by sex, age and wealth, could be related to the structure of the community. (63)

Phythian-Adams describes a number of different collective practices of the times, including the supply of wines or ale and cakes by the mayor for craft "drinkynges" at which masters and journeymen took part and other examples of "structurally integrative commensality" (1972:65). One evidence of this integrative feature, in a society replete with hierarchical differentiations of offices, ranks, degrees, and occupations, was that, despite the geographical concentration of wealth and/or occupations in different parts of the city, it was not a fragmented society. "Taken as a whole, the social topography of Coventry was remarkable chiefly for the evident intermixture of all types of person" (1972:65).[10]

This integration was symbolised in ceremonies which cut across occupation and rank, such as the holy cake, "which was consumed together in church by the parishioners after the celebration of mass even in times of famine" (Phythian-Adams, 1972:65). At other times, there was an obligation on the church deacon to serve parishioners bread and ale, especially at "Whitsun ales and wakes at the feasts of dedication" (65). There were the informal gatherings for bonfires at Midsummer and St. Peter's nights. There were the May Day celebrations which organised the unmarried into couples. There was Hock Tuesday which temporarily reversed gender inequalities, when women overpowered, bound, and ransomed men. In Coventry, there was also the annual custom of the Lord of Misrule, "which was also to be found at court, in great households, university colleges, and the Inns of Court" (67): "the indications are that within the confines of his household or even elsewhere, the civic ruler had to be seen or known to put temporarily aside his formal status, in order to become, instead, the subject of satirical government" (68).

In the early summer, public festivities either expressed the antipathy be-tween town and country, or violated "the sanctity of private property," or breached the privileges of the local land-owning class (Phythian-Adams, 1972: 68): "at such times everyday rules did not apply, while the privileged class, whose interests normally ensured their preservation, was expected to acquiesce passively in their flagrant transgression."[11]

Phythian-Adams suggests that the significance of these practices lay in the control of social tensions that were given expression. The idea suggests that they were examples of what Turner referred to as communitas, or antistruc-ture, in which social order is temporarily suspended. These ceremonies and customs had the effect, perhaps the function, of "preserving and enhancing the wholeness of the social order" (69). This all suggests that Phythian-Adams is finding, or deriving, or at least applying from anthropology, what came to be called structural functionalism:

> In a close-knit structure composed of overlapping groups or group-ings, where a change in status in one sphere so often could
> effect standing in another, ceremony performed a crucial clarify-ing role. It was a societal mechanism ensuring continuity within
> the structure, promoting cohesion and controlling some of its
> inherent conflicts, which was not only valued as contributing to
> the 'worship' of the city, but also enjoyed by contemporaries.
> (1972:69)

The year in the city of Coventry tended to fall into two halves, which Phythian-Adams characterises as ritualistic and secular. The ritualistic half was between 24–25 December and 24 June, inclusively. It included major feasts of the church, including Christmas, Lent, Easter, and Whitsun and the feasts of Corpus Christi, St. George's Day, and Ascension Day. This contrasted with the more 'secular' six months between 25 June and Christmas. According to Phythian-Adams, this division of the year was emphasised by "native pop-ular practice." For example, at Norwich, Lent was ushered in by 'the King of Christmas' on Shrove Tuesday; May games were played in London up to 24 June, and there were Morris dancers and maypoles, leading Phythian-Adams to comment: "Any attempt at analysing popular culture has to take into con-sideration the ways in which religious and vulgar symbolism thus comple-mented each other and often merged into one" (1972:71). But what is he say-ing here? What is the 'religious' here? The official church calendar? But the whole thrust of his fascinating account seems to point to Religion, understood as Christian Truth, as encompassing the whole range of activities and all sta-tuses and degrees.

As Phythian-Adams has shown, Religion was integral to the ritual process and to all aspects of the life of the community, and cannot be described as identical with the church and as a separate domain from the secular. For example, the greater use of candles in church at Christmas time was matched by a larger number of candles to be lit by smiths at their work, and there was a lot of fire-symbolism ritual, such as the burning of 'palm' leaves on Ash Wednesday, the hallowing of fire in church at Easter, the use of fresh foliage to decorate the city at summer feasts, the lighting of midsummer bonfires, and "the rural custom of rolling burning wheels down hills to mark the summer solstice" (Phythian-Adams, 1972:71).

The craft guilds performed plays at Corpus Christi, and St. George's Day featured a representation of the dragon and its defeat and death. The St. George's Day procession visited St. George's Chapel, which was associated with "the chivalrous slaughter of monsters" (Phythian-Adams, 1972:7). There was also displayed a bone of a fabulous giant boar slain by Guy of Warwick. During Lent, behaviour was controlled and if necessary punished by aldermen in a "civic enforcement of personal morality" (72). The guilds instructed that there should be no working during the twelve days of Christmas, during Easter week, or during Whitsun week.

According to Phythian-Adams, the contrast between the ritualistic half of the year and the next six months between 25 June and Christmas was "absolute" (1972:73). He says, "In this period there was no religious or popular symbolic coherence, there were no institutionalized extremes of behaviour and there were no extended holidays. Essentially this was a time for uninterrupted, normal economic activities." However, the "normal economic activities," or some of them, were "dependent on rural rhythms.... It is thus difficult to doubt the existence of a marked pre-Reformation dichotomy of the year, the two halves of which it is surely no exaggeration to denominate for convenience as respectively 'ritualistic' and 'secular'" (73). In the second half of the year, the component groups "ceremonialised themselves in private" (75). They had guild elections, the rendering of accounts, and the inaugural dinner of the new master of the butchers.

The reader should notice how his use of the term 'religious' in "religious or popular symbolic coherence" coincides with what he usually refers to as the 'ritual' half of the year. Likewise, 'the secular' half of the year corresponds to "normal economic activities," implying that the latter were neutral towards, and essentially different from, the religious (the ritualistic). It is here, I believe, that the problems engendered by projecting back onto medieval Coventry the distinction between the religious and the secular, with its modern overtones of essentialised difference, become apparent. I suggest that there would have been a clear gain for the analysis of the medieval situation if a relative dichotomy between sacred and profane had been used. Rather than claiming, as Phythian-Adams does, that one half of the year was markedly 'religious' and the other half markedly 'secular', he could instead have avoided that problematic terminology and referred instead to a *relative* absence of sacralising rituals in the second half of the year, a relative profaneness, in the legitimate sense of greater distance from the sacred, or less ritual content. This different kind of distinction is tacitly supported by much of what he goes on to say. By suggesting that the year tended to fall into two halves, such that the degree of sacralising activities (rituals) is relatively greater in one half than the other, he would have avoided an essentialising construct that divides them into the entirely modern opposition between the religious and the nonreligious. This still allows for elements of profane or ordinary utilitarian motivations in the ritual half, and for elements of ritual in the predominantly profane or secular half. It is far more like a gradation of different degrees of intensity than an opposition between the religious and the nonreligious.

It was in the ritualistic half that the practices expressed the importance of the whole community above its constitutive parts: "the ritualistic half embraced every major public ceremony...which formally interrelated separate whole groups or groupings of the social structure" (Phythian-Adams, 1972:74). It was in the ritualistic half of the year that the church feasts, popular "native" customs, the guilds, and the civic authorities were all fully committed to the renewal of the structures that bound them together.

This implies that we cannot legitimately separate out the 'political' or the 'civil' in the sense of neutrality towards religion, for what we today represent as separate were embedded in these activities in the medieval period. For example, at Christmas, which was the beginning of the 'ritualistic' period, the retiring mayor was burlesqued and parodied, but the ritual ended with "the Mayor processing as the King's representative backed by a token armed force provided by each company" (Phythian-Adams, 1972:75). The appointment of the mayor would normally be described loosely as 'political' by many historians (and anthropologists) because it has to do with civil power and its legitimation. However, there is no separate realm of politics in view here, rather a ritual process that provides rites of passage between degrees and statuses and that subordinates power to the well-being of the totality (the commonweal). If, on the other hand, 'politics' merely means 'power', then not much has been said.

The two halves of the year also represented another dichotomy. The ritualistic half in Coventry began in the centre of the city, which was

> virtually a single vast churchyard containing two parish churches and
> the Cathedral Priory...this whole consecrated area constituted a
> ritual centre for the city. It is...noteworthy that the ceremonies in
> the earlier part of the ritualistic period were mainly confined to it.
> (Phythian-Adams, 1972:76)

Starting points for major processions were the guild chapels, such as St. Nicholas, which belonged to the Corpus Christi Guild, St. John Bablake of the Trinity Guild, the "craft-cum-gild [sic] Chapel of St. George." "[D]uring the ritualistic half, therefore, there seems to have been a movement of formal ceremony from the centre outwards to the limits of the city but no farther. Nearly every other observance during this moiety was similarly confined" (77). He mentions Hock-tide games, maypoles, bonfires, and pageants.[12]

What is notable in this spatial representation is that the starting points for the ceremonies were guild chapels, which further subverts any modern distinction between religious (church) institutions and secular (work) guilds. And the procession to the boundaries symbolically marked out the whole city as a relatively sacred space—that is, relative to the contexts of time and occasion.

The distinction that Phythian-Adams makes between the ritualistic and secular halves of the year seem to me to correspond more closely to a relativising (rather than hypostatised) distinction between sacred and profane. The secular half may have been less the time of sacralising rituals than the first, but still did not amount to the secular in the modern sense of a separate domain. Nor can we talk intelligibly of the ritualistic half being the domain of 'religion' in the modern sense. We need to bear in mind that community, which the historian sees as being renewed through regular ritual processes, had a name in medieval and early modern English: the commonweal. Commonweal was thought of as an organic unity with analogy to the body and strikingly resembles the organic model of anthropological structural functionalism. The problem about how to deal with change is also salient for structural functionalism and the organic theory of society. Phythian-Adams comes very close to expressing the same point. Talking about "the intricate regularity of the pattern" of observances, he says:

> [It] bears mute witness both to the communal quality of a late medieval urban society, particularly the subordination of the parts to the working of the whole, and to the pervasive role of the pre-Reformation church and its practices in that community. Such a reconstitution also highlights the extent of the subsequent change: the destructive impact of the events of the mid-sixteenth century and the subsequent obliteration of the established rhythm of life itself. (1972:78–79)

Open-air ceremonies, games, and other practices generally were banned after the Reformation:

> Ceremony and religion together withdrew indoors from the vulgar gaze. The formalization of social structure was now passively restricted according to the hierarchical seating arrangements within the parish churches ... formal communal processions totally disappeared.... The civic body may have ceremonially observed certain church festivals, but there is no evidence that anyone else took part.... By the seventeenth century the claims of community... were yielding to class loyalties. (Phythian-Adams, 1972:80)

Phythian-Adams finishes his article with this point:

> It was no accident that the elaborate official inaugurations which had
> characterized the old secular moiety alone survived untarnished, in
> the post-Reformation world, to dominate the altered and abbreviated
> ceremonial calendar of the Coventry citizen. (80)

He is suggesting here that whereas the social order associated with an integrated community and a unifying ritual process disappeared, it left the secular as a truncated remnant to become the dominant mode of living. Society
became desacralised because only the nonsacred part remained. But perhaps
this view needs qualification. For he has described these halves as moieties of
an organic whole. If half of an organic whole disappears, then something more
is happening to the rest. I suggest that this amounts to a transformation in
secularity. In a profound sense, there is the emergence of something qualitatively new. This new kind of dominant secularity has to be put in the wider
context of the formation of the new princely state of Henry VIII, the early effects of colonial ambitions, and the later emergence of a new capitalist class.
It also has to be seen in the perspective of the transformed meaning of Religion
from encompassing Christian Truth to a privatised realm of individual, constitutionally guaranteed rights. But perhaps this transition was not immediate
and took a far longer time than Phythian-Adams allows for.

In the introduction, I discussed the representations of the medieval polity
by the historians Southern and Swanson. I will here briefly revisit that discussion to suggest how the distinction between the terms religion and secular,
on the one hand, and sacred and profane, on the other, might help the modern
reader to get a clearer picture of that polity. It will still only be an act of the
imagination, to be sure, but I believe it does bring greater—if only relatively
greater—clarity. Both Southern and Swanson, it may be recalled, emphasise
the identity of religion and the polity rather than their separation; yet Swanson frequently loses sight of this identity by aligning the medieval distinction
between church and state along the contours of the modern religion-secular
dichotomy. He frequently identifies 'religion' and 'church', which are contrasted with 'state' or the 'political order', which is 'secular'. In the light of the
actual typical usages of these terms in medieval England, let us now try to
express the relationships within the polity in terms of sacred and profane, as
indicated above.

The first thing to notice is that Religion as Christian Truth encompasses
both church and state in the medieval period. We cannot therefore simply
identify religion with church, as Swanson sometimes does. While the pope is
both a priest and a prince (having inherited the title of the Roman emperor,
pontifex maximus), the king is sacred and is anointed by God. In turn, it seems
quite wrong to suggest that 'the secular' is the state *rather than* the church. If
that were so, it would mean that the secular priesthood is not part of the

church. Furthermore, the only specifically 'religious' institutions are the monastic orders, which in this context have a specific application. But this of course does not mean that the state is 'nonreligious' or neutral to religion in the modern sense. Nor does the distinction between the ecclesiastical and civil courts mean that the former are 'religious' institutions whereas the latter are 'secular' institutions in the modern sense. These courts were distinguished by different functions, but in many cases there was hardly a distinction between heresy and treason; and the civil courts were expected to aid the ecclesiastical courts in the hunting down and punishing of heretics. Nor was the civil commonwealth nonreligious in the modern sense. What we would today call the social order was not distinct from religion but was encompassed by it. As Southern said, to be a human was to live one's life within the church-state, and the rites of passage of baptism, marriage, and death guaranteed both citizenship and salvation.

However, what one could say with more accuracy is that there existed relative degrees of sacrality and profaneness. There were continual disputes as to whether or not the pope and the priesthood were closer to God (and therefore more sacred) than the anointed king, a dispute which became central to the Reformation. There was a general sense in which the continuum between sacred and profane was framed in terms of relative distance from God in the divinely ordained hierarchy. Thus, while the skills and status of the master carpenter or stonemason were ritually and publicly sacralised, they were relatively more profane than the prince or the priest. On these same lines, it might be disputed as to whether the church institutions were relatively more sacred than the civil ones. For example, the church would presumably claim that the ecclesiastical courts were closer to the work of God and therefore more sacred than the civil courts. Even if this were true, it would not imply that the civil courts did not serve God. Even if the duties of the civil courts were relatively more profane, they were still sacred as duties and service to God. The hunting down and burning of heretics was surely a sacred duty. Church land was used for burial and was hallowed; in that context such land was more sacred than the profane or unhallowed land outside the walls of the church. But this did not mean that the land where the king held court or hunted was not in a very real sense sacred. Probably the most sacred duties in the realm were associated with service in the king's (or queen's) bedchamber. In an official document of 1691, "Duties and Salaries of State and Household Officials" (Browning, 1953:105–7), the unknown writer lists nine great officers of the crown, both ecclesiastical and lay, and explains their ranking in terms which exemplify what anthropologists might refer to as a ritual order. The writer then specifies the most important duties: "Gentlemen of the Bedchamber are nine, whereof the first is Groom of the Stole, that is . . . groom or servant of the long robe or vestment, he having the office and honour to present and put on his Majesty's first garment and shirt every morning, and to order the things of the bed-

chamber. The gentlemen of the bedchamber consist usually of the prime nobility of England, whose office in general is, each one in his turn, to wait one
week in every nine weeks in the king's bedchamber, there to lie by the king on
a pallet bed all night, and in the absence of the Groom of the Stole, to supply
his place." Again, the idea that the polity or commonweal was a 'political order'
in the modern sense of separation from religion identified with 'church' makes
no sense in the medieval context. There was no English word 'politics' in wide
usage denoting a distinct and separate domain. The commonweal was God's
order as manifested among men (and of course women, children, animals, and
minerals, as the whole cosmos was ordered by God). If all duties were performed according to degree, status, and birthright, then it was a 'politic' order,
meaning that it functioned as God intended.

Phythian-Adams, in his representation of medieval Coventry, suggested
that the abolition at the time of the Reformation of many of the traditional
pageants and ceremonies which sacralised the hierarchy of the medieval order
opened the way for a new class-based society with greater emphasis on privacy
and individualism. This process may have been under way, but there was huge
resistance too, and arguably that transformation into modernity took longer
than Phythian-Adams suggests. In his paper on the seventeenth-century theorist of the state James Harrington and his famous and influential work
Oceana, Goldie says:

> In seventeenth century Britain ... the Godly Prince of the Marsilian,
> Lutheran and Hobbesian tradition becomes translated into the pa-
> triot of civil humanist and Whig thought. In Whig England, the
> Erastian imperial theme and the theme of Christian liberty moved
> forward together. The ideal of Christian liberty needed the ideal of the
> Godly civil *imperium*. This was why a Republican like Harrington
> offered praise (as Rousseau later did) for Hobbes's civil religion: they
> all agreed that the civil commonwealth was the high priest.... It
> is tempting to identify Harrington as having failed, unlike Locke, to
> arrive at a modern liberal conception of the privacy of religion and its
> dissociation from the state. Yet for Harrington, and his Augustan
> Whig successors, 'true religion' remained a business of state....
> Whig and 'country' hostility to central state power would be tempered
> by [the] doctrine of the Godly commonwealth's duty to restrain
> both the anarchy of private 'enthusiasm' and the tyranny of popish
> priests. (Goldie, 1987:206–7)

O'Gorman has discussed whether it can be held that England in the eighteenth century was characterised by dissent, economic class, and individualism,
or alternatively whether it was an Anglican confessional church-state characterised by degree and God-ordained hierarchy (O'Gorman, 1997:160–75). The
answer seems to be both yes and no. On the one hand:

>The revisionist interpretation of English society presents a conser-
vative view of a stable and continuing church-state, one which
emphasizes the importance of traditional institutions and attitudes at
the expense of modern and 'progressive' forces such as secularism, radicalism and reform. In many ways, revisionism has been a
healthy corrective to an established historiography which, for several decades, had played down the influence of Anglicanism upon
public as well as private life in the eighteenth century.... when contemporaries discussed the relationship between the state and the
church they did so in theological terms which owed more to Hooker
and Filmer than to Locke and natural rights. (O'Gorman, 1997:165)

On the other hand, "[t]oo much emphasis upon traditional elements in British society can minimize the significance of those social currents within the
Whig polity which was helping to fashion commercial and industrial developments" (171).

Reading a historical work like E. P. Thompson's *History of the English
Working Class* (1991 [1968]) is like lifting an ornamental stone in an eighteenth-
century formal garden to find with a shock a teeming variety of insect life
struggling in the real mess of subsistence. For the moment, I only wish to sal-
vage from this two-sided picture the following point. Despite the presence of
strong elements and currents—many of them deriving from the nonconformist middle and working classes and their association with trade and manufacturing, classes which, as Thompson points out, are *in the making*—which
retrospectively we interpret as leading to secularism, capitalism, individualism,
and the constitutional separation of church and state, England in the eighteenth century was not 'modern'. The influence of the Enlightenment was
undoubtedly there,[13] and the impact of the American and French revolutions
was obviously of fundamental importance in the birth of modernity. But in
England at least, and presumably in most of Europe, much of the traditional
hierarchy surrounding king, church, and aristocracy was still in place and
continued into the nineteenth and even the twentieth century. Cannadine has
claimed that the way that the British imagined their empire well into the twentieth century reflected the way they saw themselves, which was as

>an unequal society characterized by a seamless web of layered
gradations, which were hallowed by time and precedent, which
were sanctioned by tradition and religion, which extended in a great
chain of being from the monarch at the top to the humblest subject at the bottom. (Cannadine, 2001:4)

I am arguing, therefore, that a world dominated by God and the church-
state is a world in which Religion means Christian Truth; such a world is one
in which the total hierarchical order is sacralised, and the profane is either

those parts of the order of things which are *relatively* distant from the sources of sacralisation, such as the more technical and value-free practices, or, the more definite and absolute nuance, outside the sphere of salvation and under the dominion of Satan. In both cases, the profane is defined ultimately by its relation to the total order of Christ. In contrast, the modern secular is in principle either neutral or hostile to religion. It does not require the hypothesis of God, who becomes a hypostatised option external to the world of deism and agnosticism and an unbelievable irrelevance in atheism. The secular derives from a belief in natural rationality and the world as a material system which contains the cause of its own existence. It is made up of the modern rhetorical domains of politics, economics, science, and constitutions, which formally separate religion or religions and privatise it or them.

The ambivalence between these two analytically distinct (though admittedly historically connected) concepts can be seen in Britain throughout the nineteenth century. Brian Stanley identifies four main assumptions underlying missionary thinking in the nineteenth century. The first of these

> was the belief that the cultures which missionaries were penetrating were in no sense religiously neutral—rather they were under the control of the Evil One. 'Heathen' societies were the domain of Satan in all their aspects—not merely religion, but also economics, politics, public morals, the arts, and all that is embraced by the term 'culture'. (1990:161)

This belief is virtually identical to the one held by the Protestant Samuel Purchas in the early seventeenth century, and justified in the same way by reference to the Fall, the Flood, and the Tower of Babel. On the other hand, the missionaries, by pursuing their agenda to save the souls of people they suppose to be in danger of damnation are also civilising them by making them look and behave like Europeans. In this context, the advantages and indeed necessities of capitalism, markets, trade, and manufacturing become evident. The role of commerce in this civilising process may have been ambiguous in the minds of many individual missionaries. Stanley quotes from David Livingstone's public address delivered in the Senate House of the University of Cambridge in 1857 as an example of the apparent relationship of missionary activity to the spread of commerce:

> I beg to direct you[r] attention to Africa;—I know that in a few years I shall be cut off in that country, which is now open; do not let it be shut again! I go back to Africa to make an open path for Commerce and Christianity; do you carry out the work which I have begun. I LEAVE IT TO YOU! (quoted in Stanley, 1990:70)

Isaac Schapera, in his introduction to Livingstone's *African Journals 1853–1856*, explained Livingstone's rapturous reception back in imperial Britain primarily by his geographical discoveries, which showed that Africa "was not a useless desert but a land of incalculable commercial possibilities" (Schapera, 1963:xii).

This ambiguity suggests that the religion-secular dichotomy and the relativising distinction between the sacred and the profane should be analytically separated, and that we need to keep in mind all the implications for one set of categories when there occur transformations in meaning and rhetorical usage of other sets. Let me now suggest that the distinction between sacred and profane, so fitting for constructing some kind of representation of England at least before the Reformation and arguably for long afterwards too, might also help us to understand non-Anglophone cultures better than the modern distinction between religion and the secular.

The concept of 'Islam' is represented in the following way by someone whom Abdulkader Ismail Tayob refers to as "one of the most influential leaders of contemporary Islam":

> Islam is a comprehensive system which deals with all spheres of life.
> It is a state and a homeland (or a government and a nation). It is
> morality and power (or mercy and justice). It is culture and a law (or
> knowledge and jurisprudence). It is material and wealth (or gain and
> prosperity). It is an endeavour and a call (or an army and a cause).
> And finally, it is true belief and worship. (al-Banna 1978: 2, quoted in
> Tayob, 2007: 189)

Let me give some other examples from the ethnographic study of other cultures rather than the history of England. The problem of identifying a religion from any other type of social formation which is tacitly supposed to be 'secular' in the modern sense of 'nonreligious' is sometimes commented on in passing by anthropologists and those who study non-Western cultures. In *The Ideology of Religious Studies* (2000: for example, pp. 81–87) I analysed several ethnographies where 'religion' is constructed by the (nonindigenous) anthropologist in a way that makes it virtually impossible to distinguish from the culture as a total ideological system, or a holistic set of representations in many ways analogous to Religion as the Commonweal in medieval and early modern England. I gave a range of examples such as an article by T. O. Ranger (1988) called "African Traditional Religion," a book by Benjamin C. Ray on African Religions (1976), and an article by James Cox (1995) on the meaning of the sacred in Zimbabwe. Another was Cooper who made the point in the context of indigenous North America. Generalising about the indigenous people of North America in a paper entitled "North American Traditional Religion," Cooper says:

> No tribe has a word for 'religion' as a separate sphere of exis-
> tence. Religion permeates the whole of life, including economic ac-

tivities, arts, crafts and ways of living. This is particularly true of
nature, with which native Americans have traditionally a close
and sacred relationship. Animals, birds, natural phenomena, even
the land itself, have religious significance to native Americans: all
are involved in a web of reciprocal relationships, which are sustained
through behaviour and ritual in a state of harmony. Distinctions
between natural and supernatural are often difficult to make when
assessing native American concepts. (G. Cooper, 1988:873–74)

This generalisation would also have been apposite for the kind of medieval
and early modern English society discussed above, except in the sense that, in
English, Religion specifically meant encompassing Christian Truth. But in
medieval and early modern England, there was no word for 'religion' if by that
word is meant the separation from the 'secular' in the modern sense, a nuance
which today's usages inevitably carry. I suggest that if Cooper had consistently
used the terminology of sacred and profane in the sense suggested above, and
clearly separated it from the modern religion-secular dichotomy, then his analysis would have avoided the contradiction between the title ("North American
Traditional Religion") and the content ("No tribe has a word for 'religion' as a
separate sphere of existence").

This point comes out in Armin Geertz's paper on the Hopi, "Religion and
Community in Indigenous Contexts" (2004). This is a good example of the
kind of close and detailed observation, empathy, and methodological agnosticism that is typical of the essays in many publications on 'religion' in this or
that culture. Indeed, the volume of essays in which Geertz's paper appears,[14]
by claiming to be about the study of 'religion' and 'religions', tacitly constructs
or reconstructs the observer's assumed ground of neutral, objective observation which we associate with secular sociology. This is true even though the
purpose of the book is to examine the problem of the category 'religion' itself.
In effect it could be claimed that the book, like Cooper's article cited above,
embeds the undeniable reality of 'religion' and the multiple 'religions of the
world' while simultaneously claiming to problematise the terminology. In the
early part of his essay, Geertz discusses various ideas of a community. After
considering different options he suggests a working definition: "a collectivity
of actors sharing meanings and activities in the context of a common worldview. Such a definition draws heavily on Clifford Geertz's hermeneutic and
semiotic concept of culture" (2004:194). Geertz lists the many different practices and productions of communities, including language and communication; naming and taxonomy; notions of person, kinship, gender, and age; laws,
customs, etiquette; aesthetics; world views and religion; shelter; tool making;
subsistence; and sexual reproduction.

I do not think that Geertz means that the attributes of communities that he
lists are both necessary and sufficient for the definition of community. I think

he means that this is a reasonable list of the kinds of things that people produce collectively in communities of various kinds; I don't think he intends to deny that there are communities that only produce some of these things. For my purposes, the crucial question is, what kind of a thing[15] or domain is 'religion', how is it distinguished from "world views" in his phrase "world views and religion," and should it be listed with language, kinship, and tool making as one thing or domain among others? Religion is mentioned here as one item in a long list of attributes. Yet the concept of 'religion' which figures prominently in his title and which is the declared object of study in the title of the book itself, does not get close treatment. 'Religion' as a concept seems to have little work to do in his description and analysis. Let me, however, focus on those instances where it does appear as a concept.

After a discussion of the idea of 'community' in general, comes this paragraph:

> Religious communities, on the other hand, are more specifically
> focused. In many societies communities are both religious and sec-
> ular, depending on the time and the context. In this sense, com-
> munities mark entrances into (initiation), changes during (transition
> rituals), and exits from (funerals) the community. Ritual and pag-
> eant mark important community activities and are integral to main-
> taining and shaping community norms and identity. The community
> consists as well of differentiation in the group based on function
> and merit. Religious validation adorns social markings such as gen-
> der, family, and clan and integrates these in terms of the natural
> and sacred worlds. In fact, community is often conceived as a sacred
> or semi-sacred entity in itself. (Geertz, 2004:194)

This is surely a strange paragraph. The first sentence, "Religious communities, on the other hand, are more specifically focused," would lead the reader to assume he means 'are more specifically focused than non-religious ones', and would expect a precise statement about how, specifically, religious communities differ from nonreligious ones. But Geertz immediately continues: "In many societies communities are both religious and secular, depending on the time and the context." This sentence in relation to, or perhaps in contrast to, the one that immediately preceded it seems to distinguish between communities that are wholly religious, and those that are "both religious and secular." Again, the reader would expect some clarification about how this distinction is to be made. However, Geertz goes straight on to talk as if religion means the same as ritual, as in rites of passage. But it is surely difficult to claim that rites of passage are religious rather than secular. The more one focuses on the actual usages of words, the more opaque the meanings become.

I think that an implied point that Geertz might be attempting to make here (though I admit that this is only guesswork) is that, whereas 'religion' in modern Western societies usually implies a personal and privatised faith in God separated from a secular world, and consequently implies the existence of purely voluntary associations of believers, in societies such as the Hopi it is more suitable to imagine 'religion' in terms of collective practices, such as life cycle rituals, which may or may not be legitimated with reference to collective myths. If I am correct in attributing this position, then it immediately introduces a problem: how can 'religion' have two such different meanings and yet still be a valid analytical and descriptive concept? It seems bound to offer confusion rather than clarity. After all, ritual is arguably endemic to what we call secular institutions as well, such as the courts of law, the military, the universities, or the First Lady walking the dog. Ritual surrounds and arguably sacralises the telling of the story of American destiny in its various settings, as well as the founding fathers and the artefacts that bear witness to that destiny: the struggle for freedom in the face of adversity, the defeat of the hierarchical Old World and the glorious emergence of the land of equality, and the civilising of the indigenous barbarians. But the problems packed into this paragraph, and thus in the meaning of the article as a whole, do not end there.

What does Geertz mean by the words sacred, semi-sacred, natural, or secular? How is the natural separated from the sacred? Does this imply that the natural world is *not* sacred? Is Geertz telling us that the Hopi make a distinction in their own language between 'sacred' and 'natural' worlds? Or is he making a more universal claim? And what kind of status as an analytical and descriptive category does 'semi-sacred' have? Is 'natural' similar in nuance to 'secular' and also 'profane'? It is surprising how highly esteemed academics play fast and loose with such categories as though they do not need clear articulation.

Religion does appear again later in the chapter, this time in opposition to witchcraft and sorcery. This is framed in terms of "the good religious life and the evil magic one" (Geertz, 2004:209). This is the first time in the discussion that the reader has been told that this is the meaning of religion. If this is the case, we need to know if this is a faithful translation of Hopi categories, or a rough and ready approximation of Anglophone ones. Also, how does this distinction relate to the earlier one between religion and secular? Again, from this distinction it would be logical to infer that the study of religions is the study of goodness, or of the way that humans promote goodness, and that witchcraft, like politics and economics, is not 'religion'. Does this mean that witchcraft and sorcery are therefore 'secular'? Why then do we not have special departments for studying witchcraft, in the way that we do for politics or economics? And how does this usage reflect on the idea implicit in Geertz's paper and in the book as a whole that religions are distinctive kinds of social formation? The lack of control over key organizing categories points to some unacknowledged function in their tendency to have a life of their own.

Only the Hopi themselves can tell us which English-language categories best suit their ways of thinking and their practices. Methodologically, it might have been less confusing if Geertz had weeded out the whole problematic discourse of 'religion' and its tacit distinction from the nonreligious secular, and instead employed the terms sacred and profane in the way I outlined above in the discussion of the city of Coventry, understanding 'profane' as those practices which are relatively less sacred.

The case of the Pueblo American people may offer another example, though again clearly only the Pueblo people themselves can decide which English-language categories most truthfully represent their values and practices. But Tisa Wenger's empathetic and critical approach (Wenger, 2005:89–113) does much to illuminate the situation of another ancient and sophisticated people who have been colonised by both Catholic and Protestant Europeans for centuries. In her discussion of the Pueblo people's struggle for the right, against the opposition of the white authorities, to perform their traditional dances in 1920s America, Wenger shows how they adopted the strategy of redefining their traditions as 'religion'. In this way, they hoped to save their distinctive forms of governance by appealing to the U.S. Constitution:

> Like many Native Americans in the 1920s, the Pueblo Indians of New Mexico faced multiple threats to their survival as tribes. During these years, the federal Bureau of Indian Affairs (BIA) announced policies that would have decimated Pueblo landholdings, limited the sovereignty of Pueblo governments, suppressed Native American ceremonial dancing, and severely restricted Pueblo children's participation in tribal initiation rites. On May 5, 1924, the Council of All the New Mexico Pueblos, including representatives from fourteen of the nineteen recognized Pueblos in the state, met to shape a unified response. The Council's resulting statement, an appeal 'to all Indians and to the People of the United States' linked all these policies together as threats to Pueblo religion. The Council wrote, 'We have met because our most fundamental right of religious liberty is threatened and is actually at this time being nullified ... our religion to us is sacred and is more important to us than anything else in our life.' In identifying 'religion' as their primary concern, these Pueblo leaders made use of an English-language category that had no parallel in their own languages. Like other Native American languages, the languages of the New Mexico Pueblos (Tewa, Tiwa, Keres, and Zuni) have no word that directly translates as religion. What did it mean, then, for Pueblo leaders to use the English-language concepts of religion and religious freedom in their attempts to change government policy and to appeal for public support? This article argues that Pueblo leaders of the 1920s successfully employed the American discourse on religion to legitimize and defend Pueblo identity and ways of life, and that in the process they

subtly changed the ways in which they talked about their traditional practices. (Wenger, 2005:89–90)

Wenger points out that, behind the threat to suppress dancing if the Indians did not voluntarily desist, there was

> a long history of often-violent suppression of Native American cultural practices. Most notably, the 'Religious Crimes Code' of 1883 was a BIA policy that authorized agency superintendents to use force and imprisonment to halt any Indian religious practices that they saw as immoral, subversive of government authority, or an impediment to the government's 'civilizing' policies. (2005:93)

Among the various justifications given for the suppression of Pueblo practices was that they were immoral and lewd; that they interfered with labour practices and were thus economically harmful; and that, since they included long initiation rites for young men, they interfered with school attendance and thus with state education requirements. In this way, they would interfere with the policy of assimilation. Protestant missionaries and others who equated Christianity with civility suggested that the dances, which were central to the life of many Indian nations, were barbaric and "impeded Indian progress towards 'civilization'" (Wenger, 2005:96).

The Pueblo people's earliest responses to the policy of government agencies' suppressing dance performances "did not choose to emphasize a religious freedom argument," and denied that such federal policies could apply to their own "customs" and "dances" (Wenger, 2005:94). Wenger points out that most Pueblo people had accepted a form of Catholicism, and the rites of baptism, since the Spanish colonial period. For the Pueblo people, it was Catholicism that meant 'religion', not their own customary practices (95). On the other hand, many of their most sacred values and practices were 'traditional' and not Christian:

> At least one Pueblo tribal council experimented with defending the intrinsic value of their ceremonies on quite different grounds than religious freedom. The San Ildefonso Pueblo Council asked the teacher at their day school to help them draft a letter to Commissioner Burke protesting against the dance circular. This letter attempted to communicate the significance of the Pueblo dances in language other than religion: as filial loyalty and as high art. They wrote:

>> Every Indian child is baptised in the Christian Church by the consent and request of its parents, and our children are trained in the Christian religion. But we also teach our children reverence and love for the memorials of their ancestors, and we believe we have a right to do this . . . . To us, our dances are drama, opera, and poetry. They are our heritage from men and women who

lived under different conditions than we, but whose stock we are.
As their children, we hold *sacred* [my italics] their memories.
We believe that the beauties wrought into the rhythmic form of
dances by them, as expressions of the poetry and valor of their
souls, are good rather than bad.[16]

Far from using "religion" to defend the Pueblo ceremonies,
in this statement the San Ildefonso Council applied the term not to
the indigenous practices that the BIA threatened to suppress, but
to the Catholicism that almost all the Pueblos had embraced since the
Spanish colonial period. In this formulation, the Pueblo ceremonies
were not "religion," but simply acts that were necessary for proper
respect for the ancestors and that held intrinsic artistic value. The
relevant English words are "reverence," "love," "valor" and "sacred."
So we can see that San Ildefonso leaders defended their ceremonies according to these values and the practices which represent and
express them, rather than religious freedom. (2005:94/5)

Wenger points out that, by adopting the category 'religion' to categorise
their non-Christian practices, they hoped to defend those practices from suppression, because freedom of religion is a right protected by the U.S. Constitution. In this sense, an essentially colonialist category was able to become
"an effective part of an indigenous strategy of resistance" (Wenger, 2005:91).
However, there was another side to this, for by accepting the concept of religion inscribed in the Constitution, they also invited the undermining of traditional concepts of authority and collective participation. This was because
'religion' is an autonomous practice of individual choice, and religions are
voluntary associations: "Regardless of its success, and no matter what the intentions of those who employ it, such a strategy of resistance inevitably re-
shapes the practices it defends" (91).

By appealing to the constitutional clause on religious freedom, the Pueblo
people opened themselves to the demand of the authorities that, if the dances
were to be categorised in constitutional terms as 'religious', they could not
demand participation in the rituals and initiations on the basis of the traditional authority of the elders, and so these could only be of a voluntary nature:

The religious freedom defense was somewhat effective as a discursive
strategy for protecting Pueblo traditions from outright government
suppression. Accompanying it was a degree of implicit individualism,
derived from American conceptions of religious freedom, which
forced traditionalist Pueblos to conceive of ritual responsibilities in
newly individualistic terms. (Wenger, 2005:106)

This article shows how the negotiation of colonial categories such as 'religion' between white authorities and representatives of non-Western cultures

requires detailed focus if the inherent implications of power in the changing definitions of such categories are to be understood. Wenger's paper reveals the instability of the category 'religion'. The meaning for the Pueblo people changed. Religion had previously referred to Christian Catholic Religion inherited from the Spanish colonialists. In that usage, their own older indigenous practices or customs were referred to differently "in language other than religion: filial loyalty and as high art," and expressed reverence and love for their traditions. However, under the hegemonic constructions of the modern Constitution, combined with the rhetoric of Protestant missionaries, the Pueblo people adopted 'religion' strategically to include what had previously been excluded in order to protect those same traditions. In the process, the traditions necessarily changed for they now had to be reconceptualised as individual voluntary practices, thus undermining traditional forms of collective authority.

David Chidester's historical research on the formation of the category 'religion' on the African frontier has similarly shown, albeit in a very different context, how 'religion' or the absence of 'religion' changed strategically in the way that missionaries and other colonial representatives used the term for purposes of colonial conquest and administration (Chidester, 1996, 2007). He further shows how metropolitan theorists used contradictory and inaccurate evidence derived second- or third-hand from African reportage in various ways to construct a largely mythical generic category of 'religions' which in turn passed into academic discourse. Tisa Wenger also notes a similar point when she says:

> European missionaries and colonial agents gathered the material for the emerging discipline of comparative religions—and thus for general theories of religion—hand in hand with their efforts to subdue indigenous populations. In that context, it should not be surprising that European theories of religion and related categories (such as fetish, totem, and myth) often helped to justify European colonialism. In U.S. history, theories of 'primitive religion' helped naturalize the idea that Native Americans needed to be Christianized and Americanized, thereby justifying the internal colonialism of the Indian reservation system. (2005:90)

This kind of historical evidence points to the danger of assuming that the meaning of 'religion' is stable and self-evident, and can be used uncritically in universal and essentialised applications. In their critique of what they call the "Official Account of Religious Studies" in the teaching of religion in education, I'Anson and Jasper criticise structures of representation which are fixed, hierarchical, and characterised by "accounts of religions and cultures that abstract from the messiness of contingency and change in order to produce accounts that are systematic, rational, and certain" (I'Anson & Jasper,

2006:86), and the construction of such authoritative models, "which claim to be neutral but which serve centralized state curricula and impose hegemonic closure rather than opening up a creative 'hospitality to difference' " (2006:85). And they point out how these closed, virtually state-sponsored accounts "re-inscribe assumptions that inform what Derrida . . . called a 'white mythology' " (80).

My own approach to the white mythology of 'religion' is to focus on its relationship with the myths which are produced and reproduced in reifying discourses on the 'nation', 'society', autonomous individuals, and other things that religion has been defined as excluding: those various domains such as science, the state, politics, and education which are intended to be secular in the sense of nonreligious neutrality towards religion (though both hostility and empathy are also options). It is as much the invention of the idea of the secular as nonreligious with which I am concerned, for it is the conceptualisation of this space in sociological rhetoric that tacitly indicates the profound transformation of what is meant by both 'religion' and 'secular'. Bryan Wilson has characterised 'secularisation' in this way:

> Secularization is here taken to be not merely a change in popular consciousness . . . but, more fundamentally, a radical reorganization of the structure of society. It is a process in which the major areas of social organization (economy, government, defence, law, education, health maintenance, and recreation) become differentiated and autonomous, and in which organized religion has finally relinquished the last remnants of the presidency that once it enjoyed over the whole gamut of social affairs. Inevitably, as society has become rationalized, and as what counts as worthwhile knowledge has become increasingly empirical, so the consciousness of individuals has also changed, and their forms of sociation have undergone transformation, but most conspicuously Christianity has lost its erstwhile functions of legitimating authority and polity; of informing and superintending justice and the law; of providing the basis for education; and of reinforcing social control. Social support for religion has declined and the Christian constituency has generally dwindled in most Western countries. (Wilson, 1990:587–88)

The problem with this way of representing social change is not that it is false, but that it embeds into the text the assumption of stability, continuity, and givenness of the various categories that are employed. Rather than looking at the level of concepts and categories, Wilson simply employs them as though they refer to things in the world which have always been there but which have changed their shape. The "structure of society" changed; but what this buries from view is that the very idea of a social structure is a modern essentialisation which has been produced by the changes which he hopes to describe, and which he is rhetorically persuading us—and himself—to believe. To be able to objectify a social structure in this way is also to construct an imaginary ground of neutral objectivity and factuality, not only towards 'society' but also towards 'religion'. Wilson says that the "major areas of social organization" become differentiated, which does not really help us to see that, for example, there was no well-developed and -theorised discourse of 'politics' as a domain differentiated from 'religion' until the end of the seventeenth century, or of 'economics' before the late eighteenth century, and that these rhetorical domains are part of the problematic. There is an underlying assumption generated by this kind of descriptive prose that there are societies in the world, that societies have a number of areas, and that these have become increasingly evident to scientific reason as they have become progressively differentiated. One of these areas is 'religion' which has changed its position in relation to the other areas. They are, as it were, preexistent, but they change their forms and their ways of relating to each other. They were there already, but they separated out from each other, as though they were agents growing up and coming into their own maturity. What this language fails to bring home is that these transformations were inventions, new imaginings which did not so much transform already existing entities such as societies, but invented them as rhetorical abstractions (for no one has actually seen 'a society' or 'a religion'; they are metaphysical objects) as part of a newly generated and entirely different imaginative representation of the world. Wilson's description is therefore more like a proclamation, a persuasive discourse which imaginatively constructs or reconstructs the 'objective' description for which sociologists strive.

And the discourse also constructs the sociologists and their view of their own position in relation to the things imagined to be observed. The authoritative voice of the expert social analyst suddenly becomes less so when we realise that it is an act of self-persuasion, that her and the reader's consciousness is being constructed and reproduced in and by these very forms of words, and thus is alienated in the act of objectification. Thus Bryan Wilson exemplifies the neutral, objective scholar who looks out onto history and sees the various objects of his analysis changing. What he doesn't see or convey is that his own consciousness, and the categories that organise his writing, are themselves part of the process that he is objectifying, and that we can only get close to imaginatively grasping the difference between now and then when we deconstruct the categories in which we think and attempt to understand them as rhetorical devices for persuading ourselves to see the world in a particular way. In short, the sociological consciousness and imagination, which is taken for granted and embedded in the description, is itself part of the problematic.

It is in this sense that I quoted in the introduction Roberts and Good's point, in *The Recovery of Rhetoric: Persuasive Discourse and Disciplinarity in the Human Sciences* (1993), when they argue:

[R]hetoric has played a central part in the formation, development
and legitimation of the emerging human sciences.... If we are
to understand the present-day classifications and hierarchies of the
various disciplines in the human sciences, then it is essential to
understand their rhetorical constitution. (1993:4)

The argument of this book is very much concerned with "the processes by
which disciplines establish themselves and assert their credibility through the
generation of 'commonplaces' " and the way in which "the discourses and practices of the human sciences both enact and *conceal* the persuasive strategies
essential to the establishment of knowledge about the human world" (Roberts
& Good, 1993:1–2; my italics).

In his preface to *The Social Reality of Religion*, Berger says:

The following argument is intended to be an exercise in sociological theory. Specifically, it seeks to apply a general theoretical perspective derived from the sociology of knowledge to the phenomenon of religion. While at certain points the argument moves
on levels of considerable abstraction, it never leaves ... the frame
of reference of the empirical discipline of sociology. Consequently it must rigidly bracket throughout any questions of the ultimate truth or illusion of religious propositions about the world.
There is neither explicit nor implied theology in this argument.
(1973:7)

What we should notice here is the explicit distinctions which Berger
makes, which in turn carry some further tacit assumptions as well. 'Religion' is
a "phenomenon," which means that it is a thing which can be observed from
the outside. The ground of this objectification is the sociology of knowledge,
which is explicitly distanced from theology. The implications of this methodological statement seem to be that, whereas theology can only offer partial and
metaphysical claims about ultimate truth based on speculation rather than
real knowledge, only sociology as a secular science can be objective, neutral,
and truthfully descriptive. There is a hierarchy of encompassment built into
this claim. Theology is incapable, unlike sociology, of bracketing truth claims.
It only makes them. But sociology can achieve neutrality and objectivity. It
can tell it like it is. Theology cannot encompass and subordinate the discipline
of sociology because only the latter can be based on a strictly empirical perspective, and thus only the latter can give objective, neutral description and
analysis. Theology may have things to say about metaphysical Truth, and it
undoubtedly had an important role in constructing a sacred canopy, but only
sociology can tell you accurately how and why it has done this. In assuming
that he (we) occupy this uniquely neutral and thus superior position as observers, sociologists such as Berger are actually advocating and thus construc-

ting the concept of secular knowledge. Beneath apparently modest disclaimers that sociology cannot set itself up to judge theology's truth claims, Berger (on all of our behalves) is implying its superior natural rationality.

The concept of secularisation is inherently ensnaring since we (and of course Berger) are already writing from a secular perspective (however much some of us might like to escape from it) and thus secularisation is both the object of our analysis and simultaneously the set of assumptions which guides our thinking. To challenge it, to find a way out of a circularity within which language has trapped us, we have to turn our attention to the way these categories actually operate in our own rhetoric. In the process of *inventing* the secular by means of that very activity whereby we claim to be neutrally describing what the world is really like, we are also inventing 'religions'. But I want to explore the idea that we need to invent religion and religions because without them we would not be able to invent the idea of nonreligion or 'the secular'. Contrary to the superficial impression conveyed by the appearance of historically continuous usages, 'religion' is not something that simply exists in the world, a 'phenomenon' with a stable and continuous identity, but is an ideological category with a shifting semantic content in relation to other unstable and contested categories like the secular, science, politics, the state, and so on. By writing as though 'religion' and 'theology' have always existed and that we all in principle know what is referred to, we simultaneously reproduce and authorise the nonreligious space from which we think we are writing. As academics, we construct and in that sense advocate secular values and attitudes in the very process of claiming to be describing a special set of 'religious' values and practices. Sociological theory is as much a myth and an act of faith as theology, but this is concealed by the act of rhetoric.

The circularity becomes evident in Berger's description of "the process of secularization": "By secularization we mean the process by which sectors of society and culture are removed from the domination of religious institutions and symbols" (1973:113). Here we see that the secular is defined by the removal and separation of religion. But what is meant by religion? Is he here talking about generic religion? Or is he talking about encompassing Christianity? Earlier, he made statements about religion which make it look like a generic, universal class of collective world-building activities, for example:

> Religion is the human enterprise by which a sacred cosmos is
> established.... The sacred cosmos is confronted by man as an immensely powerful reality other than himself. Yet this reality addresses itself to him and locates his life in an ultimately meaningful order. (Berger, 1973:35)

This kind of statement implies that this is a general theory about a generic religion defined in terms of humankind's various collective attempts to construct meaningful sacred canopies. Here, Christianity is tacitly constructed as one among a number of 'religions', taken as one example of humankind's multiple cultural constructions, presumably alongside other essentialisations such as Hinduism, Buddhism, Confucianism, and Islam. But these essentialised 'phenomena' are themselves produced in the same movement of discourse as 'the secular' viewpoint of sociology. Therefore when he describes the process of secularisation as the removal of religion, it is important to be clear about what is and what is not being removed. Does it imply that the secular/nonreligious as the ground of empirical rationality has always somehow been here, but has been progressively revealed as 'religion' has been rolled back? Is a secular society one in which world-building activities and the attribution of meaning by collectivities and individuals are being removed? This would be a radical and perhaps worrying proposal, because it would suggest that the ground is giving way beneath our feet. Berger has shown us that world-building activities and the construction of a sacred canopy are essential for survival. Is the secular not itself a world-building ideology, an invention of 'reality', a sacred canopy underpinned by its own practices, values, imaginings, knowledges, missions, and beliefs in salvation and progress?

It is important for my argument to draw attention to the idea of the nonreligious view of the world, which is implied throughout by the removal of 'religion' into a separated conceptual space. If religion has been transformed into an object of description, then it can only logically be described from a nonreligious ground. This nonreligious ground is not necessarily hostile to religion, and may favour it as contributing something valuable to secular society. But whether the secular take on 'religion' is thought of as neutral, favourable, or hostile, it is different because it is nonreligious. It may help to catch this act of rhetorical invention of both 'religion' and the 'nonreligious secular'—the ground of our claimed objectivity—by looking more closely at what it means to say that 'religion' has done this or that. For one thing, we should be conscious that 'religion' is an English-language word that for most of its historical usage has referred in one way or another to Christian Truth. Christianity has not until very recently, under the influence of the same objectifying processes as sociology, been represented as 'a religion', any more than does sociology represent itself as 'a religion'. They both imply encompassing claims about Truth. I believe we can get a glimpse of this process by considering how the discourse on Religion as Christian Truth shifted within the discourse of Calvinism. Whereas Catholic Christianity and the official Religion of the church-state (in the case of England, Anglicanism) encompassed all institutions and practices either by inclusion or, negatively, by exclusion (as in the case of heresy or paganism, which were only conceivable in relation to Christian Truth), this meaning became radically transformed in Puritan thought and identified with the interiority of the individual consciousness. The influence of a particular kind of Puritan consciousness, in combination with the dramatic expansion of trade, production, and consumption in the context of colonialism, was a crucial stage in the emergence of the modern paradigm that radically separated Christian Truth from the world, and made possible the secular sociology of Wilson and Berger.

This radical transformation of the meaning of Christian Truth was, at the same time, a transformation of the meaning of 'the world'. This did not and does not in itself give us the notion of nonreligious secularity, a self-subsisting material universe obeying natural laws independent of God, and an empirical model of knowledge. One could still argue that for Puritans the world was profane rather than secular in the modern sense; the profaneness of the world was defined by its distance from God. Nevertheless, it can surely be argued that this internalised conscientiousness, when combined with advances in science and the materialist, corpuscular philosophy, and when combined also with the growth of various kinds of relativism, including the discovery of many superstitions that looked like 'religions' (see the discussion of Samuel Purchas in chapter 7), did eventually come to produce what we today mean by secularism. Tawney put the influence of Calvinism like this:

> While the revelation of God to the individual soul is the center of all religion, the essence of Puritan theology was that it made it, not only the center, but the whole circumference and substance, dismissing as dross and vanity all else but this secret and solitary communion. Grace alone can save, and this grace is the direct gift of God, unmediated by any earthly institution .... To a vision thus absorbed in a single intense experience, not only religious and ecclesiastical systems, but the entire world of human relations, the whole fabric of social institutions ... reveal themselves in a new and wintry light .... Where Catholic and Anglican had caught a glimpse of the invisible, hovering like a consecration over the gross world of sense, and touching its muddy vesture with the unearthly gleam of a divine, yet familiar, beauty, the Puritan mourned for a lost Paradise and a creation sunk in sin. Where they had seen society as a mystical body, [a] compact of members varying in order and degree, but dignified by participation in the common life of Christendom, he saw a bleak antithesis between the spirit which quickeneth and an alien, indifferent or hostile world .... Puritanism had its own standards of social conduct, derived partly from the obvious interests of the commercial classes, partly from its conception of the nature of God and the destiny of man. These standards were in sharp antithesis, both to the considerable surviving elements of feudalism in English society, and to the policy of the authoritarian State, with its ideal of an ordered and graded society, whose different members were to be maintained in their traditional status by the pressure and protection of a paternal monarchy .... Puritanism became a potent force in

preparing the way for the commercial civilization which finally triumphed at the Revolution.... From the very beginning, Calvinism
had comprised two elements, which Calvin himself had fused, but
which contained the seeds of future discord. It had at once given a
whole-hearted *imprimatur* to the life of business enterprise, which
most earlier moralists had regarded with suspicion, and had laid
down upon it the restraining hand of inquisitorial discipline. At
Geneva, where Calvinism was the creed of a small and homogeneous city, the second aspect had predominated; in the many-sided
life of England, where there were numerous conflicting interests to
balance it, and where it was long politically weak, the first. Then, in
the late sixteenth and early seventeenth centuries, had come the wave
of commercial and financial expansion—companies, colonies, capitalism in textiles, capitalism in mining, capitalism in finance—on the
crest of which the English commercial classes... had climbed to
a position of dignity and affluence.... The individualism congenial
to the world of business became the distinctive characteristic of a
Puritanism which had arrived, and which, in becoming a political
force, was at once secularized and committed to a career of com-
promise. Its note was not the attempt to establish on earth a 'Kingdom of Christ', but an ideal of personal character and conduct, to
be realized by the punctual discharge both of public and private
duties.... In America, the theocracy of Massachusetts, merciless
alike to religious liberty and to economic license, was about to be
undermined by the rise of new states like Rhode Island and Pennsylvania, whose tolerant, individualist and utilitarian temper was
destined to find its greatest representative in the golden common
sense of Benjamin Franklin. (Tawney, 1962 [1926]:227–38)

This retrospective reading of the importance of Calvinism and Calvinists
in the formation of a modern view of the world indicates that it was not really a
destiny, and, as already suggested, English society in particular remained to a
considerable extent a confessional state throughout the eighteenth century and
well into the nineteenth. David Cannadine, referring to the way the British saw
their empire in the nineteenth and even the twentieth century, has argued:

Far from seeing themselves as atomized individuals with no rooted
sense of identity, or as collective classes coming into being and
struggling with each other, or as equal citizens whose modernity
engendered an unrivalled sense of progressive superiority, Britons
generally conceived of themselves as belonging to an unequal society
characterized by a seamless web of layered gradations, which were
hallowed by time and precedent, which were sanctioned by tradition

and religion, which extended in a great chain of being from the monarch at the top to the humblest subject at the bottom. That was how they saw themselves, and it was from that starting point that they tried to comprehend the distant realms and diverse society of their empire. (Cannadine, 2001:4)

This would suggest that, insofar as an ideology of individualism and economic class existed in Britain, it was still subordinated to an encompassing hierarchical ideology until quite recently. While we cannot deny the importance of the ideology of the self-made entrepreneur, the individual seeking economic salvation, derived from Calvinism or nonconformity more generally, and the new rise of a middling order on the back of manufacturing and colonial trade, historians point to a truth about Britain, that in one way or another the Anglican church-state encompassed and hallowed the traditional order of things until quite recently. In this light, it does seem significant that the term 'commonwealth' was used to describe the association of nations after the empire had mainly been disbanded. It was surely in North America that the transcendental values of individualism and economic rationalisation became the dominant discourse, and they have since been missionised throughout the world as the legitimation of U.S. imperial policy.

What Calvinists did was to provide a powerful view of the world as so distant from God that the worldly rationality that Calvinism encouraged and legitimated could, in the right circumstances, come to seem natural in a sense that did not require God as a hypothesis. In a number of the North American colonies, this view became powerfully established. As Tawney put it, instead of striving to establish a kingdom of God, or at least a theocratic state of the kind which Puritans attempted to establish in Massachusetts, this strain of Calvinism introduced an ideology of individualism and established "an ideal of personal character and conduct, to be realized by the punctual discharge of both public and private duties."

Hookyas, quoting R. K. Merton, concludes *Religion and the Rise of Modern Science* (1972) by saying:

> The Puritans, through the whole spectrum of their views... 'were the main support of the new science before the Restoration', and they left 'their indelible stamp on the next generation'. No differences about the interpretation of the facts can impair the reality of the facts themselves, which have been brought to light by historico-sociological research and which prove that 'Puritanism, and ascetic protestantism generally... played no small part in arousing a sustained interest in science'. (148–49)

Hookyas criticises Tawney for the dismal way he portrays the Puritan view of the world, disapprovingly quoting the passage "the Puritan mourned for a

lost Paradise and a creation sunk in sin" (1972:157n5) and offering a brighter
Puritan vision, attributing to English Puritanism

> anti-authoritarianism, optimism about human possibilities, rational
> empiricism, the emphasis on experience.... This does not neces-
> sarily imply that Puritanism as such produced many highly qualified
> scientists. The issue at stake here [is]...: Did Puritanism in fact
> create a spiritual climate favourable to the cultivation and freedom of
> science? The affirmative answer to this question is no modern in-
> vention of sociologists. The vindicators of the new science gave the
> same answer. (Hookyas, 1972:143)

The implications of Tawney's representation are that for the most part the
Puritans inherited the traditional Christian idea of the world as relatively
profane, but they tended to distance the world from God to such an extent that
they reduced the degree to which its institutions could be seen as sacralised by
God. However, ambiguity may be built into the Puritan view, which may be
capable of different emphases concerning the world. Optimism, humanism,
and a belief in progress and the Enlightenment were also alive, and in the
Declaration of Independence there is still a connection between "the Laws of
Nature and of Nature's God," and "Men ... are endowed by their Creator with
certain unalienable Rights." On the other hand, the humanist principle is also
asserted in the idea that men have the right to choose their own government:
"Governments are instituted among Men, deriving their just powers from the
consent of the governed," which is a radical contradiction of the European
status quo that sovereignty is given by God and sacralised by the church.

It seems reasonable therefore to suppose that Calvinists and other Dissenters, including deists and atheists, contributed to the conditions whereby a
modern ideology of secularism was able to develop from a view of the world as
profane. But this does not make them the same concepts, and their analytical
separation helps us to fine-tune distinctions and gain greater clarity and less
ideological distortion. One thing which has presumably always been clear,
even to scholars in religious studies who tend to attribute to every culture 'a
religion', or even several: the English-language category religion has for almost
all its history been inseparable from the Christian incarnation and Christian
theology, and required a process of abstraction and modern fetishism and
animism before it was ready to incarnate in different manifestations in different cultural contexts. But when this contested term is projected onto other
peoples, who think in entirely different languages, there is always ambiguity
about whether the projector is imagining 'religion' to encompass all institutions on analogy with medieval and early modern ideas, and therefore seeing
it as indistinguishable from holistic culture; or whether 'religion' is imagined
in the Calvinist mode as radically separated from the profane world; or whether
'religion' is more simply a projection of the Western religion-secular dichot-

omy, whereby religious practices are assumed to be different in kind from political, economic, and technical/instrumental ones.

Whereas the profane is a world radically distanced from God (who created it) by the Fall, the secular is a world which does not essentially depend on God for its ontological reality. The secular social world is generally represented as constructed and legitimated by humans, not by God. God has become, as it were, an optional extra licensed by the secular constitution of the nation-state. Furthermore, in the modern secular world, 'religion' ceases to mean encompassing Christian Truth, and ceases even to require a deistic god as a causal hypothesis, and becomes instead reified as 'religions' in sociology and religious studies, objects and even agents acting in the world like fetishes, multiple objects of legislation, comparison, and sociological analysis, defined by their separation from the nonreligious world of politics, state governance, and rational economic practice. These discursive formations on the profane and the secular are thus historically connected but significantly different. By analytically separating them as distinct discourses which have significant historical connections, we may be able to untangle some of the confusions about what is meant by 'religion'.

We should also pay attention to how the idea of the 'sacred' shifts in meaning and usage in this context. The shift in nuance of 'religion' does not play out in the same way as that of the 'sacred'. On the one hand, Religion is Truth which encompasses and legitimates all institutions, including those called secular. Saint Thomas More was secular, but he wore a hair shirt, and his most important duty was to hunt down and torture heretics (see Ackroyd, 1998). In this context, secular institutions—and in particular the civil magistrate such as the prince—are also *relatively* sacred, and therefore 'profane' is a relative term also. While (for example) King Henry VIII was raised in sacredness above the bishops (see chapter 5), they were more sacred than the stonemasons; yet the status, skills, and initiations of the Masonic guild were more sacred than those of the ditch diggers, and the limits of the profane world of the city and its business were sacralised by processions and feasts. While the profaneness of a fallen world increased with the Calvinists, the idea of sacrality persisted, for example, in human rights, in democracy, in artefacts and practices such as the U.S. Constitution or the Declaration of Independence.

I will argue in chapter 9 that the U.S. Constitution is an example of a document which, in its definition of the basic principles of the secular nation-state and the rights of individuals, is itself sacred. Under the First Amendment, the idea that 'the world was created by God' is a religious belief, and therefore a private right separated from the state, which is neutral towards 'religion'. More specifically, the rights and principles which the Constitution proclaims and guarantees, including the right to practice one's religion freely and without interference from the state, are sacred rights. It is not religion that is sacred here (though of course practitioners or believers will attribute sacredness to their personal faiths), but what is sacred is the right to practice religion, and this right is defined by the secular Constitution which frames the ideology of the nation-state. The democratic processes that are held to be a constitutive part of the modern nation are defended as sacred. Principles, such as equality before the law, are sacred. We cannot assume, therefore, that the sacred and 'religion' are simply and exclusively synonymous, and they need to be distinguished for descriptive and analytical purposes.

The ambiguity of all these terms—religion, secular, sacred, and profane—is attested to by the ongoing controversy about what precisely is meant by the constitutional separation of religion and the state. However, I suggest that most people who contest the meaning of the U.S. Constitution are contesting where the line should be drawn, not the conceptual separation itself. As I will argue in chapter 9, when the controversies around the interpretation of the U.S. Constitution are put into historical and epistemological context, it seems difficult to deny that a basic conceptual distinction between 'religion' as a private nonpolitical right and the secular state as a public, nonreligious sovereignty has been institutionalised. It is only in such a context that the arguments about prayers at state schools or the teaching of creationism and evolutionary theory would be controversial issues in the first place.

If the U.S. Constitution is a secular, sacred document which separates 'religion' from the state by characterising it as a private right, the idea of the nation itself is highly problematic. For the nation is surely sacred, the transcendental object of rituals of worship and sacrifice; and yet modern nationalism is rarely if ever included as 'a religion' in religious studies textbooks and syllabi. There is undoubtedly a close, complex, historical relationship between discourses on 'religion' and discourses on the 'nation', and both of these Anglophone notions have been imposed onto non-European communities that were either taken as colonies, such as Kenya or indigenous America, or threatened with colonisation, such as Japan. European languages such as English, French, Portuguese, German, and Russian were the dominant languages of what Hobsbawm calls "the apogee of nationalism, 1918–1950" (1990:131–62). The language of modern nationalism was transferred to parts of the world where entirely different concepts of the polity had been developed historically, and while on the one hand the imperial powers such as Britain and France artificially created (or tried to create) nation-states in the Middle East such as Iraq, Bahrain, Saudi Arabia, and Israel for strategic purposes, the language of nationalism was adopted by many anticolonial elites in order to create a focus for independence movements. The development of nationalism is a complex issue which has been well explored by a number of writers such as Anderson (1991), Gellner (1983), and Hobsbawm (1990), who makes this generalisation:

The Versailles settlement revealed [a] new phenomenon: the geographical spread of nationalist movements, and the divergence of the

new ones from the European pattern. Given the official commitment
of the victorious powers to Wilsonian nationalism, it was natural
that anyone claiming to speak in the name of some oppressed or
unrecognised people—and they lobbied the supreme peacemakers in
large numbers—should do so in terms of the national principle,
and especially of the right to self-determination. Yet this was more
than an effective debating argument. The leaders and ideologues of
colonial and semi-colonial liberation movements sincerely spoke
the language of European nationalism, which they had so often learnt
in or from the west, even when it did not suit their situation. And
as the radicalism of the Russian Revolution took over from that of the
French Revolution as the main ideology of global emancipation, the
right to self-determination, now embodied in Stalin's texts, hence-
forth reached those who had been beyond the range of Mazzini.
Liberation in what was not yet known as the Third World was now
seen everywhere as 'national liberation' or, among the Marxists,
'national and social liberation'. (Hobsbawm, 1990:136)

Hobsbawm does not mention the importance of written constitutions
in the formation of the modern nation-state.[17] This would have relevance
for the topic of religion since the most powerful modern constitution, that of
the United States of America, which has been used as a model for many other
nations (Bailyn, 2002) and for communities struggling to become independent nations, implies a major change in the understanding of the meaning
of the word 'religion' in the English language. The degree to which Western
colonialism encouraged the adoption of Western-style written constitutions by
the leaders of national liberation movements, which in turn incorporated a
specific concept of 'religion' separated from the public 'secular' domain, does
not seem to have attracted interest from within religious studies.

However, evidence from the Japanese historian Jun'ichi Isomae suggests
that at the time of the end of Edo in the 1850s Japan was considered by Western
nations such as Britain and America as a 'semi-barbarous nation' because it did
not have a modern constitution guaranteeing the separation of religion and
politics. This gave rise to a long internal debate among the intellectual elite
and governing class about what constituted 'religion' and what constituted the
'secular state'. There existed a real problem of translation, and though a solution was found in the Meiji Constitution of 1889, it is arguable that the confused result was part of the problem leading to the formation of state Shinto
and the cult of emperor divinity (see Isomae, 2007).[18] Today's constitution was
written (originally in English) during the occupation at the end of World War
II; it guarantees the separation of 'religion' and 'politics' (*seikyô bunri*; see
Mullins et al., 1993:75–134). To what extent this constitutional concept does
justice to indigenous Japanese forms of life, or to what extent Japanese forms

of life have converged with American ones in order to increase the fit, is debatable. It is at least arguable that Japanese capitalism has significantly different organisational principles compared to American models, in particular that human relations are ritually sacralised in importantly different ways, more in terms of face-to-face hierarchies of deference and subordination than individualism, but this is disguised from analysts because they assume that Japan has become, or is becoming, 'westernized' or 'Americanized' (Johnson, 1995; see also a discussion in Fitzgerald, 2000:160–63).

I am arguing here that there is a historically valid understanding of the sacred-profane distinction, in the English language at least, which cuts across the modern religion-secular dichotomy and consequently subverts it. To what degree it can be translated without too much distortion into non-European languages is open to argument. But its continued usage by historians, anthropologists, sociologists, and others across the spectrum of the humanities and social sciences as though it is the same distinction as that between the religion and the secular is the cause of considerable rhetorical confusion. To recover this English-language distinction, it is necessary to disentangle it from the uncritical scholarly conflation of the 'sacred' with the 'religious', and the 'profane' with the 'secular'. To do this, I have appealed to historical and ethnographic usage to show that this conflation is the result more of a lack of critical awareness than of a genuine ideological compatibility between the two pairs.

In some ways like the Hopi, the Pueblo peoples, the Japanese, and our own ancestors, contemporary Anglophone academics (like politicians, civil servants, or members of the staff at the White House) participate in relatively profane practices, such as waiting in line for lunch in the canteen, and in others which are more ritualised because they are more sacred to us (e.g., reading and listening to papers in conferences) and the society in which we flourish (graduation ceremonies). And I suggest that until we, the community of scholars, begin to take notice of how 'religion' pops in and out of our thinking and writing in a number of logically unaligned ways, which it does with a feeling of entire naturalness, then we will continue unawares to do ideological work in the construction of our own cosmology, even at the very moment that we are claiming to describe theirs. This perhaps is a sense in which society or culture, in the shape of powerful controlling categories embedded in discourses which we all in similar ways reproduce, thinks through us, setting us up (for example) as realist empiricists while all the time using us as world constructionists.

4

On Civility and Barbarity

The expression 'discourse on civility and barbarity' in the title of
this book refers to those practices by which we express our collective
sense of ourselves as civilised as opposed to a barbarous other. The
value of civility is arguably fundamental to our idea of ourselves
as human, as distinct from something short of human, a barbarian.
Civility is what literate male elites in Europe, and perhaps universally,
have represented themselves as having, in comparison with those
others who do not. The Greeks represented themselves as civilised,
and all others who could not speak the language or think and behave as Greeks were barbarous. The Romans consciously based
their own self-representations of civility on those of the Greeks and
thus, adapted to their own circumstances, continued a language
of civility and barbarity. The Roman Catholic male elite adopted this
language to express the superior civility of Christian Truth or Religion over against the barbarous superstitions of Turks, Tartars, and
all other infidels and further adapted it by conflating barbarism
with paganism and heresy. In turn, Protestants regarded Catholics as
barbarous and pagan in their superstitious practices and idolatries.
No doubt, there were and are different ways in which this fundamental dichotomy can be expressed. Many practices considered
orthodox or orthoprax have been associated with self-images of superior civility, implicitly and often explicitly compared with some inferior other. This other was usually, but not always, external, but
could also refer to internal marginals, such as gypsies and Jews, and
subordinates, such as peasants who lived in the country (hence,

paganus) rather than the city (hence, *civitas*). There is a certain degree of relativity as to what counts as inside and outside.

Given the focus of this book, it is legitimate to concentrate here on the European or Euro-American discourse on civility and barbarity. It needs to be said, though, that, unlike the religion-secular ideology of modern nation-states, the general distinction between 'our civility' and 'their barbarity' may be a near-universal. This is the bottom line of 'us' and 'them', 'our ways' and 'their (inferior) ways', and it is difficult to conceive of any human collectivity that does not have ways of formulating its own practices as superior against an inferior other.

During the nineteenth century, the European colonising powers referred to savage, barbarous, and semi-civilised nations which they justified colonising in the name of superior modern civilisation, a combination of Christianity and scientific rationality. For example, the film *The Last Samurai*, starring Tom Cruise, quite skilfully brings out the interface between the cultural assumptions of the colonisers and the colonised. Though Japan was not militarily colonised by America (at least not until 1945), the Japanese elite were divided, and the triumphant party, led by the Chōshū and Satsuma dynasties, felt compelled to accept the hegemonic values of the more powerful and turn them into instruments of their own survival. The film depicts the conflicts in Japan in the 1870s in the early Meiji period between, on the one hand, the Japanese and the Americans and, on the other, between the Japanese modernisers and the samurai, who stood for traditional values of *bushidō*. The Americans, who were perceived by the Japanese as a barbarous nation of cheap traders who smelled like pigs and did not understand the civilities of courtesy and polite conversation, were at the same time recognised as a powerful threat to Japan's independence as a nation. Barbarous or not, they needed to become more like the Americans if they were to survive. The wider context of the colonisation of much of the rest of Asia by European powers such as France and Britain helps to explain the urgency felt by a powerful section of the Japanese aristocracy. In the film, the Americans see the Japanese as barbarous and backwards, in some ways like their own Indian 'savages'. On the other hand, the Japanese modernising elite, contemptuous of the Americans, yet impressed by their power, and thus largely converted to the demands of modern rational, scientific 'civility', needed to destroy their own 'irrational' past in the form of the samurai.

The civility of *bushidō* was formulated partly in terms of the virtue of honour rather than 'trade'. *Bushidō* was not only about sword fighting. On the martial arts side, it included *kendō* (stick fighting), horsemanship, and skill with bow and arrow. But the martial arts themselves were permeated with Confucian values of subordination and the deference of juniors to seniors and women to men, the symbolism of the shrine *torii* (gate), the chanting of Buddhist monks in the temple, *chadō* (tea ceremony), and meditation on the transience of the cherry blossom (*sakura*). The American demands of modern civilisation were in the end victorious and the samurai were defeated, but the American victory in the final analysis depended on mass-produced machine guns and heavy artillery outweighing the outstanding Japanese artisanship of handmade steel and sword production (e.g., modern technology and the destruction of indigenous forms of life as the prerequisite of imperial conquest). This in turn presupposes the destruction of the social formations that sustained the traditional way of life and the victory of mass production and eventually mass consumerism. American or modern Western values of capitalism were thus victorious, and represented as the triumph of superior rationality. However, an interesting subtext of the film, represented by the contrasting behaviour of the American hero and the head of the samurai rebel army, was a questioning of the supposed superiority of easygoing American egalitarian values over against the more hierarchical and severe disciplinarian values of *bushidō*. Tom Cruise, though a disciplined American warrior, ironically begins to see that his own lack of civility is justly corrected by the deeper humanity of the severe *bushidō* codes. The film could be represented as ending with the equation of the destruction, by white American barbarians, of the morally superior civilisations of the Japanese and the indigenous Americans.[1]

It could surely be argued that the civility-barbarity dichotomy, like the opposition between Religion and superstition which closely follows its discursive contours, is about who is and who is not properly human. As Pagden (1982) points out, two supposed practices in particular—cannibalism and human sacrifice—have indicated people whose understanding of natural law is perverse. These two practices were fundamental characteristics of the barbarian in the European imagination, and accusations of such practices "contributed to the de-humanisation of the outsider, for men who ate other men were never thought to be quite human" (Pagden, 1982:81). The Greeks and the Romans had attributed these practices as essential characteristics of the enemies of civility. Christians adopted from classical literature the belief that many 'barbarous' peoples were also anthropophagi, such as Tartars, Mongols, and Thracians, and they also accused Jews and various heretical groups such as Waldensians of cannibalism. The Christian explorers and missionaries expected to find these practices (and various kinds of fabulous monsters) in America.

However, Pagden also points out that the attributions of cannibalism to neighbours are ubiquitous: the Arawak believed that the Cribs were doing it (1982:81); the Arab merchants of the Sudan attributed it to the Azande; the Mani of the Gambia believed that the Portuguese slavers ate their victims; many Africans believed that the white man had come to drink their blood; the Mexica were believed by other American peoples to eat their sacrificial victims (83). The Christian mass has also been thought by non-Christians to be cannibalistic. The distinction between civility and barbarity is therefore not confined to the Greeks, Romans, and Christians:

This seemingly stark dichotomy ... is perhaps not so very surprising as it might at first seem. The anthropologists have shown us that
few peoples have a fully articulate sense of a single undivided ge-
nus. As Lévi-Strauss once observed, 'a very great number of primitive tribes simply refer to themselves by the term for "men" in
their language, showing that in their eyes an essential characteristic of man disappears outside the limits of the group'. (Pagden,
1995:22)

The historian W. R. Jones (1971:21–52) also wants to universalise this
opposition, perhaps more from a historical than anthropological perspective.
Jones is concerned specifically with the opposition between the ideas of the
civilised man[2] and the barbarian in the writings of elite men in European
history, but he also sets it within the wider context of "the origins of civilization
in world perspective" (49), arguing that there is "considerable justification" for
a view of history as "a gradual extension of civilization outward" from an axis of
several centres "running from North Africa eastward to China" (49–50). This
view of history can be justified in part at least "in the attitudes displayed by the
apologists for civilisation toward their barbarian antagonists" (50). Apologists
are usually male members of a literate elite who have a particularly powerful
function in the self-representations of a cultural collective. One example he
gives concerns the conceptions of the Chinese elite of their tribal neighbours:
"A Chinese chronicler ... remarked of the fierce Hsiung-Nu, who troubled the
peace of the Middle Kingdom, that 'their only concern is self-advantage, and
they know nothing of propriety and righteousness'" (21).

The translated part of this sentence is referenced as originating with
B. Watson, *Records of the Grand Historian of China Translated from the Shih Chi
of Ssu-ma Ch'ien* (New York, 1961–1963), II:155. I do not mention this in order
to offer any criticism, either of the Chinese translation (I do not read Chinese)
or of the appropriateness of indicating how the barbarian-civilised dichotomy
might reasonably be thought to have relevance for the Chinese case, as well as
the European. It serves well the function of showing how the English-language
dichotomy might have analogous meanings in Chinese language and ideology.
This would be partly a problem of translation. Both Jones (who seems to read
several languages) and Watson (who has translated this piece from the Chinese) would have been acutely aware of the problems of rendering complex
concepts, such as 'civilised', 'barbarian', 'self-advantage', 'propriety', and 'righteousness', from one language to another. Even within the European languages, the words 'civilised' and 'barbaric' change their nuance from one context
to another (though one result of Jones's impeccable research has been to bring
out the continuities within the European context very strongly, a point to which
I will come back). But one suspects that this point is even more salient when
translating a Chinese word with a Confucian nuance into the English word

"righteousness," which in many contexts is strongly overlaid with biblical and monotheistic associations.

Nevertheless, while for my purposes in this book I do not have to settle these complex issues, they need at least to be broached. The sheer colonial power of Anglophone and generally Euro-American discourses makes our constructions of civility and barbarity the ones to which others are more or less forced to conform. Yet it must also be the case that many ancient and sophisticated cultures (I think in particular of Japan, a country where I lived for several years, as represented in the film discussed earlier) harbour a feeling that the Americans and British are barbarians even while being forced to adopt some of the American and British criteria of civility. Let us say that they have ambivalent attitudes towards the West, feeling a need to be like us but at the same time looking down on us.[3]

This discussion of civility and barbarity is not historically exhaustive. It is intended to show the extent to which discourses on civility and barbarity overlap with those on Religion (understood as Christian Truth) and superstition, and rationality and irrationality. It introduces the dichotomy as European, with its origins in Greece, and traces it as a Roman and then Roman Catholic discourse up to the time of the Reformation. I argue that this dichotomy is an important aspect of the way a Christian identity has been constructed, and the light that this sheds on that identity. But in following chapters, I will attempt to show that much the same dichotomy reappears in Protestant discourses in which Catholics themselves become identified with the barbarian, the irrational, and the superstitious. Furthermore, this same dichotomy reappears in Enlightenment discourses where scientific rationality becomes paradigmatic but marginalises 'religion' by privatising it and transforming it into a constitutional right guaranteed by the nonreligious state. The superiority of European scientific rationality over against the superstitious barbarity of non-Europeans thus becomes a powerful tool in the new phase of colonialism of the nineteenth century. Instead of the imposition of Catholicism in its Aristotelian-Thomist cosmological paradigm, one finds in the nineteenth century that one of the demands of civility becomes the constitutional separation of religion from politics and the establishment of a modern, Western-style nonreligious state in conformity with European scientific rationality. And during this period in the nineteenth century, the evolutionary hypothesis transforms but does not obliterate the civility-barbarity discourse. Civility belongs to Protestant Enlightenment Europe because Europe is more developed in evolutionary terms, in contrast to those prelogical primitives who are still living in darkness, as though they are evolutionary throwbacks. In short, the relationship between civility and religion changes, but the basic discourse persists.

In his article "The Image of the Barbarian in Medieval Europe" (1971), Jones is primarily concerned with the idea of civility and its dichotomous opposite, barbarity, as it has been constructed historically in the literate self-representations of Greek, Roman, and Christian elites. Jones's article is a study of the changing nuances of what he identifies as a key conceptual dichotomy in European civilisation since the ancient Greeks up to the Renaissance. What emerges from this and other expert studies is a series of overlapping dichotomies: from the Greeks and Romans, civility and barbarity, rationality and irrationality; to which were added by the Christians, Religion (Christian Truth) and superstition.

Jones gives a number of clear and useful general glosses on the fundamental opposition he is exploring, such as this one:

> Civilized man, with his urban institutions, his agrarian way of life, his technological and economic sophistication, and his conspicuous literary and plastic artistry, conceived himself as superior to these other folk with whom he sometimes competed for domination of the richer parts of the world. Long before the ancient Greeks invented the word 'barbarian' to describe the Scythians and other peoples who differed from them in not subscribing to the ideals of Greek culture, other civilized men had expressed similar sentiments towards alien peoples with whom they came into contact. (Jones, 1971:21)

Through the invention of their own self-representations as 'civilised' in contrast to the other 'barbarians', Greeks, Romans, and Christians in their differing but comparable ways were able to valorise themselves and their own practices and disciplines, and at the same time rationalise aggression towards those neighbours they deemed to be inferior. Jones acknowledges that there were "occasional efforts to idealize the barbarian and to extol his real or supposed virtues" (1971:22); however, generally,

> the pejorative implications of the word 'barbarian' were almost invariably present in its use in Graeco-Latin antiquity and in medieval Europe and Byzantium, although its precise applications and connotations reflected changing historical circumstances. (22)

Arguably, from a feminist point of view, all these European cultures have been misogynist. In all these cultures, women have been thought of as children, an idea sanctified by Aristotle. The Greek philosophers Plato and Aristotle (and other classical writers) had and still have profound authority within Catholicism and Christianity, especially through Aquinas, who took over many of Aristotle's ideas. They defined civility, rationality, and what it means to be human. Explaining the distinction in Greek between rational and irrational souls, Pagden comments, "Neither women nor children are, in Aristotle's view, fully rational, since the former lack what he calls 'authority' (akuron), while the rational faculty in the latter is only partly formed" (Pagden, 1995:21).

What defines Greek ideas and self-representations of what it means to be 'civilised'? Jones mentions the polis, the Greek language, the literary and artistic ideals of the city-state, and the cultural sophistication of the Greek poets, dramatists, and philosophers. In contrast, with some notable exceptions, the depictions of the other as "the oaf, the slave, and the predator usually passed unchallenged in the circles of the intelligentsia" (Jones, 1971:24).

For the Greeks, there may have been a stronger ethnic or racial element in their construction of the other as barbarous, whereas for Romans the difference was more weighted towards a cultural concept of difference. Whereas in the case of the Greeks, barbarians could never be civilised because they could never be Greek, Jones suggests that the Romans, through their style of colonisation, opened a larger loophole for the possibility that barbarians could become civilised. If conquered barbarians submitted themselves to Roman law, language, and the toga, then there was some conceptual possibility that they could be converted to civility, and Jones gives examples of such perceived conversions. This distinction between Greek and Roman attitudes to the barbarians is well expressed by Pagden, when he compares Aristotle and Cicero:

> Unlike... the Greek *polis*, the Roman *civitas* was crucially a civiliza-
> tion for exportation.... Where Aristotle's 'barbarians' differed
> from Cicero's 'provincials' was that whereas the former would seem
> to be immoveable in their slavery—for no amount of instruction in
> civility could restore a man's capacity for rational understanding—the
> latter could clearly be educated in the ways of civil society. This is
> why Cicero himself, always among the most chauvinist of Romans,
> could nevertheless insist that the Africans, the Spanish and the
> Gauls were entitled to just rule, despite being 'savage and barbarous
> nations'. (Pagden, 1995:22)

The Greek description of 'barbarians', that is, wild, undeveloped, and uncultivated tribes that lacked the Greeks' urbane sophistication, was consciously continued by Roman writers, whose typical examples of barbarity were the Germanic and Celtic tribes. Typically, the word 'barbarian' invoked feelings of "dread, distrust, and hatred for a variety of peoples" (Jones, 1971:23); barbarians were thought typically to be "warlike, unpredictable and cruel." Barbarians were *saevitia* and *crudelitas*. Thus the Romans continued the Greek denigration of the barbarian other, though theirs tended to emphasise morals and manners rather than language. "*Romanitas* was a cultural rather than a racial phenomenon" (Jones, 1971:24). Anybody could therefore in principle adopt "the Latin language, the toga, Roman law and religion" but even so the distinction could not be eradicated, but only lessened.

Jones mentions the Christian monk/statesman Cassiodorus Senator's (490–585 CE) distinction between *civilitas* and barbarism. Cassiodorus is quoted as saying, "The observance of the law is the sign of *civilitas*... for what is better than that people should wish to live under the rule of justice? For that brings together people from their wild state into a civilized community" (Jones, 1971:30). Cassiodorus was writing on behalf of the Gothic king Theodoric, who made a proclamation to his Gaulish subjects urging them " 'to obey Roman customs' and to relish the 'ancient freedom' by putting off 'barbarian cruelty' and wrapping themselves 'with the morals of the toga' " (Jones, 1971:30–31). Here, the Roman toga symbolises law, which in turn is virtually the same thing as Roman customs, both of which are essential for *civilitas*. Yet Cassiodorus Senator was Christian.

This is one piece of evidence that the Greek and Roman distinction between 'civility' and 'barbarity' was adopted in much the same way by Christian writers to refer to non-Christian outsiders and also to non-Christian or only nominally Christian insiders. Indeed, the distinction was strictly enforced, and the Christian identification of barbarian with 'pagan' (similar to Cicero's provincials, e.g., *paganus*, or country people, who lived outside the civilising context of the city) and also with 'heretic' was the legal mechanism whereby Christian civilisation could defend itself from its internal and its external enemies. Jones's evidence suggests that heretics and pagans attracted the same feelings of disgust and mistrust among the Christian elite as barbarians did among the Greeks and Romans. The continuity of language and meaning is emphasized in the context of the formulation of eighth- and ninth-century "Carolingian political theology and diplomacy ... by the identification of the Christian religion with the tradition of imperial Roman unity" (Jones, 1971:36). Religion here is being used specifically to mean Christianity or Christendom. The implication here is that Christian civilisation is in many important respects modelled after Roman civilisation. Religion is difficult to distinguish from civility and from rationality.

Jones refers to the distinction between civility and barbarity as the "principal distinction within the European consciousness" (1971:32). Nevertheless, continuity does not necessarily imply identity, and clearly there were Christian characteristics that made Christian civility different in expression from Roman. Jones explains how "changing conditions within Europe during the fifth, sixth and seventh centuries blurred the distinction between *romanitas* and barbarism and promoted new categories of differentiation" (1971:32). This led to the substitution of the older Roman-barbarian dichotomy with that of the Christian-barbarian dichotomy: "In his book of miracles," Gregory of Tours "employed *barbarus* as a synonym for pagan" (32).

Furthermore, the identification of the barbarian with the pagan linked it to heresy, for the barbarian was also "the Heathen or the Arian heretic" (Jones, 1971:32). This indicates an apparent difference between Romans and Roman Catholics, for with the church the problem of civility was not only expressed in terms of orthopraxy, that is, following the correct customs, but doctrinal orthodoxy. A fourth-century Christian writer, Prudentius, is quoted as saying,

"As different is the Roman from the barbarian as man is different from the animal or the speaking person from the mute, and as they who follow the teachings of God differ from those who follow senseless superstitions" (27). Notice that, while following the teachings of Christ may in a formal sense be different from being articulate, being a man, or being Roman, it is tacitly of the same kind. The crucial distinction is between being civilised and being barbarous.

For example, Jones says, "This cultural antagonism [between civility and barbarity] is vividly displayed in the actual indifference of Christian Romans towards converting the Arian and Pagan Germans to Trinitarian Christianity and in the remarks of an Arian Christian apologist of the fifth century" who insisted upon "the inadequacy of Christianity to assuage the ferocious customs of the invaders" (1971:27). After several such examples, Jones concludes, "Romanitas, whether pagan or Christian, was still juxtaposed against barbarism during the late Roman period" (28).

In the case of Christians, an emphasis on adherence to orthodox doctrinal formulations, for example, belief in the Trinity as against the Arian heresy, was of course an important feature in the definition of submission and conformity to the canons of civility. The barbarian became conflated with the idea of the pagan, heretic, heathen, and infidel in Christian thinking. Jones refers to the Christian-barbarian dichotomy of the fifth, sixth, and seventh centuries, and specifically *barbarus* as a synonym for pagan: "the Catholic Christian was distinguished from the barbarian, who was the heathen or the Arian heretic" (1971:32).

Yet the distinction suggested above between orthodoxy and orthopraxy, which may appear to be a straightforward distinction between an emphasis on 'belief' and an emphasis on 'practice', needs some further consideration. One of the earliest and clearest examples of Christian ideas about barbarity "are those provided by surviving examples of Celtic penitential literature" (Jones, 1971:33), which state clearly that the pure connotation of being a true Christian is best exemplified by a dress code. He specifically cites a sixth-century Welsh penance for wearing the hair long:

> The perfect identification of the barbarian and the pagan occurs in
> the sixth century Welsh compilation known as the 'Synod of the
> Grove of Victory', and it is repeated in later sources. A mid-seventh
> century Welsh penitential decreed a penance for the *catholicus*
> (Christian) who dared to let his hair grow in barbarian fashion
> (*in more babarico*). (Jones, 1971:33)

This suggests that, though many writers in religious studies assume that correct 'belief' is the most important feature of Christian identity, here we can see that 'belief' does not necessarily refer to a personal adherence to a proposition in the later nineteenth-century Protestant sense, influenced by modern positivist epistemology, but in the ancient Roman Catholic context also had the sense of correct *practice* (like the wearing of the Roman toga).

Bede used the word barbarian in his *Ecclesiastical History* to refer to the Scots (34–35) who plundered into Northumbria. William of Malmesbury "used the word [barbarian] . . . to describe the early Anglo-Saxons" (Jones, 1971:37). William of Malmesbury was talking about the effects of conversion to Christianity on the warlike and barbarous English. Here it seems to mean that the barbarians were civilised by being educated in submission to Christian law, morality, and codes of conduct generally. The Irish were in turn characterised as barbarians by the English (Jones, 1971:42). Since the Irish were Christian, this implies that they were not *properly* Christian as the English thought of it, since their customs were 'uncivilised'.

In the context of the later middle ages, Jones says, "Islam was not viewed as *a pagan religion* but rather as a particularly hateful and dangerous corruption of the true faith—a pernicious heresy." He says, "Christian apologists created a mythical portrait of *Islam as a perversion of true religion*, the delusions of pawns and dupes" (1971:37). At this time, for example in the context of the late fifteenth-century occupation of Constantinople by the Ottomans, "the image of the barbarian . . . was used principally to connote ferocity, brutality and cruelty" (Jones, 1971:38). This indicates the degree to which true Religion overlapped with civility and rationality in the Christian imagination and, conversely, superstition with barbarity and irrationality. The Christian meaning of the word barbarism "was used to express the condescension of some Europeans towards others who seemed less advanced or refined" (39).

It is in this context that we find the following sentence, which is full of interest: "When the ambition or arrogance of civilized man coincided with specific political, military or religious objectives, such antagonisms might be concealed behind the idealistic ventures of a civilizing or missionizing kind" (23). At a general level, it makes sense and could be true of Chinese, Greek, Roman, Muslim, or medieval Christian aggression intended to subjugate, discipline, dominate, and possibly colonise the other. It could be true also of the Protestant Christian missions within the wider context of European agencies in nineteenth- and twentieth-century colonialism (see Brian Stanley on "the gospel of civilization" in his chapter 7, "Christianity and Culture," in *The Bible and the Flag*, 1990:157–74). But do the words in the quotation from Jones— "civilizing *or* missionizing" (my italics)—have significantly different meanings? This only becomes of interest if, for example, one wanted to claim that missionising has 'religious' objectives, and that these are conceptually distinct from 'civilising' missions. How shall we distinguish between them? The same question might be asked about the differences, if any, between 'political' and 'religious' objectives. Is this just a rhetorical turn of phrase, or are there substantive and important differences between these?

It has been almost a cliché to say that Christianity is defined by belief, whereas "Hinduism," for example, is defined by practice, but it is not clear what the implications are for the history of Christianity, or how much of this is a Protestant backward-looking projection. What does it mean and what was the real significance of the issues around heresy? Charles Freeman, in *The Closing of the Western Mind*, has argued that correct doctrinal formulation became a huge issue in the church initially because of the demands of the Roman emperor Augustine, who was concerned primarily with the survival of a unified empire. According to Freeman, it was Emperor Constantine who imposed doctrinal agreement on the bishops at the Council of Nicaea in 325 because they were unable to find agreement themselves. The definition of orthodox belief was therefore, according to Freeman, from the beginning a decision made by a Roman emperor. If there were so many conflicting interpretations of the meaning of doctrinal belief among the various factions within the church, and the doctrinal formulation which emerged victorious did so as a result of the power of the Roman emperor, then this surely raises a doubt about what kind of 'belief', other than conforming to a series of practices, ordinary Christians thought they were believing. According to Jones:

> Among the clearest and earliest illustrations of the purely religious use of the word [i.e., barbarian] are those provided by surviving examples of Celtic penitential literature, which stipulated punishments for persons who served as scouts or informers to the heathen and led them to attack their fellow Christians. (Jones, 1971:33)

He describes this as "the purely religious use" of the word barbarian, by which he presumably means Christian use. Being a barbarian in this sentence is equivalent to being an informer on behalf of the other, a betrayer of one's compatriots, an outsider pretending to be an insider. 'Religious' here means knowing how to behave with loyalty towards one's own people; in short, "the purely religious use" seems to amount to understanding and performing proper Christian communal practice.

If this is the perfect identification of the barbarian with the pagan, then it constructs Christian identity in terms of customs and loyalties, such as the cutting of hair, the correct presentation of the self and the body, and loyalty to one's own people. It also reduces the power of the idea that holding correct belief as an inner private conviction, private assent to a proposition, is the crucial demarcation of 'the purely religious', and suggests instead that 'believing' or assenting to a specific doctrinal formulation should be understood as a form of public practice, a shared behavioural disposition, a collective demand for solidarity acted out in the disciplines of civility. Wearing the hair in correct fashion is essentially not so much different from the symbolism of wearing the Roman toga for Roman civility and identity and of being morally and culturally correct. This formulation takes the problem of orthodoxy away from belief in the modern positivistic sense, as being propositional—an inner mental abstraction and formulation of propositions that, to be true, must conform to their outer object—and suggests alternatively an embodied cultural practice denoting collective self-identity.

Jones does not put it explicitly in that way. But it is difficult to avoid such an inference. There are several other examples provided by Jones that tend to strengthen the view that what is 'civilitas' to the Romans and what is 'religion' to the Christians are not very different; it amounts to the laws, customs, literacy, urbanity, dress, manners, and whatever else are deemed to be the proprieties and conformities of the civilised person.

No doubt, many will say that Christianity is essentially a doctrine of salvation which transcends the distinction between civility and barbarity, and it is in this sense that Christianity is "purely religious." This soteriological sense of the meaning of 'religion' is one of the many and various ways that modern scholars use the term. But this is what is at issue, for these examples do not seem to support that interpretation. According to Jones, for Ambrose, the bishop of Milan, "Roman civilization and barbarism continued to stand in stark contrast, divided by a cultural and moral chasm so immense that Christianity could not bridge it" (1971:26). Presumably this is because being Christian is to be civilised, and some peoples were simply too barbarous and irrational to be capable of converting. And even Saint Augustine of Hippo saw it very much in terms of culture or civilisation against barbarism, a distinction which apparently was more fundamental even than the universal soteriology of redemption through Christ:

> Despite his ingenious effort to elevate contemporary discussions of
> the fate of Rome from the merely historical level to the metaphysi-
> cal, and despite his insistence on the relative unimportance of the
> barbarian sacking of Rome against the backdrop of God's plan of re-
> demption, he continued to contrast Roman civilization and barba-
> rism in the conventional manner. (Jones, 1971:27)

What we have here in this work by Jones, tacitly at least, is an idea of Religion as the practice of civility (Christian Truth) contrasted with barbarity, rather than a metaphysical plan of redemption that transcends history and culture and language. It amounts to a collective identity, a total ritual system which ideally every individual practiced from birth to death, and which encompassed, teleologically, all the practices of civility and rationality. Redemption, of course, is fundamental; but to be redeemed is to become civil and one is redeemed *from* barbarity.

During the eighth, ninth, and tenth centuries, there evolved the idea of a more or less "unified territorial existence" for "a spiritually homogeneous Christendom," as against the hostile groups of Agars, Slavs, Vikings, Magyars, and Arabs on its borders. Expressed as a dichotomy between Christians and those "heathen barbarians" (at this time, "the barbarian was usually the non-Catholic Christian or heathen") who wished to destroy Christendom, an " 'ideological conflation' was associating *Romanitas* and *Christianitas*. The *Romani* or *respublica Romana* had by the eighth and ninth centuries become equivalent to those persons who submitted themselves to the Roman or Western Church" (Jones, 1971:35).

Jones's discussion progresses towards the late middle ages, when "*barbarus* kept its classical meaning, as the opposite of Roman or Latin, only on the linguistic and literary levels" (1971:34). In this new context, it came to indicate either the vernacular languages or faults in Latin grammar and composition. This again points to a notion of Religion and civility as correct practice and literacy, which are tied to knowledge of the classical languages. The historian Bede, Jones tells us, "used the word 'barbarian' in its linguistic, moral, and religious senses during the course of writing his *Ecclesiastical History of the English Nation*" (Jones, 1971:34–35). The examples he gives from Bede suggest again that being a Christian as distinct from being a pagan is very like being a Greek or a Roman as distinct from being a barbarian. An English prince was offended by the "barbarous" speech of a foreign preacher; pagans are "puffed up with barbarous folly" (35); the Romans built a wall to prevent the barbarous Picts and Scots from ravaging the South; in describing "the slaughter in Northumbria perpetrated by the 'pagan' Penda and the 'barbarous' Cadwalla, Bede evoked the classical prejudice against the barbarian" (35)—all of these examples from Bede give weight to the idea that standards of morality, decency, literacy, correct behaviour, rational thought, and other superior attributes characterised the civilised Christian as against the pagan or barbarian.

Again and again, the logic and methodology of Jones's extremely skilful weaving together of a multitude of expert sources in different languages suggests that the term 'religion' has little or no useful descriptive content over and above indicating the kind of attributes that any construction of Christian civility would claim as against the barbarian. This is not to deny the important semantic changes that Jones is at pains to point out (1971:36). It is to question the claim that some of the changes were of a religious nature in some generic sense, and others were nonreligious, or that some were more purely religious than others. For example, we can see that converting 'barbarians' to Greek civilisational values and practices, if it were possible, would be different in some respects from the conversion to Roman civility. Since the Romans were invested in widespread colonisation, they allowed greater room for conversion to civility through the adoption of Latin and the toga. Their concept was less racially explicit than the Greek. Actually, as Jones points out, many Romans, much like the Greeks, thought that such conversion was ultimately impossible, even while the processes of colonisation and acculturation continued (24). He has also pointed out that many Christians thought in the same way. And this was also how many of the Christian Spanish conquerors thought about the indigenous peoples of America (see the discussion below).

Jones gives the reader a number of examples of the similarity between Roman civility and barbarity and Christian faith and barbarity. He shows how "Louis the Pious promoted the conversion of the Swedes, who bordered his realm," advancing missions "in order to preach and thence all of the barbarian nations would be able to take the sacrament of divine mystery more easily and more fully" (1971:36). Clearly, the idea of conversion through preaching and the administering of the sacraments are specifically Christian concepts, but it is also suggested by Jones in this context that there is also a significant "identification of the Christian religion with the tradition of imperial Roman unity," that converting the Swedes to Christianity was a policy of those who considered themselves civilised towards those whom they considered dangerous and barbaric. The Christian idea of the pagan barbarians overlapped considerably in meaning with the Roman, in the perceived "qualities of ferocity, belligerency, and cruelty" (1971:36).

In the twelfth century, William of Malmesbury "used the word [barbarian] . . . to describe the early Anglo-Saxons . . . . To the English historian, Christianity was a civilizing force capable of achieving the moral as well as the spiritual conversion of its adherents" (Jones, 1971:37). It is not clear, however, what "spiritual conversion" means here, nor how we should distinguish it from "moral conversion." The examples which Jones gives from William of Malmesbury lead the meaning of 'religion' back to Religion, and thus back to civility: conversion to Christianity abolished "the war-like habits of the English—a distinctive trait of the barbarian" (37). And he quotes from the translation from the Latin by W. Stubbs:

> In the first years of their arrival, they were barbarians in their look
> and manners, warlike in their usages, heathens in their rites; but
> after embracing the faith of Christ, slowly, by degrees, because of the
> peace they enjoyed, putting the exercise of arms in second place,
> they gave themselves entirely to the works of religion. (Jones, 1971:37)

What else could the works of Christian religion be than the practices of civility? For surely it is civility that is rational, and Christian salvation is the discovery of God's rationality. Civility is not merely a *sign* of salvation, for it is the discipline which constitutes one's correct consciousness of God's order and purposes in the world. What I infer from Jones's paper, though these words are not his, is that Christian orthodoxy is a form of orthopraxy, and that the best meaning we can give to a concept of 'correct belief' is itself a practice or lifetime set of practices.

Discussing the work of the twelfth-century Anglo-Welsh author Gerald of Wales, who composed reports on both Wales and Ireland—the *Topographia Hibernica*—for the English king, Jones says:

[H]e attempted to generalize on those social and attitudinal factors
which differentiated Ireland from its more civilized neighbor....
Despite the conversion of the Irish to Christianity long before, Gerald
complained of their failure to conform to the basic teaching of the
faith and of their vicious ignorance. Uncouth and unpredictable, the
Irish bore a clear resemblance to the barbarian of the Graeco-Latin
sources. (Jones, 1971:41)

There may be more to Christian practice and belief than the disciplines of
civility, but it is difficult to find them in Jones's account and the many examples he uses, and the reader receives the strong impression that a good part
of what is meant by failure to conform to the faith is "vicious ignorance,"
uncouthness, unpredictability, in short, barbarism.

The Irish had been Christians long before most other parts of the British
isles, so Jones describes this as "internal barbarism," meaning that a Christian,
Gerald of Wales, representing a Christian English king, is referring to other
Christian people (the Irish) as barbarians. I interpret Jones to mean the attribution of barbarity by those who saw themselves as upholders of the true
orthodox Christian faith towards those others within the borders of Christendom whom they considered to be only nominally Christian but not true
Christians. Therefore the Irish were barbarians, because they were inferior
morally and culturally, that is to say, 'uncivilised'. For Gerald of Wales, the
Irish were nominally Christian, but they were not *really* Christian because they
were not what he considered to be civilised. Besides, Jones always comes back
to the point that his notion of Christianity as "pure religion" is that Christianity
was a form of civility:

The Ciceronian idea of savagery pervaded the medieval concept
of barbarism. The barbarian was viewed as illustrative of the re-
tarded, disoriented, irrational infancy of mankind, before man
had begun to achieve better things for himself through his submission to law and the exercise of reason. (1971:42)

Thomas Aquinas's master, Albertus Magnus (thirteenth century), partly
influenced by Cicero and other classical writers, contrasted "the sweet reasonableness and tractability of civilized man with the disorderliness and irrationality of the barbarian. The barbarian, he observed, was he 'who neither
law, nor civility [*civilitas*], nor discipline disposes to virtue'" (quoted in Jones,
1971:42). Aquinas himself made the same point. So apparently did Roger
Bacon.

This leaves us still wondering what sense of Christianity as "purely religious" is left out of account here, and why we cannot simply equate being
Christian with being civilised in a particular way, a way that involves virtue, urbanity, submission to the (Christian) law, literacy, education, morality,

various forms of knowledge, and so on. This view seems strengthened when one considers Pagden's account, discussed below, of the problems that Christian theologians and lawyers had in classifying the Amerindians and their practices, and justifying their conquest and enslavement.

I want to explore further this idea that Christianity can be equated, at least for much of European history, with self-representations of civility. This becomes important again in the context of colonialism.

The previous discussion of Jones's paper on the barbarian-civilised dichotomy hopefully will have persuaded the reader to consider civility as at least a major part of what has been meant by Religion or Christian Truth, as distinguished from the barbarity of various kinds of non-Christians. This would suggest that conversion to Christianity can be thought of as a crucial stage in the attainment of civility. Civility is the cultivation through various disciplines of one's full humanity and rationality. Religion has for centuries meant Christian Truth. The implication is that Religion, civility, and rationality overlap, and the theological problem may lie in trying to show how they are different.

If Religion means, or meant, Christian Truth, what—over and above civility and rationality—does that Truth consist in? Which aspects of Catholicism and Christianity cannot be discussed in terms of 'our Christian civility' as against 'their barbarity'? For the idea of civility has packed into it the idea of 'being human' through obedience to the rational teachings of the church-state.

This viewpoint acquires additional focus in the context of the early Spanish colonisation of the Amerindians in the late fifteenth and early sixteenth centuries. The initial violence of the Spanish from the late fifteenth century was not the violence of 'religion' in the modern sense, that is, the violence frequently attributed to religion as contrasted with the rationality of the nonreligious, secular state. The Religion that hit the indigenous people of Central America in the late fifteenth century was itself an empire of a kind, the pope himself also a prince carrying the Latin title of the Roman emperors, pontifex maximus; the Spanish Christian king requiring the pope's blessing for his colonisation of the New World. This is not to say that there was no distinction internal to Christianity between church and state, but to say that it would be entirely misleading to confuse it with modern discourses on the separation of religion from politics.

The pope, Alexander VI, had in a way given his permission (through his bulls of donation) to the Spanish and the Portuguese by giving them Christian authority to rule any undiscovered pagans that they might come across. As Anthony Pagden puts it: "Alexander VI's bulls of donation granting to Ferdinand and Isabel sovereignty in the new world rested on the assumption that the pope had jurisdiction over the land of the pagans" (Pagden, 1982:37).

Pagans were divided into three kinds: in the first are

> those who live outside the Church but on lands that had once formed
> part of the Roman Empire, and thus came within the *dominium*
> of the church; in the second are those who live anywhere in the
> world, but who are lawfully subject to a Christian prince; in the
> third are the true infidels, men who dwell in lands which are nei-
> ther subject to legitimate Christian rule, nor had once been
> within the bounds of the Roman world. (Pagden, 1982:37)

The conquest and enslavement of the Amerindians followed soon after the Muslims and Jews had been expelled from Spain by the Christian king in the 1490s. The rulers of Spain were concerned to find a legal and theological answer to the question "by what right had the crown of Castile occupied and enslaved the inhabitants of territories to which it could make no prior claims based on history?" (Pagden 1982:27). To find the answer, the king consulted a select number of scholars from the law and theology faculties, who were in-vited to join his "royal confessors" (1982:27). Such theologians and lawyers as Sepúlveda, Matías de Paz, Palacios Rubios, John Mair, Vitoria, and many others recommended a number of possible strategies, all of them apparently derived from Aristotle or from the Aristotelian-Thomist synthesis, which pro-vided the overriding paradigm of all knowledge for Christendom. One of these was the Aristotelian theory of natural slavery.

Palacios Rubios was one of those who did not deny a degree of rationality to the barbarous inhabitants of America. However, this did not make him their friend and protector. In his report, he described the barbaric living standards of the Indians based, he claimed, on reliable reports (Pagden, 1982:51). He created the infamous *Requerimiento*, which was a "declaration of the Indians' obligations to submit to Spanish rule and be converted to the Christian faith, which all the conquistadores carried with them and were required to read out loud to all the Indians before attacking them" (Pagden, 1982:51). This idea that conversion could occur through a declaration of intent in a language one does not understand under threat of death seems a long way from the much later Protestant theology of the change of heart occasioned by the mysterious work-ings of the Holy Spirit while reading the Bible.

Rubios structured his report in terms of what Pagden refers to as "a number of traditional 'primitivist' topoi." They owned no property; large ap-parently unstructured groups lived together in one hut, which means that they failed to preserve both physical and moral (hierarchical, social) distance. Though they were not as savage as the Turks, "who are 'almost like animals devoid of reason'," they were still morally incapacitated. They went naked so they had no sexual modesty, and the women were assumed to be promiscuous. There was ignorance of the true role of the father, since they had a perverse descent through the female line, may have been matrilocal, and the women had too much authority in the upbringing of children:

> Underlying Palacios Rubios's critique of Amerindian sexual life was the tacit assumption, made by all Europeans at the time, and for centuries to come, that the origins of civil society were to be found in the family and, furthermore, in a family whose natural ruler was the father. Any community where, because there was no marriage, there was no proper family structure, and where women ruled over such loose unions as did exist (in the crucial sense that they were responsible for the education of the children), was not only guilty of sanctioning unnatural practices, it was no community at all but a mere horde. (Pagden, 1982:53)

The structure of the family, which Christians saw as in the nature of things and thus discoverable by natural reason, was assumed to lie in the relations among father, mother, and children, and this embodied the fundamental hierarchy of relations as they ought to be realised in the city, with magistrates as the structural equivalent of the father. The hierarchical structure of the city was, homologically, the microcosmic form of the universe and the family at different levels of organisation (Pagden, 1982:71). The good life, the realisation of rational ends in the city-state, industry, commerce, the law, and diet are all part of civility and the self-realisation of the individual and the community and are surely a way of talking about the final end of salvation. The hierarchical principle works itself through many contexts. For instance, an ability to work with stone rather than wood is an example of this higher reason and self-realisation, since stone work is highly valued. The complexity of technical accomplishments, of status considerations, of manners, of forms of government were all signs of higher civilisation of which Christianity is the apex. As mentioned above, two supposed practices in particular—cannibalism and human sacrifice—indicated people whose understanding of natural law was perverse. Most accounts of cannibalism emphasise the collapse of proper social relations, of all intelligible structure; things are not in their proper place, as a result of incest, adultery, lack of monogamy, sodomy, bestiality, and/or the subversion of male and age hierarchy and proper authority, which Christians took to be natural and God-ordained:

> Nearly all supposedly eye-witness accounts of Amerindian cannibal rituals follow closely an established pattern. The link with human sacrifice, the propitiatory rites to placate the gods, the orgiastic wine-sodden 'mingling of males with females', the total collapse of an in any case fragile social order so that the proper distinction between the social categories male/female, young/old, kin/non-kin dissolves in a tumble of bodies 'devoid of any sentiment of modesty' and

finally in the frenzied consumption of the sacrificial victim, all, or most of these—details of Livy's account of Bacchanalia—may be found, mutatis mutandis, in most European accounts of Indian cannibal festivities. (Pagden, 1982:82)

For Christians, cannibalism was a fundamental mark of barbarism for a number of reasons (Pagden, 1982:85). It involved murder and "the sin of ferocity" (86) which is of course against God's natural and divine law. Cannibalism denies the victim his natural right to a burial which itself was an essential ritual for the resurrection of the dead on the day of judgment; this latter point is connected to the deep assumption that as God incarnated into the world, and the real presence is the incarnation of God in the central act of Christian civility, so the soul is incarnate in the body and rises again with the body. As Pagden puts it, the human body is sanctified in Christian thought (1982:85) and this helps to explain the horror at the idea of eating it. But for Vitoria, there was an even more basic reason for the unnaturalness of cannibalism. It is above all a category mistake, "a failure to distinguish what is fitting as food from what is not" (Pagden, 1982:85).

That cannibalism, like sodomy, bestiality, and other barbarous practices, is a category mistake can be understood from the underlying cosmological assumptions that Christians had derived from Greek hierarchical representations of the world, and especially the Aristotelian-Thomist metaphysics. For every level of being in the cosmic hierarchy, there is an appropriate level of food, and the appropriate level is always below but not too far below. The Amerindians were reputed to eat not only creatures too high in the chain of being, but also too low, such as rats, locusts, and worms (Pagden, 1982:87). Not to understand one's proper diet (or marriage partner, or form of government) is equivalent to not knowing one's proper place in the chain of being. Every status borders on a higher and a lower. Raw food was considered relatively barbaric, and cooked animal meat a sign of civilised awareness of the food level appropriate for humans, neither too high in the natural hierarchy (which made the eating of other humans an abomination) or too low (rats). The food most worthy of humans is the cooked meat of animals. These improprieties are sins which Pagden also talks about in terms of "pollution" (1982:87).

For Christians, the preparation of food has special significance: "At the most elementary level transubstantiation was a miracle which involved the transformation of one kind of food—a wafer—into another—the flesh of Christ himself" (Pagden, 1982:88). Vitoria himself drew attention to this. Pagden seems to be suggesting that the ritual of the mass is a symbolic form of cooking.

Regarding human sacrifice, one problem that the theologian/lawyers had was that human sacrifice "had biblical support in the stories of Abraham and

Jephthah the Gileadite.... Human sacrifice may not, Vitoria conceded, be unnatural—for the urge to pay proper homage to God, even if that God is not the true one, is undeniably strong" (Pagden, 1982:90). The problem was that the Indians in sacrificing humans only had "a blurred vision of reality," and that their ignorance of the proper law of things had led them to sacrifice the wrong kind of creatures. Just as cooked animal flesh was the most fitting diet, so animal sacrifice was the most fitting sacrifice. For Vitoria, "[t]he pres-ervation of the distinction between the various levels in the scale of being was more binding than the demand that man should offer up to God all that he most valued" (1982:90). This is an interesting statement because it is another bit of evidence in favour of the view that the maintenance of the proper order of civilised life is the fundamental purpose of Christianity.

Another point that follows is that civility and barbarity are also judged in terms of levels of art, technology, agriculture, house building, the presence of cities, the sophistication of mechanics, and thus the presence of an artisan class, plus the use of letters and a literate class. Vitoria reproduced a hierar-chical list of occupations derived from Aristotle. For example, "The ability to make things, in particular the tools men require to tame their natural envi-ronment, was a further distinction between civilised man and the barbarian" (Pagden, 1982:91).

However, Christian commentators such as Las Casas and Vitoria repudi-ated many of the grossest claims of incivility of at least some Amerindian groups, such as the Mexica and the Inca. The Franciscan Jacobo de Testera in 1533 listed their accomplishments in order to argue that they could not be con-sidered natural slaves due to their supposed unreason and lack of humanity:

> How can they be incapable, with such magnificent buildings, with
> such skill in making intricate things by hand, [with] silversmiths,
> painters, merchants, tribute collectors; [with] the art of adjudication
> and [the means] to distribute *per capita* men and services, [with] a
> gentility of speech, courtesy and style, [the ability to exaggerate
> things, i.e., a gift for hyperbole?] to persuade and attract [others] with
> their services; [with] disputes, feast days, pleasures, expenses, solemn
> occasions, marriages, entails [*mayorazgos*], succession rites both *ex
> testamento* and *ab intestato*, an elective kingship, the punishment of
> crimes and excesses, [the custom] of going out to receive distin-
> guished persons when they arrive in their villages, feelings of sad-
> ness, the ability to weep [*usque ad lacrimas*] and to express gratitude
> when good manners require it. (Pagden, 1982:75)

However, though the Inca and the Mexica had arts and crafts, they did not have iron. They had achieved great things in stone, but without iron tools they were limited. Without iron, the Indians could not realise the level of civilisation required by Christians (1982:91–92).

Another crucially significant sign of barbarity for Christians was the absence of literacy:

> The absence among the Amerindian tribes of 'arts and letters' was,
> for Vitoria... proof that, like the wild beasts, Indians lived only to
> go on living. They had yet to arrive at that stage in man's develop-
> ment where they would be able to create for themselves a second
> world, in which the members of the quasi-mystical body politic
> are endowed with the ability to work in harmony with one another for
> the purpose of a higher good. (Pagden, 1982:93)

So the problem was one of classification. If the Indians were irrational and thus 'natural slaves', how could one explain the signs of relative civility of the Mexica or the Inca? But if they were rational, then how explain their canni-balism, human sacrifices, primitive agriculture, and lack of letters? (1982:93). The answer for Vitoria was that the Indians were rational, but their full po-tential had not been realised. They were more like children than natural slaves; not basically irrational, able to reason and to acquire skills, but only partially (*in potentia*). Pagden glosses Vitoria:

> True natural slaves may yet, of course, exist, along with the wild men,
> pilosi, satyrs and the like... but they will not be, as the Indians
> are, creatures capable of civilized behaviour, however crude or in-
> choate that behaviour might be. 'I understand' [wrote the jurist Diego
> de Covarrubias in 1547] 'that his [Aristotle's] words refer to men
> created by nature to wander aimlessly through the forests, without
> laws or any form of government, men who are born to serve others as
> the beasts and wild animals are. But I doubt that the Indians are
> among these, for on the evidence of those who have travelled among
> them and have known their institutions and their savagery, one
> thing is certain, and obvious, that they live in cities, in towns and
> villages, that they appoint kings whom they obey and institute
> many other things besides—which proves that they have a knowl-
> edge of the mechanical and the moral arts and a knowledge of the
> things of the world and are provided with reason.' Covarrubias
> was making much the same general observation about the psycho-
> logical implications of Indian culture as Vitoria had. (1982:96)

If the Indians were capable of rationality, and therefore human and not to be classified as natural slaves, why were they so backwards? Why did they perform human sacrifice, cannibalism, and other perversions? The suggestion already given is that they were still only in potential, and that they had not had the chance of development into the full rationality and civility that Chris-tians had achieved. If the Indians were human, which the evidence suggested they must be, then their moral and technical backwardness must be due to environment and lack of education. In this they were similar to the labouring poor of Europe (Pagden, 1982:97). Vitoria remarked that many peasants are little different from brute animals. City-less peasants were thought by the educated urban elite to be stupid and hardly able to reason. They were unable to control their passions. Yet peasants are humans nevertheless and have the potential to grow into full civil humanity:

> The word 'Indies' soon came to describe any environment in which men lived in ignorance of the Christian faith and the proper modes of human life. Jesuit missionaries spoke constantly of 'these Indies' of Asturias, of Calabria and Sicily, of the Abruzzi, regions where, they claimed, the country people lived like 'savages', polygynous and apparently polytheistic. Little wonder, too, that the word 'Indian' should have rapidly been extended to all men, regardless of their race, who deviated from the orthodox faith—even to such otherwise civilized beings as the Dutch.... The theologian Alonso de la Veracruz...who had spent many years in Mexico City, pointed out to those who claimed that the Indian was an inferior species of man, that their life-style, like that of the Spanish farmers, was due to the fact that they did not live in a true *politia*. Once brought together into political assemblies and housed in cities, their innate ability to govern themselves as human beings became immediately apparent. (Pagden, 1982:98)

However, these inequalities of civility among different peoples were a necessary part of God's design, for the functioning of the society depended on different classes endowed with different levels of potential for different kinds of necessary tasks: "The social status and obligations of the poor are very similar to those of the natural slave, with the one fundamental distinction: the poor man is not innately inferior to his master" (Pagden, 1982:98). In the final scheme of things, all humans are judged equally for their sins in the sight of God, even though inequality in this life is also natural because ordained by God.

For these kinds of reasons, Vitoria defined the Amerindians as fully human, with their rationality only partly realised, and argued that the responsibility of the Spanish Christians was to provide education and the Christian environment within which the barbarians could learn civility and gain salvation. By education, Vitoria meant (following Aristotle) the training of the speculative intellect so that it can "deduce the *secunda praecepta* of the law of nature" (Pagden, 1982:99). The first principles of the law of nature are created by God and implanted in man at birth, "but the deduction of the *secunda praecepta*, from which all the norms and promulgated laws of the community derive, depend on the operation of the human intellect" (99).

However, barbarians and pagans frequently fail to interpret the law of nature correctly. This could lead them easily into bad customs, bad systems of government, bad laws, and any number of perverse habits, to which they hold through the force of habit. Jean Bodin, summing up Aristotle's teaching, said something very similar (Pagden, 1982:100). Las Casas too pointed out that a child reared among "Saracens" could never hope to come to a knowledge of the articles of the Christian faith—and hence to a true understanding of life—" 'by the ordinary route . . . by virtue of the infused habits'. Only by training, by living continuously among Christians, 'by forming an acquired habit', would such a child be led to the truth" (102).

The Indians were not on this understanding condemned for being true to their own traditions. The problem was that the traditions departed from Christian understanding and were thus in need of correction. But the upshot of all this is that Christian civility, salvation, the ends of human life, and the idea of the fully rational individual finding the fulfilment of reason in God's order, the civil state, the (hierarchical) form of social relations, and *scientia* are all tied together into a coherent holistic system which was challenged in some important details by the realisation that people lived in America who could not be easily fitted into established categories. Furthermore, the response of expert theological and legal testimony reveals to us the degree to which Christian Religion is fundamentally identical to a concept of civility defined against the other's barbarity.

While the arguments of Las Casas, Vitoria, and other Dominicans and Jesuits against the theory of natural slavery in some technical sense prevailed, in practice not much changed. As Pagden points out:

> Nearly a century after Vitoria delivered *de indis*, the Franciscan Juan de Silva explained in the same Aristotelian terms as Vitoria had employed that the Indians were still incapable of understanding either the natural world or the moral order, incapable, as he put it, of distinguishing 'between the right and wrong or between a thistle and a lettuce'. (1982:103)

Though Indians have a rational and immortal soul, they are intellectually in a state of childhood:

> For the obvious deduction to be drawn from all that has been said is that the Indian is no 'third species' but some variety of fully grown child whose rational faculties are complete but still potential rather than actual . . . . Children . . . were regarded by Aristotle as little more than animals so long as their reason remained in a state of becoming. (Pagden, 1982:104)

This made the Amerindians' social status technically different from a slave but in practice tied to the bottom of an authoritarian social order, and fit to serve and labour. The barbarian, by definition an outsider, should be educated and governed by the Christians:

The 'barbarism' of the Indian thus conferred on the Spaniards political *dominium* but only so long as it was exercised in the Indians',
and not in the Spaniards', favour. So long, indeed, as the Indians
remained as children the Spaniards had a duty to take charge
of them. (Pagden, 1982:105)

It has been shown above by Pagden that the acknowledgement by men like
Palacios Rubios that the Amerindians had a small degree of rationality did not
mean that they could be treated as fully human. J. H. Parry in *The Spanish
Theory of Empire in the Sixteenth Century* (1940), talking of the justifications
offered for conquest by Rubios, who was a civil jurist, and the Spanish canonist
Matías de Paz, a Dominican, says that they argued

that the Indians were rational beings and naturally free both before
and after conversion and that their paganism by itself gave no ground
for war against them. Both writers proceeded to qualify this declaration, however, by restating the doctrine, associated with the name
of Henricus de Segusia, Cardinal of Ostia, of universal papal dominion in temporal as in spiritual matters, thus basing the rights of
the Spanish conquerors upon a papal grant overriding the 'natural
rights' of the Indians: 'The authority of the Supreme Pontiff alone
may give to our Catholic and invincible King the right to govern these
Indies, with political, but not despotic, rule, and so keep them per-
petually under his dominion.' The doctrine of papal sovereignty was a
commonplace among canonists of the fifteenth and early sixteenth
centuries, while the medieval conception of the world as a homogeneous Christendom with an infidel fringe still lingered. It involved
the belief that infidels might retain their lands and possessions
only by the favour of the Church. If they should refuse to recognize
papal authority, the Pope might direct the steps necessary for
bringing them into obedience—even to the extent of appointing
Christian rulers over them, with the proviso, however, that such appointed rule might be 'politicum' only and not 'despoticum'. (Parry,
1940:12–13)

It is significant that, as Parry points out, "Ostiensis [cardinal of Ostia] had
had in mind the infidels of the Near East" (1940:13). This would be consistent
with the discourse on civility and barbarity we have followed above.

The conquest of America introduced a new set of theoretical problems for
Christendom since it challenged the predominant Christian view of the extent
or structure of the world based on biblical and classical accounts. Here were
people who looked much like human beings but who seemed to have polities
or forms of life entirely independent of the supposed history of humankind
as depicted in the Bible and the teachings of the church fathers. Parry thus

adds that "this doctrine as applied by Palacios Rubios to the New World became a confused mixture of humanitarianism, papal absolutism, and Spanish imperialism" (1940:13). As Pagden has put it:

> The simple fact of America posed a conceptual problem for Christendom. How could the Pope claim authority over Amerindians who were until recently completely unknown to Christians and who themselves had had no contact with or knowledge of Europe, which until now had been the centre of the world? The early colonization was a confrontation between a previously unknown people and a feudal European polity that itself recognized no modern distinction between Church and State, and whatever or whoever subsisted outside of its cognitive borders could not properly *exist* except as irrational barbarians, demons or savages, marginal beings arguably fit to be slaves. (Pagden, 1982)

The king of Spain was no doubt genuinely concerned that his rule of America should be legitimate in Christian terms. He had received disturbing accounts of what the Christian Spanish conquistadores were doing to the Indians, especially from Las Casas, a Dominican friar who lived in America. He was the most important chronicler and eyewitness of the terrible things that were done to the indigenous people. It was Las Casas who mainly drew the king of Spain's attention to the massacres, tortures, and cruel enslavement of the Indians. It should be added that Las Casas did not object to the enslavement of black Africans, and encouraged their importation into America to save the indigenous people. As already mentioned, Las Casas believed that the Amerindians were partly rational, but undeveloped like children, and needed paternalistic discipline and nurture to bring them to Christ.

This gives us another insight into the degree to which Christian conversion was thought of in terms of being civilised and rational. Parry points out, "The government, conscious of its responsibilities, kept a tight hold upon the Indies almost from the first; the conquistadores, adventurers, crusaders, quickly gave way to administrators, lawyers and judges, both secular and ecclesiastical" (Parry, 1940:1).

The distinction between secular and ecclesiastical here was the orthodox distinction between institutions which had different functions but which were both encompassed by Christian Truth. This is not the modern distinction between religion and the secular. Later, he says:

> The close connection between Church and State in Spain made it especially necessary for Spanish theologians to proceed with caution. Significantly, the first writer to attack the problem by suggesting a *secular* justification for Spanish imperialism was not a Spaniard. John Major (or Mair), a Scottish Dominican with no personal or

practical interest whatever in the Indies, felt impelled to write in
support of the Spanish enterprise, and to begin with an emphatic
denial of universal papal sovereignty: ' . . . for the supreme pontificate
was first established by Christ; but He granted no temporal monarchy'. (Parry, 1940:13; my italics)

Parry comments that this statement was supported by examples of the
freedom of the kingdoms of France and Spain from outside interference in
temporal matters. Parry seems legitimately to be equating 'secular' with temporal here, as distinct from ecclesiastical. This would be consistent with the
point that the secular or temporal in the meaning of the times was not neutral or 'nonreligious' in the modern sense. All were by definition orthodox
Christians.

It is important to bear in mind that the Reformation was occurring while
many of these debates among Catholic theologian and lawyers were under way
in the early sixteenth century. Luther and Calvin, who both rejected the authority of Aristotle and Aquinas, as well as the authority of the pope, did not
think that the civil government should be neutral towards religion in the
modern sense of nonreligious neutrality.

Another writer, Forrester, in his article on church and state in the thinking
of Luther and Calvin (in Strauss & Cropsey, 1963:277–313), summarises Luther's and Calvin's general understanding of Christian Truth and the form of
government:

> God's sovereignty in the world is total. The necessity for temporal
> government is correlative to the necessity that God's Will should be
> observed among sinful men; its limits are defined by the fact that
> political authority is *delegated* authority, subordinate to, and depen-
> dent on, the sovereignty of God; its worldly autonomy arises from its
> direct dependence on the Will of God. In short, all political power
> flows from God and is to serve Him. (Forrester, 1963:293–94)

Forrester points out that there were three general conceptions of the relation between church and state which both Luther and Calvin criticised as
inconsistent with the New Testament. One was the attempt which they attributed to the papal authorities to absorb the functions of the state and to deny
any real autonomy to the state. A second was the attempt by some rulers to
dominate the functioning of the church and to arrogate spiritual powers which
properly belonged to the church. And a third was the philosophy of radical
groups such as the Anabaptists who virtually denied the existence of a legitimate civil authority in the divine order of things and people. None of these
alternative conceptions implies a neutral, nonreligious, 'secular' world or 'civil'
authority in the sense that is indifferent to Christian Truth or somehow independent of it. The point is that Religion, understood as Christian Truth,

encompasses both church and state, regardless of the internal disputes over the demarcation of functions they might have been conceived to have in any particular empirical example.

Parry, in his discussion of the Spanish Catholic debates at around the same time that Luther and Calvin were inaugurating the Reformation in the early sixteenth century, says:

> At this point, however, his [Major's] thought took a curious turn which made him a precursor of Sepúlveda as well as of Vitoria and Bellarmine. Leaving his theological ground, he found a second justification of conquest in the duty of bringing civilization ... to a barbarous people. Aristotle, naturally, was his authority, quoted with all the affectionate familiarity of the medieval schoolmen.... 'Those people live like animals ... it is evident that some men are by nature free, and others servile. In the natural order of things the qualities of some men are such that, in their own interests, it is right and just that they should serve, while others, living freely, exercise their natural authority and command.' Major was the first publicist to apply the Aristotelian theory of natural servitude to the natives of the New World or to any entire race. (Parry, 1940:18)

Talking of Sepúlveda's theory of a natural aristocracy's right to rule, again derived from Aristotle, the right and duty of natural Christian superiors to rule barbarians, and the duty of inferiors to obey, Parry says:

> The corollary of natural aristocracy was natural servitude—since the more perfect should hold sway over the less; the Aristotelian theory, interpreted in the same way by Sepúlveda as by Major, received full weight in *Democrates Alter*, and was made to constitute a general mandate for civilised nations to subdue by force of arms, if no other means were possible, those peoples ' ... who require, by their own nature and in their own interests, to be placed under the authority of civilised and virtuous princes or nations; so that they may learn from the might, wisdom and law of their conquerors, to practise better morals, worthier customs, and a more civilised way of life'. (1940:18)

This idea of natural servitude (the natural slave) derived from Aristotle was debated by the theologians. As both Jones and Pagden also pointed out in their discussions of the discourse on civility and barbarity, the conflation of barbarians and pagans meant that some of the same condescension towards external 'others' was applied to rustic peasants internal to Christendom who were too stupid to achieve Christian rationality. This idea was expressed by the Spanish Christian Mesa, who felt that it was not only non-Europeans who were suitable as slaves: the people of Normandy were also. There was a popular analogy among the literate elite between the external barbarians, such as the savages and pagans of America, and the internal barbarians, such as the pagan peasants of the European villages. They lacked reason and were like animals; it was in their nature to serve and obey, though they were capable of salvation since they were men.

Pagden points out that, for Mesa, the justification of why slavery was appropriate for the Indians was based on their servile disposition, including:

> their lack of understanding and mental capacity, and their lack of
> perseverance in following the faith and observing good customs;
> for that is natural servitude according to the Philosopher. Or, he says,
> perhaps they are slaves by nature because of the nature of the
> land; because there are some lands where the configuration of the
> stars makes slaves of the inhabitants, and they could not be ruled if
> there was not some measure of slavery there, as in France where
> the people of Normandy, which is a part of the Dauphinage, have
> always been ruled like slaves. (Pagden, 1982:50)

One of the theologians, Vitoria, denied that the Amerindians were natural slaves. In his critique of the applicability of Aristotle's category 'the natural slave' to the Amerindians, Vitoria pointed out that these people were fully capable of trade and commerce, an essential characteristic of human civility. This view was shared by Las Casas. But Vitoria thought that they should be treated like the serfs in Spain, and also like children who were only partly rational. This amounted to a justification of the *encomienda* system which was imposed on the Indians and in which, technically, they were not slaves but serfs.

There is clearly a problem for the Spanish theologians and lawyers about the relative authority of church and state, pope and king. But the relation between church and state differed from the late eighteenth-century Enlightenment ideology that church and state, religion and politics, should be completely separated as it is in modern constitutions. This is apparent in the following by Parry:

> In order that they [the Indians] might learn from the missionaries,
> and prepare themselves for entry into the Church, it was necessary
> to place them under civilised government and tutelage, with or
> without their consent. Something of Saint Augustine's doctrine of
> the relation between Civitas Dei and Civitas Terrena entered into
> Sepúlveda's thought—the Scriptures needed the protection of the
> secular sword—the fate of missionaries, in Sepúlveda's own day, in
> Florida and on the Pearl Coast, provided a tragic example. Civiliza
> tion and Christianity went hand in hand; conquest was a religious duty.
> (Parry, 1940:37)

Here, the function of the secular arm to provide military protection for the missionaries, the Dominican friars who were and still are called in English 'the religious', is a "religious duty." One can see the problems of terminology here, where a modern sense of 'religious' is being used to describe the duties of secular personnel who are distinguished from 'the religious' in the older sense.

Furthermore, Parry's formulation "Civilization and Christianity went hand in hand" is ambiguous, because it suggests that the two were not identical but overlapped. However, one interpretation is that the phrase seems intended to make the point that, just as one cannot ultimately distinguish between the duties of the secular and the religious in terms of Religion (some duties may have a higher degree of sacredness, but in the final analysis they are all Christian duties), so also one cannot effectively distinguish the paradigmatic concepts 'civilisation' and 'Christianity'.

The form of colonial control imposed on the indigenous peoples incorporated many of the features of the feudal order of Spain, though with the indigenous peoples forming a new bottom class of virtual slavery. The virtue of work for the barbarian was, as Pagden points out in his discussion of Gregorio's argument in favour of a kind of qualified slavery, part of the process of salvation, which is coextensive with being human. As Pagden paraphrases him, "In exchange for their labour—hard work was, in any case, part of the civilizing process—the Indians would learn through Spanish example to live 'like men'" (Pagden, 1982:49).

Some background knowledge of the systems of government as they were actually institutionalised throws an ironic light on the European discourse on civility and barbarity. The *Columbia Encyclopedia* (2004) gives the following succinct descriptions of some of the relevant institutions which were either justified or condemned by Catholic intellectuals:

Encomienda: [Span. *encomendar* = to entrust], system of tributary labor established in Spanish America. Developed as a means of securing an adequate and cheap labor supply, the *encomienda* was first used over the conquered Moors of Spain. Transplanted to the New World, it gave the conquistador control over the native populations by requiring them to pay tribute from their lands, which were "granted" to deserving subjects of the Spanish crown. The natives often rendered personal services as well. In return the grantee was theoretically obligated to protect his wards, to instruct them in the Christian faith, and to defend their right to use the land for their own subsistence. When first applied in the West Indies, this labor system wrought such hardship that the population was soon decimated. This resulted in efforts by the Spanish king and the Dominican order to suppress *encomiendas*, but the need of the conquerors to reward their supporters led to de facto recognition of the practice. The crown prevented the *encomienda* from becoming hereditary, and with the New Laws (1542) promulgated by Las Casas, the system gradually died out, to be replaced by the *repartimiento* and finally debt peonage. Similar systems of land and labor apportionment were adopted by other colonial powers, notably the Portuguese, the Dutch, and the French.

Repartimiento: in Spanish colonial practice, usually, the distribution of indigenous people for forced labor. In a broader sense it referred to any official distribution of goods, property, services, and the like. From as early as 1499, deserving Spaniards were allotted pieces of land, receiving at the same time the native people living on them; these allotments were known as *encomiendas* . . . and the process was the *repartimiento*; the two words were often used interchangeably. The *encomienda* was almost always accompanied by a system of forced labor and other assessments exacted from the indigenous people. The system endured and was the core of *peonage* in New Spain. The assessment of forced labor was called the *mita* in Peru and the *cuatequil* in Mexico.

The entry on "peonage" gives the reader a sense of the continuity of these institutions through the various historical vicissitudes, so that it becomes more difficult to distance our more recent discourses on religion and civility from those that occurred in the past:

Peonage: system of involuntary servitude based on the indebtedness of the laborer (the peon) to his creditor. It was prevalent in Spanish America, especially in Mexico, Guatemala, Ecuador, and Peru. The system arose because labor was needed to support the agricultural, industrial, mining, and public-works activities of the conquerors and settlers in the Americas. With the Spanish conquest of the West Indies, the *encomienda*, establishing proprietary rights over the natives, was instituted. In 1542 the New Laws of Bartolemé de Las Casas were promulgated, defining natives as free subjects of the king and prohibiting forced labor. Black slave labor and wage labor were substituted. Since the natives had no wage tradition and the amount paid was very small, the New Laws were largely ignored. To force natives to work, a system of the *repartimiento* [assessment] and the *mita* was adopted; it gave the state the right to force its citizens, upon payment of a wage, to perform work necessary for the state. In practice, this meant that the native spent about one fourth of a year in public employment, but the remaining three fourths he was free to cultivate his own fields and provide for his own needs. Abuses under the system were frequent and severe, but the *repartimiento* was far less harsh and coercive than the slavery of debt peonage that followed independence from Spain in 1821. Forced labor had not yet included the working of plantation crops—sugar, cacao, cochineal, and indigo; their increasing value brought greater demand for labor control, and in the nineteenth cent[ury] the cultivation of other crops on a large scale required a continuous and cheap labor supply. To force natives to work, the plantations got them into debt by giving advances on wages and by requiring the purchase of necessities from company-owned stores. As the natives fell into debt and lost their own land, they were reduced to peonage and forced to work for the same employer until his debts and the debts of his ancestors were paid, a virtual impossibility. He became virtually a serf, but without the serf's customary rights. In Mexico a decree against peonage was issued in 1915, but the practice persisted. Partly to alleviate it, Lázaro Cárdenas instituted the *ejido* in 1936. In that year, too, debt peonage was abolished in Guatemala. In the United States after the Civil War, peonage existed in most southern states as it had in the Southwest after its acquisition from Mexico. Not only blacks and Mexicans but whites as well found themselves enmeshed. By 1910 court decisions had outlawed peonage, but as late as 1960 some sharecroppers in southern states were pressured to continue working for the same master to pay off old debts or to pay taxes, which some states had levied to preserve the sharecropping system.

Technically, under the *encomienda* system, the Indians were not slaves but serfs. However, this technicality did not make much practical difference. Las Casas, in shock and misery at the suffering inflicted by his own people upon the indigenous people, and fundamentally against the *encomienda* system, went into a monastery for eight years to seek solace from God, and he emerged with the inspiration of the *congregación*. The *congregación* was a kind of planned city first set out by Las Casas with the purpose of teaching the residents Christian civility in a gentler and more humane way than the *encomienda* (Blume, 2007). It should however be remembered that, while Las Casas praised the human attributes of the Indians highly, he also sought to convert them to Christianity and thus to save them from perdition. He thus made them dependent on the Roman church, its rites, language, and ideology of order. His organisation of the *congregación* reproduced much of the Spanish feudal order, with the church building at the centre of the town, and all activities and relationships subsumed under Christian Truth. Furthermore, while personal devotion was a central part of Las Casas's practice and motivation, he was in the service of God, the pope, and the king, as well as the Indians. And Las Casas apparently had no moral qualms about importing black African slaves in order to save the indigenous Americans from slavery.

Blume (2007) has indicated the difference in the conception of 'religion' then operating, compared to the modern Protestant one. She contrasts the totalising Christian world of Las Casas and the violence it inflicted with the modern Protestant form of internal colonial violence of Rios Montt, the Guatemalan dictator who as recently as 1982 inaugurated massacres in an attempt to destroy indigenous forms of life. Rios Montt was committed to the Protestant ethic of individual religiosity, opposed to the indigenous collectivisation of the Maya, and sought to break both their communal beliefs and their anticapitalist economic base of discrete *milpa* farming. It is in Rios Montt that the fully formed capitalist state finds its true warrior, a dictator willing to use all means necessary to impose a religious and secular individualism that would benefit both his desire for absolute power and the absolute power of the market (I have glossed Blume here).

That the *encomienda* was first formalised in the context of the subordination of the Moors and then exported to America after the unification of Spain and the expulsion of Muslims, indicates that the early beginnings of modern colonialism and the cultural and military hegemony that it inaugurated was strongly linked with aggression against Muslims and the geographical consolidation of Christendom. However, I do not mean to infer that, because the consolidation of Christendom led to violent and ruthless colonialism (vividly described by Las Casas) that this is the same as saying that 'religion' was a fig leaf for 'political' power and 'economic' exploitation.

Modern English-language terminology, when it is used to describe the world as it was imagined in an earlier time, or even in what we now retrospectively see as the very early beginnings of modernity, almost automatically confuses the issues. One of the problems of terminology is that Aristotle's *Politics* was a text of major importance to Aquinas and consequently authoritative to all those Spanish lawyers and theologians who were engaged with these issues. The English-language title *Politics* irresistibly suggests a significant identity of meaning with the modern category. But there is a definitive difference. As already noted, the modern English-language category 'politics' implies a nonreligious domain separated from 'religion'. Yet it seems quite clear from Parry's and Pagden's accounts that, in the minds of the fifteenth- and sixteenth-century churchmen, what Aristotle meant by politics did not imply this modern idea. For Aristotle, politics was encompassed by the Good (*summum bonum*). For Aquinas, Religion, understood as Christian Truth, and theology, as the exposition of that Truth, encompassed all knowledge, including philosophy and science. These were teleological conceptions in which all facts were also values. Natural reason, while in some significant senses independent of revelation and thus in theory available to all humans, was still implanted by God. Politics was not a separate activity distinguishable from theology as it is in the modern constitutional thinking of the Western Anglophone world. There was no conceivable distinction between two separate spheres, religion and the nonreligious secular. The most that could be said is that there were things that could only be had from revelation that natural reason alone could not give. But the knowledge derived from natural reason was still legitimated by the church, which derived its authority from Christ.

Pagden vividly describes how the dehumanising effects of the *encomienda* system were in practice enslaving and destroying the life of the Indians:

> The cultural and social demands of the *encomienda* may ... have been directly responsible for some of the features of Indian life which the Europeans found most reprehensible; suicide, infanticide, induced abortions and what the Spanish generally referred to as the Indians' 'lack of charity', their willingness to abandon the sick or the old, even to mock the sufferings of the dying. For similar cases were recorded on Franciscan mission stations in California in the eighteenth century, and have been observed today among the Ik, an East African tribe displaced by the creation of a game reserve from their tribal homelands. (Pagden, 1982:35)

"Indians everywhere," Pagden argues, " ... were to live in emulation of their Christian rulers, in huts each housing a single nuclear family grouped around, not the log cabin and the dance floor, but the Church and the chapter house." Instead of practising their own disciplines of civility, they were forced to live in "artificial families composed of a single lineage through the male line" (Pagden, 1982:35).

The institutionalisation of the Spanish *encomienda* system inevitably raises the question: to what extent was enforced enculturation an important part of Christian conversion? Was this similar to the claim of the fourteenth-century Byzantine emperor, recently quoted by the current pope, that Islam was evil because it converted people by the sword?[4] What does this imply for 'belief'?

Pagden draws our attention to the point made earlier that, technically, the Indians became serfs not slaves:

> But although the *encomienda* failed dismally in practice ... although the colonists behaved as though their Indians were merely slaves, to be sold or exchanged like any other form of merchandise, there was a distinction in law ... between the *encomienda* and true civil slavery. (1982:36)

Critics such as Las Casas, Montesino, and Vitoria did not want to challenge the authority of the king, and though Las Casas despaired of the violence imposed within the *encomienda* system, he preferred that the Indians were not technically slaves. These Christians were angry about the violent and exploitative behaviour of the colonists. But this raised questions about what kind of authority the Crown did have in America, what were the limits of the temporal and spiritual power of emperor and pope.

For us today, it may seem like a fine distinction to make for Vitoria to argue that, while the Amerindians were barbaric and like children who required the disciplines of Christian civility to lead them to salvation, they were not natural slaves. But this was in fact a challenge to one detail of a sacred corpus. Aristotle had been virtually sanctified by the church, and his philosophy was fundamental to the exposition of true faith and Christian *scientia*: "For it was clear to most Europeans that the Indians lacked a proper understanding of reality.... [T]hey lacked, that is, any *scientia*, because science is precisely the ability to draw conclusions from stated premises" (Pagden, 1982:102), and *scientia* is part of theology. It is really the ability to reason correctly, and this underpins all proper understanding and therefore is the unifying principle of the total order of the world and human life. "Only through training his mind to the point where he would be able to interpret correctly the real world of nature in which he lived, would the Indian ever acquire an understanding of the mysteries of the Christian faith" (Pagden, 1982:103).

It appears that understanding the Christian mysteries is the fulfilment of the movement of reason, but the same reason underlies the ability to live in cities, to form a state, to practice morality, to have a (written) tradition, to have technical accomplishments such as architecture, to have literacy, to marry and raise children, to eat the proper food, and so on. These practices amount to civility as against barbarity. To repeat an earlier question in a slightly different way: can we find a conceptual wedge to insert between the meaning of Religion, understood as Christian Truth, and the meaning of civility?

This is not the end of the story, for the language of civility and barbarity continues in Protestantism, and then again in the nineteenth-century colonisation of the world and the evolutionary hypothesis that primitives are pre-logical survivals of earlier stages of human development. This discourse was shared by theists, atheists, and agnostics. The discussion at the beginning of this chapter of the film *The Last Samurai* indicates quite accurately how degrees of civility continued to be associated in the nineteenth century, in part at least, with levels of technology. We should also consider that the Japanese were pressured to create a constitution which defined a modern secular state and provided a guarantee of freedom of worship or religion. That the Japanese did not organise their cosmos in such terms is suggested by their need to debate the meaning of these terms, and to argue over the most equivalent indigenous vocabulary (Isomae, 2002, 2007).

5

Luther, Calvin, and Henry VIII's *Formularies of Faith*

Throughout this book, I am concerned with the methodological problem of using our own contemporary English-language categories to classify, describe, and analyse texts and forms of life both from earlier periods of European history and in non-European cultures. My interest here derives from perplexing issues in contemporary discourses on religion and the secular, and my focus is on a range of connected categories which we frequently use to talk about 'other cultures', in which expression I am including our own European past. I put the problem in the context of 'other cultures' because it draws attention to the parallels and analogies between historiographical and ethnographical description. One point that I wish to highlight is that, even in the work of the most professional and self-critical scholars, the apparent innocence of words which in everyday use we take for granted systematically misrepresents the past, or at least re-represents the past in ways which serve wider contemporary interests. There is of course no conscious conspiracy here. The idea that this could be a conspiracy is absurd. Apart from the paranoia implied by such an idea, the more serious point is that conspiracy implies conscious intent, whereas my argument is based on the more reasonable idea that it is the *lack* of conscious intent that makes the reproduction of discourses so effective in naturalising our own ways of seeing the world by making them seem basic to all human existence.

In the previous chapters, I discussed discourses on civility and Christian Truth in the work of such writers as Jones, Parry, and Pagden. Parry's and Pagden's subject was the Spanish Catholic response to the dilemmas posed by the conquest and subjugation of the indigenous peoples of America, and I argued that it is difficult to drive any kind of conceptual wedge between Religion and the ideological order of human relations. There is no 'society' separated from 'religion', as though an expression like 'the relation between religion and society' could have any legitimate meaning. The dominant notions of Christian civility in the thinking of the Spanish theologians and lawyers who were confronted by indigenous Americans' difference was highly inclusive and concerned diet, dress, levels of technology, architecture, forms of courtesy, morality, ceremonies and rites of passage, arrangement of space and time, family structure, conceptions of legitimate authority, gender, and relationship with the natural environment. When looked at through the discourses on civility and barbarity, we find a continuum of concerns and assumptions in which the major distinction is between Christian Truth and pagan superstition. And I suggested that the discourse on civility and barbarity underpins and unifies what we in the modern world have separated.

I have suggested that the distinction between Christian Truth and superstition is therefore virtually the same as the distinction between rationality and irrationality, and that science and politics are encompassed by Religion and therefore not conceived as separate domains. The paradigmatic change from which our own Anglophone discourses grew seems to have emerged as clearly articulated rhetoric in the late seventeenth century and as powerfully institutionalised in late eighteenth-century America.[1] This change is not the result only of internal developments peculiar to Europe but has a colonial dimension and context. The individuals who supported Dissent were often merchants and those whose prosperity depended directly or indirectly on overseas investments. The contemporary constructions of 'religion' and 'religions', I suggest, is not the neutral and objective science that it has been represented as being but part of an ideological paradigm that has authorised, and perhaps still does authorise, the assumption that modern practices of politics and economics are in principle inherently rational and in the nature of things. I hope to problematise this assumption about ubiquitous religion and religions by showing that (a) there are good reasons for thinking that our ancestors had an entirely different view of the meaning of 'religion', and (b) our own scholarly practices tend to hide this by constructing a past which conforms too uncritically to what we assume to be the 'natural' generic categories in which we think today.

In chapters 6 and 8, I will analyse this problem of the construction of 'religion' in the context of two volumes of the series *English Historical Documents* (Williams, 1967; Browning, 1953). In this present chapter, I analyse an important set of documents published by Henry VIII and his bishops during the period after the break with Rome and the foundation of the Church of England: *Formularies of Faith Put Forth by Authority during the Reign of Henry VIII* (Lloyd, 1825).

I imagine that, to do any kind of historiographical (or ethnographical) work, one is compelled to use the current categories of one's own language embedded as they are in current discourses but, provided the historian or anthropologist is critically aware of the dangers, he or she will at least be able to reproduce the *imaginaire* (in the sense outlined in a footnote to chapter 1) dominant at the historical moment of the past or dominant in the language and consciousness of contemporary non-Europeans. It might be argued that to question the use of such basic categories as religion, politics, economics, and the secular state in the description of our past or other people's present would be to defy common sense and make the historiographic and ethnographic tasks impossible. However, if this is true, then I would argue in turn that we should ask ourselves about our modern culturally determined motives for producing historiography or ethnography at all. This issue has been discussed at length by other authors. I arrive at it as an issue from a critique of the field of religious studies and the questions I have raised about the ideological function of modern discourses on 'religion' and which pervade not only academic writings throughout the humanities but also our wider public discourses.

Before continuing, it seems necessary to say something about the founders of the Reformation and their views on issues to do with the relation between church and state. I am not concerned specifically with the direct degree of influence that Luther and Calvin may or may not have had on the English Reformation of Henry VIII. Henry did not want to break with Rome and considered himself to be a Catholic, but this in turn required him and his bishops to reformulate the idea of what constituted the Catholic Church and the proper relations between church and state. My main interest here is to argue that, whatever differences did or did not exist among Luther, Calvin, the Catholic Church, Henry VIII, and his bishops on the correct understanding of the relation between church and state, none of them thought in terms of a modern separation between religion and a neutral, nonreligious polity. If they talked at all about the autonomy of the state, they meant *relative* autonomy from the power of the church as an institution, not autonomy from Religion understood as Christian Truth.

The implication of this is that it is seriously misleading, without a great deal of explicit explanation and special pleading, to apply to that era the English-language terms 'politics' or 'economics' or 'civil society', for these terms are all today heavily impregnated with an entirely different concept of 'the secular'. On the other hand, I do not deny that it is in this period of plantations, colonies, and overseas trade expansion that we might retrospectively detect the early beginnings of a reformulation that much later was to emerge as a fully articulated paradigm shift which divides the world into two distinct domains, one 'religious' and the other nonreligious and either neutral or hostile to religion.

As the two most influential voices of the Reformation, the views of Luther and Calvin on the meaning of 'religion', church and state, civil society, and the secular power clearly need to be considered in a historical review of this kind. The scholarly commentaries on and interpretations of these seminal thinkers are overwhelmingly vast, but for my purposes it is unnecessary to become submerged in such a huge and disputatious literature. I am only here concerned to make some relevant, accurate, and reasonably uncontroversial generalisations as a background to the analysis of the English-language texts, especially those written by Protestants. For this more-limited purpose, I have relied for the most part on the clear and concise exposition by Duncan B. Forrester in his article "Luther and Calvin" in Strauss and Cropsey (1963:277–313). Forrester shows that, despite some important differences of emphasis between Luther and Calvin, some of which I will mention here, there is a general and unsurprising sense in which their views coincide on the matter of the nature of the state in relation to their Reformed views of the church and the meaning of Religion.

Perhaps the first thing that should be said is that for both these thinkers there is no conception of 'politics' as something distinct from theology, nor of a modern understanding of a secular realm that, by being radically separated from 'religion' is itself conceived as 'nonreligious'. Forrester says: "In their thought there is no trace of the relativism or indifference which is often the basis of toleration. Nor is their doctrine of the two kingdoms another way of stating the modern concept of the separation of Church and State" (Forrester, 1963:301).

Everything they said that has relevance to any field that might be constructed as 'politics' flows from their understanding of God's word as revealed in the Bible, especially the New Testament. Consistent with this, Religion meant Christian Truth, a Truth that encompasses all human life and knowledge. While there are significant adjustments of the concept of the state that derive from their critique of the Catholic Church and their rejection of some important aspects of the Aristotelian-Thomist synthesis, there is no sense in their writings of a state or civil authority which is neutral in terms of Religion, nor a concept of the world based on an independent set of principles. Anything in what we call 'nature' or 'morality' or 'law' is for both Luther and Calvin derived from God and determined by God's sovereign purposes. Forrester summarises their general understanding of Christian Truth with characteristic clarity:

> God's sovereignty in the world is total. The necessity for temporal government is correlative to the necessity that God's Will should be observed among sinful men; its limits are defined by the fact that political authority is *delegated* authority, subordinate to, and dependent on, the sovereignty of God; its worldly autonomy arises from its direct dependence on the Will of God. In short, all political power flows from God and is to serve Him. (1963:293–94)

Forrester points out that there were three general conceptions of the relation between church and state which both Luther and Calvin criticised as inconsistent with the New Testament. One was the attempt, which they attributed to the papal authorities, to absorb the functions of the state and to deny any real autonomy to the state. The second was the attempt by some rulers to dominate the functioning of the church and to arrogate spiritual powers which properly belonged to the church. And the third was the philosophy of radical groups, such as the Anabaptists, who virtually denied the existence of a legitimate civil authority in the divine order of things and people. It should be noticed that none of these alternative conceptions necessarily implies a 'secular' world or 'civil' authority that is indifferent to Christian Truth or somehow independent of it.

Though Luther and Calvin placed different emphases on the degree of definition to which the legitimate state should conform, both believed that the state had a God-ordained function in human life and that in some real sense it had autonomy and required a specific realm of duties and skills by which God could be served. The civil power was "ordained" by God to punish heresy, to maintain order by force if necessary, and to protect and even in some extreme circumstances to reform the church. Since all power derives from God, so the ruler is a minister of God. In this sense the civil power "may even be called *divine*, for rulers, both Luther and Calvin suggest, are sometimes even called in Scripture 'gods' " (e.g., in Psalm 82; Forrester, 1963:294). Forrester points out that there is no notion of popular sovereignty nor a contract theory of government here. They both demand obedience to the state authorities. All subjects have an absolute duty of obedience to the civil authority except in extreme instances where that authority tries to coerce its subjects to perform acts that are clearly sinful and against the teaching of Christ and the apostles as found in the New Testament. Yet even here there is no right of active rebellion, only the right to refuse to act in a sinful manner. In such circumstances, one must passively accept one's persecution by a sinful civil power with faith in God's goodness and the justice of the world to come.

The ruler is not responsible for deciding what constitutes true Religion; this is the responsibility of the church. The church's responsibility is to teach and preach so that the ruler may understand what it means to be a Christian and therefore rule as a Christian ruler. But it is not the function of the church to arrogate to itself the actual functions of the state. There exists a kind of mutual interdependence of function between church and civil governance; doubtless, the actual manner in which this would be formulated in practice would differ according to different local contexts, such as the traditions of a specific polity. But the crucial point for my purposes is that the legitimacy of both church and state derived from and is encompassed by God and therefore by Religion in the sense that Religion means Christian Truth.

According to Forrester, Luther lays greater stress on the invisibility of the church, and is not so clearly prescriptive as Calvin about the form and function of the visible church except in relation to doctrine, preaching, and the sacraments. Apart from these three matters, which are the essential function and concern of the church, the magistracy may "organize the external polity of the Church as seems most convenient to it; it may do as it wills with the property of the Church; and the temporal authorities, if Christian, may even be recognized as 'bishops' with authority over the external affairs of the visible Church" (1963:286–87). Luther, unlike Calvin, did not find a clear model of church organisation and discipline in the Bible, and left such matters more to the traditions that existed. In this sense it might be held that for Luther the matters of salvation are more indifferent to the order of things in the visible church. Forrester sees Luther as less consistent than Calvin on such matters. For example, concerning the proper order of marriage, Luther could be quite radical, almost indifferent:

> What is the proper procedure for us nowadays in matters of marriage and divorce? I have said that this should be left to the lawyers and be made subject to secular government. For marriage is a rather secular and outward thing, having to do with wife and children, house and home, and with other matters which belong to the realm of govern-ment, all of which have been completely subjected to reason (Genesis 1.28). Therefore we should not tamper with what the government and wise men decide and prescribe on the basis of the laws and of reason. Christ is not functioning here (Matthew 5.31–32) as a lawyer or gov-ernor, to set down or prescribe any regulation for outward conduct. (Forrester, 1963:307, quoting from Luther's Commentary on the Sermon on the Mount)

Such a statement might lead the modern reader to see a source for the later, more clearly articulated distinction between an indifferent and neutral state and a concept of religion as merely inner and private and radically separated in the form of voluntary association. In contrast, Calvin is far more prescriptive about the form of the church, believing that clear guidance for the governance of the church can be found in scripture.

However, there is for both reformers a division of functions which are complementary. For example, the church has the power to excommunicate even secular governors and rulers, for as Christians they are subject to the dis-ciplines of the church (Forrester, 1963:287). At the same time, the secular governor, or 'godly prince', has the responsibility not only to regulate public behaviour (which must be consistent with Christian principles) but also to de-fend the true church and even, in extremis, to purge it and restore it to its true Christian form (288). The ruler should give material support for the church and its ministers, and thus encourage sound doctrine and a truly Christian organisation.

The state then is not neutral or indifferent, not even in Luther, and does not consist of a 'nonreligious' realm in the modern sense. The state and the monarch are the servants of God and have the responsibility of ensuring "the nearest approximation to the 'good life' which is possible in a fallen world" (Forrester, 1963:294). After preaching, the next highest office in the service of God is that of the ruler, whose office, as we have seen "may even be called 'divine'" (294). It follows that it is the duty of the citizen to obey the ruler, and the grounds for disobedience are very narrow indeed. The only justification for disobedience is if the ruler should require the subject to perform an action which is clearly contrary to the will of God. Even in such a situation, the refusal to obey can only be passive disobedience and not active rebellion, and the subject must endure with Christian humility and patience whatever punishment is inflicted by the ruler.

The encompassment by Christian Truth of what we separate out as civil or secular in the modern sense of nonreligious is seen in the teaching of 'vocation', and the hierarchical ordering of human relations. In the eyes of God, and with regard to salvation and the need for God's forgiveness, all men are equal. But with regard to life in the fallen world, there is no equality. Forrester says:

> [A]s regards life in this world, equality disappears and is replaced by order and rank, and men find themselves in various 'stations' or 'vocations' in which they are required to serve God by serving their neighbor.... Each man has a variety of different functions in society which are to be seen as divine vocations. One man, for example, may have the vocations of husband, father, farmer, and citizen, each with its specific duties and obligations. (1963:307)

In this sense, what we call the social order is a divinely instituted order, encompassed by Christian Truth, and all people must follow their vocation, understood as their degree and station in life with its specific duties.

Before discussing Henry VIII's *Formularies*, I want briefly to look at this issue from the point of view of political theory, with special reference to the term 'state'. Quentin Skinner holds:

> With Bodin's insistence in his *Six Books* that it ought to be obvious to any Prince that 'wars made for matters of religion' are not in fact 'grounded upon matters directly touching his estate', we hear for the first time the authentic tones of the modern theorist of the State.... The Latin term *status* had ... been employed by legal and scholastic writers throughout the later Middle Ages in a variety of political contexts. But even if we feel justified in assuming that *status* should be translated in these cases as 'State'—an assumption which perhaps tends to be made rather readily by some medieval historians—it is clear that what is at issue is very different from the modern idea of the State. (Skinner, vol. 2, 1978:352–53)[2]

But what does Skinner mean by "political contexts" here? I assume that the meaning of 'politics' is not historically constant; it does not run essentially unchanged from Aristotle up to the present. If something approximating to the modern usage of 'state' first appears in Bodin in 1576, then we might expect the term 'politics', even if it existed in a minor key in English translation at the time, to be changing in nuance. The term 'politics' may well have been used in English in the sixteenth century but arguably it was not until the later seventeenth century that it was being used in English in the modern sense to refer to a practice radically separated from and neutral towards 'religion'. But to achieve this change in the nuance of 'politics' and 'the state', it would be reasonable to suppose that the meaning of 'religion' was also in the process of transformation, because their semantic fields were linked in specific ways. But in Skinner's text, we do not know from this translation of Bodin what the nuance of 'matters of religion' should be taken to be.

In an earlier discussion of Bodin in the same volume, Skinner represents Bodin's *The Six Books of the Commonwealth* (1576) as his "greatest work of political theory" in which Bodin uses an expression such as "all sorts of religions" (Skinner, 1978:248). This could all too easily be thought by the modern reader to be an early example of a modern generic usage of the concept of 'religions', as in 'world religions' or 'the religious experience of mankind'. However, this would surely be mistaken, because Skinner also draws the reader's attention to Bodin's *Colloquium of the Seven*, which is made up (as Skinner informs us) of six dialogues which are "evidently intended to represent the whole spectrum of serious religious opinion," which comprises the viewpoints of a Lutheran, a sceptic, an exponent of natural religion, a Calvinist, a Jew, and a convert to Islam (246). This narrows down the range of possibilities for what Bodin intended to mean, or what Skinner intends to mean, by "serious religious opinion" to three of the positions. The Lutheran and the Calvinist are presumably defined strictly in the context of different interpretations of Christian Truth. In the cases of the sceptic, the Jew, and the convert to Islam, the formulation of scepticism, the application of 'religion' to the Jew, and the understanding of Islam by a convert from Christianity could presumably at that time also only be properly grasped in relation to current renderings of Christian Truth. The exponent of 'natural religion' was presumably, like Lord Herbert of Cherbury in the middle of the seventeenth century, working out of a Christian monotheistic context towards what retrospectively we might see as an early harbinger of a modern generic concept which did not fully emerge until the eighteenth century. The meaning of these terms are all interlinked. After all, it was common for writers well into the nineteenth century, in English at least, to refer to non-Christians as having superstitions rather than Religion. Usages of the term 'religions' in what appears to be an early modern generic usage—as for example in the previously mentioned work of Samuel Purchas, *Purchas his Pilgrimage; or, Relations of the World and the*

Religions observed in all Ages and Places (1626 edition, first published in 1613, and discussed in chapter 7)—was arguably an ironic usage, given that throughout that work the term 'religions' when applied to pagans and savages is interchangeable with 'superstitions'. Yet surely the genealogy of 'the state' and 'politics' is interdependent with these other changes.

C. H. Williams, in his editing of volume 5 of *English Historical Documents*, to be discussed further in chapter 6, includes only an edited version of the *Formularies*, and I have therefore used the 1825 edition of C. Lloyd under the title *Formularies of Faith Put Forth by Authority during the Reign of Henry VIII*. This contains a preface by the editor, followed by the preface of King Henry VIII (xv–xxxii) to the original *Institution of a Christian Man* and *Articles about Religion* (1536); *The Institution of a Christian Man* (1537); and *A Necessary Doctrine and Erudition for Any Christian Man* (1543). I am not here concerned with the degree to which Henry's *Formularies of Faith* do or do not precisely translate into Protestantism, nor with the extent to which they in some respects retain aspects consistent with a form of Catholicism.

In the *Formularies*, we are given an insight into how the bishops and their master, the king, conceive the church in relation to the rest of the world. The Catholic Church is declared the mystical body of the faithful, and no church is superior to any other:

> And I believe that this holy church is Catholic, that is to say that it cannot be coarcted or restrained within the limits or bonds of any one town, city, province, region, or country; but that it is dispersed and spread universally throughout all the whole world. Insomuch that in what part so ever of the world, be it in Africa, Asia, or Europe, there may be found any number of people . . . which do believe in one God the Father, Creator of all things, and in Lord Jesus Christ his Son, and in one Holy Ghost. (Lloyd, 1825:54–55)

The church of Rome is only one of the churches of the Catholic Church. There is great diversity in the churches of different nations in their "observation of such outward rites, ceremonies, traditions and ordinances" but nevertheless "the unity of this one catholic church is a mere spiritual unity" consisting in uniform doctrines and practices (Lloyd, 1825:54–55). However, no one who is "out of this catholic church" can receive salvation:

> [L]ike as all the people and beasts, which at the time of Noah's Flood were out of his ark or ship, were all drowned and perished, even so all the people of the world, be they Jews, Turks, Saracens, or of any other nation, whatsoever it be, which, either for their infidelity, heresy, or schism, or for their indurateness and obstinate persevering in mortal sin . . . shall utterly perish, and be damned for ever. (1825:59)

Noah's ark is here a metaphor for the church which saves. The ark and the Flood were, however, believed in literally, and constitute an important stage in the dispersal of the descendants of Adam and Eve and of Noah himself to different parts of the world. Adam and Eve's expulsion from the Garden of Eden, the scattering of the descendants of Noah as a result of the Flood, and the Tower of Babel provided three of the main reference points for thinking about and understanding the reason that, in the succeeding years of exploration and colonial expansion, so many peoples would be discovered who fell outside the Christian dispensation. Christian writers of travels and voyages such as Samuel Purchas would continue to try to link the peoples of Asia, Africa, and America as descendants of the sons of Noah or as lost tribes. And we saw in Pagden and Parry in chapter 4 that the problem for the Spanish lawyer/theologians was that the discovery of America and the peoples living there put the biblical account in jeopardy, and put into question the humanity of the Amerindians.

If Henry remained loyal to many of the Catholic practices, and if he defined the Anglican church as Catholic, he certainly opened the way to Protestantism which became more clearly established under Edward VI and Elizabeth I. Henry's agents Thomas Cromwell, Thomas Cranmer, and Edward Seymour were all sympathetic to the Reformation and had close relationships with German and other Reformers. The *Catholic Encyclopedia* says:

> In 1535 Henry sent agents to negotiate an agreement with the Reformers in Germany, and in 1537 he was led by Cromwell, in connivance with Cranmer, into further negotiations with the Protestant princes assembled at Smalkald. He wrote to Melanchthon to congratulate him on the work which he had done for religion, and invited him to England. Melanchthon was unable to come, but in 1538 three German divines, Burkhardt, Boyneburg, and Myconius, were sent to London, where they remained some months, and held conferences with the Anglican bishops and clergy. The Germans presented as a basis of agreement a number of Articles based on the Lutheran Confession of Augsburg. On the doctrinal part of these articles, the first thirteen, both parties came to an agreement [Letter of Myconius to Cromwell, 8 September 1538]. On the second part, the 'Abuses' [viz., private masses, celibacy of the clergy, invocation of saints] the King would not give way, and finally dissolved the conference. Although the negotiations thus formally came to an end, the Thirteen Articles on which agreement with the Germans had been made were kept by Archbishop Cranmer, and afterwards by Archbishop Parker, and were used as test articles to which the preachers whom they licensed were required to subscribe. Eventually they became the nucleus of the Articles of Religion which were authorized under

Edward VI and Elizabeth. Hence the almost verbatim correspondence between these Articles and the Lutheran Confession of Augsburg, from which they were originally taken. ("Anglicanism," *Catholic Encyclopedia*)

The term 'religion' with which we are almost obsessed today, and which has been transformed into a ubiquitous object to be studied by specialist departments in nonreligious secular universities, appears occasionally rather than frequently in sixteenth-century documents. The reason may be that, in a sense, everything was Religion in the sixteenth century. 'Religion' is not mentioned once in the whole commentary on the Paternoster (Lloyd, 1825:178–203), nor in those on the Ave Maria (1825:204–8), the Articles of Justification (1825:209–10), or the Article of Purgatory (1825:210–11).

In his short preface to the 1825 edition, editor C. Lloyd uses the word 'religious' once, and it seems more like a modern usage: "the moral or religious practice of mankind" (v). Otherwise, he refers to such matters as "the errors of Popery," "the pure doctrines of Protestantism," and "the rise and progress of Protestant opinions in the country": "It is in these works ... that they may trace the last departure of that darkness, which had so long obscured the genuine form of Christianity, that they may hail the re-appearance of the pure light of the gospel" (Lloyd, 1825:v).

King Henry's preface (Lloyd, 1825:xv–xxxii) concerns equally salvation *and* what we call the social order. Writing of "the most holy word and commandments of God ... in such things as doth concern our religion," the king notes:

> such diversity in opinions, as have grown and sprung in our realm, as
> well concerning certain articles necessary to our salvation, as also
> touching certain other honest and commendable ceremonies, rites,
> and usages now of long time used and accustomed in our churches,
> for conservation of an honest policy and decent and seemly
> order ... being very desirous to eschew not only the danger of souls,
> but also the outward unquietness which by occasion of the said di-
> versity of opinions ... might perchance have ensued. (1825:xv)

The expression 'our religion' here could mistakenly be seen as question begging, because it is Religion that is at stake. But the expression does not imply that there are a number of different religions of which Christianity is one. It refers to the correct interpretation and understanding of Christian Truth. These documents are designed to tell the reader what true Religion is and how it should be practised. In this case, it is not anti-Catholic as such but is reformist in certain ways. There is, of course, no distinction of the modern kind here between religion and politics. It is about "conservation of *an honest policy* and decent and seemly order" (my italics), but 'policy' is not a separate domain from religion but prudent action in any domain, its prudency being in conformity with reason and civility, which of course originate with God. Henry mentions several times the question of salvation and also "the honest ceremonies and good and *politic* orders" and the need for "unity and concord" (Lloyd, 1825:xvi; my italics).

At that period of history, the commonweal was frequently referred to as 'the politic body' and, like other uses of 'politic' as an adjective implies fitting, well-ordered, and God-given—though it can also have more negative connotations, in the sense of crafty or cunning. (The *Oxford English Dictionary* gives prudent, judicious, expedient, shrewd, skilfully contrived, cunning, and scheming.) Divine purpose was realised through submission to one's status and duties in the creation of a harmonious whole. This was a politic state of affairs. Worship could be politic too. We moderns did not invent cynicism, and neither did Machiavelli; however, it would be wrong to say, as we might today, that 'religion' is here being used as a mask in order to manipulate 'political power'.

The word 'politic' here is a long way from contemporary usages such as 'politics' and was not a domain but an attribute. For 'politics' as a contemporary noun implies a domain separated off from another domain named 'religion', and another one called 'economic science', and another one called 'secular law'. The modern separation of religion and politics, or church and state, is the most important because it rests on a distinction or, more strongly, on an opposition between religion and nonreligion. The prolonged attempts by various intellectuals to imagine religion and politics as separate required that both politics and religion have different natures or essences. By being essentially separated, they can then be thought of as having problematic interrelations. But this cannot make much sense when referring to an idea of a totality of human relations made by and for God, in which the king is head of the church; the bishops (lords spiritual) are in the Parliament with the rest of the nobility (lords temporal) and play a leading role in government; and the ministers read state-authorised homilies in the form of sermons on civil obedience.

In the *Formularies of Faith*, Henry and his bishops have divided the articles into two: those that are directly necessary to our salvation, and those less important practices "as have been of a long continuance for a decent order and honest policy, prudently instituted" (Lloyd, 1825:xvi). He therefore seems to make a distinction between personal salvation and public order. Yet the logic of the *Formularies of Faith* is not pointed in that direction, for the *Formularies* are very much concerned with the disciplines of civility, with institutions such as marriage and the family and other facets of what we call the social order, and in that sense might arguably be taken to be concerned with collective salvation as well as individual salvation. *A Necessary Doctrine and Erudition for Any Christian Man* is as much concerned with legitimate authority, status, duty, and obedience as anything, drawing an explicit analogy among Christ as King and Father of all, Henry as king and father of his subjects, and the father as head of the family with authority over wife and children. In effect, the *Formularies* assert the traditional hierarchical order of the commonweal, which makes it virtually impossible to drive a wedge between Religion and commonweal.

Belief in the three creeds, the Nicaean, the Athanasian, and the Common, is essential for salvation. People who do not believe "cannot be the very members of Christ and his espouse the Church, but be very infidels or heretics, and members of the Devil" (Lloyd, 1825:xviii). It seems clear here that public assent to the creeds is a matter simultaneously of heresy and the authority of the state. One might say that the church-state of medieval times is in transformation to the state church of the early modern nation.

The people "ought and must most reverently and *religiously* observe and keep" the Articles of Faith (1825:xviii). And referring to the Sacrament of the Altar, Henry says, "every man ought... *religiously* to try and search his own conscience" (xxv). "Religiously" here is an adverb referring to the attitude with which a practice is performed. The practice is not done 'religiously' because it is an aspect of 'a religion', but because certain actions require complete devotion, preeminently service to God, which in turn implies service to those with authority from God. Of course, Anglophone dictionaries written by Protestants include definitions that define 'religiously' in terms of worship of God, or in terms of 'religion', which is virtually tautological. But most dictionaries or compendiums include meanings for 'religiously' which do not necessarily imply belief in or worship of God in the Christian sense at all, and which thus suggest a persistent strain of meaning which may be a survival from an original Latin nuance of *religio*. Various dictionaries, such as Ainsworth (1740), Riddle and Arnold (1847), and Simpson (1977), as well as the expected theistic definitions in terms of belief in God, also define 'religiously' in such terms as faithfully, strictly, exactly, conscientiously, scrupulously, carefully, nicely, cautiously, with integrity, and with conscientious exactness.[3]

For Christians, complete devotion is demanded by God, and so the exemplary kinds of actions done religiously are those directed towards God. But it should be borne in mind that the importance of these practices derives also from the interests of the state, as presumably was also true of classical Rome. Such uses of 'religiously' in the context of these texts suggest, in conformity with the explicit analogy made among Christ as Lord and Father of all people, the king as lord and father of his subjects, and the father as head of the family, that all duties—for example, to the king, to one's master or lord, a wife to a husband or children to their father—ought to be performed religiously in the sense of conscientiously, scrupulously, and exactly.

At the same time, a 'politic' action is one which is suitable and appropriate to the circumstances, and thus as relevant to those actions that we might today judge to be 'religious' as to those we might judge to be 'political'. Since a politic action is presumably one done scrupulously, with exact attention to detail, then there seems to be considerable overlap between the usages of 'politic' and 'religious' or 'religiously', and hardly an essential distinction. There is no modern dichotomy in the *Formularies* between religion and politics. Some dichotomies appear in Henry's comments between Christian Religion (e.g., Truth) and superstition (being a heretic or an infidel; Lloyd, 1825:xviii); between "inward spiritual motions and graces of God" and "outward and civil works" (xxvii); between the superstition and idolatry of worshipping images, and images as "representers of virtue and stirrers of men's minds" (xxviii); between heaven "to reign in glory with Christ," and earth, "this transitory world" (xxix).

In their own preface addressing the king in *The Institution of a Christian Man*, the bishops refer to "the right institution and education of your people in the knowledge of Christ's true religion" (Lloyd, 1825:23). The expression 'Christ's true religion' is standard. In this context, it is made virtually to stand as the equivalent of "the whole sum of all those things which appertain unto the profession of a Christian man" (23). Another way of expressing this, I suggest, would be in terms of the disciplines of Christian civility. One can see how impossible it is to privatise such religion, since this is a matter of state, of the commonweal, of the totality of social relations, of duty. Also, "Christ's true religion" is contrasted with "all errors, doubts, superstitions and abuses" (23).

'Faith' is another word sometimes used in the same sense: "that faith is the very fountain and chief ground of our religion" (Lloyd, 1825:25). Faith is not confined to the inner, individual, private assent to a doctrine of personal salvation; it is a commitment to practice the Christian disciplines of civility, which are collectively imagined and policed.

The bishops make reference to "the clergy of this your most noble realm, as well religious as other" (Lloyd, 1825:26). Here, "religious" refers to 'regulars', the monks, friars, and nuns living in religious houses, in contrast to the secular priests. After the closure of the monasteries, they became a dying class in England and other Protestant states but continued to flourish in Catholic ones. (The language of 'the religious' is still evident in Anglicanism.)

Then there is this: "Bodily sickness and adversity . . . be sent unto me by his hand and his visitation . . . to save me, and to reduce me again by penance unto the right way of his laws and his religion" (Lloyd, 1825:31–32). To explain sickness as a punishment and a moral awakening is to attribute purpose to what today we would think of us as neutral, nonreligious, material processes. It may be that humans have always attributed some kind of mystical purpose behind natural events such as diseases and earthquakes, but in this context it is not a capricious or arbitrary explanation. Everything in nature has an intended purpose, which is the unfolding into actuality of its potentiality. When viewed *sub specie aeternitatis*, God is the final cause towards whom all subordinate purposes are moving. But some are perversions by the devil.

Again, we can get a good idea of what 'religion' means by seeing with what it is contrasted: "neither will I glory or put my confidence in any other man or creature of this world, be it in heaven, hell or here in earth, nor in any craft of magic, sorcery, charms, witchcrafts, or any other false arts, subtiled and invented by the Devil" (Lloyd, 1825:32).

We have seen that the king was now head of the church and head of state. It is interesting that the bishops declare, "Jesus, that is to say, my Saviour and my Christ, that is to say, mine anointed King and Priest, and my Lord.... For he hath done and fulfilled the very office both of a Priest, and of a King, and of a Lord" (Lloyd, 1825:32). If Jesus is thought of as priest and king combined, isn't that also true of Henry, who is also lord, king, and head of the church in England? It is easy to lose track of the subject of such epithets as King, Priest, and Lord.

The language of sin is like that of pollution, as when the bishops, talking about the virgin birth (which they affirm), write:

> And I believe that this conception and nativity of our said Saviour was ordained to be thus pure, holy, and undefiled, to the intent that all filthiness and malediction... and all the filthiness and malice of the sins of the whole world, as well original as actual, should thereby be purified, purged, and made clean. (Lloyd, 1825:37)

This is typical language, for example, "the penitent and contrite man must first acknowledge the filthiness and abomination of his own sin" (1825:97); and

> Know you also, that God hath not called us unto uncleanness and filthiness of life, but unto holiness and sanctimony. And therefore I do exhort you all, and in the name of God command you, to eschew all fornication and adultery, all uncleanness and carnal concupiscence, all filthiness and unpure living in fleshly lusts of the body. (276)

We also get another typical usage of 'religiously' in the commentary on the sacrament of marriage: the husband and wife ought to believe that wedlock, according to the sacrament, "is a state and manner... being the same virtuously and religiously, according to the law of God" (Lloyd, 1825:91). Surely this sacrament is one of the keys by which Christian soteriological doctrine is locked in at the level of social institution (see also 1825:269). This sacrament determines who can marry whom and what the relationship means. The rules of incest, whom one can and cannot marry, the "degrees of consanguinity and affinity," are listed (270). The marriage union is analogous to the union of Christ and the church (272). Women are subject to their husbands as the church is subject to Christ. The sacrament of monogamous marriage is one of the fundamental disciplines of Christian civility. And the commentary on the Sacrament of the Altar warns that one should be in the right condition before accepting this sacrament, for it "is to be used with all due reverence and honour; and that every man ought first to prove and examine himself, and religiously to try to search his own conscience" (100).

Christ's religion is contrasted with sin, infidelity, heresy, schism, damnation, "naughty weeds" (Lloyd, 1825:75); "chaff, or stinking and naughty
weeds" (75–76); filthiness, abominations, "horrible errors and false prophets"
(76); "the filthiness and abomination of his own sin" (97); and "infidel princes" (113). It is against these excrescences, pollutions, and barbarities that the
disciplines of Christian civility were to be practised. Christ's religion, which is
the harmonious garden that these barbarous infidelities threaten, is thus very
much concerned with a total ordering of life.

The document also talks about the division of functions between the ecclesiastical and civil authorities:

> Christ and his apostles did institute and ordain in the New Testa-
> ment, that besides the civil powers and governance of kings and
> princes [which is called *potestas gladii*, the power of the sword], there
> should also be continually in the church militant certain other min-
> isters or officers, which should have special power, authority and
> commission, under Christ, to preach and teach the word of God unto
> his people; to dispense and administer the sacraments of God unto
> them. (Lloyd, 1825:101)

However:

> it is out of all doubt that the priests and bishops never had any
> authority by the gospel to punish any man by corporal violence, and
> therefore they were often times moved of necessity to require
> Christian princes to ... constrain and reduce inobedient persons unto
> the obedience and good order of the church. (Lloyd, 1825:113)

The point here is that the power of physical coercion and punishment
belongs to kings and princes, and they have had the power in the past to license
the priests to have certain powers. But kings and princes can also "constrain all
the power and jurisdiction which was given and assigned unto priests and
bishops ... as shall be necessary, wholesome, and expedient for the weal of their
realms, the repressing of vice, and the increase of Christ's faith and religion"
(Lloyd, 1825:114). The "weal of their realms" means the commonweal, which is
clearly ordered, and ought to be ordered, through "the increase of Christ's faith
and religion." Kings and princes are responsible. The thrust of this argument
is against the authority and power of the pope and the ecclesiastical hierarchy
in the realm of the sword. Kings and princes alone have the power:

> God hath constituted and made Christian kings and princes to be as
> the chief heads and overlookers over the said priests and bishops, to
> cause them to administer their office and power ... purely and sin-
> cerely.... And God hath also commanded the said priests and

bishops to obey, with all humbleness and reverence, all the laws
made by the said princes. (Lloyd, 1825:121)

The "pretended monarchy of the Bishop of Rome" is responsible for "the
notable decay of Christ's true and perfect religion among us" (121–22).

The detailed interpretations of some of the Ten Commandments—especially the Fifth Commandment to "honour thy father and mother"—contained
in *The Institution of a Christian Man* make the conceptual separation of religion and civil society problematic, to say the least, both in the sense that the
commandments are understood to support the formal order and authority
of the state, and in the sense that they reveal the conception of everyday hierarchical relations. The order of the cosmos, the order of the state, and the
order of the family are all seen as analogues in the discourses of those times.
As in all societies, the daily practices of etiquette were taken so much for
granted that they are frequently not mentioned. Yet there is an argument
deriving from anthropology that we need to see the informal and the formal
together simultaneously to get close to understanding what people of the time
would understand. If 'salvation' is understood as the disciplines of civility, then
the everyday courtesies, dress codes, gendered forms of address, occupations,
and orders of state would all be integral to what we have separated out as
religion. This explains why official state policy was routinely announced in the
churches, jut as bishops played leading roles in Parliament and in the king's
court.

Apart from the reference to "mother" in the Fifth Commandment and the
reference to "wife" in relation to "wedlock" in the commentary on the sanctity
of marriage, the language throughout is male gendered. Women are subject to
their husbands as the church is subject to Christ (Lloyd, 1825:271). The word
'father' is not only meant to refer to the "natural" father but also the "spiritual
father, by whom we be spiritually regenerated and nourished in Christ; and all
other governors and rulers under whom we be nourished and brought up, or
ordered and guided" (1825:148). And talking about honour and duty, "This is
the very honour and duty which not only the children do owe unto their
parents, but also all subjects and inferiors to their heads and rulers" (148). This
lengthy commentary makes it plain that obedience to parents means obedience
to the established authorities, and disobedience is both a sin and a crime
punishable in the Old Testament by serious penalties:

For scripture taketh princes to be as it were, fathers ... to their subjects. And by scripture it appeareth, that it appertaineth unto the
office of princes to see that the right religion and true doctrine of
Christ may be maintained and taught; and that their subjects may be
well ruled and governed by good and just laws; and to provide and
care for them, that all things necessary for them may be plenteous;

and that the people and the common weal may increase; and to defend them from oppression and invasion . . . and to shew towards them fatherly pity. And finally . . . to correct them that be evil . . . . And therefore all their subjects must . . . be bound by this commandment, not only to honour and obey the said princes, according as subjects are bound to do . . . as to their natural lords; but they must also love them as children do love their fathers . . . even like as the health of the head is more to be tendered than the health of any other member. (Lloyd, 1825:153)

The power of the prince, in this case Henry, is in this way linked to the entire set of hierarchical relations and duties of Christ's true religion which are embedded in the commonweal or order of people. In *A Necessary Doctrine and Erudition for Any Christian Man: Set forth by the King's Majesty of England* (Lloyd, 1825), it is written: "For the truth is that God constituted and ordained the authority of Christian kings and princes to be the most high and supreme above all other powers and officers in this world, in the regiment and government of their people." Henry lists the duties of the prince to rule, to punish, "to procure the public weal and common peace . . . but specially and principally to defend the faith of Christ and his religion" (1825:286). Much of the description of God's power and will, and the proper attitude of submission, obedience, and trust, is also tacitly if not explicitly a description of how Henry thought of the king's own power and his subjects' proper attitude to their earthly lord.

All such power and duty are divinely ordained, in which case there is no sense in which religion and society are thought of as separate domains in the way that modern usages would lead us to believe. Authority based on the senior-junior principle is everywhere divinely ordained, and the ultimate authority below God is the king in his domain. All older men should be respected and obeyed as one would respect and obey one's natural father: "reverence to old men, and to all such as be their masters and tutors . . . and so as fathers must be honoured and obeyed" (Lloyd, 1825:156). The king is a father to the nation; and God is the Father of the world. The chains of command and obedience also embrace masters and servants: "this commandment doth also contain the honour and obedience of the servants unto their masters" (1825:155). Servants should obey their masters as they would obey Christ. Scripture provides many examples "of the great vengeance of God that have fallen upon rebels and such as have been disobedient unto their princes" (154). The analogous senior-junior relationships—father-son, king-subject, Christ-believer, husband-wife, master-servant, teacher-pupil—construct the universe of relations on the basis of a kind of fictive kinship.[4]

One comment on the Paternoster continues the analogy between "our sovereign Lord the King" and Christ "the king and prince of all princes":

> If our sovereign Lord the King would say to any of us, Take me for
> your father, and so call me; what joy in heart, what comfort, what
> confidence would we conceive of so favourable and gracious words.
> Much more then incomparably have we cause to rejoice that the king
> and prince of all princes sheweth unto us this grace and goodness, to
> make us his children. (Lloyd, 1825:181)

I had to read this several times to be clear that it is Henry who is the sovereign
lord the king, and Christ who is the King and Prince of princes. Of course, it is
an analogy and Christ's grace and goodness are "incomparably" more, which
in a sense defeats the analogy, which to be meaningful has to be based on an
element of comparability. But there can be no doubt that this language sacralises the king by *suggesting* comparability even while denying it.

When one unpacks the meaning of faith and Religion in these important
texts, it seems problematic how they came to acquire their modern generic universality. We will see how this application eventually occurred though when we
look at the colonial expansion and the travel and voyage literature. Where "our
religion" is used in *The King's Book: A Necessary Doctrine and Erudition for any
Christian Man: Set Forth by the King's Majesty of England* (Lloyd, 1825:213ff.), it is
unavoidably identified with the contents of doctrine. Faith is "the beginning,
entry, and introduction unto all Christian religion and godliness" (1825:222).
This faith is described by Saint Paul as "the perfect faith of a true Christian
man, and containeth the obedience to the whole doctrine and religion of
Christ." The first article of the faith is belief in the triune God: "there is but one
very God, three persons, the Father, the Son, and the Holy Ghost" (223).

Religion cannot be applied then to "the blind, ignorant, and obstinate Jews,
replete with envy and malice, as the very members of the Devil, by whom they
were provoked and induced" (Lloyd, 1825:233). Though the words superstition,
irrationality, and barbarity are not actually used, they are plainly implied. They
profane the Truth, and as such they are defined by the Truth. Their externality is
not a modern neutrality but a kind of encompassment, similar to the way Satan
is an angel encompassed by God, but a fallen angel. The infidels, pagans, and
heretics are excluded because they are damned; but they are included in the
sense that Christ's purpose and judgment finally determine everything.

Religion is composed also of the belief that the church is Christ's mystical
body, and that at the day of judgment the dead shall be physically resurrected
(Lloyd, 1825:234, 236, 251). The belief in bodily resurrection is another re-
minder for the modern reader of the profoundly different sense of selfhood
implied in contrast, for example, to the later Cartesian dualism and its dis-
embodied mind. The whole discussion relentlessly pins the meaning of faith
and Religion to the definition of orthodoxy and the true disciplines of salvation.
There is also evidence perhaps of the rise of nationalism, the nation-state, the
national church:

> And therefore the Church of Rome, being but a several church . . .
> doeth great wrong to all other churches, and doeth only by force . . .
> support an unjust usurpation: for that church hath no more right
> to that name than the church of France, Spain, England or Portugal
> which we justly call catholic churches. (Lloyd, 1825:247)

These churches "profess and teach the faith and religion of Christ" (248).

> And as all Christian people, as well spiritual as temporal, be bound to
> believe, honour and obey our saviour Jesus Christ, the only head of
> the universal church, so likewise they be by his commandment
> bound to honour and obey, next unto himself, Christian kings and
> princes. (248)

The term "spiritual" here refers to a status of persons (men), also often referred to as ecclesiastical, which is distinguished from those whose status is "temporal" or civil. This is not the same as the modern distinction between 'religion' and 'the secular', since Religion as Christian Truth encompasses all statuses. Nor is it precisely the same as 'sacred' and 'profane' because the king and his status are sacred, as can be determined from the frequency which, in other documents, he (and in the case of the queen, she) is addressed as 'sacred'.

I am picking out the rare uses of the word 'religion' from these documents. One could argue that, in the sixteenth century, 'religion' is used rarely, and where it is used it is tightly drawn and specified and embedded in the practices of Christendom, whereas the opposite seems to hold today. Today, religion is used so openly and prolifically that it seems obvious that its meaning and ideological function have changed greatly, and that therefore there is danger of confusion in projecting our meanings back into earlier eras.

That the meaning of 'religious' has changed dramatically becomes clear when Henry considers the appointment of "ecclesiastical ministers" and the usurped powers of the church of Rome (Lloyd, 1825:278ff.). He goes through the various councils, arguing that none of them gave authority to the primacy of Rome. During the later councils, such as Constance, Basil, and Florence, there were schisms, bishops and princes were divided,

> [a]nd the great part of the learned men that were there were of the
> later institute religious, and therefore obsequent to the pleasure and
> will of the bishops of Rome, and brought up only in this later
> scholastic doctrine, and little exercised or learned in the holy scrip-
> tures, or in the old ancient doctors and writers. (Lloyd, 1825:285)

In this passage, the 'religious' are the monks, friars, and nuns who, by serving the will of the pope, fell into superstition and, presumably, damnation. The religious in this instance are irreligious.

The sacrament of marriage makes it impossible to separate religion from married life, and therefore from the order of things and people. Baptism is virtually the bestowal of human citizenship on the infant and thus the point where Christian Truth and social order are locked together, and this continues with marriage. The sacrament determines who can marry whom and what kind of relationship it is.

The description of God's power and will and the proper attitude towards God of submission, obedience, and trust, might have been a description of how Henry expected his subjects to view and submit to his own power (Lloyd, 1825:291). The patriarchal world order assumed and reauthorised in the *Formularies of Faith* is found reasserted in the seventeenth century by Filmer in his *Patriarcha* (1991 [1680]), the text that occasioned the first of Locke's *Two Treatises on Government* (1988 [1690]). Filmer makes it explicit that, just as God is Father and Lord of the world, so the king is father and lord of his realm and subjects, and a man is father and lord of his family. While many aspects of patriarchy continue up to the present, with women only winning the right to vote in Britain after the First World War and in France after the Second World War, the virtue of a kind of egalitarianism was at least partly articulated in seventeenth-century Newtonian cosmology and Cartesian rationalism, and in eighteenth-century Enlightenment writings, for example those of Thomas Paine and a whole spectrum of American writers (see chapter 9). However, it is necessary to take into account that, in the seventeenth century, Religion and nation were almost synonymous, and our Protestant Religion continued to encompass a church-state (see chapters 6 and 8). Also, few seventeenth-century theorisations of the state could be described as secular in the modern sense. Goldie argues that the language of 'civil religion' and its synthesis of civility and piety stemmed from the Reformers' theology of the church-state and "were among the most pervasive" concepts in early modern Europe (Goldie, 1987:199). This was so to the extent that even Locke has been read less as the modern inventor of the absolute distinction between the religious and the civil society and more as belonging to a post-Reformation tradition of the identification of true Religion with the state. And even well into the eighteenth century, as O'Gorman argued, English society was still to a large extent a "confessional state":

> England in the early eighteenth century was a confessional state, a
> state in which one official confession of faith, Anglicanism, was es-
> tablished by statute and enforced through the law—a faith, moreover,
> in theory accepted and practiced by the vast majority of the popula-
> tion. (O'Gorman, 1997:163)

In coming chapters, I will consider the textual evidence for the degree that generic religion of the modern kind was conceivable during the eighteenth century.

6

English Historical Documents, 1485–1558

T. F. Mayer, in his introduction to a republication of Thomas Starkey's "A Dialogue between Pole and Lupset," published originally around 1539 (Mayer, 1989), says that to understand the meaning of the dialogue and its topic, we have to understand

> Starkey's humanist practice of inventing reality through language. He did this in the twin sense of constructing a vision of a self-sufficient England, a vision which Starkey intended would persuade his readers to bring this world into existence, and of preparing a manifesto of political reform. (Mayer, 1989:xiii)

The topic is the commonweal or commonwealth, and the implication is that Henry's break with Rome and the institution of the Anglican church-state had exacerbated tensions within the order of things and persons to a dangerous level. Rhetoric on the commonweal was designed to convince people that, even in the new context of post-Reformation England, there existed a God-ordained order of degree and deference that was threatened by dissent within the politic body.

According to Mayer, Starkey acted as an advisor to Thomas Cromwell, and therefore to the king, on various aspects of policy regarding the dissolution of the monasteries and how to deal with dissent. He had trained in rhetoric in Italy and France and was therefore aware of the latest in humanist learning. There was apparently a perceived need for various methods of persuasion that the new order which Henry was instigating was the morally correct one.

On the other hand, the ideal of the commonweal is represented in the "Dialogue" as under attack from Dissent, greed, and selfishness generally, which to be persuasive must have been referring to an ideal that was already in some form widely disseminated. Starkey's ability to persuade, which was partly underwritten by an appeal to Aristotle, must surely have depended to some extent on an imaginative connection with what people already widely believed at the time. This seems especially true given that the commonweal is described as being in a state of dangerous decay and requires reinvigorating with moral purpose and submission to the God-ordained holistic order. Or was this the skill of rhetoric, that one conceals one's own inventiveness by speaking as though it is obvious what one means?

The evidence is that the hierarchical view of the world as a macrocosmic great chain of being reproduced microcosmically in the human gradations of degree and rank was well embedded in the discourse of the lawyer/theologians discussed in chapter 4 by Pagden and Parry. Thus, while the discourses on the commonweal were undoubtedly rhetorical acts of persuasion, they did not occur in a vacuum and seem to have been a dominant ideology in the minds of people, much in the way that the values of democracy and liberal capitalism are rhetorically generated and widely appropriated in our own day. And this leads me to question some of the historian's own use of language. For, as I have argued in earlier parts of this book, Anglo-American historians and anthropologists tend, more or less inevitably, to build their models of the past— or of non-European cultures—in terms of Anglophone categories. While many of the same scholars are methodologically sophisticated, and aware of the problems of translation and interpretation, nevertheless very basic and powerful organising categories, such as religion, the secular, politics, the state, or economics, get applied to cultures which did not think or act in those categories.

In the "Dialogue" in question, there is no usage of such categories which we moderns would think of as 'normal'. In his introduction, Mayer says that Starkey was given "a lucrative benefice" in London to add to his collection of preferments. In the thought of the day, this would have made him a secular priest, or the Anglican equivalent, but not a religious. These were the most frequent usages of the terms 'religious' and 'secular'. Yet the editor, whose far greater knowledge and expertise I respect, makes the following statement: "Cromwell talked seriously with Starkey and no doubt asked his advice on religious affairs" (Mayer, 1989:viii). This could mean that Cromwell asked his advice on affairs of the monasteries, for these were the religious houses. But it is difficult to judge because Mayer uses the term 'religious' in other ways which confuse the issue. For example:

> [Starkey] . . . sent Henry an uncompromising manifesto which . . . told
> the king how to deal with religious dissent, defended the religiously

conservative and moderate, and made several suggestions about how to disburse the proceeds of the dissolution of the monasteries. (Mayer, 1989:viii)

There are other examples of the use of the word 'religious' which also are difficult to decipher. One of Pole's clients "had escaped from England for religious reasons" (1989:xiv); and he refers to "Religious conservatives among the bishops" (xiv).

This lack of clarity about language is evident in Mayer's use of 'political' and 'politic' too. For some reason, the editor reverses the more usual expression of the time 'the politic body' and calls it the 'body politic', an expression which is still current (Mayer, 1989:xiii). By reversing these two words, 'politic' ceases to be an adjective and appears to become a noun. He says that Starkey's training in Italy and France equipped him "with the most novel political concepts" (1989:viii). The problem is that, if the actual contents of the "Dialogue between Pole and Lupset" are anything to go by, there was no concept of 'political' as distinct from 'religious' in the discourses of the day. One is therefore bound to ask about the historian's rhetorical purpose, conscious or unconscious, in framing his discussion of the text in these categories at all.

In this chapter, I analyse the construction by another modern historian of English society, Williams (1967), in the transition between the late medieval and early modern period, which includes the era of the Reformation. I am not a historian and do not have any original new historiography to add. My purpose is parasitic on the work of historians, and in that sense I approach it with respect for their specialist knowledge of a specific historical period and what their findings can teach me about the changing usages of categories in historical time. I marvel at the erudition of the authors and editors of the works that I analyse and am not motivated by a critical attitude towards their historiographical expertise itself, which would be inappropriate. My concern is methodological; I am interested in the way that modern categories such as 'religion' are reproduced in the organisation of our view of the past, such that they take on an appearance of permanence, as though essentially in the nature of things. The paradox is that historians, like anthropologists in the study of contemporary non-European cultures, are usually more aware than their critics of the dangers of projecting modern ways of thinking into those worlds that had different forms of thought and spoke a different language. Yet even in the texts of highly knowledgeable and methodologically sophisticated writers, such projections seem to be unavoidable.

It is presumably an occupational hazard for historians to describe and analyse a previous historical era with the categories of the contemporary one. Williams is aware of the problem when, in his general introduction, discussing "class distinctions" in late feudal and early modern society, he tells us it is important "to avoid the crude error of reading back all the implications of nineteenth century ideology into a period inspired by very different ways of thought" (Williams, 1967:26).

Not much later in the narrative, Williams warns us against projecting our own notions of class and class war: "To read back into the period any such notions is to reveal a complete misunderstanding of the early Tudor period" (Williams, 1967:30). And on the next page, in discussing problems related to what has been called "the agrarian revolution" as an explanation for the rise in prices without a corresponding rise in wages, he says: "it might be suggested in passing that there is probably more risk than profit in applying terms which have gained currency in one situation to a set of circumstances in another where the similarities are probably very superficial" (31). Yet in his general introduction and in the introductions to each section of documents, Williams constantly uses modern categories which, if in existence then, had a significantly different logic of use, and sometimes were not really in use at all.

Williams divides the documents into six sections, and it must have been extremely difficult to know which texts to place in which subsection, and which categories to use for dividing up the subsections in the first place:

Part I: The Writing of History
Part II: The Land
Part III: Commonweal
   A: The Structure of Society
   B: The Theory of Commonweal
   C: Leaders in Society
Part IV: Government and Administration
   A: The Crown
   B: The Secretariat
   C: Chamber and Household
   D: The King's Council
   E: The Conciliar Courts
   F: The Common Law
   G: Parliament
   H: Local Government
   I: Theory of Government
Part V: Religion
   A: The Eve of the Reformation
   B: The King's Private Matter
   C: The Breach with Rome
   D: Confiscation of Church Wealth
   E: Doctrine under Henry VIII
   F: The English Bible
   G: Heresy

H: The Church under Edward VI
I: The Church under Mary
Part VI: Daily Life in Town and Country
    A: Life in the Country
    B: Life in the Town
    C: Industry and Industrial Conditions
    D: Money
    E: Poverty & the Poor Law
    F: Bringing Up the Young

It can be noticed that Williams does not use the word 'politics' as a sub-section, and this would presumably be because, like 'class distinctions' and 'class war', it would constitute a methodologically crude (to use his word) way of importing nineteenth-century nuances back into a period that did not think or act in such terms. Yet he does sometimes use it in his own introductions to the different subsections. 'Politics' as a noun was rare in the period, in fact I found no instance of it any of the documents which I read (a considerable number) in the whole volume (the adjective 'politic' was more common and had a different nuance from the modern noun). In his general introduction, the editor frequently refers to both religion and politics as though they are or were essentially different domains though with a problematic interface. His early assertion (and I don't suppose he intended this as a comprehensive definition) that "Politics is the struggle for power: it is also the means for getting things done" is vacuous. For one could argue that struggling for power is so endemic in the struggle for survival that using the word 'politics' to describe so many different potential contexts of power renders it descriptively and analytically useless. On the other hand, since in modern usage it is heavily overlaid with (though not exhausted by) nuances of instrumental rationality, bureaucracy, constitutions, political parties, class divisions, elections, representative government, and a concept of the nation-state as essentially 'secular' and separated from 'religion', there is a constant danger and temptation of inadvertently projecting these characteristics back into the documentary material. Indeed, this happens constantly, as I will show. The editor writes about "the political history of these years" (Williams, 1967:2); "the innovations in religion and politics" (1967:4); "from 1529 onwards Englishmen were at the mercy of rulers wholly committed to great adventures in religion and politics" (5); "kaleidoscopic changes in religion and politics" (5); "[d]uring Henry VII's reign the rehabilitation of the kingship was a major problem of politics" (18); and the examples can be multiplied.

    Even in the editor's own words, the usages seem unsustainable. The nature of kingship and the state render this language of 'religion and politics' impossible. For the king, referred to by such epithets as "our most dread sovereign Lord," "the king's royal majesty," and quite frequently "our most sacred king," is in 1534 both the head of state and also the head of the Church of England.

Words such as 'religion', 'religious', 'politic', and 'secular' had different applications from the modern ones. In modern Anglophone usage, they have been rendered into distinct domains with different logics. Religion has retreated from its pervasive, encompassing reality in this earlier period, which is textually represented by Williams's selection of documents, and has become a relatively marginal, privatised domain, and this retreat has facilitated the emergence of a new civil domain that has been imagined as 'nonreligion' in terms of civil society, the state, secular knowledge, and the dominating rationality of self-interest and markets. We might today think of these modern practices and ideals as sacred or sacrosanct, and arguably the right to practice one's religion is a sacred principle today. But there is no concept of the nonreligious in these documents, and I suspect it would have been meaningless to contemporaries of the time.

This points to another difficulty in Williams's editorial usage. For example, part III is given over to documents that are concerned with the commonweal and is divided into three subsections:

Part III: Commonweal
   A: The Structure of Society
   B: The Theory of Commonweal
   C: Leaders in Society

One can understand the difficulty for any modern scholar of doing any writing or thinking without using the term 'society'. Yet there are a number of problems with equating the term society or "the structure of society"—an expression which the editor employs quite frequently—with commonweal. One problem, which has been discussed by the historian John Bossy (1985:170–71), is that 'society' and 'societies' are modern essentialisations, in some ways parallel to 'religion' and 'religions'. The idea of 'a society' hardly existed before the seventeenth century, except in such a context as 'on Christmas day I enjoyed the society of Mrs Brown'. It was a word of relationship, not a reified object which could be lined up alongside a number of other similar objects and compared. The idea of 'the structure of society' is perhaps dependent on, or provides the basis for, the nineteenth-century idea of 'sociology' or 'social science', which is itself understood by sociologists as a secular science in the sense of nonreligious and neutral towards religion (I have discussed this point in greater detail in chapter 3). But the idea that the commonweal of the sixteenth and seventeenth centuries could have been neutral towards religion is clearly wrong if the actual documents themselves are to be believed. The reified idea of society as a possible object, or as multiple possible objects, of study presupposes a separation from 'religion' which, I shall argue here, was hardly conceivable in the period that this volume covers.

There is therefore a problem in the editorial separation of commonweal from Religion. For practical purposes, some distinctions have to be made, but one has to consider whether or not the practical pressures of finding a way of distributing texts within a book like this outweighs the methodological issues involved. For it seems to me that the texts chosen to exemplify discourses on the "Commonweal" in part III, and the texts chosen to exemplify "Religion" in part V, do not themselves substantively underwrite the separation. The actual contents of the texts in both sections support the idea that 'Religion' and 'commonweal' were, for the people who were writing these documents, virtually indistinguishable. There was, therefore, no viable notion of 'a society' distinct from 'a religion', any more than there was a church defined, say, by its concern with the 'supernatural' as distinct from a state defined by its concern with the things of 'this world'. The internal distinctions and divisions of function of different institutions were not made in these terms. Whatever sympathy one has for the historian with the enormous task of bringing such texts to the reading public in some manageable form, the methodological point still stands.

The whole of part V is given over to "Religion." This category may be useful for the editor, but it is misleading. We can see from the table of contents that the editor is following a largely modern idea of what constitutes religion, one aspect of which is the tacit equation of 'church' and 'religion', and the (unsuccessful) attempt to keep it separate from 'politics' or 'the state':

Part V: Religion
    A: The Eve of the Reformation
    B: The King's Private Matter
    C: The Breach with Rome
    D: Confiscation of Church Wealth
    E: Doctrine under Henry VIII
    F: The English Bible
    G: Heresy
    H: The Church under Edward VI
    I: The Church under Mary

Analysis of the documents themselves indicates that the term Religion is used fairly infrequently. It is virtually synonymous with Christian Truth or piety and while this is the root of modern usage the sixteenth-century usages have a different logic from the modern one. For most English-speaking people throughout the sixteenth and seventeenth centuries, and probably this is true for much of the eighteenth and nineteenth as well, 'Religion' meant Christian Truth, and since most English-language discourses on 'religion', as it is understood in English, were written by Protestants, Religion meant Protestant Truth as against Catholic and other superstitions. Religion permeated everything. It was usually contrasted not with 'the secular' (which also had a different usage), but with superstition. Superstition, however, was not the opposite of Religion in the sense that the secular is the opposite of religion in today's usages. Superstition was error in 'religion', confusion in the matters of salvation and redemption, a state of being lost and damned. It was a state of irrationality and barbarity. It was even a case of not being human, as the Spanish discourses on the Amerindians often suggested.

One of the habitual ways of thinking in the modern English language has been in terms of the separation of church and state and of religion from politics. I think we have to take seriously the idea that, when we talk about the dichotomous relationship, we are not talking about two preexisting domains defined by essentially different aims and characteristics that collided, each side struggling against the predominance of the other, and were now to be separated again. There is frequently an assumption that the words 'religious' and 'secular' each have a single continuous meaning historically, and that they are essentially different.

The problem is that the meaning of the terms changed and therefore it can be misleading to assume a simple and unproblematic continuity. The 'religious' was a status term referring to monastics. The 'secular' was most commonly used to refer to the secular priesthood, though there was a legitimate extension of the meaning to a more general reference to secular offices. Another way of making this distinction was between the spiritual and the temporal, as in lords spiritual (bishops) and lords temporal (landed gentry). However, in the understanding of the time, both the spiritual and the temporal as categories of people were subsumed in the higher unity of God and his redemptive purposes. Thus they were all members of Parliament, they were all members of the church, bishops helped to formulate state policy, and the king was God's vicar on earth. Furthermore, they largely belonged to the same degree of landed nobility.

A similar point can be made about the distinction between ecclesiastical courts and civil courts, or between canon law and civil law. These were important distinctions within their rightful context, but, as we will see from reading the documents, they were brought together and united at a higher level in the totality of Christendom.

Actually, 'religion' and 'politics' had to be constructed as distinct domains in the very process of separation. So 'separation' does not describe the historical reality, but only pretends to; the word implies that religion and politics have always been with us, but that we moderns are the first to understand this clearly, and what needs to be done with them. They need to be separated in language and thought because they are already separated in reality, but our ancestors did not understand that. They had not progressed as far as we have. They were still caught up in historical struggle, whereas we have finally emerged out of the jungle of confusion and can see the entire landscape. There is still a bit of thicket clearing to be done here and there, a few aimlessly wandering tribes who don't know how to organise themselves properly, a few lost souls that need Euro-American aid, but fundamentally the historical madness is thinning out. But, instead, I would say that their 'separation' is rhetorical, and as such has been their genesis. In that sense, they are invented categories, not preexisting generic domains that have always existed in all languages.

It could perhaps be argued that church and state never have been completely separated in England, since the monarch is still the official head of both; yet it is also true that there are many ways in which religion and politics today have been defined that make them mutually exclusive and inhabiting distinct domains. If anybody were to say that "politics is her religion," it would probably be taken metaphorically or ironically, because everyone knows that politics and religion don't mix. It is because they have been separated ideologically that the points at which they seem to get entangled can cause such commentary in the media and in the courts.

There is no doubt that church and state were merged in the figure of the sixteenth-century monarch, which is why I have tried consistently to use the term 'church-state'. We can arrive at a sense of awe at the exercise of kingly power when we consider the statement put out by the cowed abbot and monks of Peterborough Monastery soon before the Dissolution in 1534. It is a remarkable statement, no doubt under pressure and threat, and it clarifies the absolute degree to which the king's power is acknowledged above everyone's, including the bishop of Rome and the archbishops of Canterbury and York:

> [E]veryone of us, in his prayers and supplications to be made according to custom, will commend to God, and to the people in their prayers, first of all the King as Supreme Head of the Church of England, then Queen Anne and her off-spring, and then lastly the Archbishops of Canterbury and York, with the other orders of the clergy as shall seem fit. (Williams, 1967:777–78)

Thomas Cromwell's First Injunctions of 1536 (Williams, 1967:805–8), in which there is no mention of the word 'religion', make the same point as the abbot and monks had. Cromwell demands the obedience of those "having cure of souls" for

> the abolishing and extirpation of the Bishop of Rome's pretensed and usurped power and jurisdiction within this realm, and for the establishment and confirmation of the king's authority and jurisdiction within the same . . . the King's power is within his dominion the highest power and potentate under God, to whom all men within the same dominion by God's commandments owe most loyalty and obedience, afore and above all other powers and potentates on earth. (1967:805–6)

The relation between the authority of the church and the authority of the state has been reformulated into an identification of "the Christian religion and duty" with the power of the national state embodied in the king. It is to the king's "laws and decrees" that they swear absolute submission, not to the bishop of Rome.

In this sense, Williams is misleading when he says, "The most significant change comes about in 1534 when parliament decides that the king is not only head of *the secular state* but is also the only supreme head on earth of the Church of England" (1967:19; my italics). Nobody can deny that church and state were distinguished in medieval thought in the analogous way that, in law, distinctions were made between ecclesiastical and civil courts, clergy and laity, and lords spiritual and lords temporal. However, neither the civil courts nor the lords temporal were 'nonreligious' or neutral towards religion in the modern sense. The state could not have been secular in the modern sense, which is arguably defined by its essential *exclusion* of religion. Whatever we may think about the secular, which is a complex term with many components, its bottom line is that it is nonreligious. How else could we claim to have a science of religions? Today, we are aware of their problematic relationship, a relationship that implies their separation as distinct domains. This is the reason that, for example, there is such protest when Anglican bishops are deemed to have ventured into politics; or when Muslim imams, who are thought of as 'religious' figures in English-speaking Western countries (though probably not in Arabic ones), are accused of orchestrating 'political' opposition to Anglo-American attempts to impose 'democratic freedom' on Arab states. But in sixteenth- and seventeenth-century England, bishops were lords spiritual and participated in the government of the commonweal, which was the realisation of God's order on earth. The pope was a prince and the king of England was Christ's vicar and head of the English church. To attempt to distinguish between sixteenth-century church and state in the categories of today violates the structure of language and meaning and threatens to confuse rather than clarify.

It is unsurprising that, in his general introduction, many of the editor's own references to 'religion' and 'religious' come in section VII, general intro-duction, "The Church" (Williams, 1967:35ff.). Here are some examples:

religious experience (35)
the religious situation on the eve of the Reformation (37)
the religious causes at issue (37)
the religious innovations (37)
religious changes (37)
problems of religious history in the early sixteenth century (38)
the statutes dealing with religion (38)

What do 'religion' and 'religious' mean in these examples? I infer that Wil-liams is using the terms in a more general sense of the Reformation as a widespread movement of theological, liturgical, pastoral, and administrative reform. But his usages do not reflect the usages or the understanding of the time. They reflect our idea that 'religion' is a special kind of generic thing defined by a special kind of psychological 'experience' more reminiscent of William James; or that 'religions' are ubiquitous things in the plural; or that 'religious' attributes are distinguishable from 'political' attributes. But in the sixteenth century and for long after, the "situation," "causes," "innovations," "changes," and "problems" that the editor qualifies as "religious" were not meaningfully so, for the predominant meaning of 'religious' was not a special psychology but an institutionalised status. Of course, if politics only means 'power' and 'getting things done', then one might say that these events were political. They were certainly to do with *policy*. Luther's goal was also to destroy the power of the pope who was also a prince, and one effect of this was to change the power and state administration of German principalities. But it introduces a misleading issue when we evoke a question about whether Luther's (or the pope's) aims were religious *or* political.

Williams rightly points out that the driving force, or at least one of the driving forces, for Henry was concern about the succession and the need for an heir. This was referred to as the "king's private matter," which included both the problem of succession and the validity of his marriage to Catherine of Aragon. As such, it was a matter of both church and state simultaneously. Could this be one of the English Reformation's "religious causes at issue"? Or was this a 'political' matter?

In his introduction to the documents in part V, "Religion," and referring especially to those in section B, which are selected for their concern with the king's matter, Williams comments that, *if* they seem at first sight "more relevant to the political history of the period than they do to the history of the Church, a closer study of their contents will soon modify such an impression" (1967:633). Presumably, Williams is saying that, if we closely study these documents, we will realise either that they are religious *and* political, or that they are *even more* religious than we might have suspected! Yet the editor also claims that "the breach with Rome was far less concerned with problems of religion than it was with questions of law and politics" (1967:44). This claim does not sit well with the previously quoted view. But I can't help thinking that it is a mistake to keep insisting on the distinction in these matters, even when the distinction is first set up and then found wanting. Yes, this is about both religion and politics, but fused together into a different totalizing discourse and therefore neither.

We know that Henry was not a supporter of Luther, and detested his theological and liturgical proposals. Henry wished to remain a Catholic in terms of liturgy and doctrine, except insofar as he would be forced to change these elements to bring about the necessary reforms to break the authority of the pope. Williams comments, "[H]is religious beliefs remained in essentials what they had been before political necessity forced him to reject the primacy of the Pope" (1967:57).

There are a number of problems with this. For one thing, it is difficult to understand how a belief in Christendom could have remained essentially the same without allegiance to the pope. Surely, a rejection of the pope's authority changes everything. And which are the 'religious', as distinct from the 'political', elements of this? And why would Williams use 'political' when, talking about people who were "indifferent to the religious causes at issue," he refers to "[t]heir indifference to religious changes coupled with the prevailing political idea that the duty of the subject to the Prince should be one of unquestioning obedience" (37). Is it the intended implication that obedience was political duty but not religious duty? It is difficult to derive any clear sense from this as to how the distinction actually works, if at all. Another historian, Kinney, comments that "obedience is always a holy act" (Kinney, 1975:47). Obedience of a servant to a master, of a wife to a husband, of a pupil to a teacher, of a subject to a prince, of lower degree to higher degree, were analogous to the obedience of a Christian to God. The whole social order was wrapped in divinity and teleologically determined by God's scheme of redemption.

Christian marriage, whether of princes or subjects, can be classified as 'religious' in modern terms because it is a rite of passage, takes place in a church, is blessed by a priest, and is a solemn oath taken before God. Yet, in the royal house, "the giving and taking in marriage was a powerful instrument of policy" (Williams, 1967:40). Henry VIII's father, Henry VII, had, on the death of his eldest son, Rupert, planned to marry his own daughter-in-law to stop the return of her dowry to Spain. Was this religion or politics? Henry VIII's own marriage to Catherine of Aragon "was a marriage for reasons of state if ever there was one": "It would have been quite in keeping with these ideas if Henry looked upon it as part of his royal prerogative to set aside a childless marriage in order to assure the future of the dynasty" (1967:40).

Religion or politics? Henry had to challenge canon law and the pope's interpretation of it. He also had to formulate a theological argument which tacitly challenged the pope's power to give the dispensation to marry Catherine of Aragon, the widow of his deceased brother. It seems obvious that we are not here dealing with a struggle between politicians and bishops, occupying separate domains of politics and religion. In today's terminology, the church was a political institution and Parliament was full of priests.

Then, was Thomas More's opposition to the king, or the widespread opposition to the English Bible, political or religious? The editor says that William Tyndale foretold "how great an influence it would have in the spreading of ideas critical of the contemporary church" (Williams, 1967:46). Among the reactions to its publication were public burnings and excommunications. Is such a response religious or political? More useful descriptive and analytical categories are badly needed to untangle this circular and confusing discourse.

It seems a kind of irony that, when we read the historical documents that have been selected by Williams to illustrate 'religion', we rarely actually find either of the words 'religion' or 'politics'. And this is equally true about the selection of documents placed in the section on commonweal, which Williams thinks is partly about "social structure." That is not say that they do not appear, but that their usage is both scarcer and clearer than our own. When Religion is mentioned in its noun form, it refers usually in an uncomplicated way to revealed Christian Truth, for example, the return to such Truth through the reformation of the church. Thus Archbishop Cranmer, writing to Wolfgang Capito, refers to "the reformation of religion and the clergy" (1967:794). But this does not mean that religion was the business of the clergy and that politics was the business of politicians. There is surely a different nuance in such statements. After all, presumably, the reform to which he was referring was a reform either of the religious or the secular clergy, or perhaps of both.

'The religious' usually refers to the status of the monastics, and 'politic' tends to appear in the expression 'the politic body' which, as we have seen in the introduction to the commonweal, is not 'politics' in the modern sense of a distinct domain, secular or nonreligious, but in the sense of policy formed wisely for human salvation, godly living, and the solution of conflicts, especially between governments. Such policy was not formulated without reference to what we refer to as religious beliefs, because everything thought and done ought to be in the service of God. In the Ten Articles of 1536, which Williams says is one of the essential documents "in which declarations of faith were put forward" during Henry VIII's reign, honest policy means "decent and seemly order" in church and commonwealth, as in the following, where the document concerns

> certain articles necessary to our salvation, as also touching certain
> other honest and commendable ceremonies, rites, and usages now of
> long time used and accustomed in our churches, for conservation of
> an honest policy and decent and seemly order. (Williams, 1967:795)

The uses of 'religiously' (adverb) and 'politic' (adjective) are not mutually exclusive in the way that our modern idea of a domain of politics is constructed on the exclusion of a domain of religion, the domain of religion in turn being constructed by the exclusion of politics.

The Ten Articles concern some essential observances, which have been commanded expressly by God, and other time-honoured customs, which are approved but not essential to salvation and must be interpreted in a correct Protestant way. The essential observances comprise "The Creeds," "The Sacrament of Baptism," "The Sacrament of Penance," "The Sacrament of the Altar" (referring to the Eucharist), and "Justification." Inessential but time-honoured customs are discussed under the headings "And First Images" (about idolatry), "Of Honouring Saints," "Of Praying to Saints," "Of Rites and Ceremonies," and "Of Purgatory." In none of these articles is there any mention of 'religion'. The word simply doesn't appear. Nor does the word 'politics'. But one could say that rites and ceremonies were a matter of policy.

The first article concerning faith gives us a good idea what religion meant to the writer, even though the word does not appear. People who deny the "infallible word of God" in the three creeds (the apostles' Common Creed, the Nicaean, and the Athanasian) "cannot be the very members of Christ and his espouse the Church, but be very infidels and heretics, and members of the Devil" (Williams, 1967:796). The opposite of religion is not the secular or politics or the state, but infidelity and heresy, superstition and idolatry.

The word 'spiritual' is contained in an expression that is ritually repeated in slightly varied ways at the start of each article, along the lines that "the people are committed to the spiritual charge of the Bishops." This is a common usage for 'spiritual'. Another usage found in the section on penance is "I chastise and subdue my carnal body, and the affections of the same, and make them obedient unto the *spirit*" (Williams, 1967:800; my italics). A third example is found in "Justification," where the writer is talking about "good works ... not only outward and civil works, but also the inward *spiritual* motions and graces of the Holy Ghost" (801; my italics). A fourth example is in the article "Of Rites and Ceremonies": "to put us in remembrance of those *spiritual* things that they do signify" (804; my italics).

There are two uses of 'religiously': in the article concerning faith in the statement "they [the people] ought and must most reverently and religiously observe" (Williams, 1967:797); and in the article concerning the Eucharist, where it says, "every man ought ... religiously to try and search his own conscience before he shall receive the same" (801). It seems to me that this usage could be closest to the Latin *religio*, that when something is done *religiously* it is done with seriousness, solemnity, care, attention, reverence (as J. Z. Smith has also pointed out). In these cases, it is observing the sacraments and one's own conscience that should be done religiously.

In Cromwell's First Injunctions of 1536 (Williams, 1967:805–8), there is no mention of religion. He is concerned with the power and majesty of the king, which is expressed in such terms as "sovereign lord and king," or "the authority of the king's majesty." Like the Ten Articles, on which Cromwell comments in his Injunctions, he is putting forward a Protestant document. For example, he refers to the Ten Articles and the injunction to perform rites and pilgrimages as remembrances but not superstitions (e.g., not believing that they are magically efficacious). If "certain laudable ceremonies, rites and usages" are performed without superstition, then they are "meet and convenient to be kept and used for a decent and politic order" (1967:806). It seems clear that the idea of a 'politic order' is not the same as a modern 'political order'.

Even if we were able to reserve 'religion' for matters strictly of liturgy, doctrine, and church administration, we would still be confused by the editor's use of language, for he says that doctrinal problems and questions of church discipline became matters for "legislation by parliament. Between 1530 and

1547 they were political issues" (Williams, 1967:57). It was mainly bishops in Parliament and in convocation who took responsibility for them. Thus, at the time that the bishops were doing the parliamentary and legal work, Thomas Cromwell was made the king's vicar general in spiritual matters in 1535. The lack of fit between our categories and theirs, which at one level has been acknowledged by Williams, does not inhibit him from a largely uncontrolled usage and a consequent deterioration of meaning:

> the main interest in English religion and politics is concerned with
>   questions of faith and doctrine (60)
> the religious changes under Edward VI (60)
> Somerset's religious outlook (61)
> Northumberland's religious ideas and his policy (61)
> Henry's religious policy (61)
> the whole of the religious history of England since 1529 (63)

We can only guess at what he means.

Part III: Commonweal. Section A: The Structure of Society

If Williams's section on the commonweal was based on its approximation to modern society and politics, and its definitive distinction from religion, we would expect to find a different domain of discourse. Of course, there is a sense in which discourses on the commonwealth have their own characteristic concerns, but this is not because they are about a different topic but because they are looking at Christian Truth from a slightly different perspective. One can hardly find the kind of ideological separation of the modern religion-politics dichotomy. Williams, a social historian, might be an anthropologist when he observes:

> Thus while society in the early Tudor period must be presented as a
> complex of relationships inherited from the middle ages and there-
> fore, to a large degree, stereo-typed by custom and tradition, it must
> not be forgotten that this pattern was being subjected to the modi-
> fying influence of change, in part the result of late medieval factors,
> in part the direct product of the political, religious and economic
> transformations which were the distinctive features of early 6th
> century conditions. (1967:223)

On the face of it, Williams's point might seem straightforward, but it isn't because none of the terminology in today's usage is the same. The term "economic transformations" may seem intuitively meaningful to us today and there is a widespread assumption that 'economics' is simply a universal fact of human life. But this, I suggest, is to make the same mistake as the one about 'class', about which Williams himself warned his readers. Something similar can be said about his use of "political"; if it means 'politic' then it can refer to any practice; if it means 'pertaining to the political domain' then there was no concept of a political domain separated from a religious or an economic one. On the other hand, reverting to my argument in chapter 3, it might be possible to argue that there were practices that were relatively profane. One could set up a range of practices under a category like 'exchange'. At one end, the king knighting a loyal subject would be a symbolic act whereby a kind of sacrality was conferred on someone in exchange for services. At the other end were largely profane monetary exchanges. These latter were not amoral or natural in the way that modern ideology would have us believe; such exchanges still had implications deriving from Christian morality, such as the restrictions on usury. But this would be a different kind of claim which would still need to be distinguished from the modern religion-secular distinction.

On the meaning of 'religious' dominant at the time, "religious ... trans-transformations" might have referred to transformations of religious houses, but it is not clear that Williams wants to say that. If he wants to refer to the transformation of the Roman Catholic into the Anglican church-state, then it seems apparent that in modern meanings it is neither religious nor political.

Williams says that land was of supreme importance "as a source not only of wealth, but also, what was more important in such a society, of power" (1967:224). If politics is equated with power and its transformations, and given that the religious houses were huge land owners, then in that sense they were also political, the controllers of land-based power. With the dissolution of the religious houses came the concentration of land and power in the state and the king, but also the emergence of a conception of Christian Religion defined by a doctrine of the sacraments that placed the king by analogy with God on earth and with the head of the national church. And if economics is here equivalent to 'wealth', then the major source of 'economic' transformation is the changing status of land.

The term 'commonweal' seems to define the confluence of everything we separate out as religion, on the one hand, and political economy, on the other. The editor refers to the idea of the commonweal as the early Tudor "anthropomorphic theory of society" (Williams, 1967:26). This discourse was a detailed analogy of society to the human body, with individuals being by analogy parts of the body, identified by their natures, qualities, and functions. Teleologically constituted, this idealised body was ultimately united and harmonious, provided each member fulfilled his or her own duties and functions regularly and correctly. Tyndale and most early Reformers accepted this metaphor. It was frequently referred to as 'the politic body' and, like other uses of 'politic' as an adjective implies fitting, well ordered, and God-given—though it can also have more negative connotations, in the sense of crafty or cunning. Divine purpose was realised through submission to one's status and duties in the creation of a harmonious whole. The word 'politic' here is a long way from contemporary usages and needs to be kept separate. For 'politics' as a contemporary noun implies a domain separated off from another domain named 'religion'. But this cannot make much sense when referring to an idea of a body of men (women and children had a problematic status in this body) made by and for Christ, in which bishops are in the government and the king is head of the church.

Duties which devolved on one as a result of one's place in the great body were referred to as one's 'vocation'. A vocation was not a freely chosen career but God-ordained work of a kind suitable for one's station in life. A change of status was possible, however, for individuals with a special vocation and with the help and recognition of a high-ranking patron. There was a new section of aristocracy resented by the older nobility, and also a new middling order of bankers, merchants, industrialists—the rich men of the towns (Williams, 1967:32). The latter usually bought land and adopted the traditional lifestyle of the landed gentry, for they desired status in the dominant terms of the times; yet they may also have taken new business skills into landed estates and contributed to the gradual transition to capitalist forms of labour, organisation, and investment (1967:32). Williams points out:

> Rural England was experiencing the beginnings of a breakdown of
> personal relationship of lord and man which had been the main
> feature of medieval organization; it was now being replaced by the
> less intimate relationship of landlord and tenant farmer, and farmer
> and hired labourer. (1967:27)

On the other hand, there was not much mobility for the vast number of people, and not enough to challenge the overall order of people and things. Anthropologists have shown how rituals, individual and collective, can construct symbolic universes, including the social order, and presumably medieval and early modern society were full of prescriptions on the demarcation of status, such as dress, carriage, use of language, to whom one could speak, where one could enter, precedence, wealth, and so on. Sumptuary laws covered many such matters, and heralds were "the arbiters of established titles of dignity" (Williams, 1967:28).

It is notable that the documents in this section never themselves refer to 'society' or 'economics', nor do they refer to 'religion'. Instead, in the space reserved by the twentieth-century historian as "the structure of society," the actual texts selected by Williams reveal a typical concern with (in the words typical of the age employed by the sixteenth-century authors, either quoted or glossed):

> wearing costly apparel
> the reversal of attainders

authority and power by his [the king's] letters patent

forfeiture of estates

a grant of arms

heraldic visitation and the bearing of arms in relation to noble estates

creation of peers

the estates and orders of their empire [this refers to monarchs and kings]

civil administration

nobility of estates and orders

family wills and origins

forfeiture of goods and chattels

my father was a yeoman [Latimer's first sermon preached before King
Edward VI]

lease of the site of the late monastery

manumissions of bondmen and villains

stealing of wards to marry the children to

ungodly marrying

punishment of such as shall take away maidens that be inheritors

lands, tenements, and hereditaments or other great substances in goods
and chattels moveable

buying and selling of maidens for advantageous marriage

One item selected by the editor for this group, *The Fortress of the Faithful* by
T. Becon (Williams, 1967:268–71), is a satire concerning who is a true gentleman. The interest of this passage is that it defends the ideal of the commonweal on analogy with a body, an organic whole, functioning according to
virtues practised by gentlemen and nobility in which the highest value is the
common good:

> Without the true gentlemen the commonweal can no more safely be
> than the body without eyes. For as the eyes are the principal comfort
> of an whole body, so likewise are the true gentlemen of the com-
> monweal.... For their principal respect is not unto their own private
> lucre and singular commodity but their whole study is how they may
> profit the commonweal and do goods to many. (Williams, 1967:268)

This virtuous order is being undermined by unscrupulous "unnoble nobility"
and those who glory in the title of gentleman

> who think all nobility to consist in the abundance of worldly goods, in
> wearing of gold chains and costly apparel, in having fair houses and
> pleasant gardens ... they poll, they pill, they wake, they rake, they
> sweat, they fret, they gripe, they nip, they face, they brase, they
> semble, they dissemble. (268)

They are the "very caterpillars of the commonweal."

In this satirical reflection on the rise of a false nobility, which in modern parlance we might refer to as nouveau riche, or socially upwardly mobile, there is no sense of an economic sphere in the sense of a value-neutral, or even value-positive, enterprise culture, or the formation of a middle class. The dominant ideal which is being defended is the idea of a realm, a commonweal, analogous to an organic, hierarchical body in which men of different estates, degrees, and ranks, by living according to those virtues suitable to their stations, maintain and increase the realm, a true, God-given order that can be undermined by selfish pseudogentlemen who do not understand the realm of ends.

In this article, there are repeated references to "the commonweal," "the realm," "worldly goods," "nobility," "the renown, worship and honour of true gentlemen," "the common people," "virtue," "godly gifts of the mind" (such as justice, mercy, liberality, kindness, gentleness, hospitality for the poor), "multitude of riches," "the realm of England," "the commons" (meaning also "the people"), "the rich men of this world," "the king's majesty and his most honourable council," "the rich worldlings," and "despisers of God's holy ordinance." This is what a twentieth-century historian labels "the structure of society." The terms that most closely approximate to society are commonweal and realm; but we can also see that whereas 'society' is an abstract generic concept, these terms are more specific and particular, for they define not any society but this society with its specific conception of hierarchy, duty, and so on. And at this time, as Bossy has shown, when the term 'society' was used at all, it referred either to small organisations called societies, or more usually to more personal concrete sets of relationships, and had not yet become a generic abstraction—though it was soon to do so, or at least to appear to do so, as the work of Samuel Purchas discussed in chapter 7 suggests. Potential ambiguities in the dominant discourse of the times were to work loose like a rhetorical knot that begins to lose its grip in the context of the seventeenth century, especially the development of the North American colonial scene, but also in the context of colonial expansion and ambition more widely.

The editor's short discussion of *A Supplication of the Poore Commons, 1546* (Williams, 1967:276–92) continues to employ a distinction between the religious and the social, as in "there can be detected some traces of the disappointment with the actual results of [the] social and religious changes of Henry VIII's reign" (Williams, 1967:276; it was the final year of Henry's life). He adds the interesting comment, "In the new order the monk has gone, but his place has been taken by the sturdy extortioner and the possessors." If this essay constitutes a theory of the commonweal, which in turn is part of (or identical with?) the structure of society, then we should note that the God of the Bible, and the king as head of church and state, are the basic referents of this theory in the construction of the organic analogy. References to Religion as such are, as usual, very scarce. The text itself contains only one reference to "the Christian religion," and there are two references to the "superstitious religious," referring specifically to the monks, nuns, friars, canons, and hermits. But there are no references to the secular, to society, to politics, or to economics.

The idea of the commonweal valorises what we might call hierarchy in the Dumontian explication of that term, but in terms of estate, degree, and vocation. It is a supplication to the king concerning "this your majesty's realm," and the "miserable poverty" and the "wretched estate" of the king's subjects, the cause of the poverty being "the great and infinite number of valiant and sturdy beggars which had, by their subtle and crafty demeanour in begging, gotten into their hands more than the third part of the yearly revenues and possessions of this your highness' realm" (Williams, 1967:276). These sturdy beggars, the "monks, friars, canons, hermits and nuns" are "the superstitious religious"; he laments that even some "secular men" voted in Parliament for this law. Note that both 'the religious' and 'the secular' sit in Parliament with the right to vote. Parliament is not a 'secular' institution as distinct from the church as a 'religious' institution.

The king is addressed as "merciful father over this your natural country," and the writer and his like as "your loving and obedient subjects." Later he says, "Let us be unto your highness as the inferior members of the body to their head" (Williams, 1967:286). There is a deep sense of grievance, of having been cheated, by the thought that people, deluded by the holiness of 'the religious', might walk a hundred miles barefoot to offer them alms. But this problem has now been righted by the king.

The writer makes references to Pharisees, Jews, Ephesians, Saint Paul, Saint Mark, Saint Peter, and scripture generally to justify the belief that the king governs by the power and legitimacy of God, which in turn justifies obedience to the king (which is therefore virtually the same as obedience to God), and that it is a "devilish enterprise ... to rebel against your highness, our most natural sovereign and liege lord" (Williams, 1967:276).

This is a Protestant tract, expressing hatred of "our forefathers' popish traditions," and inveighs against "Pope, pardons, lighting of candles to images, knocking and kneeling to them, with running hither and thither on pilgrimage," along with "purgatory horseleeches" and "beastly buggery" (Williams, 1967:276). Remember that these documents have been editorially selected for a section not on Religion but on "the structure of society." The writer, Cooper, is defending the translation of the Bible into English against the claims of the remaining apologists for their own control of scripture and its interpretation. He contrasts the Reformation started by "our natural Prince" (277), the king, with their desire "for the maintenance of their popish traditions and purgatory patrimony." These Catholics, the remnants of 'the religious', who are equivalent to sturdy beggars—have managed to get a law passed which would deprive people who spend less than £10 per year of the right to have an English Bible in their house. By analogy, he argues, with the word of God as the food of the soul, servants in the king's household would not be allowed food unless they were "clothed in velvet with chains of gold about their necks" (278).

God is "our most merciful Father," but so is Henry, and it is sometimes difficult to disentangle in this prose God from the king. I am not saying that at the level of official theology there is no distinction. It is carefully maintained. But in the popular imagination and in much usages of language, there appears to be a fusion. There is no doubt that the king is in some significant sense considered to be sacred.

Having been offered the scriptures in English, and the decree that an English Bible should be placed in every parish church to be freely and equally available to all "of what degree soever he were"—"degree" being the operative concept rather than class—the writer complains that this offer has been resisted: "there is no small number of churches that hath no Bible at all" (Williams, 1967:279). In other churches, where there is one, this "wicked generation" of priests "would pluck it either into quire or else into some pew where poor men durst not presume to come." Here we get an indication of how salvation through the church has only ambivalently been an egalitarian soteriology, despite the claims of official theology that all are equal in the eyes of God, but is qualified by rank and wealth. The seating arrangements in the church symbolise this.

In the following quote, the writer is not himself confusing what is owed to God and what is owed to the king, but the modern reader might be forgiven for losing track of the distinction sometimes:

> If we have therefore rejected this merciful proffer [of free access to the English Bible] of our most merciful Father when he used your highness as his instrument to publish and set forth his most living Word, wherein he declared the inestimable love that he bears towards us, in that he gave his only Son to be an acceptable sacrifice for our sins; and the unspeakable mercy which caused him to accept us as just, even for his Son's sake, without our works or deservings; let us now humbly fall down prostrate before his majesty with perfect repentance of this, the contempt of his merciful gift; most humbly beseeching him of his infinite goodness tenderly to behold the dolours of our hearts for that we neglect so merciful a proffer; and to forget our obstinacy therein, giving your highness such desire of our salvation that you will as favourably restore unto us the scripture in our English tongue as you did at the first translation hereof set it abroad. (Williams, 1967:279)

While reading this, I found it difficult to decide before whom "we" are prostrating and to whose infinite goodness we are supplicating. This passage refers throughout to God, "our most merciful Father," generally until the switch to "your highness." But earlier, the author had referred to the king as "a merciful father of this your natural country," and there is a clear analogy between the Father and the father, between "the Lord Jesu" (Williams, 1967:279) and "our gracious Prince," here referring to the king rather than to Jesus the Prince of Peace. Furthermore, just as God gave his "command-ments," so also "his highness" gives his commandments (279).

But this is not all of it, for there is an egalitarian thread of salvation after all. Cooper politely points out that even the "most dear sovereign . . . shall stand before the judgement seat of God" (Williams, 1967:284). This ambiguity be-tween hierarchy and equality runs through Christian thought, and may itself be a significant source of later social theorising. But the possibility of confu-sion, if not between God and the king, then between God's laws and the king's laws, comes out in this extract:

> [T]hey say your highness's laws are God's laws, and we are as much bound to observe them as the law of God given by Moses. Truth it is, most dear Lord, that we are bound by the commandment of God to obey your highness and all your laws set forth by your High Court of Parliament. (Williams, 1967:287)

Clearly, government by king and Parliament is encompassed by the commandment and thus legitimation of God in these sentences. But is this a theory of 'society'? The subjects of wealth, rents, fines, leases, extortions, usury, benefices, land, food, are not in the slightest separated out into a separate domain called 'economics'. This is not just a semantic point. It is surely about what is valued and given importance. Anthropologists might say that politics and economics are 'embedded' in primitive institutions (and they sometimes say that about religion, though Durkheim it seems to me has created an am-biguous understanding of 'religion'). They might imply that evolution will make explicit what is now only implicit. I do not think this is the best model for understanding this. However difficult it might be to describe or explain the shift from the medieval concept of the world which Southern calls the "church-state," through the early modern configuration of the English state church, through to the modern idea of separate religious and secular domains, we can at least see that the changes are fundamental and amount to a paradigm shift in which new categories emerge in new configurations and replace previous categories and configurations. This is a change of cosmology.

The commonweal as Christian Truth is expressed by William Tyndale in "The Parable of the Wicked Mammon" (reprinted in Williams, 1967:292–94.) Williams gives his own title for this piece as "Thoughts on Social Responsi-bilities from the Works of William Tyndale," which seems suitably anaemic when compared with Tyndale's own language. That there was no separation of religion and society or politics in Tyndale's mind can be seen straightaway in the first sentence: "As pertaining to good works, understand that all works are good that are done within the law of God, in faith, and with thanksgiving to God" (Williams, 1967:292).

Again, there is no mention of 'religion', 'politics', 'economics', or any of the other words so commonly used in the modern humanities. There are uses of "spirit" here which are different from the usual references to lords spiritual and temporal and deriving from the third person of the Trinity, the Holy Ghost or Spirit. The world which Tyndale sees is, like the previous vision of Cooper, analogous to an organic body with hierarchically arranged functions. He is concerned with an understanding of good works defined by subservience to the status quo, or relative degrees, high or low:

> God looketh first on thy heart...he looketh with what heart thou workest, and not what thou workest; how thou acceptest the degree that he hath put the[e] in, and not of what degree thou art, whether thou be an apostle or a shoemaker.... Now that thou ministerest in the kitchen, and art but a kitchen page, receivest all things of the hand of God; knowest that God hath put the[e] in that office; sub- mittest thyself to his will; and servest thy master not as a man, but as Christ himself, with a pure heart. (Williams, 1967:293)

Masters also have duties to their servants: "nurture them as thy own sons with the Lord's nurture, that they may see in Christ a cause why they ought lovingly to obey" (294).

There is equality as well as hierarchy, but equality is not in this world but in the next, in the sight of God: "as great in his sight is a servant as a master" (Williams, 1967:294). One might argue that the millenarian movements and much of the agitation in seventeenth-century England were attempts to resolve this tension between a commonweal based on degree and estate and an egal- itarian soteriology. This tension can still be found in late eighteenth-century Methodism (Thompson, 1963).[1] It is surely arguable that salvation is as much a collective concern as an individual one.

The analogy of the relationship between fathers and sons to masters and servants is also applied to that between landlords and tenants. But all men are sons of God the Father. By use of analogical relationships or fictive kinship, the whole commonweal is bound to God, who is the highest degree as well as the *summum bonum*. We couldn't get a clearer idea of the fusion of religion and society at this level of ideology, and no mention of either. There is no clear reason that this document should be here rather than in the part about "Religion."

The body analogy comes out clearly here:

> Let kings and head officers...punish sin, and that with mercy, even with the same sorrow and grief of mind as they would cut off a finger

or a joint, leg or an arm, of their own body, if there were such disease
in them, that either they must be cut off, or else all the body must
perish. (Williams, 1967:293)

A little later, Tyndale writes, "remember that we are all members of one body"
(293).

The analogy of the body is not with society but with the commonweal. And
it demonstrates the subordination of every function, profession, trade, and
occupation to the overriding value of the totality, the end of the commonweal
being Christ himself:

Let every man of whatsoever craft or occupation he be of, whether
brewer, baker, tailor, victualler, merchant, or husbandman, refer his
craft and occupation unto the commonwealth, and serve his brethren
as he would do Christ himself. (Williams, 1967:293)

What we have separated out and valorised as 'economics' is here a subordinate
aspect of the commonweal. Referring to the various crafts and occupations:
"Let him buy and sell truly.... And let your superfluities succour the poor, of
which sort shall ever be some in all towns, and cities, and villages" (293).

Tyndale's theory is a form of preaching or exhortation to his fellow English
Christians to act in accordance with the ideal of the commonweal. Presumably,
there is an anxiety that the ideal is being undermined, perhaps by the emergence of a new group of land owners and 'gentlemen' who are too interested in
profit. Perhaps there is a rise in the rates of usury. For one reason or another,
there is a belief that it is in a state of decay.

The Nature of the Commonweal: Starkey's "Dialogue between Pole and Lupset"

The editor, C. H. Williams, tells us that this was written before 1539, though
not printed until 1871. He refers to it as "the functional theory of society." The
commonweal is here usually referred to as the "politic body." There is also an
analogy between the relationship of soul to body, on the one hand, and "civil
order" and "politic law" to the "politic body," on the other hand. The "civil
order" and "politic law," administered by rulers and officers, is analogous to
the soul of the individual man. As the soul keeps the body in good functioning
order, so civil order and politic law properly administered keep the politic body
properly functioning.

Starkey's thought seems closer to theory. Rather than being just a homily
based on a popular metaphor, as Tyndale's largely seems, there is a greater
degree of objectification, or reification perhaps, in Starkey. Pole develops the
body analogy very explicitly and in the process "this politic body" does seem to

become reified in language, rather than merely being a metaphor. There is ambiguity here.

"Politic" here seems clearly to have the nuance of well ordered, appropriate, wise, orderly, and proper. It seems similar to what anthropologists have sometimes called "'ritual order,'" or what the anthropologist Maurice Bloch calls a "total ritual system" (Bloch, 1992:2); or perhaps 'customary practices' might correspond as well, except that there is the sense of a rhetorically constructed holistic system of representations bringing things together, rather than simply a relatively unconnected series of discrete customs and practices.

Throughout Starkey's "Dialogue," we find expressions in the mouths of Pole and Lupset such as "all civility and politic rule" (301), "politic state" (297), and "commonalty" (297). Pole talks about "the true commonweal" (296). When Pole talks about "civil order" and "politic law," I take it that "order" and "law" are nouns and "civil" and "politic" are adjectives. 'Civil' does not seem easily distinguishable from 'politic' in the sense of the health, peace, happiness, and well-being of the people. Both civil and politic have that sense of being well adjusted, appropriate, and in conformity with traditional practice. They refer to what I have called the disciplines of civility. There is also the expression "the order of nature" (297) within which the analogy with the body anchors the politic state. Talking of this politic body:

> [T]his body hath his parts, which resemble also the body of man, of which the most general to our purpose be these: the heart, head, hands and feet. The heart thereof is the king, prince, ruler of the state ... whethersoever it be one of or many, according to the governance of the commonalty and politic state. For some be governed by a prince alone, some by a council of certain wise men, and some by the whole people together ... like as all wit, reason and sense, feeling, life, and all other natural power, springeth out of the heart, so from the princes and rulers of the state cometh all laws, order and policy, all justice, virtue and honesty, to the rest of this politic body. (Starkey, quoted in Williams, 1967:297)

It is worth pausing here to reflect that there is a greater sense of relativity, comparison, and objectification than in the extracts from Tyndale. Different forms of government are compared. This suggests something closer to comparative political theory as we might understand it. Both Starkey and Pole lived and studied in Padua, were well read in classical and contemporary political theory, and were advisors to Henry VIII and Thomas Cromwell (see Zeeveld, 1948:111–27). On the other hand, you cannot claim that, because Starkey was a Renaissance humanist and intellectual who had studied in Padua, that therefore this concept was merely an abstraction peculiar to an intellectual class of theorists—for the model permeated the sixteenth-century thinking of the ruling elites. Also, it is difficult to see, given the analogy of the body and the function of the head, how the whole people together could rule. If he had in mind some kind of democracy, the metaphor of the body would collapse because the point of the metaphor is not equality but inequality and functional hierarchy. Theologically, it could be held that equality only exists after death when the soul stands before God to be judged.

"To the head, with the eyes, ears, and other senses therein, resembled may be right well the under officers by princes appointed, forasmuch as they should ever observe and diligently wait for the weal of the rest of this body" (Williams, 1967:297). Here, the analogy evokes the 'weal' of the body, meaning its well-being, with the head subordinate to the heart. The hands and feet are also necessary to the politic functioning of the body: "To the hands are resembled both craftsmen and warriors . . . to the feet, the ploughmen and tillers"; "the strength of these parts altogether is of necessity required, without the which the health of the whole cannot long be maintained" (297).

The metaphor of bodily well-being implies the possibility of disease, and the metaphor is extended to explain the cause of such disease in the politic, or should one say impolitic, body. Disease can occur when

> the parts of this body agree not together: the head agreeth not to the
> feet, nor feet to the hands; no one part agreeth to other; the tem-
> poralty grudgeth against the spiritualty, the commons against the
> nobles, and subjects against their rulers . . . . The parts of the body be
> not knit together as it were with spirit and life. (Williams, 1967:299)

The distinction here between the "spiritualty" and the "temporalty" is that between the lords spiritual and lords temporal, which we have already encountered as a basic way of classifying the bishops and the other lords, who all sit in Parliament and participate in law making. As already noted, this is not like the modern separation of church and state at all, nor is it the separation of religion and politics. On the contrary, the analogy reproduces the fusion of religion and politics in the politic body or commonweal.[2] Pole says, "this is so manifest it needeth no proof." This may be described by the expert as either "dialectic" or "persuasive" rhetoric, and it can also be suggested that it was persuasive because the analogy would have appeared 'natural' to readers. Presumably, markets and motivations of enlightened self-interest seem as persuasively natural to our own intelligentsia today.

The "offices" of, for example, ploughmen and labourers (who are the feet) or artificers and craftsmen (who are the hands) are also "duties." What we call status is a degree, an office, and a duty. What we would separate out as 'economics' or economic theory is here thought of as a moral issue stemming from the harmonious or inharmonious working of the politic body or commonweal. Scarcity, want, and high prices, he argues, are caused by lack of productivity, itself due to vices such as idleness and gluttony:

[T]hose many and great waste grounds here in our country, the great lack of victual and the scarceness thereof, and dearth of all things worked by man's hand, do not only show the great negligence of the rest of our people, but...doth argue and declare manifest lack of diligence.... If our artificers applied themselves to labour as diligently as they do in other countries [he mentions France, Italy, and Spain] we should not have things...so scarce and so dear. (Starkey, quoted in Williams, 1967:299–300)

Another problem with the commonweal is the growth of privacy and the consequent reduction of public commitment. For example, increasingly, "every man privately in his own house hath his master to instruct his children in letters," which undermines that "common discipline and public exercise" that is necessary for a commonweal. And this instruction should be "not only in virtue and learning, but also in the feats of war" (Starkey in Williams, 1967:301).

Since the closing of the monasteries, it was now necessary according to Pole to open new institutions for such instruction for "the nobility," and such institutions should have some similar qualities to the old monasteries. For just as "the exercise of a monastical life among religious men...hath done much good to the virtuous living of Christian minds," so similarly the new institutions for the nobility; "even life as these monks and religious men there living together exercise a certain monastical discipline and life, so the nobles, being brought up together, should learn there the discipline of the commonweal" (Starkey in Williams, 1967:301). This common training of the nobility in institutions with some similarity to the old monastic institutions would make youthful nobility "true lords and masters" and "the people would be glad to be governed by them" (301). The use of "religious men" refers fairly clearly to the regulars: the monks and friars.

Lupset agrees with this part of Pole's argument, that the health of the commonweal is undermined by those who "highly esteem their own private pleasure and weal" (Starkey, quoted in Williams, 1967:302). It has to be said, though, that Pole seems to be arguing that the wealth of the whole depends on the wealth of individuals, and that if one wants to understand the commonweal it is necessary to "first find out that thing which is the wealth of every particular part" (302). Lupset notes this ambiguity, pointing out that if, as Pole seems to be arguing, the commonweal depends on the particular weal of each person, then this might encourage individuals to think first of their own private well-being, on the assumption that the common weal will follow.

Pole's answer is a fudge—if "everyman" were not "blinded with the love of themselves" but healed themselves, or were healed and corrected "by politic persons," they would grow in their love of the commonweal. The phrase "politic persons" certainly doesn't mean politicians in the modern sense. It could be interpreted to refer to an ideal category of persons who have a sense of, and can advise on and direct, politic behaviour, that is, behaviour that is directed towards the good of all (e.g., the politic body): "like as overmuch regard of particular weal destroyeth the common, so convenient and mean regard thereof maintaineth and setteth forward the same" (Starkey, quoted in Williams, 1967:302).

To what extent would it be legitimate to see the early stirrings of modern individualism in this concern of Pole's? I would guess very little. The problem of selfishness was a moral problem within Christianity which had no necessary link with the modern ideology of individualism. Arguably, it was not until the influence of Calvinism, when the linkage of spiritual and economic salvation had become more strongly established, that it is possible to detect the emergence of a powerful discourse on the individual. Such a discourse presupposes the contingent confluence of a number of other factors, including the wider context of colonialism; the Enlightenment in Scotland, France, and America; and the development of a language of human rights. These in turn required a new concept of the separation of 'religion' from 'politics' or the 'nonreligious' state, which had not yet been formulated.

7

Samuel Purchas,
His Pilgrimage

In early seventeenth-century English, a process of reification and multiplication of 'religion' and 'religions' had begun. It has often been pointed out by historians that the fragmentation of Christendom into different churches and sects gave rise to increasingly frequent use of 'religions,' referring to different sectarian churches and their different interpretations of Christian Truth. This process of reification, it seems, was compounded by the consolidation of princely states as independent and competing nation-states with their own national churches. In the entry under "toleration" in F. L. Cross's *Dictionary of the Christian Church* (1958:1364–65), we find:

> Christianity, which claims to be the only true religion, has always been dogmatically intolerant. Dissent ('heresy') within its own ranks, has been anathematized time and again in the history of the Church. St. Augustine went so far as to demand corporal punishment for heretics and schismatics; and this became the normal procedure in the Middle Ages when, owing to the intimate connection between Church and state, Catholic and citizen were virtually synonymous terms, and the heretic was thus considered a revolutionary endangering the foundations of society. The regular penalty in the Middle Ages was death.

Cross points out that the Reformers themselves, such as Luther and Calvin,

were as intolerant to Dissenters as the Catholic Church, and the
maxim of the Peace of Augsburg (*cuius regio eius religio*), which recognised only one religion, either Catholicism or Lutheranism, in a
state to the exclusion of all others, was virtually the principle adopted
also in England under Elizabeth I. (1958:1365)

The Peace of Augsburg (1555) between Ferdinand I and the Electors recognised
the existence of both Catholicism and Lutheranism (but not Calvinism) in
Germany, providing that in each land subjects should follow the religion of
their ruler. This policy continued as the basis of the ecclesiastical settlement in
the German Empire until the Treaty of Westphalia in 1648.

I do not read *religio* here in the Latin expression *eius religio* to have the
nuance of the modern generic 'religions of the world'. I take the Latin *religio*
here to refer to different interpretations, and therefore practices, of Christian
Truth. As we saw in the Anglican *Formularies of Faith* of Henry VIII and his
bishops, the universal church of Christ was not denied; the point at issue
concerned how that church should be understood and how power should be
legitimated. Religions were Christian confessions or persuasions, and the different conceptions of the church-state expressed those confessions of Christ in
specific but changing contexts of power. Nevertheless, there cannot be much
doubt that this internal fragmentation encouraged the development of the idea
of 'religions' in the plural as discrete reifications. Furthermore, the identification of one confession with one sovereign church-state consolidated the concept of 'nations' which already existed in the sense of 'peoples'. Thus to talk
about someone's *religion* was increasingly to talk about his or her *nation*. The
Catholic church was de facto becoming fragmented into different national
church-states.

To talk about Religion was also to talk about commonweal or commonwealth. In sixteenth- and seventeenth-century discourses, the commonweal
was Religion thought of from the point of view of the 'politic body', the constitutional form of human relations. The idea that Religion was essentially
separate from the politic body, in the form of religion as against a secular
(nonreligious) politics and state, was an idea that was not formulated rhetorically in English until the late seventeenth century. This transition was of fundamental importance to our confused modern ideas about religion. Yet I will
argue in chapter 9 that it was in the North American colonies that a clear
separation between 'religion' as a private nonpolitical right and the 'state' as
the public arena of nonreligious politics first became established as a dominant
discourse, enshrined in various bills of rights and state constitutions.

One factor which may have been the most fundamental driver of change in
conceptions of the church-state was the competition for trade and the processes of colonisation, alongside the development of new ways of classifying
the world and its contents that was such an important part of the Enlight-

enment. The Portuguese, followed by the Spanish, were far ahead of the French or the English in establishing American colonies (Jensen, 1955:3ff.). Since the middle of the fifteenth century, the papacy had been issuing bulls confirming Portuguese possession of their discoveries, and in 1494 the Portuguese and Spanish made a treaty dividing the New World between them. The inflow of gold and silver had the effect of raising prices in Europe, creating problems for the poor and adding impetus to the growth of commercial capitalism. English activity in overseas trade and colonisation was sporadic and began with raids on the ships of larger powers, raids which did not themselves lead to successful colonisation (Jensen, 1955:13). An example of a merchant capitalist was Sir Thomas Smythe; he was a heavy investor in the Muscovy and Levant companies and one of the organisers of the East India Company, which received its charter in 1600. He was also involved in founding the Virginia Company. Merrill Jensen comments that "when English colonies were at last founded, they were not established by courtiers and favourites of the Queen but by merchant capitalists" (Jensen, 1955:15). English colonisation did not really begin until after the peace with Spain in 1604. However, the idea of English colonisation had been promoted since the 1550s: "By 1584, when Hakluyt wrote his *Discourse Concerning Western Planting* . . . most of the basic ideas concerning the purpose and importance of English colonies had been clearly defined" (Jensen, 1955:15).

The effort to colonise Ireland in many ways acted as a model for colonisation of the New World. The typical words used in relation to the New World plantations were first used in the context of Ireland, 'planting', 'plantation', 'colony', and 'native': "the promotion literature of the 17th century had its ancestry in the advertising issued by 16th century speculators in Irish lands" (Jensen, 1955:16).

From 1604, it took only thirty years to plant thirteen permanent English colonies. The initial motives were often commercial. New England industry developed with ship building and thus international commerce, and the growth of the colonies went with the involvement in world trade. This included trade with the West Indies and also the African slave trade. Fishing also became hugely important to the emergence of the New England colonies: "The cod fisheries loomed ever larger in the economy of the seaport towns and the 'Sacred Cod' of Massachusetts in time came to rival the Puritan God as a matter of concern" (Jensen, 1955:21).

But, arguably, Dissent was as important for colonisation. As historian Ethyn Williams Kirby has put it in a paper on the Quakers: "dissent meant more than refusal to worship in the parish church: it severed the sectarian from the body politic. Church and State being one, he who remained without the walls of the former found himself thrust out of the latter" (Kirby, 1935:401). The first poor Dissenters, called Separatists, landed in New England rather than Virginia as intended. They quickly "drew up a church covenant, the

'Mayflower Compact', which served as the basis of the government of the colony until it was absorbed by Massachusetts at the end of the century" (Jensen, 1955:19).

In 1630, the Massachusetts Bay colony was founded. It was ordered according to a Puritan biblical concept which did not recognise a distinction between church and state nor between religion and politics. The Dissenters did not tolerate dissent themselves, and consequently were "constantly tormented by men who came to the colony and dissented from the Puritan vision of the ideal Commonwealth" (Jensen, 1955:20). Given the importance of dissent and trade, it is difficult not to see that there was an intimate connection between constitutional developments in the colonies and those in the metropolis. Given the variety of different kinds of Dissenters, and their different concepts of church and state, it is not so surprising that the different colonies generated a number of different experimental constitutions; nor that in such circumstances, combined with the prosperity of the American colonists from trading, 'religion' increasingly became bracketed out from the practices that promoted material survival. Puritan leaders tried to maintain the idea of a Puritan commonwealth, but gradually during the seventeenth century a wealthy merchant class, many of whom were not members of the church, increased in power, and by 1691 all property owners regardless of their confession had the right to participate in government.

Different colonies developed different ideas about government and different constitutional arrangements. Merrill Jensen says:

> The relationship of Church to State was a basic element in the political conflict of the New England colonies. Rhode Island resolutely offered religious freedom from the start. With equal resolution the colonies of Connecticut and Massachusetts denied it. (Jensen, 1955:21)

The English landed gentry (as distinct from merchants mainly interested in trade) were interested in colonies where they could transplant feudal forms of hierarchy and land tenure. Maryland was an example, where the founders typically "had no desire for a trading company charter that provided for government of the company by a majority vote of the stockholders" (Jensen, 1955:22). But the attempt to found a medieval empire failed.

From the Elizabethan era onwards, there was patently a great consciousness of, and interest in, the life of the American colonies. But it was not only America; trade and exploration over much of the globe had already been established by the reign of the Stuarts in the early seventeenth century. In 1599, Richard Hakluyt, an explorer and a personal friend of many of the English pirates and colonisers, such as Sir Francis Drake and Sir Walter Raleigh, compiled three large volumes of voyage and travel narratives, *The Principal Navigations, Voyages, Traffiques, and Discoveries of the English Nation, Made by*

Sea or Overland to the Remote and Farthest Distant Quarters of the Earth, at Any Time within the Compasse of These 1600 Yeres: Divided into Three Severall Volumes, according to the Positions of the Regions, Whereunto They Were Directed, "by Richard Hakluyt, Preacher, and Sometime Student of Christ-church in Oxford, London, 1599". Hakluyt's dedication to the First Edition, reproduced in the 1809 reprint, is 'to Sir Francis Walsingham Knight, Principall Secretaries to Her Majestie, Chancellor of the Dutchie of Lancaster, and one of her Majesties Most Honourable Privie Councell.' He says in this Dedication that when at Oxford he read 'whatsoever printed or written discoveries and voyages I found extant either in the Greek, Latine, Italian, Spanish, Portugall, French, or English languages, and in my publicke lectures was the first that produced and shewed both the olde imperfectly composed, and the new lately reformed Mappes, Globes, Spheares, and other instruments of this Art.' (pages unnumbered). While in France with Sir Edward Stafford, Hakluyt became aware of the prestige and praise acquired by other nations for their "discoveries and notable enterprises," and the general condemnation of the English for their apparent lack of these. Gathering these stories together and publishing them was intended to place English achievements and acts of heroism and discovery alongside those of other nations. It was also intended to encourage and increase England's own discoveries and colonising activities. In the second edition dedicated to the Lord Charles Howard, which he dedicates "with all humilitie and reverence", he refers to Howard's gallantry as "Chiefe and Sole Commander under her sacred and royalle Majestie". He points out the importance of the "breeding up of skilful Seamen and Mariners" (1809 [1599]:xiii), and he calls for lectures on navigation to be made available to increase knowledge in the way that lectures in Seville had strengthened the knowledge and skills of Spanish mariners. An account of the whole battle, translated from the Latin of the Dutch writer Emanuel van Meteren, takes pride of place in the second volume. The importance of the English defeat of the armada must partly be found in the preeminence of the Spanish in the arts of ship building, exploration, and discovery, and the huge wealth and prestige that their success won for them.

Accounts of voyages and discoveries by crusaders, seamen, navigators, explorers, merchants, friars, and various kinds of emissaries will tend to place the emphasis, the viewpoint, in different places. Many of the narratives, especially the sixteenth-century ones, are about trade and commerce in foreign lands, and contain masses of detail on trade routes, currencies, coins, weights and measures in different places, designs of river boats and sea-going vessels, length and direction of journeys, exchange rates, import customs, local institutions, and judicial systems (or their lack) that affect vulnerable trade and traders. Some of the pieces published include letters of company servants to their masters in England explaining delays, making requests for specific goods to be shipped for specific markets, descriptions of prevailing fashions in colour or fabric in Persia or China, advice on gift giving and which gifts prevail as the most prestigious in the court of the Mogul emperor or the court of the emperor of China, notes on manufacturing techniques in Siam and numerous other places, pleas for help against imprisonment by capricious local rulers, suggestions for new methods, routes, and contacts, and descriptions of anything from local topography to local customs that might have an impact on the success or failure of ventures.

The extent to which the state and its most powerful representatives were involved in promoting English interests abroad is well testified by the official correspondence which Hakluyt published, not least that of Queen Elizabeth. There are letters from Elizabeth to the "Emperour of Russia," "the great Sophie of Persia," "the greate Turke," "the king of China," "the Emperour of Morocco," "the Emperour of Ethiopia." These formal letters are usually about the mutual benefits of trade and commerce, the safety and responsibilities of English merchants, or pleas for clemency and the release of English prisoners from unjust imprisonment. Another important kind of queen's document is the granting of letters patent to individual and family interests, for example to Sir Walter Raleigh for the planting of new lands in Virginia in 1584, or "letters patent granted by the Queenes Maiestie to the right worshipful company of the English merchants for the Levant, 1592"; or "a Patent granted to certaine merchants of Exeter . . . for trade to the River of Senega and Gambia in Guinea, 1588."

The correspondence and documents that Hakluyt published vividly brings to light the importance for Elizabethan England of the burgeoning international trade, the regular communications already being established by heads of state around the world, the competition over advantageous trading agreements in the Levant, in Russia, in Turkey, in Mogul India, in what we now call Southeast Asia, in China and Japan. Equally important is the competition for the wealth of the Americas. So important is this context of expanding world contact and knowledge, and the consequent stretching of indigenous English language categories, that the increasingly multiple applications of 'religion' render any assumptions about its meaning problematic. Indeed, the argument I am pursuing here is that generic 'religion' and 'religions', in conjunction with 'politics' and 'economics', are categories in the making. English-language Religion—and presumably in all European languages—is in the crucible of transformation, and the emergence of discourses on the religions of the world link a modern and premodern cosmology and ideology. But it hasn't arrived yet in Hakluyt in 1599. Religion, in the sense of Christian Truth, is a self-evident reality that rarely needs mention. I have read several of these fascinating stories based on journals kept by the travellers. The word 'religion' rarely occurs at this stage, and when it does, it is in the formal sense of 'our true Religion', meaning our Christian faith, in distinction from all the superstitions of Catholics, infidels, and pagans.

There are two interesting documents written in medieval Latin and placed at the beginning of volume 1 which are reports written by friars, both of whom had been sent by powerful people as emissaries to the Tartars and Mongols. Pope Innocent IV sent four friars "with letters Apostolicall" to the Tartars (Hakluyt, 1809 [1599]:59), exhorting them to stop slaughtering and to receive the Christian faith; one of the friars, Iohannes de Plano Carpini, was the writer of the 1246 account. Another friar, William de Rubruqui, had been sent by the king of France in 1253. Their brief seems to have been to observe and negotiate with the Tartars and Mongols, who represented a threat to the security of Christendom since the attacks by Genghis Khan. Though some expressions used suggest that their purpose was to proselytise the Christian faith, the treatment that they both received from the other people, whether 'Mahometan' or otherwise, made this aim look merely apologetic and with minimal chance of success. One is most struck by their vulnerability and lack of prestige. Perhaps their most urgent purpose was the collecting of information about a potentially dangerous enemy and an attempt to open up communications and negotiations.

The reports of these friars read in many ways like attempts at ethnographic description of what we today might refer to as the cultures, customs, and social institutions of the various groups of people that the travellers encountered. The term 'Christian', like 'Turk', 'Saracen', 'Mahometan', or 'Tartar', seems mainly to be used as something like an ethnic category, rather than as a private confession of faith. They refer to collectivities or 'nations', what we might call 'tribes', societies, or cultures. These travel journals are astonishing for the hardships the friars suffered, and apparently survived, in their journeying through many lands: Eastern Europe, the Black Sea, the Middle East, and the Far East of Siberia, Mongolia, and China.

There are many fascinating aspects to these narratives, but of significance for the discussion here are the leading categories which do or do not order them. One advantage of these documents is that the medieval Latin accounts and the late sixteenth-century English translations are published side by side. I am not a specialist in Latin, but it is easy enough to search for a specific word, such as *religio*. I couldn't find a single mention of this word in either report. And in the Elizabethan English translations of the medieval Latin almost never do modern words, or old words with modern meanings, such as politics, economics, or secular appear. There is more talk in general of superstitions, idolatry, and customs. More interestingly, these narratives attempt to describe specific institutions and practices in considerable detail. Religion is extremely rarely referred to, in fact only twice. Occasionally we hear of the superstitions of the pagans, for example, in "Of their Superstitious traditions" (Hakluyt, 1809 [1599]:62), but more rarely of 'religion'. Well into the second account written by William de Rubruqui, we suddenly get the expression (in the English translation) "the religion of Mahomet," and he says: "I wonder what devil carried the religion of Mahomet thither" to Bulgaria. The original Latin from which this is a translation goes: "Et mirror quis Diabolus portavit illuc legem Machometi" (Hakluyt, 1809 [1599]:94).

Legem is derived from *lex* which is usually translated as law. Here it has been translated as religion. A few pages later, we find: "Those Bulgarians are most wicked Saracens, more earnestly professing the damnable religion of Mahomet, than any other nation whatsoever" (Hakluyt, 1809 [1599]:120). The Latin from which this is translated reads: "Et illi Bulgari sunt pessimi Saraceni, fortius tenentes legem Machometi, quam aliqui alij."

In the discussion of *legem Machometi*, we learn that "Mahometan law" suggests not a privately held faith in the modern sense of an individual's 'religion' but the rules, customs, and legitimated authority of a group of people, a 'nation' or tribe, a collective identity, observed as a totality and including everything that both friars describe: methods of production, topography, means of cooking and diet, dress, design of houses, language, writing or lack of writing, rulers and other categories or ranks of people, punishments, treatment of foreigners, customs of gift giving and receiving, marriages and funerals, treatment of women, upbringing of children, fighting techniques and weapons, habits of peace and war, relations with neighbouring peoples, genealogies of rulers and their senior subordinates, wealth, inheritance, modes of livelihood, and many other issues. This translation of *legem Machometi* as "Mahometan religion" suggests that in the late Elizabethan age there was the tentative beginning of a tendency that became more popular in the seventeenth century to refer to 'religion' beyond the meaning of Christian Truth and to apply it analogically to what we today might refer to as non-Christian faiths.[1] However, the implication could be that Religion understood as Christian Truth was a word of similar import, that refers not only to something deeply personal concerning life after death and salvation of the soul, but something approaching an ethnic or cultural identity, something about one's own culture that defines an identity in a more totalising sense. The idea of a personal faith, which undoubtedly sustained the friars in their journeys, cannot be easily separated from their identity as Christians in the sense that they represent a different law or civilisation or set of practices from the various groups encountered and described. I suggested in a previous chapter that Religion as Christian Truth is the discourse on 'our' civility as distinguished from 'their' barbarity, and that the disciplines of salvation are an integral part of this more total civilisational identity. Perhaps here 'law' is another way of talking about a total way of life and is being used in an extended analogical sense to refer to the law/religion/superstitions of pagans. It also overlaps with our term 'ethnicity', and interestingly (as I show below) Samuel Purchas frequently uses the term 'ethnikes' in his own writing to refer to pagans.

One point that seems of great interest is the degree to which gift exchange is emphasised by both of these accounts and in others, such as the travel narratives of Martin Baumgarten (1507) and the journal of Sir Thomas Roe, James I's ambassador to the Mogul emperor of India in the early seventeenth century, both reprinted in Churchill and Churchill, *A Collection of Voyages and Travels* (1704). In all these cases, the Christian traveller is worried by his inability to give appropriate gifts. It is the giving and taking of gifts which indicate a person's value and degree, and the value and status of his ruler. The ability to give valued gifts is as much a sign of a person's identity and an indication of how he should be treated as any other aspect of his situation. Its universality is particularly striking, though it irritates Protestants, sometimes mainly because they are poorer and cannot get the prestige for Christian England that they desire. Again, in the rare cases where 'religion' is used, it tends to refer to ethnic identity, customs, and way of life generally.

In the early seventeenth century, a Protestant minister, Samuel Purchas, who had admired Hakluyt (also an ordained minister), retold many of these stories in his own words. He additionally collected and translated many more himself. The title is a good summary of the contents and worth quoting at length: *Purchas, his Pilgrimage; or, Relations of the World and the Religions Observed in all Ages and places Discovered, from the Creation unto this Present. Contayning a Theologicall and Geographicall Histories of Asia, Africa, and America, with the Ilands adjacent, Declaring the ancient Religions before the Flood, the Heathenish, Jewish, and Saracenicall in all Ages Since, in those parts professed, with their several opinions, Idols, Oracles, Temples, Priests, Fasts, Feasts, Sacrifices, and Rites Religious: Their beginnings, Proceedings, Alterations, Sects, Orders and Successions. With briefe Descriptions of the Countries, Nations, States, Discoueries; Private and Publicke Customes, and the most remarkable Rarities of Nature, or Humane Industrie, in the same.*

The fourth edition (1626) has a dedicatory epistle "To His Most Excellent Majestie Charles[2] by the Grace of God, King of Great Brittaine, France and Ireland, Defender of the Faith etc," in which Purchas mentions that the first edition (1613) had been dedicated to Charles's father, James I. Purchas boasts that King James had told Purchas that he had read his book seven times and that he kept a copy on his bedside table. If this is true, then it brings home vividly the importance to the English and their rulers and literate elites of the growth of foreign trade and commerce generally, and of knowledge of other peoples in the world. Indeed, when one considers the vast amounts of fascinating (if often dubious) information available about the Middle East, Turkey, India, China, Japan, the Americas, and many other regions, mixed up with fable, satire, misrepresentation, and scurrilous comment, the interconnectedness of the world in the early seventeenth century becomes powerfully evident. Even when satirising, sneering at, and fulminating against heathen superstitions in regions as diverse as South and East Asia or the Americas, it is often the Catholic Church that is the main target. It needs to be borne in mind that England was still a small power which felt threatened by many more powerful polities in the world, not only by its main trading rivals the Portuguese, Dutch, and French. Englishmen and other Europeans in the court of the Mogul emperor, or the shogun of Japan, or the grand mufti in Turkey, were highly vulnerable, often relatively impoverished, and not of the great consequence or high status that they subsequently came to attribute to themselves in succeeding centuries.

There is also in Purchas's work a dedicatory epistle which plays with the terms 'religion', 'religions', 'religious', and 'irreligious': "To the Most Reverend Father in God, George by the Divine Providence, Lord Archbishop of Canterburie, Primate of all England and Metropolitane, one of his Majesties Most Honourable Privie Councell." He refers to the first edition of the book: "Above thirteene yeares are passed since your Graces auspicious name graced the Frontispiece of the Pilgrimage, which Promising the World and her Religions in four parts, hath (onely and that four times) performed One." At one point he refers to "the Argument it selfe being of Religions (though irreligious) to a Most Reverend and Religious Prelate" (pages unnumbered).

My own interpretation of this is that the *Pilgrimage*, which is both the short name for his book and also the (Christian) spirit in which it was written, had been intended to present "the World and her Religions," but had only truly managed to demonstrate one (Christianity, through Purchas's act of pilgrimage). These 'religions' that he intends to describe are, in truth, "irreligious" (superstitions), but they have been offered to a "Religious Prelate." This play on words extends and stretches their circumference of usage.

The work is made up of eight books, each divided into many chapters, the total having 1047 (quarto?) pages, each page having sixty-two lines of print. There is a 35-page index of subjects at the back, each page divided into three columns. The author tells us that he has only relied for travel narratives on authors he has seen with his own eyes. The names of these authors are listed alphabetically in the "Catalogue of the Authors" at the beginning of the book, and there are 8 pages of these named sources divided into three columns. Since one full column has about fifty names, there must be over one thousand authors he has read, translated from numerous languages. Many of these are ancient authors of Greece and Rome, while some are contemporaries and anything in between.

The contents of the book indicate a well-developed vocabulary of religion and religions, which is in contrast to the paucity of such a vocabulary in Hakluyt a few years earlier. J. Z. Smith ("Religion, Religions, Religious," 1998) has pointed out that both Richard Eden in his *Treatyse of the New India* (1553) and Pedro Cieza de Leó in *Crónica del Perú* (also 1553) describe the indigenous peoples in the Canary Islands and Peru as having no religion at all (Smith, 1998:269). Smith points out that the absence of 'religion' suggests "an implicit universality" on the grounds that both Eden and Cieza "find its alleged

absence noteworthy." Samuel Purchas seems to exemplify what Smith refers
to as "the major expansion of the use and understanding of the term" (269).
However, as the analysis by Pagden and Parry of the disputes of the Spanish
lawyer/theologians suggests (see chapter 4 of this book), an absence of religion
was an absence of Christian Truth and all that was implied by that absence—
an absence of civility and rationality. The Protestant Purchas, despite the
multiplication of 'religions', is in many ways still within the same thought-
world as the fifteenth- and sixteenth-century Catholics; for an absence of Religion as Christian Truth is fundamentally a multiplication of superstitions.
However, as I go on here to show, there is an ambiguity between 'religions'
meaning 'superstitions' and 'religions as a generic mode of description. It can
also be noted that as late as 1787, Thomas Jefferson in *Notes on the State of
Virginia* could find no religion among the North American indigenous peoples.
Furthermore, the "implicit universality" to which Smith refers derives from
the presumed universality of humanity contained in the biblical narrative of
the Creation, the Fall, the descent of the nations from the original created man
and woman, and their dispersal through the narratives of the Flood and the
Tower of Babel. The problem that America and its indigenous inhabitants
posed was that they were not present in the knowledge possessed by Christians. It was from this absence that the doubts about their humanity arose.

Here are some examples of what appear like modern generic uses of
'religion' and 'religions': "Asia: The First Booke. Of the first beginnings of the
World and Religion: and of the Regions and Religions of Babylonia, Assyria,
Syria, Phoenicia, and Palestina." Chapter IIII (Purchas, 1626 [1613]:17) is explicitly a "history of religions." We seem to have here a modern discourse on
world religions as early as 1613 (the original publication date). Purchas spends
considerable time discussing and clarifying the meaning of 'religion':

> For what else is Religion, but the Schoole, wherein we learne Mans
> dutie towards God, and the way to be linked most straitly to him? And
> what are all the Exercises of Religion, but acknowledgements of the
> Godhead, of the Creation of the World, of the Provident order
> therein, and ordering thereof, of the Soules immortalitie, of Mans fall
> and imperfection, of our Soveriegne and Supreame good ... whereas
> neither Art nor Industry, nor civill Society hath bound men as men
> together yet the grounds of these things have bound them as men, by
> the mere bond of humane Nature, to God, in some or other Religion.
> (Purchas, 1626 [1613]:26)

This passage defines Religion in terms not unlike the 'natural religion' of
Herbert of Cherbury, which is essentially a Protestant view of what the Bible
teaches but strategically omitting any explicit Christology—though the
Christology is really there, deeply embedded in the text. Arguably we have here
an early version of the theology lying behind nineteenth-century Protestant

founders of the science of religion such as Max Muller and C. P. Tiele. It seems, for instance, to acknowledge other religions in the expression "some or other Religion." Furthermore, it suggests a function for religion, which is to bind people together as the ground of 'civil society', art, and industry. However, the term 'civil society' should probably be read in the spirit of 'proper human relations' or 'civilised human interaction' rather than in the sense of societies as bounded wholes in the more modern conception. Or alternatively it is a phrase on the cusp of transition from the relational to the substantial (see Bossy, 1985:170–71; Dumont, 1986). Furthermore, a great deal is included in Purchas's definition of 'religion'. I will show that there are many examples of ambiguity in this respect, for while Purchas frequently uses the term 'religions' (and also 'religious' to refer to people whose practices remind him of the Christian monastics), he also uses the terms to refer to those who are most closely connected to rites and devotions to idols, gods, goddesses, and 'Devilles'.

The whole theoretical structure of the book is explicitly derived from the Bible and the narratives of the Fall, the Flood, and the Tower of Babel. The first five or six chapters might be called the theory and method section, and they make it clear that biblical Christianity frames the whole collection of narratives that Purchas has constructed. The 'religions' in the plural are 'superstitions', and the two words oscillate throughout the text as alternatives. There is only one true Religion, and this religion can explain, on the basis of the Bible, how these fallen versions of religion can be found in so many different forms all over the world. The religions of the world are represented as mistakes, misunderstandings, superstitions, and lies resulting from lack of contact and a falling away from the true sources of revelation. They are also products of the devil. In this sense, many peoples are accused of devil worship. The existence of these religion-like superstitions must be explained according to the revelation of true Religion. Thus at one point he remarks about his task, "my scope is to declare as well false as true Religions (it being not Theologicall but Historicall, or rather Historically Theologicall)" (Purchas, 1626 [1613]:47).

This is a pilgrimage, and Purchas refers to himself as a pilgrim, reading thousands of journals and travel narratives, travelling around the world in his imagination, collecting and translating and reproducing a vast range of data about the cultures, customs, and beliefs of the different regions of the world. It is an attempt to theorise a history of the world on the basis of deduction from biblical narrative:

Chapter I: Of God, One in Nature, Three in Persons, The Father, Sonne, and Holy Ghost
Chapter II: Of the Creation of the World
Chapter III: Of Man, considered in his first state wherein he was created: and of Paradise, the place of his habitation

Chapter IIII: Of the word Religion: and of the Religion of our first Parents
   before the Fall
Chapter V: Of the fall of Man: and of Original Sin

These chapters set the scene theoretically and theologically, and provide an
anchor for the narrative that from this point looks at how Religion developed
after the Fall:

Chapter VI: Of the Reliques of the Divine Image after the fall, whereby
   naturally men addict themselves unto some Religion: and what was the
   Religion of the World before the Floud

The Flood acts as another narrative switch, for it is after that event that the
world is repeopled ("Of the repeopling of the World") and divided by "Tongues
and Nations." The narrative then goes in chapter X to "Of Babylonia: the
originall of Idolatrie: and the Chaldeans."

While religion and religions are apparently Purchas's main concern, his
vast collection of narratives is as much concerned with government, polity (for
example, the "Hebrew Polity"), manners and customs, arts and inventions,
topography and geography, computations of time, festivals, calendars, gifts,
tithes, sects, hierarchies, monarchs, dynasties, superstitions, marriages, funerals, natural wonders, journeys, nations, names, provinces, cities, commodities,
rivers, shipping, castles, attire, language, writing, astrology, philosophy, medicine, magistrates, courts, revenues, wives, concubines, gift exchange, trade,
sea battles, seasons, creatures useful and fabulous, plants, fruits, drugs, spices,
the varieties of sea, islands, libraries, civil wars, successions and genealogies,
empires, schools, lakes, soils, climate, metals, mines, secular and religious
priests and men and women like priests, buildings, buildings like churches,
palaces, magicians, giants, conquests, oracles, nuns, sorcerers, enchanters,
penances, and punishments.

These are the English words he uses, by and large, to tell the stories and to
order the data from every place where travellers have been and where they now
are. It is a compendium of quite detailed descriptions and amounts to a world
ethnography, geography, and history. Religion is both the one true Religion in
contrast to all the varieties of superstitions, and it is also a generic category that
includes superstitions *as* religions.

Purchas also describes his work as a "Mappe" of "infinitely diversified
superstitions." The importance of geography and maps for Purchas is con-
firmed by the title of chapter XI: "A Geographicall Narration of the Whole
Earth in generall, and more particularly of Asia" (Purchas, 1626 [1613]:39–40).
The book contains reproductions of various maps then current, thus reflecting
the colonial expansion of Europe through sea travel, trade, and conquest, and
the new ways of imagining the world. "This earth, together with the Waters,
make one Globe and huge Ball, resting on itselfe, supported by the Almightie

hand of God" (Purchas, 1626 [1613]:41). Though the ancients, "skilfull in Geographie," tried to measure the earth, it was not until "our time" that "the science of Geographie" was perfected as a result of the circumnavigations of Spaniards, English, and Dutch and its true extent discovered, with the discovery of "America, Mexicana, and America Peruvania, and Terra Australis, or the land lying toward the South Pole" (41). This more perfect knowledge of the world "wee hope and pray may be for the further enlargement of the Kingdome of Christ Iesus, and propagation of his Gospell" (41).

A particularly interesting example is "Mercators Mappe or Topography of Paradise" (Purchas, 1626 [1613]:16) which locates the Garden of Eden, Adam and Eve, and the tree of knowledge in the area which we today call the Middle East, or the ancient Orient, between Syria, Mesopotamia, and Arabia.[3] "Paradisus" is represented as having a geographical location in the Holy Land, and it seems significant that this should be shown on a map produced by the leading map maker of his age (developed by the German Gerardus Mercator in 1569) in a world that was demanding more accurate maps for the proliferation of sea voyages then being undertaken. It underlines the degree to which European expansion of trade and colonisation was conceived as a fundamentally Christian enterprise. Indeed, how else might it have been conceived?

The letter "To the Reader" states the intention, methodology, and general structure of the work:

> I here bring Religion from Paradise to the Ark, and thence follow her round about the World, and (for her sake) observe the world itself, with the several Countries and Peoples therein; the Chiefe Empires and States; their private and publique Customes; their manifold chances and changes; also the wonderfull effects of Nature; Events of Divine and Human Providence; Rarities of Art; and whatsoever I find by relations of Historians, as I passe, most worthie the writing. (Purchas, 1626 [1613]:pages unnumbered)

This huge task may seem overly ambitious, but it is methodologically significant for its interdisciplinarity, one might say its holistic concept of knowledge, and its assumption that whatever 'religion' is, it is embedded in a complex range of human activities. What we would call the 'interdisciplinarity' is indicated when he says:

> If thou demandest what profit may be hereof; I answer, that here students of all sorts may find matter fitting their studies: The naturall Philosophers may observe the different constitution and commixtion of Elements, their diverse working in diverse places, the varietie of heavenly influence, of the yearely seasons, of the Creatures in Aire, Water, Earth: They which delight in State-affaires, may observe the varieties of States and Kingdomes, with their differing Lawes,

Polities, and Customes, their Beginnings and Endings.... The studious of Geographie may somewhat be helped...not that we intend
an exact Geographie, in mentioning every Citie with the degrees of
Longitude and Latitude, but yet limiting every Countrie in his true
situation and bounds; and performing happily more than some,
which take upon them the title of Geographers.

So "natural Philosophers," "They which delight in State-affaires," and the
"studious of Geographie" can all find relevant and useful things here. Yet
nevertheless "Religion is my proper aime, and therefore I insist longer on the
description of whatsoever I find belonging thereto," a point which suggests a
distinction between 'religion' and these other (profane?) matters, and which
raises for us today the spectre of an ancient definitional issue: what will be
included as 'religion'? For one keeps seeing ambiguity in Purchas's conception, that on the one hand Religion encompasses the world as Christian Truth,
and the whole narrative is framed by the biblical accounts; yet on the other
hand the phrase "whatsoever I find belonging thereto" suggests that some
things are outside of 'religion'.

A connected ambiguity is in the way religions oscillate with superstitions,
and we will see that what Purchas refers to as superstitious practices are not
confined to 'gods' and "Devills" but include customs which do not have any
obvious 'theological' referent. At these times, it seems that for Purchas the
customs of non-Christian people, such as their traditions of marriage or ac-
countancy, are superstitions because they are not Protestant Christian customs.

There can be no doubt that Purchas is an English nationalist in some quite
straightforward sense, and that he wishes to justify international trade and
especially English trade over against Portuguese and Dutch trade. His interest
in the acquisition of knowledge to replace "fables" may not be framed only in
terms of trade. In chapter II of the fifth book, "Of later Indian Discoveries and
an Apologie for the English Trade in the East Indies" (Purchas, 1626
[1613]:483), he opposes fables to the truth that can be discovered empirically as
a result of the endeavours of seamen to open up the world and gain knowledge
of others: "After this glut of Fables (which commonly attend whatsoever is
farre distant in Time or Place) the Indian Truth will be more welcome"
(Purchas, 1626 [1613]:483).

The "Portugals," the "Hollanders," and the English "are the triumviri,
which of all the European Nations have subdued those seas." He gives a brief
history of the successful Portuguese, and lists their many "conquests" in Asia,
Africa, and America, which

besides their Empire over the Seas, and Riches by Merchandise,
made Portugall the least part of the Portugall Crowne.... And worthy of praise they are, that being so small and poore a Nation, have
thus enlarged their State and Sovereigntie. But whiles they sought a

Monopoly of Indian Merchandise...not only (I know not by what right) forbidding the Indians to Trade their Owne Seas. (Purchas, 1626 [1613]:483)

He continues by listing the Dutch colonial acquisitions, and discusses these in section II, "Of the English Trade there; many arguments in defence of it" (Purchas, 1626 [1613]:484). He lists the successes of the English trade in various parts of the world. He says that there are many people who traduce and detract "our Traffique." But Purchas is a defender of English ambitions, including "this Indian adventure," for "Honor and Gaine [are] breaking through all obstacles, and opening all Parts of the World to every part" (484).

Purchas gives a number of reasons for defending "the Indian Societie"[4] (by which he almost undoubtedly means the East India Company), which some critics "affirme gainfull to the Adventurers, but with publike detriment to the State" (Purchas, 1626 [1613]:484). The criticism that he wishes to counter here is that the company brings wealth and advantage to a small number of individuals at the expense of the state or body politic, and is an example of the growth of individual selfishness over the good of the whole commonwealth. Against this view, he argues in effect that individual entrepreneurs, to whom he refers as "the Private Adventurers," are also patriots and their gain is all of our gain. The establishment of the company is consonant with the law of God "who hath given the Earth to the Sonnes of Men"; with the law of nature, "which by mutual offices insinuateth a Generall Good"; and with the law of nations, "which flourish most in communicating their Superfluities, by Exchange for Necessaries," a point especially pertinent for an island country (484). This is bordering on what we would call an economic theory, and again links the early justifications for overseas adventures with the wealth that accrues from trade and exchange.[5] But wealth is not justifiable if separated from honour and nobility; the company is also justified because it was "Nobly borne" of "Renowned Elizabeth, who by her Letters Patent, for the Honour of her Realm of England, for the increase of her Navigation, for the advancement of the Trade of Merchandise...first conceived, and gave first breath, to their Societie" (484). This "Virgin Mother" is praised by Purchas with hyperbole, as is James I, her successor.

Furthermore, the English are superior in their attitudes to other nations, for they are interested in factories, not fortresses, and unlike (by implication) the Portuguese and Dutch, do not annoy either Christian or heathen, and do not "make prey of Christians and Ethnikes unprovoked" (Purchas, 1626 [1613]:485):

And is it not a profit to our Nation, to vent [vend?] Clothes, Iron, Lead, and other Commodities? To set on worke so many of all Trades and Professions? To employ so many Mariners? To build so many, so able, so capable Ships? To enrich the Kings coffers and Publike

Treasurie, in Customes, Imports, and other Duties? Yea, that by enriching the Private Adventurers, the State hath so many more serviceable Members for the good of the Whole Bodie?

This last expression, "the good of the Whole Bodie," reminds the modern reader that the late medieval and early modern view of the organic common-wealth is still powerful in England and in Europe generally. The common-wealth is represented on analogy to a body, each member functioning for the health of the whole, hence the 'politic body'. Organic analogies were commonly made between God as the King of all, the king as the father of the nation, and the father as the natural authority within the family. These homologies anchor the nation and its family-like unity and harmony into Christian Truth and thus into the nature of things. However, perhaps the thrust of his advocacy, while definitely patriotic and concerned with the fame, glory, and prosperity of the English nation, is also arguing here for the pursuit of trade and profit by en-trepreneurial individuals. Purchas was an Anglican and not a Puritan in any obvious sense, but the idea that Christian salvation and economic salvation are linked was presumably circulating and, in this burgeoning context of a world increasingly connected by trade, may have been tipping the balance incre-mentally in favour of individual entrepreneurship linked to nationalistic glory.

Purchas goes on to argue that this expansion of trade and commerce can lead to peaceful and profitable relations of England with other great nations:

And is it for the honor of our Nation, that the English Name hath pierced the remotest Countries, and filled the Indians with admira-tion of the English? That Asia clothes us with her Silkes, fedes us with her Spices, cures us with her Drugges, adornes us with her Iewels, and almost adores the English Valour? That Turkie is made so neere, whiles our Indian Ocean makes our way to the Persian, the Mogoll, the Japan Monarchs, Awfulle Names of Greatnesse, not heard by our Ancestors, now delighting in our new Amitie, These and other Mighty Easterne Potentates entertaining commerce of Letters, and Embassies, with Great Britaines Greatest Sovereign? (Purchas, 1626 [1613]:485)

In his nationalist fervour, he praises the English seamen's victories in the Indian Ocean; but he also uses the language of 'East' and 'West': residents of "the Eastern World" were "Spectators of the Western Worth" (Purchas, 1626 [1613]:585). He justifies English victories and glories as "Christian justice." But there are also practical reasons: "I adde, that in the present estate of things, Necessitie may bee alledged for a Vertue" (485).

He continues in section III with more "Answers to objections made against the Indian Trade and Societie, with other Arguments for it" (Purchas, 1626 [1613]:486). One is that our mariners will be unemployed and will take to

"Pyracies": "Better our Men should carrie forreine Silver into Those parts, to bring Money and Wares for the publicke benefit, than all this money to be interecepted by strangers" (486). Sea trade brings "Gaine and Glorie." Also, it can be justified for "Propagation of Religion": "What shoulde I speake of the highest worke of Conscience, in propagating Christian Religion, and warring upon the regions and legions of Infernall Powers, captivating Silly Soules in Ethnike darkness?" (486). This is an interesting expression in the context of the earlier reference to the "Awfulle Names of Greatnesse." This should perhaps be read as "the dreaded men of Heathen power." Furthermore, admittedly playing on words, the propagation of the Christian Religion is "Merchandise, the gaine of Soules; settling learned Ministers in their Factories, to be Factors for Christ; then might we looke for a Blessing: Yea, now we have great Hopes, that Iapan may yeeld silver" (487).

This play is also revealing, for it indicates a double meaning in words such as merchandise and factories, linking productivity of trade with missionary activity. English trade, he argues, is more innocent than that of the Portuguese or Dutch. Of course, there will be evil things done too, but this is inevitable: "it is Puritanisme in Politie, to conceit any Great Good, without some Evills attendant, in any Enterprise whatsoever" (Purchas, 1626 [1613]:487).

Another argument in favour of enterprise in seeking foreign trade and commerce, "which to me was not the least, and here was placed first, [is] the Increase of Learning and Knowledge.... How little have we knowne of the World, and the Wonders of God in the World, had not the Sea opened us a Passage into all Lands" (Purchas, 1626 [1613]:487). Amongst the most important for Purchas is geography, which is knowledge of the world that God created as in the Genesis account. What we would call secular knowledge of the world ("Increase of Learning and Knowledge") is simultaneously knowledge of "the Wonders of God in the World," made possible in Purchas's rhetoric by a miracle: "the Sea opened us a Passage into all Lands," which evokes the parting of the Red Sea and the flight from the captivity in Egypt. Another image of divine delivery is the sailor who is "the true Pegasus, that with his wing-like sailes flies over the World; which hath helped to deliver Andromeda [geography] before chained to the Rockes, and ready to be devoured of that Monster Ignorance" (487). He then pays tribute to Sir Thomas Smith, governor of the East India Company.

The first few chapters of the book laboriously spell out the Christological framework for the whole theory of humanity. Purchas makes it clear and explicit that all the data in the book, gathered from hundreds of texts in several languages, are placed in a biblical and trinitarian context. Comparing himself with "the Poets" such as Homer, Virgil, and Ovid who "were wont to lay the Foundations and First Beginnings of their Poeticall Fabrikes, with invocation of their gods and Muses," so Purchas would so far imitate their manner...in a History of Religion, which should have God to be the Alpha and Omega; the Efficient from whom; the End to whom it proceedeth; the Matter of whom, the Forme by whom...I could not but make a Religion to begin this discourse of Religion.

And he prays that the holy Trinity will

guide me in this Perambulation of the World, so to take view of the Times, Places, and Customs therein, as may testifie my religious bond to him...that in beholding this Mappe of so infinitely diversified Superstitions, we may be more thankfull for...that true and only Religion, which Christ by his Bloud hath procured, by his Word revealed, by his Spirit sealed, and will reward eternally in the Heavens. (Purchas, 1626 [1613]:1–2)

Religion, then, is revealed Christian Truth, and there is only one of these. It is universal in the sense that there cannot be alternative truths, only systems and practices that erroneously appear like Truth but which are actually false superstitions. However, though revealed, there is also a natural religion asserted here:

The Heavens declare the glory of God; and, The Invisible things of him, that is, his eternall Power and Godhead, are seene by the Creation of the World being considered in his Workes. God hath not...left himselfe without witnesse, who besides the testimonie of Nature, written in our hearts, hath added those of Scripture and the Creature. (Purchas, 1626 [1613]:2)

This is not yet the natural history of David Hume, which constructs what we today would call a secular nonreligious space for objective and rational observation of the 'religious history of mankind'. It is more the natural religion of Herbert of Cherbury, of Muller and Tiele as suggested earlier. For Purchas, God and Christian Truth encompass everything, including what he can say about it. There is, rather, a sense of the world as relatively profaned, a result of the Fall and the devil. The conception of the profane world is therefore not nonreligious in the quite different sense of the modern secular since it is defined by Christian Truth. Yet we can perhaps see a semantic gap widening in his play on words, mentioned earlier, where merchandise and factories are linked with Christian conversion and the planting of Christian 'factors' in factories.

Each person, he says, has an impression of deity in his mind, and this is "a remnant of integritie after the Fall of Adam" (Purchas, 1626 [1613]:2). And a little later, "Religion in itself is naturall, written in the hearts of all men, which will (as here we shew) rather be of a false than no Religion" (17). Here he quite explicitly defines 'religion' ambiguously as true and false. We have true Religion; they have false 'religions', e.g., superstitions. Yet behind this is a universal concept of humanity, for everyone is inherently capable of receiving the dim images of Truth in their hearts, and it is as a result of great calamitous events such as the Fall, the Flood, and the Tower of Babel, that some humans have drifted further from the Truth than others, and have been less able to hear the gospel by being geographically separated around the world: "although the true Religion can bee but one, and that which God himselfe teacheth . . . all other Religions being but strayings from him, whereby men wander in the darke, and in labyrinths of error" (Purchas, 1626 [1613]:27).

This God is not knowable in any direct sense, only "as through a Glasse darkely, that wee may with Moses have some glancing view of his hinder parts." So this conception of natural religion is biblically framed. Thus superstitions are more or less inaccurate attempts to recreate this remnant of Truth left imprinted on our hearts, some closer intimations to Christ's revelation and some more distant: "That dreadfull Mysterie of the Trinitie" which "is averred against all Hereticks, Iewes and Infidels" (Purchas, 1626 [1613]:4). All classes of men are bound up in the creation of the world and the whole cosmic drama of salvation and redemption, but only Christians have the full picture. Yet even "hereticks," "Iewes," "Infidels," and "Ethnikes" (a common word in Purchas's writing that refers to pagans or, in today's language, indigenous peoples) may have some vague idea of the truth about sin and salvation but are, in different degrees, wrapped in the darkness of superstition.

I think we must recognise that, while on the one hand Religion as Christian Truth is an encompassing, cultural totality fused with nature and with the commonwealth (which it would be generally wrong to think of in today's understanding of 'politics' as a separate nonreligious domain), yet the language that the Protestant Purchas uses in his *Pilgrimage* works ambiguously towards a degree of differentiation between religion and "politie" and religion and knowledge of things like geography. There is an ambiguity throughout on this point, and the ambiguity turns in part on the status of the fallen world, and the degree to which the profane is *relatively* distanced from God's Truth, on the one hand, and, on the other, it is an object of discovery and description that has interest in and for itself.

Sometimes his use of language suggests a shift towards a later and clearer distinction between Religion and the state, or Religion and the natural sciences, that is to say, towards modern categories generally. For example, before the Fall, Adam knew God and God's law in his heart: "Nature was his Schoolmaster . . . that taught him (without learning) all the Rules of Divine Learning, of Politicall, Oeconomical, and Morall wisdom" (Purchas, 1626 [1613]:18). He uses the relation of the prince to the "Bodie Politike" as one of a number of organic metaphors to relate the part to the whole. That God's Truth

underlies all human relations and therefore all legitimate polities is unavoidable; errors in the behaviour of princes are themselves accounted for by the lack
of true godliness of the prince. Yet at the same time true Religion is a matter of
the heart in the first place; outward rites and observances are just that: "outward." But it might be claimed that in a rudimentary sense this tends to loosen
the fusion of church and state, or of religion and geography, and makes room
for the idea that others, including Penn or Locke, were to articulate, that religion and civil government are essentially different from each other, the one
concerned with the inner, the other with the outer, the one with eternal life and
the individual, the other with the temporal and the political. Thus, talking of
Religion as the basis for "policie," Purchas still makes concessions to the
notion that they are inseparable, compared for example with Locke's claim in *A
Letter concerning Toleration* (1689) that they have nothing essentially to do with
each other. And yet there is a proliferation of references to politics and even
politicians. Talking about the universality of martyrdom, even in the false
religions: "How many Martyrs hath Religion, yea, Superstition, yeelded? But
who will lay downe his life to seale some Politician's authority?" And in a side
note, Purchas points out, "Not only the Religion hath had martyrs; but Iewish,
Turkish, Ethnike, Heretical Superstitions and Idolatries." Religion, then, even
in its false varieties, is derived from true Religion, demands the loyalty that can
lead to martyrdom, expresses itself similarly in ceremonies and customs, and
is deeper and more permanent than "politicall ordinances" (Purchas, 1626
[1613]:27). The word "politicall" here has more the nuance of 'politic' in the
negative sense of clever, cunning, and devious, rather than a distinct (nonreligious) domain of human rational action; yet it may also be a shift in nuance
towards the latter.

Another way to think of Purchas's usages of 'religion', or another strand of
his usage, is the holistic model of the commonwealth projected onto others. In
English, the commonweal since the sixteenth century has been thought of
increasingly as coterminous with the nation, that is, with our Protestant Religion, 'our' being the collective identity of the English nation. One of the most
central modern English-language discourses on 'religions' in religious studies,
historiography, and anthropology derives from this kind of holistic sixteenth-
and seventeenth-century discourse, though the term has become progressively
more abstract, objectified, and consciously or unconsciously manipulated.
Deriving from the Samuel Purchas kind of usage in the context of early colonialism, we get the modern generic 'religion' and the plural 'religions' as
things that exist in the world, in principle embedded as a cosmology and a
symbolic system of values and practices in any culture at any period of human
history. This usage of 'religion' seems very close to, if less theorised than, later
anthropological uses of 'culture'.[6] These become multiple reified objects virtually coterminous with the symbolic life of reified 'societies', 'nations', and
'ethnikes', which can be described and compared as systems of beliefs and

practices. With Purchas, these 'religions' are still also 'superstitions' though at times he seems to forget this and adopts a mode of description which does not look so much different from the writing of many twentieth-century anthropologists and others interested in knowledge rather than fables about the world.

Samuel Purchas's willingness to use the term 'religion' ambiguously suggests a more general loosening up in contemporary discourses. Though this was partly a result of the multiplication of sectarian churches, the tensions between true Protestant Religion and the Catholic church centred on King Charles and his Catholic wife, Henrietta Maria, the fear of a Catholic invasion and/or insurrection, the development of American colonies, and their experiments with different concepts of church and state, leading to the separation of 'religion' and 'government' or 'politics'.

Purchas was a church vicar, as was Hakluyt. And in his view, history—including what we would separate out as the 'natural' history, the 'political' history, and the 'religious' history—is all part of the working of God's power, justice, and providence in the world which he created. Not the least part of this big picture of fallen man (as will be unsurprising to women, they are excluded from much of this world, and yet in the more ethnographic parts, there is a lot about women) is the Catholic church, which is classified along with other heathenish superstitions:

> He which admireth and almost adoreth the Capuchine, Jesuite, or other Romanists, for selfe-inflicted whippings, fastings, watchings, vowes of obedience, povertie, and single life ... may see, in all these, the Romanists equaled by Heathens, if not out-stripped .... Here also the Reader may see most of their Popish Rites, derived out of Chaldean, Egyptian and other Fountaines of Paganism. (Purchas, 1626 [1613]:pages unnumbered)

The implication here is that truth can only properly be discerned from the Protestant perspective—which perhaps is the forerunner of the idea that only what we today would call 'secular' scholars can be objective in their descriptions and analyses—and that here in this book can be found a catalogue of idolatries, impieties, superstitions, "Devilish monsters of iniquitie" "obtruded under Religious Sacred Mantle." If Religion is Truth, then the classification of all these under the mantle of religion is a deception. If they are 'religion' or 'religions' at all, they are false religions—pseudoreligions or quasi religions in contemporary terminology. What does seem to be true is that 'religion' is a highly ambiguous concept in this text. There are degrees of separation from true (Protestant) Religion, degrees of superstition, which on the basis of the book as a whole might be schematised roughly as Roman Catholic, "Mahometanism" (paganism with letters), and other "Ethnikes" (paganism without letters).

Later, he considers various discourses on the origin of idolatry and superstition, suggesting Babylonia as the original location. Following Lactantius
on the etymology of the Latin word *superstitio*, Purchas says that it referred to
those who honoured their ancestors and

> celebrated their Images in their houses, as household gods. Such
> Authors of New Rites and Deifiers of dead men they called Super-
> stitious: but those who followed the publikely-received and ancient
> Deities, were called Religious, according to that verse of Virgil.
> (Purchas, 1626 [1613]:46)

The distinction between *religio* and *superstitio* was of importance to Protestants
in relation to their own perceived superior rationality as against Catholics and
other peoples. Purchas draws a link between the original idolatry of Babylon
and that of Rome: "And this Romane Babylon, now Tyrant of the West, is the
heire of elder Babylon . . . in these devotions, that then and still Babylon might
be the Mother of Whoredomes and all Abominations" (46).

That there is a concept of universal humanity in this Protestant interpretation is evident. The relation of the prince to "the Bodie Politike" is one of a
number of organic metaphors and analogies he uses here, to relate the part to
the whole. This organic metaphor applies universally, as when he states in a
discussion of Adam and Eve:

> Our first Parents are to be considered not as singular persons
> only . . . but as the roote of Mankind, which had received originalle
> righteousnesse, to keep or to lose to them and theirs, as a perpetuall
> inheritance. As in the Bodie Politike, the Act of the Prince is reputed
> the Act of the Whole . . . so stands it betwixt us and Adam our naturall
> Prince, the Burgesse of the Worlde, the Head of this human Bodie
> and Generation, the Root and Fountain of our Humanitie. (Purchas,
> 1626 [1613]:24)

True Religion, then, is the true relation of the creation to God, relationships
being conveyed through the idea of part to whole, on the analogy with the relation
between prince and body politic, and Adam and the whole of humanity. After the
Fall, this true relation was lost, but relics of the divine image remained on the
human memory, and from this dim relic of memory various distorted 'religions'
or superstitions (i.e., false religions) developed, like addictions; hence the title of
chapter VI (Purchas, 1626 [1613]:25): "Of the Reliques of the Divine Image after
the fall, whereby naturally men addict themselves unto some Religion: and what
was the Religion of the World before the Floud." Apparently, all people everywhere have an instinct to worship God in some way:

> The wit no sooner conceiveth that there is a God, but the Will in-
> ferreth that he ought to be worshipped. What Philosophers, or what

Politicians ever taught the Easterne and Westerne Islands, discovered
in this last age of the World, this necessitie of Religion?

So all groups of humans, some of them recently discovered, in one way or
another exhibit the necessity of religion and this "natural zeale of that which
they esteeme Religion, beyond all things else esteemed most naturall" (Purchas, 1626 [1613]:26).

There are a number of things to note here. One is, as we have already
seen, that a concept of religion based on biblical Christianity is fundamental.
This Religion, which is most completely revealed through the Bible, is based
on the divine image which lies as a residual memory on human hearts. In
this sense, it is a natural religion. What does 'natural' mean here? Nature is
encompassed by God, and therefore epistemologically and ontologically by
Religion, Christian Truth. We do not yet have nature as a nonreligious independent system, an object of empirical knowledge independent of the will of
God. Nature, it is true, is fallen, and thus the connection with God has been
broken, an ambiguity which arguably helped the development of a view of
nature as altogether distinct from God. But in Purchas, nature is still part of
the redemptive plan of God, Christ offers the world redemption, and authoritative statements about the natural state of humans are still biblical. Another
point is that all order in the world derives from God, including the sense of
unity within 'civil society', for this solidarity could not be produced by art or
industry or politicians qua politicians. Yet this also represents an idea of the
politician as a specific kind of actor in society, and civil society while theoretically dependent on God is to some extent being reified as a separate concept.

Purchas is definitely in possession of the idea, which is still pervasive in
the language of religious studies, world religions, and indeed in the sociology
of religion, that there is Religion itself, which manifests itself as separate
religions. It is also a Protestant concept in the sense that this Religion is
imprinted on the heart, and that it manifests itself in outward observances of
various kinds, these being the rituals, ceremonies, and customs: "Religion it
selfe is in the heart, and produceth those outward ceremoniall effects thereof . . . it is . . . naturall most of all . . . to observe some kind of Religion" (Purchas,
1626 [1613]:26–27).

So we see that for Purchas there are two models, or perhaps one should say
tendencies or potentials towards two models. On the one hand, Religion refers
to the proper organic relations of all order in the world to God, in which ideally
everything and every person has its proper God-given degree, status, and
function in the service of the whole; but also, on the other hand, true Religion
is inner, concerned with the individual's relation to God and the afterlife, as
against outer Religion as mere external, ceremonial, magical performance and
irrational superstition. It seems to me that this ambiguity between the organic
holistic analogy and the idea of true Religion as essentially inward runs

through modernity, with the latter finding expression in the U.S. Constitution. It is the same ambiguity as that between early Protestants, such as those who travelled to America in the *Mayflower* to establish a church-state or ideal Puritan commonwealth in which Religion would encompass what we have separated out as the political, and those who, like William Penn, stressed the inward as against the outward, the soul as against matter, and religion as against the civil magistracy. In both of these ideas, one can see a distinction between relative degrees of sacrality and relative degrees of profaneness. But in the latter, the profane has become or is becoming essentialised into a nonreligious world of neutral matter, scientific knowledge, and secular governance which has nothing essentially to do with religion.

These two discourses, or what retrospectively from my modern position I *read* as two different discourses, were for writers in the seventeenth century only tendencies or different emphases from which modern essentialised polarities were beginning to emerge. An analogous bifurcation in the meaning of Protestantism can be found with reference to the work of Mary Turner (2002:17–29) in the contrast between the Anglican priests and the Methodist and Baptist missionaries in Barbados. The Anglicans saw slaves as barbarians, perhaps not much different from the natural slaves which the Spanish theologians and lawyers inherited from Aristotle, whose irrationality made them a special category of underclass in the holistic hierarchy of the plantation, and the Anglicans were not concerned to convert the slaves to Christian civility, leaving them instead to their dehumanised status as beings beyond redemption. On the other hand, Baptist and Methodist missionaries ambiguously both did and did not support an interpretation of the gospel which ordains us all to our allotted positions in life. Their greater readiness to treat slaves as equally open to salvation and redemption suggested also that slaves should be free to redeem their standing through economic activity. This emphasis was surely crucial in embedding economic theory in the natural order of things, and as a consequence (either intended or unintended) facilitated the various moves to abolish slave labour and transform slaves into a wage-earning class.

Perhaps I am reading too much ambiguity between two different emphases in Purchas as a result of retrospective reading. I stress that these later developments do not exist in Purchas in any explicit sense, and can only be noted as tendencies within his work and, more generally, within Protestantism. These discourses, in combination with a number of other diverse factors which may be only contingently connected, have passed historically into the hegemonic structures of colonial and capitalist ideology.

Even so, the discourse on civility and barbarity in one way or another runs through Protestant discourses, and Purchas is no exception. Purchas's descriptions of Muslims in his "Third Booke: Of the Arabians, Saracens, Turkes, and of the Ancient Inhabitants of Asia Minor: and of their Religions" is accompanied by hatred, contempt, and incessant negative comment. Perhaps at

this early stage of the colonial process, when Arabic polities were not less powerful than European ones, and the racism of nineteenth- and twentieth-century
Orientalists, anthropologists, and missionaries had not yet found its day, the
abuse that Purchas expresses may be more analogous to communist invective
against capitalists and vice versa during the Cold War. Nor is it much worse than
what Purchas, as a Protestant, says about Catholics. While Purchas frequently
uses the term 'sacred' to refer to non-Christians, as in "sacred customs of the
Heathens," it is clear that this usage is either ironic or, more straightforwardly,
has the nuance of "taken as sacred" by those people. For it is inherent in his
"discourse on Religion" that all but Protestant Christian practices are corrupt:

> The Divine . . . may here contemplate the workes of God, not in cre-
> ation alone, but in his justice and Providence, pursuing sinne ev-
> erywhere with such dreadful plagues; both bodily, in rooting up and
> pulling downe the mightiest Empires; and especially in Spiritual
> Judgements, giving up so great a part of the World unto the efficacie
> of Errour in strong delusions, that having forsaken the Fountaine
> of Living Waters, they should dig unto themselves these broke pits
> that can hold no water, devout in their Superstitions, and super-
> stitious in their devotions, agreeing all in this, that there should be
> a Religion, disagreeing from each other, and the Truth, in the prac-
> tice thereof. (Purchas, 1626 [1613]:pages unnumbered)

The expression "the Divine" here does not refer to God, but to any hypothetical
Protestant priest who ought to be interested in the knowledge amassed during
Purchas's pilgrimage, just as his pilgrimage amasses knowledge that may be
useful for experts in various branches of the human sciences. For the knowledge of the world presented by Purchas is encompassed by Christian Truth,
even if it does surely represent a move towards what we think of as secular,
factual, objective knowledge of other peoples and of the world as a natural
domain.

On the basis of his chapters on Christian Truth, India, Japan, "Mahu-
metanism," and the indigenous peoples of the Americas, I would make the
following generalisation. Purchas's motivations can be divided into five: (1) to
gather and relate facts and observations drawn from many sources, including
voyage observations and travel journals, into an informative compendium of
knowledge about the world; (2) to develop a biblical and Protestant Christian
interpretation of the world, and to fit the various narratives and data into that
interpretive framework; (3) to polemicise not only the peoples of the Middle
East, India, Japan, and the Americas, but also the Catholic church and its
practices, thus constructing a superior Protestant position and viewpoint; (4) to
justify trade and exchange as promoting peace and wealth; and (5) to promote a
patriotic nationalism in competition with other European nations. It seems
reasonable therefore to see this work not simply as a rhetoric of Protestant

triumphalism and Catholic irrationality and barbarism, nor simply as a patriotic justification of English successes or failures in competing for trade, merchandise, and glory, but also as an early attempt at comparative ethnography, or comparative religion. The following provides the reader with a taste of how some of these different objectives get combined:

> The Grecians burned their dead Parents, the Indians intombed them in their own bowels...that which mooved both, and began either Custome, one and the same principle of pietie and religious duty, howsoever diversely expressed. Yea, even the most lascivious, cruell, beastly, and Devillish observations, were grounded upon this one principle, That God must be served: which service they measured by their owne Crooked rules, everywhere disagreeing, and yet meeting in One Center, the necessitie of Religion. (Purchas, 1626 [1613]:27)

The flavour of his polemics against Catholics, which pervade the descriptions of 'the other' throughout, can be captured in the paragraphs with which he begins and finishes his chapters on Japan: "5th Booke: Ch. XV. A larger Relation of some principall Ilands of Asia, and first of the Ilands of Iapon." The subtitle, "A Preface touching the Iesuits, and a description of Iapon, with some of their strange customes" (Purchas, 1626 [1613]:586), leaves it unclear—I suspect deliberately—whose strange customs are to be described, the Japanese or the Catholics. In his opening sentence, Purchas plays on Jesuit gains in the East as compensation for Catholic losses in Europe, presumably as a result of the Reformation:

> The Iesuits have not more fixed the eyes of the World upon them in the Western parts, than they have fixed their owne eyes on the Eastern: here seeking to repaire, with their untempered Morter, the ruines of their Falling Babylon; there laying a new foundation of their after-hopes: here, by their Politike Mysteries and Mystical Policies, endeavouring to recover; there, by new Conquests to make supply of their losses: here, for busy intruding into affaires of state, suspected by their owne, hated by their Adversaries; there, by seeming to neglect Greatnesse, and to contemn Riches, of the mightiest are not feared, whiles Others believe, observe and admire them. Both here and there they spare not to compass both Sea and Land, to win Proselytes; every of their Residences or Colledges, being as so many Forts to establish this new Roman Monarchie, but with unlike advantage. (Purchas, 1626 [1613]:586)

On the other hand, Purchas expresses gratitude, if that word is applicable, for their travels and their knowledge of geography, "for furthering Geographie with knowledge of a New World" (586). And furthermore, their sort of Christianity is better than no Christianity at all:

Neither are the wounds of Popish Superstition so absolutely mortall, as the Ethnike Atheism; the one having no foundation at all; the other shewing the true foundation: although their Babylonish slime even here supply the roome of better mortar, besides their stubble, hay and wood built upon it. (568)

He therefore thanks the Jesuits for providing knowledge upon which his own account will draw. As a matter of interest in passing, I should mention that he also acknowledges Will Adams as a source—"Our countrey-man William Adams . . . now lives there, and hath done these many yeares"—and in the margin refers to news from Adams "in a letter which brought home by the last Indian Fleet, bearing date from Firando [Hirado?] October 1611" (Purchas, 1626 [1613]:586).

Among many fascinating glimpses of Japan and the activities of Europeans in Japan, through the Protestant fulminations we are given an insight into the dispute about trade between Macao and Nagasaki pursued by the Portuguese and more fully disclosed by the Portuguese Rodrigues, known as the Interpreter due to his position as a fluent Japanese speaker in service to the effective rulers of Japan Toyotomi Hideyoshi (1536–1598) and Tokugawa Ieyasu (1542–1616). In an absorbing book based on contemporary accounts of Rodrigues, Michael Cooper says of him:

During his fifty-six years in Japan and China, he won the friendship of the rulers Toyotomi Hideyoshi and Tokugawa Ieyasu, took an active role in the silk trade between China and Japan, and for some years was the most influential European in Nagasaki ("Nagasacke"), or, for that matter, in the entire country. He somehow found time to compose the first grammar of the Japanese language ever to be published, and in his old age wrote a lengthy account of Japanese culture that has astonished modern readers by its discernment and wealth of detail. He travelled widely throughout China, was involved in the Rites controversy, conducted official business on behalf of Macao, and finally took part in skirmishes between Ming defenders and Manchu invaders. (Cooper, 1974:9)

Purchas mentions—as related by Rodrigues the Interpreter—the dispute about the silk trade, and says that the Jesuits were accused by the emperor and "the Governour of Firando" (presumably referring to Hirado, the small island near Nagasaki where the Dutch were allowed to have the sole foreign trading station after the expulsion of the Catholics) of "being under the cloake of Religion, Merchants" (Purchas, 1626 [1613]:601).

Purchas comments that after the Jesuits had been banished from Japan, their churches were all taken down, and the "Reliques of these crucified persons were reserved as great Holies: as great Follies, I should have said"

(Purchas, 1626 [1613]:601). He then says that in 1585 the Jesuits wanted "to make the Iaponites to know the magnificence of Europe" by encouraging "the Kings of Bungo, Arima and Omur" to send their "Embassadours" to the pope "(then Gregorie the thirteenth) with Letters of devotion to his Holinesse." This "Iesuites policie" was designed "principally to enrich themselves with Gifts and Priviledges" (602). It isn't entirely clear who would be enriched— "themselves"—but presumably Purchas means the Jesuits by the local rulers and governors who were to be made aware of the power and magnificence of either the pope or Europe generally.

Purchas finishes his chapter on Japan with an attack on the Jesuits and a wish that they had not been expelled. On the contrary, he would like to see them all go there:

> But for a farewell to these Iaponian Jesuites, I like their being there
> so well, that I could wish all that Societie were Preaching in that
> Iland, or acting the Scripture-stories upon the Stage... or, if you like
> that rather, a whipping themselves in their vain-glorious Processions
> (which is another of their Iaponian Lectures) that so they might in
> some measure expiate the crimes of their European brethren; or any
> way else, so that our Europe were well ride of such vermine. (Pur-
> chas, 1626 [1613]:602)

The list of contents of the third book gives the reader a good idea of how anti-Muslim and anti-Catholic polemics are mixed with the attempt to order knowledge in a systematic way, with the term 'religion' operating ambiguously between these two, because while on the one hand it can be read ironically as referring to 'superstitions', yet the term also takes on the role of a category for organising knowledge:

The Thirde Booke: Of the Arabians, Saracens, Turkes, and of the Ancient Inhabitants of Asia Minor: and of their Religions

Ch. I. Of Arabia and of the ancient Religions, Rites and Customes thereof
Ch. II. Of the Saracene Name, Nation, and proceeding in Armes: and the Succession of their Chalifaes
Ch. III. The Life of Mahumet, Mahammed, or Muhammed, the Saracen Law-giver
Ch. IIII. Of the Alcoran, or Alfurcan, Containing the Mahumetan Law: the summe and contents thereof
Ch. V. Other Muhameticall Speculations, and explanations of their Law, collected out of their own Commentaries of that Argument
Ch. VI. Of the Pilgrimage to Mecca
Ch. VII. Of the Successors of Mahomet, of their different Sects, and of the dispersing of that Religion, through the World

Purchas uses rite, custom, nation, sect, holiness, priest, law, 'religious', and 'religion' in the list of contents to order his flow of 'facts' as well as his invective. He is also struggling with proper names and a variety of spellings. Throughout, he variously uses Mahomet, Mohamed, Mahumet, and Muhammed to refer to the Prophet, whom he also calls "the false Prophet" (Purchas, 1626 [1613]:260); Muhammedans, Muslimos, and Muslemans to refer to Muslims; and refers to Islam as the Mahometan religion, which is also referred to as "his pretence of Religion," "his new Religion," and "his false Religion." There is contempt for, but also perhaps fear of, Islam (a word I have not found here) in Purchas's text. Here he admits the widespread use of Arabic, while denigrating that language as the result of "that first confusion and babbling at Babel":

> The Arabike tongue is now the common language of the East, especially among such as embrace the Mahometan Religion: this language [is] in the first division of tongues, according to Epiphanius . . . .
> It is now the most universall in the world . . . since that first confusion and babbling at Babel. (Purchas, 1626 [1613]:229)

Furthermore, he recognises that, from the viewpoint of Muslims, it is Christians and others who are the infidels and heretics. In a section where Purchas is attempting, on the basis of a variety of sources, to derive the identity and descent of the Saracens, he says, "And Erpenius saith . . . all the Muhammedans generally call themselves Muslimos, or Muslemans, which signifieth Beleevers, as if all else were infidells or Heretikes" (230).

The descriptions of Muslim people seem more distorted than those of India because they are accompanied by hatred, contempt, and incessant negative comment: "This name Saracene may well befit that course of life which they embraced. In the more Southerly parts of Arabia, they are more civill and rich, dwelling in cities, and have quicke trade, which are all wanting about Medina and Mecca" (Purchas, 1626 [1613]:230). The use of "civill" here does not refer to civil society in the modern reified sense as distinct from 'religion' or the church. It seems to be a way of indicating superior civilisation or urban sophistication as against tribal Bedouin society. "Civill" indicates civility, or sophistication, "dwelling in cities," in contrast to those whom the prophet Jeremy "reckoneth their tents, Camels, and Flockes, as their greatest wealth" (Purchas, 1626 [1613]:230).

One can easily get the hostile mood of Purchas's approach to what we today refer to as Islam even by only reading the margin notes. Here are some examples, listed by page number:

241. Fortalicium fidei reckoneth another genealogie: and the Saracen Chronicle continueth this, even from Adam; not agreeing with themselves or any truth.

242. This mutiny, according to others, hapned many yeeres after that Mahumet had under the cloak of Religion furthered his ambition and rebellion.

242. ⁷Mahomet a Thefe and Murtherer. An Adulterer. A Wittall.

254. Mahomet guiltie of his witchcraft, often speaketh of it: that he may not bee thought such a one.

254. Such tales as these of Abraham, Salomon, etc. you shall find both in the Iewish and Popish legends, as if the Iew, Papist, and Mahumetan, had contended for the whetstone: which anyone that readeth shall finde.

255. In diverse places of the Alcoran, the better to colour his filthinesse, he hath dispersed good SENTENCES, like Roses scattered on a dunghil, and flowers in a puddle.... Others he hath of another sort, establishing his owne Tyrannie and Religion.

264. mahumetisme

272. They (Mahumetans) pretend visions and miracles, etc. But have not antichrist and all Idolaters their miracles? faith have ever relation to the word of God.

In the last item, Purchas is referring to Muhammad's tomb in Medina, at which pilgrims pray.

After relating stories which contain a lot of interesting details (though of doubtful accuracy) of pilgrimages, rites, important buildings, traditions, famous people, and legendary events, there is an interesting passage which links

the thinking behind both Catholic and Islamic practices and serves to con-
solidate the discourse on superior Protestant civility and rationality. A mile
from the city of Medina is a house where Muhammad is reputed to have lived,
and a "Mosquita" where he is believed to have prayed. In the middle of the
mosque, there is

> a Tombe made of Lime and Stone foursquare, and full of sand,
> wherein they say was buried that blessed Camell which Mahomet was
> always wont to ride upon. Even still, (as one Mr. Simons a Merchant
> and beholder thereof reported to me) they have a superstitious cus-
> tome at Cairo of carrying the leg of Mahomets Camell (as they af-
> firme) in a Coach, the women in zeale of their blinde devotion,
> hurling their Shashes to receive them some holy and blessed touch,
> for their Mahumeticall edification: as the Papists ascribe no small
> holinesse to the touch of our Ladies image at Loretto with their
> beades, or other implements of their superstition, as my friend Mr.
> Barkley, an eye-witnesse, hath told me. Marvell much we may, that
> the souldiers that crucified Christ, and parted his garments by lot,
> and Judas which kissed him, and the Devill also which carried his
> bodie out of the wildernesses, and set it on a pinnacle of the Temple,
> did not from such holy touches acquire much holinesse. But here a
> good intent was wanting, which though the Mahumetans have, yet a
> Camels leg is not so holy as our Ladies image; Grant it: but they
> pretend Tradition and Devotion no lesse than these: and otherwise,
> there is as little warrant for that house and Image of our Ladie that
> they are true, as of the other.... If Christ himselfe should thus be
> honoured, where, in all the Christian world are such Vowes, Pil-
> grimages, and Devotions in his name, as here to the supposed Lady
> of Loretto? As if they would rather be Mariani than Christiani in their
> Religion. But who brought us now to Loretto? Nay, who can but in
> reading the one, thinke of the other, both being frequented so gen-
> erally in Pilgrimages, Offerings, and I know not what Superstitions?
> Only in this is Loretto worse, that it abuses more holy names of God,
> and his Saints, to like unholy holies.... Yea, the very narration of the
> Saracenicall and Turkish Rites by us in this Booke, shall bee suffi-
> cient to them which know the Popish, in many things to discern and
> acknowledge the kindred, and like hellish descent both...howsoever
> their heads looke contrarie, one towards Christ, the other towards
> Mahomet. (272)

This last quote is rambling, and reads like an uncorrected draft, as though
we are listening to Purchas's tumbling thoughts, perhaps late at night while
working by candlelight. But it illustrates a number of Purchas's motivations
and intentions:

A. the general one of using a variety of different kinds of informants and sources to build up what we would call a database, an informative compendium of useful knowledge about the world, more and more of which is being 'discovered', observed, lived in, traded with, threatened by, competed with

B. to place all these data, and to interpret them, within a biblical Protestant Christian framework, which can be described as his theoretical paradigm

C. to polemicise not only the "Mahumetans" but also Catholics and their practices

One result of these intentions is to develop an idea of Protestant Christianity, or Protestant Christians, as inherently more rational, less superstitious, closer to the Truth, and superior in moral and intellectual identity. It is the development of a discourse on Protestant civility as against the barbarism of all others, including and perhaps in particular the Catholics. The Catholics and the Muslims are equally enemies in his writing, and much of his desire to know and to inform seems to be on the principle that one needs to know one's enemies if one is going to defeat them.

Sometimes, Purchas uses the term 'magic' to distinguish between true Religion and superstition, as when discussing various kinds of "Heremites" among the Muslims of Egypt, including one very wealthy and powerful hermit who had "Magick-bookes," and who called "Magicke" the "true science" (Purchas, 1626 [1613]:277). 'Religion' often seems to mean something equivalent to 'customs' or 'practices'. A "superstitious custome" is surely a magical ritual. "Holy" and "blessed" are used generically to describe these practices; "holy touch" conveys the idea of, or belief in, a magical power that can be transmitted from a camel's leg, a statue of the Virgin, Christ's garments after his crucifixion, or Christ's body both dead and alive. Thus we get "unholy holies," things that are holy to Catholics and to Muslims are unholy in the light of (Protestant) Truth. "Pilgrimages," "rites," "vows," "devotions," and "offerings" are words which connect what Muslims in Medina or Cairo and Catholics in Loretto in Italy do: they are similar and comparable because we cannot think of one, he says, without thinking of the other.

> 276. Mahomet, having with Word and Sword published his Alcoran . . . his followers after his death succeeding in his place, succeeded him in Tyrannie. Eubocar, surnamed Abdulla, undertooke the defence of that faithlesse Faith and Kingdome, and that (as his Predecessor had done) partlie by subtiltie, partly by force.

In this statement, tyranny and force are built into the narration of the very beginnings of Islam.

He also uses sects, factions, and religions interchangeably:

274. For the Alcoran being . . . read diversely, was cause of different sects
among them.

These sects each followed different copies of the Qur'an, each being authorised
by "foure great Doctors of the Mahumetan Law" (274). He then continues to
discuss these sects as "factions": "But two principall factions Mahumetan, at
this day" (274). These two "principall factions" are located either in "Turkie,"
"Arabia," Africa (Leshari), or Persia and Corosan (Imamia). But in Egypt there
are reputed to be four: "by Leo's judgement, all which follow the rule Leshari or
Hashari are Catholic Mahumetans" (274). However, the same author, Leo, also
affirms

that in Cairo and all Egypt are foure Religions different from each
other, in Spirituall or Ecclesiastical Ceremonies, and also concerning
their Civill and Canon Law . . . . As for those other sects, it seemeth
that they are for the most part long since vanished: and those differences which remaine consist rather in diversitie of rules, and order
of profession, than in differing Sects and Heresies of Religion. (274–
276)

Though these distinctions are not at all clear in meaning, Purchas is
struggling to find terminology in an attempt at description and analysis. He
uses the English-language terminology to hand and tries to bring order into his
data. Religions, factions, and sects seem to mean the same thing here; but how
in Purchas's mind do "differing Sects and Heresies of Religion" differ from
"diversitie of rules, and order of profession"? Perhaps he had in mind the
difference between a Catholic heresy such as Albigensianism and an order
within the church like the Franciscans, who are different from the Benedic-
tines? Here he distinguishes between "sect" and "Religious Order":

277. But these hermits we cannot so well reckon a Sect, as a Religious
Order; of which sort there are divers in these Mahumetane nations.

Sects are apparently distinguished by their different versions of the Qur'an:
"the Saracens of the East differ in their Alcoran from those of the West,
making the first five Chapters but one; and that they differ in the exposition
thereof, and in the same Schools or Universities, one Sect condemneth another" (Purchas, 1626 [1613]:277). Purchas also distinguishes "Mahumetan
Professors" according to their "Nations," meaning Arabs, Persians, Turks, and
Tartars (277).

The mixture of a serious attempt at description and analysis with anti-
Islamic vitriol can be well seen in this sentence, with which he begins chapter
VIII:

278. Although some may thinke, that I have been so tedious, in the
relation of the Mahumetan opinions and Superstitions that, to

> speake any thing more, would seeme but as powring water into the
> full sea: Yet... this Saracenicall Religion hath sustained her chances
> and changes, according to the diversitie of times and places where it
> is and hath been professed: so doe I hold it fit, as we have seene the
> foundation, to behold also the frames and fabriques thereon buil-
> ded, and from that Fountaine (or Sinke-hole rather) of Superstition,
> to lead you along the gutters and streames thus derived.

He attributes preeminence to the Turks among the "Mahumetan nations," and
he asserts the need to link narratives of the "briefe Historie of that Nation, and
the proceedings of their State, to ascribe their theories and opinions, and then
their practice and rites of Religion" (Purchas, 1626 [1613]:278).

This sounds like a conscious methodological intention to narrate these
different aspects together, and therefore a degree of differentiation between the
proceedings of their state and the practice and rites of religion. He emphasises
"the discovery of their Religion" in the context of the narrative of the nation,
which implies a distinction and a unity. There is not much specialist vocabulary available for talking about the state, civil society, politics, economics.
When talking about their ancient, pre-Islamic worship of fire, air, water, and
earth, he refers to their "Religion."

One could claim that there is an attempt in this book to create what we
would call an objective, secular narrative of events and facts, even though it is
framed by biblical Christianity and steeped in Protestant polemics, hyperbole,
and insult. Here is a description of the Turkish attitude to "the Booke of their
Law" which, according to Purchas's source, Anthony Menavinus, "who lived a
long time in the Turkish Court," is called "Musaph" or "Curaam,"

> which Georgiovitz reckonethe another booke; not the Alcoran; it is in
> Arabike; and they hold unlawful to translate it into the vulgar.... I
> could thinke it likely that this containeth some Extracts and Glosses
> hereof; or is to their Alcoran, as our service booke to our Bible....
> The ignorance of the Arabike hath caused much mis-calling of words
> and names. They have it in such reverence, that they will not touch it,
> except they be washed from top to toe: and it is read in their Churches
> by one with a loud voice, the people giving devout attendance without
> any noyse... and after he hath read it, he kisseth it, and touchest his
> eyes with it, and with great solemnitie it is carried into the due place.
> (Purchas, 1626 [1613]:297)

Bracketing any possible mistakes, this is a straightforward description of a
ritual practice. Look at the words he uses, and the Christian terminology by
analogy: church, Bible, service book, reverence, solemnity. There is also the
usage of "the more religious" which may not refer to "the religious" but to a
degree of devotion, e.g., talking about times of prayer, he says these are per-

formed seven times each day: one of these is "duely observed on the Friday by all, at other times by the more religious" (Purchas, 1626 [1613]:298). "[I]n their fast or Lent they abstaine very religiously" (300). The use of "religiously" here has the same ambiguity noted earlier. It is performed religiously because it is an act ordained by God; or alternatively because it is a ritual practice which is performed conscientiously and with exactitude in the sense of *religio*. On the other hand, "The wives and women servants...are in their habite and behaviour modest: and where himselfe dwelt, the Father-in-Law had not seene the face of his Daughter-in-law...so religiously doe they veyle themselves" (Purchas, 1626 [1613]:300). This use of "religiously" seems consistent with the more general nuance of *religio*, doing things with great seriousness or solemnity. It is very much about ritual practice.

Talking about the diet and drinking habits of the Turks under the title "Of the Turkish Manners, their Civill and Morall behaviour," Purchas says, "Opium they much use, it seemes for the giddinesse and turbulent dreames it causeth, which they (as all kinde of stupefying astonishment and madnesse) religiously affect" (Purchas, 1626 [1613]:304). It isn't clear to whom or what "they" refer here, or the meaning of "religiously affect," but I interpret it ironically as superstitious madness masquerading as 'religion'.

Sometimes, "nation" and "religion" are used almost interchangeably, as houses were built "for all Strangers and Pilgrims of any Nation or Religion" (307).

The ambiguity of 'religion' comes out here: "The places of most Religion to the Turkes abroad, are those which Mahumet himselfe polluted with his irreligion: as Mecca, Medina etc." (306). He might have said the places which are "most sacred to the Turks" are those which Muhammad profaned. That there is so little about abstract belief in God, and that religion is talked about in terms of practices of a wide variety, suggests what religion meant to Purchas as a Protestant Christian. It is about practice, the right way to live, the disciplines of civility or barbarity, rather than about abstract beliefs. Of course, belief is involved, but superstition is wrongheaded practice. There are nuances of belief.

Purchas also has to acknowledge that, from the "Mahometan" viewpoint, Christians are "Infidels":

> After this they all kneel and prostrate themselves on the ground, the Meizin observing a long ceremonie, in which with a loud voice hee prayeth GOD to inspire the Christians, Iewes, Greekes, and generally all Infidels to turne to their Law. (Purchas, 1626 [1613]:309)

Note here the use of the word "Law." He could have said "to turne to their Religion." Again, we can see that the term 'religion' has many possibilities, and these are being teased out at a time and in a context where descriptive and analytical categories are required. Another point to note is that this is a genuinely sobering observation and is not accompanied by some vicious aside. In some parts of his text, Purchas is objectively assessing the other point of view.

He also uses the mediaeval and early modern distinction between the religious as in 'regulars' and the secular priests. For example, opening chapter XIIII, he says, "After the discourse of their Regulars (which in estimation of devotion have with the Turkes, and therefore in this history, first place) their secular priests follow to be considered" (Purchas, 1626 [1613]:319). Here he is discussing the reports of a source called Septemcastrensis, who lived among the Turks and who says that there are many divisions among them:

> And besides their differences in ceremonies, there are saith he, four sects, differeing in maine grounds of Religion .... One of these sects is that of Priests, holding that none can be saved, but by the Law of Mahomet. The second of their religious Dermschler ... are of opinion, that the Law profiteth nothing, but the grace of God. (314–315)

He makes it clear that the priests are the seculars. The 'religious' he calls "Regulars." A king, Amurath II,

> going to stoole in the night, the boords gave way, and he fell in, staying on a crosse Timber, where this religious man in their wonted habite appeared to him .... This after so affected the King, that himself became a religious man, till the necessitie of State-affaires compelled him to resume his government. (Purchas, 1626 [1613]:314–15)

"[T]his religious man" who wears a habit presumably refers to what Purchas takes to be the equivalent of a Christian regular (monk or friar); the experience leads the king to enter a religious order, which he then must leave in order to return to his secular duties, the duties of state affairs. However, this seems clearly not to mean that the king ceased to be 'religious' in the modern sense of a secular neutrality towards religion.

On the matter of what we would call church-state relations in Turkey, we have seen that Purchas, an ordained minister of the Anglican church, dedicates his book first to the king and second to the archbishop of Canterbury, thus suggesting that the Church of England is a part of the state, and a hierarchically lower part at that. And when he mentions an English monarch, as he does here, he uses hyperbole:

> Master Harborn, sometime Embassador into Turkie for Englands Queen (the world's wonder, our western Hesperus, that shined so far over and beyond all Christendome, into the East; but my words are too base to usher in that renowned name) Elizabeth. (Purchas, 1626 [1613]:320)

He then reports the relation in Turkey as follows:

> The Turkes doe hold for head and chiefe of their Religion the Mufti (the choice of whom is made by the Great Turke himselfe) .... His

> authoritie is so esteemed, that the Emperour will never alter a de-
> termination made by him. He intermedleth in all matters as best he
> liketh, whether they be civill or criminall, yea, or of State. And yet
> he hath no power to command.... The Grand Signior, to shew that
> he is religious and just, doth serve himself of the authorities of
> this Mufti, in affaires of warre and peace, demanding his judgment.
> (Purchas, 1626 [1613]:320)

He goes on to say that the mufti warned the emperor that the Moors in Spain
should be protected against the Christians: "hee was so bold with the Emperour, as to tell him to his face, that if he did neglect the cause of those
Mahumetans, hee might be thereunto by his subjects compelled" (320).

I think we can deduce various things from this. One is that the power of the
Turkish emperor is legendary and is not something to joke about even for a
Protestant Englishman. This in turn highlights the stupendous power of the
mufti. The whole discourse also makes no bones about a distinction between
'religion' and 'state'. This is unsurprising and should not be confused with a
modern distinction between the religious and the secular since clearly neither in
England nor in Turkey is the state 'nonreligious' in the modern sense. It is a
division of functions within a total sacralised order of power and hierarchy. But
whereas, for Purchas, the king is above the archbishop of Canterbury, in the case
of Turkey, the equivalent of the archbishop of Canterbury is in some respects
above the king. Purchas is attempting to find a language for discussing and
analysing these issues comparatively, when he says about the mufti:

> In the Booke of the Policie of the Turkish Empire, it is said, that the
> Mufties authoritie is like to that of the Iewish High Priest, or Roman
> Pope. I rather esteeme it like to that of the Patriarckes of Alexandria,
> Antioch, etc. as binding not on all Mahumetans, but the Turkes only.
> (Purchas, 1626 [1613]:320–21)

But the relative power of mufti and emperor is not clear, for he goes on to say,
"His authoritie, saith Soranzo, is so great, that none will openly contradict the
Mufties sentence: but yet if the Emperour be settled in a resolution, the Mufti,
with feare or flattery inclines unto him" (321).

There is no logical place to end a discussion and analysis of this fascinating
book. I choose this relatively arbitrary ending, hoping to have shown that, while
the book is framed by Religion as Christian Truth derived from biblical narratives,
the *Pilgrimage* strives for words to categorise new ethnographic knowledge. In
this striving, the ambiguity of terminology becomes apparent, and the fundamental
trope of encompassing Protestant Truth frequently loosens and accumulates
alternative usages that, in retrospect, suggest the development of modern generic
usages. But we cannot without great qualification say that this has been articulated yet, only that we think retrospectively that we can detect its emergence.

8

English Historical Documents, 1660–1832

The contrast between the usages of 'religion' and related categories in the sixteenth century (chapter 6) and those of Samuel Purchas in the early seventeenth century (chapter 7) suggest both a proliferation and shifts in nuance. What seems to have happened is that the greater consciousness of the forms of life of non-European peoples, which was the concern of Purchas in his pilgrimage around the world, led to a proliferation by analogy of usages of English-language (or more generally European) categories in the attempt to organise new knowledge. In general terms and to some extent, this shift seems consistent with Jonathan Z. Smith's argument that an "essentially Catholic understanding of 'religion' in close proximity to ritual" was becoming transformed into something more like the eighteenth-century definition by Samuel Johnson: "To know God, and to render him a reasonable service, are the two principal objects of religion . . . . Man appears to be formed to adore, but not to comprehend, the Supreme Being" (quoted in Smith, 1998:271). Smith characterises this as a shift "to belief as the defining characteristic of religion," and suggests that these tendencies "were exacerbated by the schismatic tendencies of the various Protestantisms, with their rival claims to authority, as well as the growing awareness of the existence of a multitude of articulate, non-Christian traditions" (271).

However, insofar as one early seventeenth-century writer such as Purchas can be taken as valid evidence, the most that can be said is that there is considerable ambiguity. Despite the evidence of a move towards a more generic concept of religion, a major and even defining trope in Purchas's discourse remains the opposition between 'religions' and 'superstitions', which can also be read as an opposition between Religion as Protestant Christian Truth and 'religions' as falsehoods, Satanic deceptions, and barbarous irrationality. Furthermore, despite this evidence, and despite the revolutionary turmoil of the mid-seventeenth century, with its proliferation of radical theologies of dissent, I want to show in this present chapter that much of the usage after the Restoration of 1660, in England at least, suggests a powerful and significant continuity in the dominant discourses of the male elite.

I have argued that, by looking at discursive usages not only of 'religion' in isolation but of categories having significant connection with religion—for example, 'secular', 'politic' and 'politics', 'state', and 'commonweal'—a rather different and more conservative pattern emerges. My thesis in this respect is that the major change in the understanding of 'religion' had to wait for clear articulation of the binary distinctions between religion and science, religion and politics, religion and the state, which in modern language have come to be constructed as essentially different in kind, what in shorthand gets called the religion-secular dichotomy. These binaries also required a consolidation of shifts in meaning of other dichotomies, such as natural and supernatural, mind and matter, or soul and body. While these kinds of distinctions were clearly articulated by English writers such as William Penn and John Locke soon after the Restoration, it was in the eighteenth-century North American colonial context that they became most powerfully formulated in some of the state bills of rights and constitutions (see chapter 9). In contrast, and despite the establishment of Dissenting churches and a growing culture of scientific empiricism and Enlightenment attitudes to knowledge, the church-state arguably continued in England as the regnant discourse well into the nineteenth century.

The problems that were encountered in volume 5 of *English Historical Documents*, discussed in chapter 6, are to some extent repeated in volume 8, *1660–1714*, edited by Andrew Browning (1953). That is to say, the editor felt compelled to classify and discuss the texts which form the basis of his knowledge according to modern categories such as religion, politics, and economics, even though he was aware that the texts themselves do not support this way of constructing our collective past. In his editor's introduction, Browning says: "The church ... found it hard to distinguish between the religious and the political aspects of its success" (1953:3).

But he might equally have said that 'the state' found it hard to distinguish between the religious and the political aspects of its success. Everyone found it difficult to make this distinction in anything like the modern sense, even though the language was being developed at this time. For as we will see by looking closely at the use of language, though the church and state are distinguished in seventeenth-century English language, and while there are some obvious differences, say, in the day-to-day ecclesiastical duties of a parish priest and the civil duties of a magistrate, I suggest that the difference between them is not equivalent at all to the modern distinction between 'religion' and the modern nonreligious state which is constitutionally protected from, or neutral towards, 'religion'. On the other hand, when we look at a minority of individual English writers of the late seventeenth and early eighteenth centuries, such as Benjamin Hoadly, an Anglican bishop who had such radical views on the separation of church and state that he was frequently cited by American revolutionaries (Hoadly, 1710, 1718; see also Bailyn, 1967:37), or when we look at some of the more radical charters of states such as Pennsylvania even from the late seventeenth century, we can in retrospect see a clear distinction between freedom of religion and the legitimate powers of the civil governor.

In one publication (four volumes) of 1704, *A Collection of Voyages and Travels, Some now first printed from Original Manuscripts* (Churchill & Churchill, 1704), there are articles translated from many different languages. Some of these had appeared in Hakluyt (1599), for example, the account by the German nobleman Martin Baumgarten, translated from Latin, of his travels in 1507 through Egypt, Arabia, Palestine, and Syria. However, for texts translated for the first time, methodologically speaking, I can only take the language as typical of the early eighteenth century, when the work was published. One thing that becomes clear immediately is that there are various usages that I have not found in the Browning volume, which covers the same period. For example, the first article is a translation from Spanish of a book by a Dominican friar, R. F. F. Dominic Fernandez Navarette, who in 1646 had been sent by his order to the Philippines and had then transferred to China, where he learnt Chinese and studied "their Histories," "the points in controversy among the Missionaries," and various facts about "that mighty Monarchy." The title of his book has been translated into English as *An Account of the Empire of China, Historical, Political, Moral and Religious*. This translation indicates that distinctions between 'political' and 'religious' were current in English in 1704. Again, the context is one of European expansion and new knowledge of other peoples.

However, the texts in the Browning volume indicate that such language was developing only in certain contexts, and was not the most general or dominant at the time. Ideas about governance and control over much of the trade and plantations reflected the organic hierarchy of the home ideology. The classificatory distinctions which the editor makes among documents concerned with the monarchy, Parliament, and the church does not reflect any really clear distinction in the minds of the authors of most of these documents that church means 'religion' and Parliament means 'politics'. The evidence from the terminology and the use of language generally here is that we are still entering into the *imaginaire* of a people who do not think in modern terms. And even in eighteenth-century America, there were many aspects of public life which made a clear distinction problematic (see chapter 9).

Browning immediately follows this point about the difficulty for the church in distinguishing between the religious and the political with a comment about "the decay of religion" and the "decline in moral standards and in ideas of good behaviour" (1953:3). The problem here is to know what is meant by the decay of "religion." What exactly was decaying? The implication of his claim may be that 'religion' was making way for the 'secular' state. But this could be a very distant backwards projection, a judgment based on hindsight. We will see from reading some of the texts that Browning has selected as representative of the thought of the era that Religion still encompassed the nation as it had in the rhetoric of the previous century, and in a sense helped to define an emergent concept of the nation-state, for the relatively few references to Religion are usually in the sense of 'our Protestant Religion', which is tied closely to the national interest and binds together all institutions equally, including the monarchy, the parliament, and the church. One might go so far as to say that in the minds of many of the elite, our Protestant Religion and the nation are two sides of the same coin.[1] We will have more chance of finding the emergence of the modern distinction in American thinking, even though some of this derived from English nonconformists like Locke and Penn.

In his essay on James Harrington, seventeenth-century theories of the state, and the power of what he calls "civil religion" deriving from various sources including Luther, Goldie says:

> In most political drama of Christendom between Dante and Hegel, the primary drama of Christendom was the liberation of the prince and the patriot from the priest. As Sir Robert Molesworth expressed it in the 1690's, in a manifesto which was to be much admired throughout the enlightenment, 'the character of the priest will give place to that of true patriot'. (Goldie, 1987:200, citing Molesworth, *An Account of Denmark*, 1694)

Goldie claims that Locke can be read as belonging to that Protestant tradition in which he also includes Harrington, Hobbes, and Hegel, in which

> the mission of the state, of the Godly Prince, was to realise in the commonwealth the religion which, in its corrupt medieval form, had held all commonwealths under its tutelage. The superstitions of the medieval church were seen to be reflections of the impingement of clericalism upon ordinary life; conversely, true religion had a necessary relationship with the right ordering of the commonwealth. For instance, Locke's exclusion of papists from toleration, too often seen as a quaint reminder of anti-Catholic prejudice lurking in an otherwise canonically liberal and secular mind, is an intrinsic outcome of the Lutheran conception of the state. Papists are not patriots .... In this sense, Locke does not advocate just the liberal

privatisation of religion, but has a doctrine of civil religion. (Goldie, 1987:201)

If that is true, then for the purposes of my argument in this book I will try to have it both ways, and argue that Locke has been read in both ways and that the idea of the privatised religion of the individual as against the public non-religious state was the most influential understanding of his work. But Goldie makes us aware that there was an alternative tradition of thinking about the state which was strong in the seventeenth century. Goldie argues that the language of civil religion and its synthesis of civility and piety "were among the most pervasive" in early modern Europe (1987:199). Goldie takes James Harrington, the author of *Oceana* (1656), to be one instance of this broad stream of early modern theorists whose conceptualisation of civil religion incorporated those practices and institutions that we separate out as secular society. Secularisation for them was the sacralisation of ordinary life not through the encompassment of priestly virtue but through the transformation of all men into priests and all human relations into the law of God.

The nation-state in the texts edited by the historian Browning is surely sacralised in the person of the monarch and increasingly the Parliament, and the quote from Sir Robert Molesworth and the observations of Goldie suggest that national patriotism at least of an elite class centred on the court predates the 1780s, which is Hobsbawm's (1990) dating of the earliest beginnings of modern nationalism. An aspect of these changes of nuance, whereby 'religion' meaning Christian Truth is becoming pluralised, and there is an anticipation of a concept of political economy as something independent of religion, is the development of trade and plantations, which we will see was now a very explicit concern for the king and others with influence. This is reflected in the editor's inclusion of a whole section on "Trade and Plantations." This again attests to the growing influence of overseas investments, often by people with Dissenting backgrounds, matched by the *imagined* separation of religion and politics by an articulate few, such as John Locke and William Penn, both of whom had overseas interests.[2]

A good case in point would be Lord Anthony Ashley Cooper, first Earl of Shaftesbury, who was a Protestant, educated largely by Puritan tutors, and who supported toleration. In 1663, Shaftesbury was one of eight lords proprietors given title to a huge tract of land in North America, which eventually became the province of Carolina. He was made lord chancellor in 1672 (until 1673) and first lord of trade until 1676. It was in 1672 that the Council of Trade and the Council of Foreign Plantations, which had been established by Charles II in 1660, became combined as the Board of Trade and Plantations. Shaftesbury was a patron to John Locke, who served as secretary of the Board of Trade and Plantations and secretary to the lords and proprietors of the Carolinas. It may have been at Shaftesbury's prompting that Locke composed the bulk of the *Two*

Treatises of Government (1689–1690). The degree to which Locke influenced the direction of American constitutionalism has been debated by historians (see Hartz, 1955; Macpherson, 1962; Bailyn, 1965; Pocock, 1975; Dworetz, 1990), but he is generally credited with some of the earliest articulations in the English language of some of the most important principles of modern constitutions. It was also around this time that William Penn was drafting constitutions for Pennsylvania.

Pagden, in his book *The Fall of Natural Man* (1982), has shown how Spanish theologians, working within the dominant Aristotelian-Thomist paradigm of Christendom, debated the classification of the indigenous peoples of the Americas and the justification for conquest and slavery. I argued in chapter 4 that such a paradigm could not have found any conceptual space for an idea of civil governance that was 'nonreligious' in the modern sense of being neutral, indifferent, or hostile towards religion. This was reflected in the paternalistic systems of governance imposed on the indigenous colonised Indians, essentially a transplantation of the dominant Catholic paradigm which was a holistic, hierarchical, and patriarchal concept in which Religion encompassed all other institutions, and defined the order of things in a totalising way. The English Protestant nation was also still holistic in its dominant conceptions in the seventeenth and eighteenth centuries, and many Puritan Dissenters escaped from England to try to found holistic colonial communities dominated by a single vision of God's order. However, the Dissenting traditions in England also produced a liberal model of the constitutional separation of religion from politics of the kind which Locke advocated and which the Quaker William Penn took with him to Pennsylvania. This, I would argue, was a fundamental element in the creation of a new paradigm on which our modern ideas of secular, objective knowledge and rational politics and economics depend. What the reading of these texts suggests is that this was not so much the realisation through progress of a truly rational human existence but a chance configuration of different elements that now mystifyingly underpins the dominant American world order.

In the late sixteenth and early seventeenth centuries, the published collections of travel writings of Hakluyt and Purchas, discussed in the last chapter, reflect the huge growth of interest in overseas trade and encounters with other peoples. For example, Purchas dedicated the first edition of his *Pilgrimage* in 1613 to James I, and the second edition in 1626 to Charles I, which indicates the growth in consciousness among different ranks and degrees of English people of the new world, not only the Americas and the West Indies but, equally important, the East Indies, a generic term for South, Southeast, and East Asia. And the Dutch during this period were enjoying a rapid ascendancy in the conveyance of trade around the world, making Amsterdam the most important entrepôt and financial centre in Northern Europe.

It is true that, in hindsight, we can detect, or think we can detect, semantic shifts caused by more general changes that were laying the foundations of modernity, and perhaps it is in this sense that Browning, referring to the English civil war period, the execution of Charles I of England, and the proliferation of radical groups that questioned all established conventions of thought and practice, says, "All accepted codes, in fact, had been shaken. And the later Stuart world hardly knew by what lights to guide its conduct" (1953:3).

The effervescence of radical thought challenging the status quo is reflected in An Act for Preventing the Frequent Abuses in Printing Seditious, Treasonable, and Unlicensed Books and Pamphlets and for Regulating of Printing and Printing Presses (1662; published in Browning, 1953:67):

> [B]y the general licentiousness of the late times many evil-disposed
> persons have been encouraged to print and sell heretical, schis
> matical, blasphemous, seditious and treasonable books, pamphlets
> and papers, and still do continue such their unlawful and exorbitant
> practice, to the high dishonour of Almighty God, the endangering
> [of] the peace of these kingdoms, and raising a disaffection to his
> most excellent Majesty and his government, for prevention whereof
> no surer means can be devised than by reducing and limiting the
> number of printing presses . . . by and with the consent and advice of
> the Lords Spiritual and Temporal and Commons in this present
> Parliament assembled.

It can be noticed that Parliament is made up of "the Lords Spiritual and Temporal and Commons," which indicates that bishops (the lords spiritual) were fully involved in the making of laws. We will see below that all members of the Parliament took holy communion actually in the Parliament itself, and that sermons were regularly being preached in Parliament and laws were still being promulgated from the church pulpits. The distinction here between heresy and treason is not much clearer now than it was in Henry VIII's time. There is no notion of a *nonreligious* society here, except possibly in the very stretched and different sense that the monastic orders had been abolished, and, in that sense only, a Protestant nation is nonreligious. But this is hardly what is implied by the nonreligious 'secular' of contemporary rhetoric.

Also it needs to be remembered that the revolutionary interlude of the mid-seventeenth century was in some sense being reversed, for we are talking about the Restoration, and though far-reaching changes had irreversibly been instigated in what it was possible to think by the impeachment and execution of Charles I, those shifts seem glacial, and we are still concerned with a premodern[3] hierarchical society in which religion and politics are one and the same thing, church and Parliament different but interdependent institutions encompassed by Christian Truth, and the idea of their separation is only beginning to emerge in the minds of a few influential individuals. The inter-regnum and the rule of Oliver Cromwell established a different vision of Christian Truth, but it was still a vision of a world encompassed by Religion. Browning points out, "The revival of the practice of touching for the king's evil was symptomatic of a real change in popular feeling" (1953:49). This change does not seem to be towards modernity but away from it.

In Browning's selection of documents in part I, "The Monarchy, the Royal Prerogative. Act for the Preservation of the King, 1661," offices for employ-ment are described as ecclesiastical, civil, and military (1953:64). There is the expression "in church or state." The distinction between church and state is there, and there are other examples, but this piece of rhetoric does not yet, I believe, suggest a separation in the sense that we would understand it.

"Sir Robert Filmer's Justification of the Prerogative 1680" challenges the claims published by "schoolmen and other divines" that

> mankind is naturally endowed and born with freedom from all
> subjection, and at liberty to choose what form of government
> it please . . . . This tenet was first hatched in the schools of good
> divinity, and hath been fostered by succeeding papists. The
> divines of the reformed churches have entertained it. (Browning,
> 1953:70–71)

According to Filmer (who was one of Locke's main targets in his articulation in the *First Treatise on Government* [1689][4] and in his advocacy of the distinction between privatised religion and the political state in *A Letter concerning Toler-ation*), the problem with their argument was that they forgot that

> the desire of liberty was the cause of the fall of Adam . . . . Upon the
> grounds of this doctrine both Jesuits and some of the zealous fa-
> vourers of the Geneva discipline have built a perilous conclusion,
> which is that the people or multitude have power to punish or deprive
> the prince if he transgress the laws of the kingdom. (70–71)

Filmer considers the argument of Bellarmine, which is based on "the equality of mankind in general." Filmer's repudiation of these doctrines is based on an analogy between fatherhood and kingship: "I see not . . . how the children of Adam, or of any man else, can be free from subjection to their parents. And this subordination of children is the fountain of all regal authority by the ordination of God himself." For Filmer, "civil power not only in general is by divine institution, but even the assigning of it specifically to the eldest parent" (Browning, 1953:71).

The contemporary reader might be misled by this quote to imagine that Cardinal Bellarmine was advocating social equality, or a freedom from sub-ordination and subjection to authority. It perhaps should be clarified that this was not an argument between a libertarian (Bellarmine) and an authoritarian

(Filmer). This was an argument about the relative power of kings and popes over secular affairs. Bellarmine was not a libertarian in today's sense. At the apex of his career, Bellarmine was head of the Holy Office of the Inquisition. He had been educated by Jesuits in Padua in the 1560s, and lectured on the *Summa* of Aquinas at Louvain, where he was ordained in the order. His first book, *De scriptoribus ecclesiasticis* (Rome, 1613), was a study of the fathers and medieval theologians. Later, between 1581 and 1593, he published *Disputationes de controversiis christianae fidei*. In this work he argued that, among the different forms of possible secular government, monarchy is the best; however, he also argued for the indirect power of the pope over secular authorities. He asserted the doctrine that the pope is the supreme judge in matters of faith and morals. Though the pope had no direct jurisdiction in secular affairs, Bellarmine contends that he does have the power to depose kings, absolve subjects from their allegiance, and alter civil laws in those cases where necessary for the good of the souls in his care as chief pastor. He entered into a public dispute with King James VI of Scotland (James I of England) concerning the power of kings, arguing, against James's strong assertion of the divine right of kings, that the first allegiance of bishops was not to the king but to the pope. He also argued with the Scottish juror John Barclay, who had published in a work called *De Regno el Regali Potestate* (1600) a strong defence of the rights of kings and against the usurpation of temporal power by the pope.

It was Bellarmine who, as inquisitor, oversaw the trial and burning of Giordano Bruno. Bruno (1548–1600) was an Italian philosopher, priest, astronomer/astrologer, and occultist. Burned at the stake as a heretic for his theological ideas, Bruno is seen by some as a martyr to the cause of free thought. At fifteen, Bruno had entered the Dominican order, taking the name of Giordano. He continued his studies, completed his novitiate, and became an ordained priest in 1572. Bruno's ideas were heterodox and he was denounced to the Inquisition, which had prepared a total of 130 charges against him. He was imprisoned in Rome for six years before he was tried. His trial was overseen by Bellarmine, who demanded a full recantation, which Bruno refused. Consequently, he was declared a heretic and handed over to secular authorities. A month or so later, he was brought to the Campo de' Fiori, a central Roman market square, his tongue in a gag, hung upside down naked, and burned alive, on 17 February 1600. In 1616, Bellarmine also became involved in the Copernican controversy, and it was he who administered the controversial admonition to Galileo not to hold or defend the Copernican theory.

We can see that Filmer's argument about the subjection of children to the father's authority is an argument about the right of kings to complete obedience by their subjects, and against the right of rebellion. He was arguing against Bellarmine's claim that, in cases where subjects are forced into sin by their monarch, then the pope has the right to absolve them from the sin of rebellion and can even depose a monarch.

Note Filmer's use of the word "ordination" of regal authority by God. Kings, like priests, are ordained. And "civil power" is authorised by God, and thus can hardly have been nonreligious, at least in Filmer's mind. Filmer uses the expression "the natural institution of regal authority": "as kingly power is by the law of God, so it hath no inferior law to limit it." It is the same "law of nature" that gives fathers and princes their legitimate authority (72): "there were kings long before there were any laws. For a long time the word of the king was the only law . . . . In all aristocracies the nobles are above the laws, and in all democracies the people" (72; this is my earliest finding of 'democracy'). Locke's *First Treatise on Government* (1689/1690) targeted Sir Robert Filmer's *Patriarcha* (probably published in 1680), in which these arguments appeared and which reasserted the principles that Locke, in many ways a revolutionary ahead of his time, wished to challenge with his radical statement of the separation of religion from the nonreligious state, an argument also clearly expressed in *A Letter Concerning Toleration* (1689).[5] What seems clear from all the texts which Browning has selected and classified under "The Monarchy" is that it is all inseparable from encompassing Religion, and not about religion in the modern sense as a private faith separated from the state.

In An Act for the Security of the Crown, 1696 (Browning, 1953:74–75), we find the expression "the reformed religion": "the welfare and safety of this kingdom and the reformed religion do next under God entirely depend upon the preservation of your Majesty's royal person and government." However, this should not be read in the sense of 'a religion', for religion is still Christian Truth, but the authoritative interpretation of it has been reformed, such that Catholics are heretics, and the Protestant king is its defender and sacred guardian. Civility has been restored and the barbaric practices of the Catholics repulsed. The act condemns a conspiracy of papists who "encourage an invasion from France to subvert our religion, laws and liberty" and determines the importance of acting "to the utmost of our power in the support and defence of his Majesty's most *sacred* person and government" (my italics, Browning, 1953:75). Here a parliamentary act (which would be classified as 'political' by modernists) proclaims the sacrality of the king and his government.

In section C, "Limitations of the Prerogative," Charles II, in his "Speech in support of his Declaration of Indulgence to the House of Commons 1673" (Browning, 1953:77) says: "I will preserve the true reformed Protestant religion and the Church as it is now established in this kingdom, and that no man's property or liberty shall ever be invaded." The ideas of religion, liberty, and property are tightly bound up together in these post-Restoration discourses. Liberty does not mean the freedom to do what one wants, but the right to hold property and not be under the jurisdiction of Rome. And when challenged (very deferentially yet directly) that he could not make laws, only Parliament could do that, Charles II stated that he did not "pretend to the right of suspending any laws wherein property, rights or liberties of any of his subjects are concerned, nor to alter anything in the established doctrine or discipline of the Church of England" (78). The king's major stated aim is to "secure the peace of the Church and Kingdom" (79).

An address to the king by members of Parliament refer to him as "your sacred Majesty": "We, your Majesty's most humble and loyal subjects, the knights, citizens and burgesses in this Parliament assembled, do render to your sacred Majesty" (Browning, 1953:79). Modern readers might suppose that this is mere hyperbole and rhetoric, especially since the beheading of his father not so many years before. No doubt, this cataclysmic act had long-term consequences. Yet even today the queen of England has not lost all her charisma of office, even though vilification by the press and the Muppets, and the royal family's likeness to a TV soap opera, has considerably reduced the prestige of royalty. Today, many ordinary Americans would feel a sense of awe in entering the Oval Office of the White House to meet the elected president of the United States, reputed to be the most powerful man in the world. In the seventeenth century, all great rank and degree had charisma, and the taboos surrounding the king's bodily presence could induce a sense of awe. This perhaps explains the propensity to use the epithet 'sacred', and the popular belief in the king's healing touch.

The expression "the religion now established" (Browning, 1953:79) still refers to Christ's Truth, but in these usages it seems formal. 'Religion' is not used in these texts otherwise. "Matters ecclesiastical" is one way church business is put. But this again is not a generic concept of religion, but a specific reference to an indigenous institution.

Again, we find the usage "your sacred Majesty" (Browning, 1953:79). Another form of address is: "We, your Majesty's most loyal subjects, the Lords Spiritual and Temporal and Commons in this parliament assembled" (79–80). The reference to the distinction between the lords spiritual and temporal, who form the sacred government of the king, who is the head of the church as well as the state, is another indication that this was not a world conceived to be divided between two distinct spheres, the religious and the nonreligious. The taking of the oaths of allegiance and supremacy as demanded by Parliament had to be accompanied by the receiving of the sacraments, "of the Lord's Supper according to the laws and usage of the Church of England" (80). This therefore is simultaneously a religious and a political act, or rather neither in the modern sense. It is only conceivable in its own language, which is not the language of a religious sphere separated from a nonreligious state.

James II, concerned about representing the trading interests of England, refers to "the honour of this nation and the figure it ought to make in the world" (Browning, 1953:82). The Parliament in replying thanks the king for "your great care and conduct in the suppression of the late rebellion, which threatened the overthrow of this government both in Church and State and the utter extirpation of our religion by law established, which is most dear unto us"

(82). The expression "both in Church and State" indicates some separation in the minds of those who made this statement. Yet, at the same time, "religion" here tacitly holds church and state together, and is not identified more with one than the other, but is surely the cement in which both the other institutions have their common being. On the other hand, while Christian Truth is universal, the church is national. Again, the separation of the universal Catholic religion and the national church-state may constitute a further loosening of the rhetorical structure of these discourses. Yet the expression "this government both in Church and State" indicates the extent to which the concept of Religion is merged in the concept of the nation in the dominant rhetoric, and perhaps we could say that encompassing Religion, in the sense of Our Protestant Religion, is the midwife in the transition from universal Christendom to nationalism. In a sense the nation, as symbolised by the king-in-parliament, has become the transcendental object of devotion. It needs to be borne in mind that these texts have been placed by the editor in the section on "The Monarchy." But it seems that they might equally have been placed in the sections on either the Church or Parliament.

Chief Justice Herbert, in "The case of Godden and Hales 1686" (Browning, 1953:83), reminds us again of the analogy between the king's authority as "the supreme lawgiver" and God's: "There is no law whatsoever but may be dispensed with by the supreme lawgiver, as the laws of God may be dispensed with by God himself, as it appears by God's command to Abraham to offer up his son Isaac." It is interesting, but not unusual, that the chief justice uses a precedent from the Old Testament to support his legal arguments. We saw in the dispute between Bellarmine and Filmer that the present order of things is legitimated or challenged by events described in the Old Testament. This indicates a different concept of time, which is not a linear concept of progress towards some liberal enlightenment of greater knowledge, but an attempt to maintain the order of things as they are believed to have been revealed for all time. Arguably, the different concept of time is one of the most fundamental differences between them and us, with all its many implications for self-consciousness.

The king orders "the right reverend the bishops" to ensure that the "Declaration of Indulgence" (1688; Browning, 1953:83) be read in all churches. How can one separate church and state here? To attempt to redescribe this as the relation between religion and politics would make no sense. But the issue is being aired and debated so much that one suspects that the concepts are shifting their nuances. Yet in the "Petition of the Seven Bishops 1688," signed by William Canterbury and others in protest at the illegality of the king's "Declaration of Indulgence" without the agreement of Parliament, there is no sense that they are involved in a 'political' act except in the uninformative sense that they are engaged in power. If this is all politics means, then it is part of the definition of what it means to be alive and leaves everything to be settled.

I would appeal again to the strategic distinction between relative degrees of sacred and profane. The bishops are lords ecclesiastical, and they are members of Parliament. You could say (though it seems that they wouldn't have) that the bishops had political power. But their conception seems to be structured more in terms of "the whole nation, both in Church and State" (Browning, 1953:84). They represent church, nation, and government simultaneously.

This late seventeenth-century conception of the sovereignty of Parliament, or of the king-in-parliament, has been usefully, if briefly, put into a slightly longer time frame by Bernard Bailyn (1967). Talking about the concept of representation in England, Bailyn explains how elective representation to Parliament changed between the medieval period and the eighteenth century. Representatives in medieval parliaments stood only for the local interests of their own residential community, for their immediate constituents: "representatives of the commons in the medieval parliaments did not speak for that estate in general or for any other body or group larger than the specific one that had elected them" (Bailyn, 1967:163). But by the time of the mid- to late eighteenth century, these restrictions on representation had changed, and members were not only parochial but had become spokesmen for wider interests: "Symbolically incorporating the state, Parliament in effect had become the nation for purposes of government, and its members virtually if not actually ... spoke for all as well as the group that had chosen them" (163). Bailyn quotes Edmund Burke, who said that Parliament was not

> a congress of ambassadors from different and hostile interests, which
> interests each must maintain, as an agent and an advocate, against
> other agents and advocates; but Parliament is a deliberative assem-
> bly of one nation, with one interests, that of the whole, where not
> local purposes ... ought to guide, but the general good, resulting
> from the general reason of the whole. (quoted in Bailyn, 1967:163)

This provides a useful longer-term perspective within which to place the picture of the sovereign power of the king-in-parliament in the late seventeenth and early eighteenth centuries. For it shows how, on the one hand, church and state are encompassed holistically by Religion and nation throughout this period, and simultaneously how the term 'sacred' is used most frequently to refer to the king, and by extension to the king-in-parliament as the sovereign power. Even with the Whig-Tory two-party system developing, it is difficult to identify any real demarcation between religion and politics.

In section D, "Organs of Central Government," one document shows that the court is another institution in which men of different status, function, and degree mingle, unaware of any notion that some of them are 'religious' functionaries and some are 'nonreligious'. Distinctions between spiritual and temporal, or ecclesiastical and lay jurisdiction do not correspond with our notions of the religious and the nonreligious secular. These latter concepts have not yet appeared in any of the texts so far discussed. In "Duties and salaries of State and Household Officials, 1691," we see that the ecclesiastics, the military, and the men of civil rank are all represented:

> The court of the King of England is a monarchy within a monarchy, consisting of ecclesiastical, civil and military persons and government. For the ecclesiastical government of the king's court there is first of all a dean of the king's chapel, who is usually some grave, learned prelate chosen by the king; for as the king's palace is exempt from all inferior temporal jurisdiction so is his chapel from all spiritual. (Browning, 1953:105)

In this article on the duties and salaries of state and household officials, the writer lists nine great officers of the Crown: lord high steward of England; lord high chancellor; lord high treasurer; lord president of the King's Privy Council; lord privy seal; lord great chamberlain; lord high constable; earl marshal; lord high admiral. These are wonderful-sounding titles and certainly invoke ritual status in the social anthropological sense. We can see the separation of functions where the head authority of the civil government does not have authority over that of the chapel; nor does he have authority over the king's bedchamber or his stable:

> For the civil government of the king's court the chief officer is . . . the Lord Steward of the King's Household . . . . He hath authority over all officers and servants of the king's house except those of his Majesty's chapel, chamber and stable. (Browning, 1953:105)

Furthermore, the lord chamberlain, who is civil, *does* have authority over the chaplains. It is the lord chamberlain who has "oversight of" officers belonging to the king's chamber, officers of the wardrobe, sergeants-at-arms, all physicians, apothecaries, chirurgeons, and barbers. "To him also belongeth the oversight of the chaplains, though himself be a layman" (105).

Notice that, on the one hand, the ecclesiastical and the civil are conceptually separated; and the chapel and the dean represent ecclesiastical government. Yet the dean is appointed by the lord chamberlain, who is within the civil category. All are encompassed by the king and his household, which represents the state. But the church is also within the state. Religion (Protestant Truth), which is not used here specifically, refers to and encompasses the whole ritual order of things.

In one speech in the Parliament, "Speech of Sir Charles Sedley in the Commons on the extravagance of the Civil List, 1691" (Browning, 1953:108), we can see the division between the king and the Parliament over expenditures, but this in itself says nothing about a distinction between a religious and a secular authority. However, what it does reinforce is the perceived inseparable identity between the nation's interests as against other nations, and the

Protestant Religion: "we shall give and [the people of England] will cheerfully pay whatever his majesty can want to secure the Protestant religion, to keep out the king of France, aye, and King James too" (108).

Arguably, it has historically been the transference of a holistic concept of the order of things implied by Religion from the universality of the Catholic church to the nation-state that provided the early transition from the empires without borders to the imagined community of the nation which Benedict Anderson and most other scholars date later, from the late eighteenth or early nineteenth centuries (Anderson, 1991; Gellner, 1983; Hobsbawm, 1990). However, Greenfeld (1992) sees the beginnings of the modern nation in Henry VIII's nationalisation of the church. What all these historians would agree on is that something new was being imagined. This is also true of Religion. While Christian Truth still retained the idea of a total hierarchical order of things, that order had been transferred from a universal to a bounded entity, the nation, increasingly separated from other similar and competing bounded entities, such as France or Holland. There is also an indication (see below) of a transfer of sacrality, or at least of a widening of sacrality, from the king to the Parliament, which will eventually be connected to the idea of the will of the people and the nation-state in the modern sense. It is there that contemporary formulations of the sacred secular perhaps had their early beginnings.

In section E, "Determination of the Succession," the sense of two alternative 'religions' normally only emerges in a comparative and/or alternating context between Protestant and Catholic. One text, an "Anonymous Account of the Popish Plot, 1678" (Browning, 1953:109) exemplifies the concerns of the era. The plot amounted to

> no less than the murder of the king, the subversion of our religion, laws and properties, the introducing of popery and a tyrannical arbitrary government by an army, our common and statute laws to be abolished and annihilated, and a mixture of military and civil law introduced.

Here king, religion, law, and property are all found in the same sentence. In my terms, they are the disciplines of (Protestant English) civility threatened by the barbarities and irrationalities of popery. That they are distinguished in no way implies that they are distinguished in accordance with our modern notions. Also, the expression "our religion" implies the religion of this nation. But the pluralisation of religions has entered the language in this way: it is said that Mr Oates was determined at an earlier stage in his life to try the Catholic religion ("that religion") and, if it was found to be as corrupt as Protestants say, "he would renounce that religion and return again to the Protestant Church" (Browning, 1953:109). (The Jesuits are singled out again as dangerous.) This going backwards and forwards between two 'religions' tends to loosen their commonality and creates a sense of two distinct entities. Yet in the same text the anonymous author also uses the term "Christendom" (Browning, 1953: 109), which strengthens the impression that we are witnessing the early transformation of an established discourse on encompassing Christian Truth into a plurality of religions. But this plurality is still nothing like the modern generic pluralisation.

At the same time, in the Exclusion Bill, 1680: An Act for Securing of the Protestant Religion by Disabling James, Duke of York, to Inherit the Imperial Crown of England and Ireland and the Dominions and Territories Thereunto Belonging (Browning, 1953:113), we find the king's person and his government addressed as sacred:

> James, Duke of York, is notoriously known to have been per-
> verted from the Protestant to the Popish religion, whereby not only
> great encouragement hath been given to the popish party to enter
> into and carry on most devilish and horrid plots and conspiracies for
> the destruction of his Majesty's sacred person and government,
> and for the extirpation of the true Protestant religion, but also, if the
> said duke should succeed to the imperial crown of this realm,
> nothing is more manifest than that a total change of religion within
> these kingdoms would ensue. (Browning, 1953:113)

As usual, our notion that religion and politics are separate, the latter being nonreligious according to the logic of such a separation, is entirely absent; for this act

> shall be openly read in every cathedral, collegiate church, parish
> church and chapel within the aforesaid kingdoms, dominions and
> territories by the several respective parsons, vicars, curates, and
> readers thereof, who are hereby required, immediately after divine
> service in the forenoon, to read the same twice in every year... and
> upon Easter Day. (Browning, 1953:114)

Given that the preceding documents were classified under the section on "The Monarchy," it seems unconvincing and misleading to write, as some historians do, as though monarchy is about politics in any modern sense. It is clearly about power, but this does not say very much at all. Moving from the section on monarchy to the section on Parliament does not substantially change the language.

What we find in the section of documents in part II, "Parliament. A: Summons and Duration," is a clear identification of Parliament and government with nation and Religion, that is, Protestant Christian Truth, but the ways in which this is talked about has some degree of variation.

In the "Articles of Impeachment against the earl of Danby, 1678," the third charge included that he traitorously intended "to deprive his sacred Majesty" of the meeting of parliaments and "their safe and wholesome councils"

(Browning, 1953:199). Parliament wishes to "proceed to perfect these matters now before us, which tend to the safety and honour of your sacred person and government, and to the preservation of the true Protestant religion" ("Address of the Commons for the Removal of the earl of Halifax 1680," in Browning, 1953:180–81).

Variations on the expression "your [his Majesty's] sacred person" is standard usage by Parliament and by petitioners (Browning, 1953:204–5). For example, in a petition from Scottish representatives (in part VII, "Scotland: B. Reconstruction in Church and State, the Petition of Scottish representatives in London to Charles II, 1660," in Browning, 1953:605), the same language is used: "May it please your sacred Majesty." The language is that of deferential hierarchy: "We, the noblemen, gentlemen and burgesses of your Majesty's ancient kingdom of Scotland ... do in obedience to your Majesty's command humbly offer"; "And as we humbly conceive that the sole power of calling and holding of Parliaments ... doth reside in your Majesty."

Here, what today is separated out as 'politics'—i.e., the reconvening of the Scottish Parliament—is the prerogative of a sacred majesty who is the apex of the hierarchy. The sacrality of the king and his headship of church and state also come out strongly in the language used in the Act of Rescissory, 1661 (Acts of the Parliaments of Scotland, VII:86–87), described as an "Act Rescinding and Annulling the Pretended Parliaments in the years 1640, 1641, etc." For example:

> the sacred person and royal authority of the King's Majesty and
> his royal father of blessed memory ... the sacred right inherent
> to the imperial crown (which his Majesty holds immediately
> from God Almighty alone) ... such has been the madness and delu-
> sion of these times that even religion itself, which holds the right
> of kings to be sacred and inviolable, hath been pretended unto
> for warrant of all these injurious violations and encroachments ...
> upon and against his Majesty's just power, authority and govern-
> ment ... that sovereign power, authority, prerogative and right of
> government which by the law of God and the ancient laws and con-
> stitutions of this kingdom doth reside in and belong to the King's
> Majesty. (606)

Here it is made explicit again that the king's sovereignty, government, and constitutions are legitimated by the law of God.

The "Order of Council for the Restoration of Episcopacy, 1661" (register of the Privy Council of Scotland, 3rd series, 1:30–32) uses similar language:

> his Majesty, having respect to the Glory of God and the good and
> interest of the Protestant religion ... hath been pleased ... to declare
> unto his Council his firm resolution to interpose his royal authority

for restoring of this Church to its right government by bishops. (Browning, 1953:608)

And in Act for Raising a Militia, 1663 (Acts of the Parliaments of Scotland, VII:480–81), the language is repeated:

> A Humble tender to his sacred Majesty of the duty and loyalty of his ancient kingdom of Scotland. For as much as the Estates of Parliament, upon consideration of the great blessings this kingdom enjoyeth under the protection of his Majesty's authority and the administrations of his royal government . . . have by their several addresses to his sacred Majesty made offer of their lives and fortunes and all that is dearest to them for the advancement of the royal honour, authority and greatness . . . do cheerfully recognize his Majesty's royal prerogative [to raise an army]. (Browning, 1953:610)

The language of sacrality here legitimates the king's powers, and it seems to have little conceptual connection with what we mean by politics today in modern liberal democracies.

This language continued when Queen Anne came to the throne in 1702. For example, the clergymen of the Diocese of Canterbury, writing to thank Queen Anne, address her as "your most sacred Majesty." They thank her for "continuing to preserve our most holy religion in the Church of England, and the Protestant Succession as established by law" (Browning, 1953:422). In 1707, this language of the sacrality of government encompassed by Religion is still in force: "We, your majesty's most dutiful and obedient subjects, the Lords Spiritual and Temporal and Commons in Parliament assembled" (Browning, 1953:182).

In 1710, Henry Sacheverell, a "Doctor of Divinity," preached a sermon at St. Paul's and also at the assizes (courts for the administration of civil and criminal justice) held in Derby in 1709, that cast aspersions on the Glorious Revolution of the late William III and Mary by citing "diverse texts and passages of Holy Scripture." The "Articles of Impeachment against Henry Sacheverell, 1710" (Browning, 1953:205) first established rhetorically the official position:

> [T]he happy and blessed consequences of the said revolution are the enjoyment of the light of God's true religion established among us, and the laws and liberties of the kingdom; the uniting her Majesty's Protestant subjects in interest and affection by a legal indulgence or toleration granted to dissenters; the preservation of her Majesty's sacred person . . . and the prospect of happiness to future ages by the settlement of the succession of the crown in the Protestant line, and the union of the two kingdoms.

Parliament considered these sermons to have been

> a wicked, malicious and seditious intention to undermine and sub-
> vert her Majesty's government and the Protestant succession as by
> law established, to defame her Majesty's administration, to asperse
> the memory of his late Majesty, to traduce and condemn the late
> happy revolution, to contradict and arraign the resolutions of both
> Houses of Parliament, to create jealousies and divisions among her
> Majesty's subjects, and to incite them to sedition and rebellion.
> (Browning, 1953:206)

Clearly, Parliament was concerned as much with "true religion," "her
majesty's sacred person," and the succession settlement as with anything else.
Furthermore, and equally significantly, the doctor of divinity was preaching
what we retrospectively might have described as a 'political' opinion both in a
church as a sermon and in the assizes. Thus, the law (the assizes, Parliament
as legislature) and the church are both contexts in which holding and expressing opinions on the state and its formation and constitution are not separated
into either religion or secular politics. The issue is one of loyalty or sedition.

As we have seen, one aspect of the definition of the nation is the definition
of true Religion, and this is articulated as our Protestant Religion, the 'our'
being definitive of the nation and the religion simultaneously. But who are
we? Presumably, we comprise powerful groups of literate men with interests
in prestige, rank, and wealth, rather than a truly modern (mythical) nation of
(in principle) equals in the modern sense; there is also implied the definition
of true Religion (Protestantism) as against superstitious heresies, especially
Catholicism. Throughout these sections in Browning, there are references to
the dangers of destabilisation either from sectarian malcontents inside the
nation or from papists who might be inside or outside, but are finally associated with outside irrational and malevolent powers. The dominant trope is the
distinction between the sacred king and his nation and government, on the one
hand, and the profane, on the other. Due to

> the dissolution of the last parliament, and by the frequent proroga-
> tions of the present parliament ... the papists have been greatly
> encouraged to carry on their hellish and damnable conspiracies
> against your royal person and government and the Protestant reli-
> gion now established among us. (Browning, 1953:206)

The language here can be thought of in terms of the distinction between
Catholic or sectarian barbarity, and the disciplines of civility that constitute the
nation and its true Religion, including all those practices that constitute the
legitimate state.

In "Declaration of Charles II to his people, 1681" (Browning, 1953:185), the
king is explaining why he dissolved the two previous parliaments, and indicates

that he was concerned with "the weighty consideration either of preserving the established religion and the liberty and property of our subjects at home, or of supporting our neighbours and allies abroad." But he also talks about "the preservation of the general peace in Christendom." The term Christendom is still used occasionally, though presumably its meaning is now weaker.

The necessity for "the security of the Protestant religion" (Browning, 1953: 185) could surely as easily be read as the necessity for the security of the state, or the necessity of the security of the monarchy, or the necessity of the security of the Parliament and the interests of its dominant men. All of the following expressions implicitly or explicitly identify the security of Religion, nation, state, and interests such as property against the disorderly, dangerous, and malicious counterinterests of dissidents:

Parliament passed a vote which refers (negatively) to "the prosecution of Protestant dissenters . . . a weakening of the Protestant interest, an encouragement to Popery" (186)

"the Protestant interest" repeated

"the religion established" (i.e., Protestant religion)

the king reminds Parliament that "religion, liberty and property were all lost and gone when the monarchy was shaken off" (186)

various disorders in the city threatened "ruin to the government of both Church and State" (189)

Danby was lord high treasurer of England. In "Articles of Impeachment against the earl of Danby, 1678" (Browning, 1953:198), the Parliament sought to impeach Danby for six charges, for example, charge 2 was: "That he hath traitorously endeavoured to subvert the ancient and well-established form of government in this kingdom, and instead thereof to introduce an arbitrary and tyrannical way of government." The fourth charge was: "That he is popishly affected, and hath traitorously concealed . . . the late horrid and bloody plot and conspiracy contrived by the papists . . . tending to the destruction of the king's sacred person and the subversion of the Protestant religion" (199). The fifth and sixth charges concerned the improper uses of state revenue.

One of the main tensions between king and Parliament concerned who had the right to control and raise taxes. Whereas the writers at the time of Henry VIII were keen to stress the king as the absolute power in the nation-state, now it is increasingly claimed that Parliament has that power. In the text "Earl of Shaftesbury's observations on elections" (c. 1680), the Earl of Shaftesbury is discussing whether the rights of various parts of the country to send representatives to Parliament lies with an act of Parliament itself, or with the king. He admits that the legal position is unclear to him. However, "[i]t is . . . a thing of very dangerous consequence to have such a power lodged in the king alone," and he points out that power lodged in the king alone "would be in effect to choose his own parliament" (Browning, 1953:211). Here we can see the clashes of perceived interests that led earlier to the impeachment and execution of Charles I, which we might retrospectively interpret as the progressive emergence of parliamentary democracy. At around this time, the two-party system of Tories and Whigs was emerging. But on the other hand, the kind of rhetoric which he invokes to sway people's minds is not reminiscent of a modern politician:

> The Parliament of England is that supreme and absolute power
> which gives life and motion to the English government. It directs and
> actuates all its various procedures, is the parent of our peace, de-
> fender of our faith and foundation of our properties; and as the
> constitution of this great spring and *primum mobile* of affairs is in
> strength and beauty, so will also all acts and performances which
> are derived from it bear a suitable proportion and similitude....
> It is from the fruit of this great council that we must expect our
> nutriment, and from its branches our protection. (Browning,
> 1953:211)

This could not be a clearer, even if tacit, equation of encompassing Religion with Parliament, which is the defender of the faith, the first mover, the life-giving organism. But it also seems to indicate a shift in the architectonics of the holistic vision, and the partial transference of sacrality from king and government to parliamentary government. In retrospect, we see this perhaps as a step in the direction of modernity.

In his introduction to part IV, "The Church," the editor says:

> Of all the institutions in England that which gained most from the
> Restoration was the Church. In its case indeed, something more
> than a restoration was effected, for the position accorded to it after
> 1660 was loftier and more secure than any it had previously
> enjoyed.... Of this restored Church the restored Monarch was ac-
> cepted without question as the supreme governor.... The Church
> gloried in its submission to the King, and endeavoured by every
> means within its power to exalt his authority. The King on his part
> was expected to use that authority to maintain the rights and pri-
> vileges of the Church. (Browning, 1953:359)

Conflict between them arose, however, because the king strove to enlarge the area of toleration for Catholics against the interests of the national church. Note the editor's incongruous use of 'religious' and 'political':

> The reply of the Church party was the so-called Clarendon Code, a
> series of four statutes, which not merely defined the position of the
> Church, but imposed heavy disabilities, both religious and political,
> on all who failed to conform to it. (Browning, 1953:359–60)

The editor seems instinctively to have assumed that his meaning here was self-evident and did not need explanation. But the texts that he selected do not seem to correspond to the descriptive categories he is using, and do not allow any obvious meaning to this statement. Usually, scholarly use of categories that are embedded in modern paradigmatic assumptions are instinctive rather than conscious or intentional. It is a practice that provides the reader with a safe haven from the sense of lack of direction when confronted with difference.

James II introduced a second "Declaration of Indulgence" in 1687, giving a degree of toleration to both Catholics and nonconformists. But the nonconformists, not being given to monarchy or Catholicism,

> preferred to accept the overtures now made to them by the indignant Anglicans, and join the alliance in the general interests of Protestantism and political liberty on which the Revolution was based.... The Toleration Act thus mitigated the religious, but not the political disabilities of the Dissenters. (Browning, 1953:360)

By "religious," the editor Browning here means their Christian practice, and by "political" he means qualifying themselves for office. It may be true that the Toleration Act was itself another incremental push in the conceptualisation that these are or should be two separate domains. There is a gap between the interpretation of 'religion' that the Dissenters hold and their ability to hold office. Yet the editor is using the terms as though they were already so thought of, and as though we can think of them unproblematically in this way. I would argue that the conceptual breach is in the process of being made, and is not yet an established distinction. Dissent pushed men and women to search for new ways of thinking about institutional arrangements.

"Meanwhile the established Church and other religious organisations had settled down to live more or less peaceably together" (Browning, 1953:361). These are effectively Anglicans, Protestant nonconformists, and Catholics. So at this time "religion" still fundamentally refers to the various Christian practices or confessions. Yet the expression "religious organisations" to refer to something different from monasteries is a new one. For example, the Friends (Quakers), who arguably had the most radical vision of an alternative order of things, and whose disciplines of civility challenged so many of the hierarchical assumptions of the time, were probably not referred to as "the *Religious* Society of Friends" until 1793 in an address to King George III.[6] This change in title indicates a significant but later change in the nuance of the word and its relation to other areas of practice such as politics and economics.

Browning says that the Church of England's "victory over Puritanism had been achieved at the expense of subservience to political authority little in keeping with a high level of spiritual life" (Browning, 1953:361). These remarks of the editor's, and his unguarded use of the terms spiritual and political, actually do not clarify the epoch nor his meaning. To what does "political authority" refer here? If it merely means power and the exercise of power, few people would think that the spiritual jurisdiction was not concerned with power. Is it supposed to imply an authority that was imagined as 'nonreligious'? But these texts do not appear to use the word politics at this stage, and as has been shown, the state could not have been described as nonreligious without introducing a contradiction. And to what does the editor refer in the expression "a high level of spiritual life"? In one of the texts in this section of Browning's book, "spiritual" (Browning, 1953:367) is used in an "act of spiritual jurisdiction," for which are given as examples excommunication and absolution, and this is synonymous with "ecclesiastical jurisdiction" (368). In this sense, "spiritual jurisdiction" is the exercise of power by specific people—"pious presbyters of the diocese" (368)—in a specific institutional location (the church, ecclesiastical government, the diocese).

This again does not mean that, retrospectively, we cannot read into the situation early movements towards the modern essentialisation of these as separate spheres. In section A, "Toleration and Persecution," we see that Charles II's attempts to settle the matter of the relation between church and state can be seen in such documents as the Worcester House Declaration (1660), the Declaration in Favour of Toleration (1662), the Clarendon Code, which includes the Corporation Act (1661), the Act of Uniformity (1662), the Five Mile Act (1665), and the Conventicle Act (1670). There is also his "Declaration of Indulgence" (1672). It could be argued that these acts are stages in the formative processes that have come to be constitutive of this slowly emerging divergence. This is significantly different from the implied assumption that 'religion' and 'politics' are simply two generic arenas of ubiquitous human activity that were previously obfuscated by some kind of linguistic shortcoming but are now becoming revealed.

This ambiguous situation can be felt in the "Worcester House Declaration 1660: His Majesty's Declaration to all His Loving Subjects of His Kingdom of England and Dominion of Wales concerning Ecclesiastical Affairs" (Browning, 1953:365). It begins: "How much the peace of the State is concerned in the peace of the Church, and how difficult a thing it is to preserve order and government in civil whilst there is no order or government in ecclesiastical affairs, is evident to the world" (365). The distinction here is between civil and ecclesiastical affairs. The reason that peace in the one is dependent on peace in the other is that they are enmeshed with each other through the mediation of Religion. He refers to "the Protestant Religion" frequently, as in "we declared how much we desired the advancement and propagation of the Protestant religion," and refers to religion also as "faith" and "profession."

When the king talks about "zeal for the peace of the Church and State" (Browning, 1953:365), he is solidly linking them, yet simply to continue with rhetorical usage that names them separately, at a time when issues such as toleration are engendering the idea that religion and politics are (or should be) distinct and separate, is likely to engender a subtle sense in the contemporary reader's or listener's imagination of there already being two separate entities which are closely interdependent. The position of the king as someone who is closely linked to Catholic continental Europe but who must legitimate the Church of England as the national church of his kingdom inevitably increases the relativity between different 'religions' in the sense of Christian churches or confessions. He also uses the term "persuasions." But on the other hand, he only seems to recognise two, as when he refers dualistically to "either persuasion":

> We must for the honour of all those of either persuasion with whom we have conferred declare that the professions and desires of all for the advancement of piety and true godliness are the same, their professions of zeal for the peace of the Church the same, of affection and duty to us the same; they all approve episcopacy; they all approve a set form of liturgy; and they all disapprove and dislike the sin of sacrilege and the alienation of the revenue of the Church. (Browning, 1953:366)

Charles refers frequently to "practice" and "exercise," as in "the exercise of our religion in our own chapel" (Browning, 1953:366) or "to encourage the exercises of religion, both public and private" (367). Also see his use of "holy exercises" (367). He frequently distinguishes between ecclesiastical and civil government. As seen above, "spiritual" (367) is used typically in relation to the jurisdiction exercised over excommunication and absolution. On the other hand, he refers to the divisions within the Protestant persuasion as "the reformed churches" (369).

On discussing "ceremonies . . . which have been introduced by the wisdom and authority of the Church for edification and improvement of piety" (Browning, 1953:369), Charles acknowledges "the private consciences of those who are grieved with the use of some ceremonies" (369). One such problem is the reception of "the sacrament of the Lord's Supper" while kneeling, sitting, or standing (the king himself would always kneel, he says). Also he is concerned about "the use of the surplice," "the oath of canonical obedience," the taking of university degrees, and so on. He is tolerant and liberal in his attitude to all of these. Sometimes he refers to "Christian religion" rather than "the Christian Religion," for example, "the blessed gift of charity which is a vital part of Christian religion" (Browning, 1953:368); though one can also find the latter, as in "the propagation of the Protestant religion" (370). Whichever way he expresses it, religion is always Christian, Protestant, and established by law. And even here it might be said that the law, both civil and ecclesiastical, *is* Christian. It is not as though law, as one separate and fundamental aspect of the nonreligious state, has established Religion as another domain, which would be the modern and different nuance whereby the secular constitution establishes the citizens private right to practice his or her religion.

I have found no mention of politics, economics, or modern generic religions throughout the texts chosen by the editor to represent the thinking of the period. The predominant terms are ecclesiastical, church, state, Parliament, monarch, sacred, civil, and Religion in the encompassing sense of our Christian Truth, or that which binds the nation together.

In his "Declaration in Favour of Toleration" (1662), the king renews his commitment to his earlier Act of Indemnity and reassures those who doubt that he will never "decline from the religious observance of it" (Browning, 1953:372). Here, "religious" seems to have the nuance of correct, unwavering, committed observance, for it is an act of Parliament that he promises to observe religiously. This seems consistent with the Roman usage of *religio*, in the sense conjectured earlier. The king reaffirms his commitment to "the uniformity of the Church of England in discipline, ceremony and government" (373), but at the same time he will not persecute unnecessarily those who, living peaceably, "do not conform thereunto through scruple and tenderness of misguided conscience, but modestly and without scandal perform their devotions in their own way" (373). He also rejects "that most pernicious and injurious scandal, so artificially spread and fomented, of our favour to papists" (373). Here, it is admittedly difficult not to see a very early sense in which toleration clears a small space for the neutrality of the state towards religion understood as a separate private practice. Yet it is noticeable that, throughout these important documents, there is no hint of the modern vocabulary of politics, economics, or religion as generic ideas, nor any usage of the term secular. Sacred, as has been pointed out, is used mainly in relation to the king and the government. The language of the church is more typically found, for example, in the following important act of Parliament: An Act for the Uniformity of Public Prayers and Administration of Sacraments, and Other Rites and Ceremonies; and for Establishing the Form of Making, Ordaining and Consecrating Bishops, Priests and Deacons in the Church of England. The act proclaims "an universal agreement in the public worship of Almighty God" (377).

When the expression "spiritual promotions" (Browning, 1953:379) is used, as in "shall ipso facto be deprived of all his spiritual promotions," the act is referring to "any ecclesiastical benefice or promotion," such as a parsonage or a vicarage. Again, the modern nuance of the term spiritual, as in 'spirituality' as a private quest for special experiences, is entirely absent from this usage. Here it is aligned with other terms, as in how the *spiritualty* is distinct from the *temporalty*, or the ecclesiastical is distinct from the civil.

One might have expected to find the word 'spirituality', however, in the language of the religion of the heart of some Dissident sects, referring for instance to the movement of the spirit within. Yet it can be noted in passing that Bunyan, in *The Pilgrim's Progress*, which was published around this time in 1678, in the edition edited by N. H. Keeble (1984), only uses the word spiritual once as far as I can ascertain. In contrast, Keeble uses the word to explain Bunyan's meaning twelve times in his introduction and eleven times in the notes at the end of the text.[7]

It is interesting and significant to note who are specified to swear by the Act of Uniformity:

> every dean, canon, and prebendary of every Cathedral or collegiate church, and all masters and other heads, fellows, chaplains and tutors of or in any college, hall, house of learning or hospital, every public professor and reader in either of the universities and in every college elsewhere, and every parson, vicar, curate, lecturer, and every other person in Holy Orders, and every schoolmaster keeping any public or private school, and every person instructing or teaching any youth in any house or private family as a tutor or schoolmaster, who upon the first day of May which shall be in the year of our Lord God one thousand six hundred sixty two, or at any time thereafter, shall be incumbent or have possession of any deanery, canonry, prebend, mastership, headship, fellowship, professor's place or reader's place, parsonage, vicarage, or any other ecclesiastical dignity or promotion, or of any curate's place, lecture or school, or shall instruct or teach any youth as tutor or schoolmaster, shall before the Feast Day of Saint Bartholomew ... subscribe the declaration. (Browning, 1953:379)

It could validly be argued that this statement and the oath of allegiance are only necessary because they presuppose the fissures in the body politic which the act is attempting to hold together. Reading it this way is to acknowledge the major shifts in the conceptualisation of both 'religion' and 'politics' that are moving as powerful currents as a result of many causes, the cause of nonconformity and toleration acting as explicit manifestations. However, read from the other side, this and kindred documents indicate the degree to which the modern configuration centred on the opposition between religion and nonreligion has not yet emerged as the dominant discourse. The people specified have to declare against taking up arms against the king, and to conform to the liturgy of the Church of England. Heresy and rebellion against the king are not clearly distinguished, since both are subversive of Religion, which embraces all. Though the threat of republicanism and regicide is a massive issue in the emergence of modernity, it is not in itself modern. For many, popular conceptions of a republican alternative to monarchy will be conceived as another and more righteous form of God's rule on earth. Though a distinction is made between church and state, as in "any change or alteration of government either in Church or State" (Browning, 1953:380), yet allegiance to the liturgy of the Church of England and to the king are demanded in the same sentence, and the people specified do not in any way get distinguished in terms of 'religious' or 'nonreligious'. Even time, as in "before the Feast Day of Saint Bartholo-mew," wraps all together in the same overarching set of Christian assump-tions. Fellows, scholars, schoolmasters, tutors, and governors are all equally specified to "subscribe unto the Nine and Thirty Articles of religion" (381). Lecturers are, like parsons and vicars, in holy orders.

By 1670 and the Conventicle Act (Browning, 1953:384), there is increasing opposition to uniformity from "the growing and dangerous practices of sedi-tious sectaries" who attend "any assembly, conventicle or meeting under col-our or pretence of any exercise of religion in other manner than according to the liturgy and practice of the Church of England."

The word "sacred" comes up in a petition from some people in Man-chester for a special licence to practice nonconformity under the 1672 "De-claration of Indulgence" (Browning, 1953:388). They refer to "your sacred majesty" twice. They request a minister "of the Presbyterian persuasion . . . to exercise his ministerial function among us."

The Test Acts of 1673 and 1678 hardly mention 'religion' and never the other words. All members of "the House of Peers" and "the House of Com-mons" had to make the oath and declaration "at the table in the middle of the . . . House, and whilst a full . . . House is therewith their Speaker in his place." They were required to declare

> that I do believe that in the sacrament of the Lord's Supper there is
> not any transubstantiation of the elements of bread and wine into
> the body and blood of Christ at or after the consecration . . . and that
> the invocation or adoration of the Virgin Mary or any Other Saint
> and the sacrifice of the mass, as they are now used in the Church of
> Rome, are superstitious and idolatrous. (Browning, 1953:392)

The document goes on to renounce the authority of the pope. This is in Par-liament.

Now, clearly, the Test Acts were in reaction to perceived threats from Catholics, but the language is not about religion, politics, economics, or the secular, but about legitimate authority in church and state, with the king's authority overriding both. This is about power, and the legitimation of power, but not about 'religion' as distinct from 'politics' or vice versa.

Archbishop Sancroft, writing to Bishop Compton in 1681 to "hurrah" the king's determination to vigorously prosecute "all Papists and popish recu-sants," considers it an act of piety of His Majesty, a "pious purpose" (Brown-ing, 1953:394–95).

James II, in his 1687 "Declaration of Indulgence," grants "the free exercise of their religion," and talks about the need for tolerance in order to safeguard trade, among other things. It is his opinion "that conscience ought not to be constrained, nor people forced in matters of mere religion" because this enforced uniformity "destroys" "the interest of government" by "spoiling trade, depopulating countries and discouraging strangers" (Browning, 1953:396). This is a quite startlingly explicit connection among toleration, successful trade, and the (tacit) interests of the class that was developing England's co-lonial power. The use of the word "mere" in "mere religion" as distinguished from the importance of "the interest of government" is difficult to interpret, although it surely can be argued that this is an early sign of the distinction which Locke and Penn were articulating around this time. James continues:

> and add that to the perfect enjoyment of their property, which has never been in any case invaded by us since our coming to the crown; which being the two things men value most, shall ever be preserved in these kingdoms, during our reign over them, as the truest methods of their peace and our glory . . . . We therefore, out of our princely care and affection unto all our loving subjects that they may live at ease and quiet, and for the increase of trade and en-couragement of strangers, have thought fit by virtue of our royal prerogative to issue forth this our declaration of indulgence.
> (Browning, 1953:396)

The importance which James gives to property, the increase of trade, and the encouragement of strangers seems very noticeable. In granting toleration, he says that "all our subjects may enjoy . . . their religious assemblies." This seems like a different use of 'religious' from the common one of the time. Bunyan, in his *Pilgrim's Progress* (1984 [1678, 1684]), uses "religious" about nine times, for example, in the expressions "becoming religious" and "reli-gious fraternity." I do not think that Bunyan means by religious fraternity "monastery." However, there is no idea of a modern secular world in Bunyan and "religious" here would be better understood in contrast to "prophane." Locke uses the term to refer to voluntary "religious" associations, and in Locke there is an explicit idea of a polity which is nonreligious because it is not concerned with religion which, despite Goldie's argument about civil reli-gion, is an entirely different domain in Locke's formulation. King James's language feeds into the impression that there is shifting nuance here and there. Here the personal confession of the individual is being distinguished from the interests of government, from trade, and from public duty, and there is the sense that freedom of religion is being granted in order to protect the government:

> And to the end that by the liberty here granted the peace and security of our government in the practice thereof may not be endan-gered . . . we do freely give them leave to meet and to serve God after

their own way and manner ... so that they take especial care that
nothing be preached or taught amongst them which may anyways
tend to alienate the hearts of our people from us or our government.
(Browning, 1953:396)

It is difficult to read this without, from the privileged position of hindsight,
seeing a conceptual widening, a breakthrough in the expression of religion as a
matter of private conscience separated from (though subordinate to) the interests of government. (On the other hand, the distinction between preaching
and teaching presumably would still have had a different nuance then, since
only twenty-odd years earlier all lecturers were in holy orders and all teachers
had to swear to the Act of Uniformity.) "Conscience" is increasingly a key word
in these texts, and "trade" is beginning to enter the texts too. For example, the
mayor, aldermen, councilmen, gentlemen, and burgesses of the city of Gloucester wrote, thanking the king for "liberty of conscience" and linking it positively to trade: "Since it hath not been in the power of human policies to
reunite us in one judgment in matters of religion," the king has taken "the
wisest and most Christian expedient," thus giving "new life and vigour to your
people and trade" (Browning, 1953:398).

James, or those advisors and speech makers who had the power to put
words into the king's mouth, reissued the same "Declaration of Indulgence"
in 1688 in order to counteract rumours that he had changed his mind. To
this, he added a section of text which clearly links the following advantages
to liberty of conscience: commanding the trade of the world; establishing the
peace, greatness, safety, and honour of the country; and improvement to the
good management and functioning of the fleet and the army (Browning,
1953:399–400). There are also two other factors, one a suggestion of something approaching a theory of merit, that men (I assume women were excluded) should be promoted to service on the basis of merit rather than on the
basis of their having passed or failed "the burden and constraint of oaths and
tests"; and a self-representation of the king not as an oppressor but as a father.

This is surely a remarkable statement and it makes clear what is not clear
in other documents, which is that liberty of conscience, "the free exercise of
their religion," is clearly connected in powerful minds with increasing trade,
the growing strength of the national interest and position in the world. This
is a national enterprise, and the honour and prestige of the nation through
successful trade and self-assertion in the world are incrementally becoming the
dominant virtues and motives for action. The word 'religion' has not in this
context become anything like a modern generic concept. It is still Religion
understood as Christian Truth, but a Truth which is bifurcating in two directions: as our Protestant Religion, it is the nation, and all priests are patriots
and all citizens are priests; but it is also becoming to some degree privatised
through the concept of "liberty of conscience"; we men are all Christians, the

king seems to imply, but we all have our different individual ways of expressing that. What truly unites us is the nation, and a desire for its greater glory and prosperity. It is as though there were two religions, the nation and the privatised conscience. It may be this bifurcation that is the source of the modern alienation of the individual. The anxiety about the existence of God is a function of the privatisation of 'belief', in which God is becoming marginalised from the scientific conception of the material world in some ways like the individual conscience in Dissent and nonconformity is becoming marginalised from the central affairs of the nation-state.

There is also the sentence "not only good Christians will join in this, but whoever is concerned for the increase of the wealth and power of this nation." This sounds like a tacit extension of the idea of religion and toleration beyond Christianity, perhaps towards Jews.

In the following year, Locke published *A Letter concerning Toleration*, which is centrally concerned with the toleration of differences between sectarian viewpoints. The argument is framed by Christian, though liberal Christian, suppositions:

> The Toleration of those that differ from others in matters of Religion,
> is so agreeable to the gospel of Jesus Christ, and to the genuine
> Reason of Mankind, that it seems monstrous for men to be blind, as
> not to perceive the Necessity and Advantage of it. (Locke, 1689:7)

Here, Locke makes an influential distinction between Religion and government, and in the process he redefines the meaning of both Religion and the commonwealth:

> I esteem it above all things necessary to distinguish exactly the
> Business of Civil Government from that of Religion, and to settle the
> just Bounds that lie between the one and the other. If this be not
> done, there can be no end put to the Controversies that will be always
> arising, between those that have, or at least pretend to have, on
> the one side, a Concernment for the Interest of Mens Souls, and on
> the other side, a Care of the Commonwealth. (1689:8)

As mentioned earlier in relation to his patron the nonconformist Earl of Shaftesbury, Locke served as secretary of the Board of Trade and Plantations and secretary to the lords and proprietors of the Carolinas. It seems important to notice how the distinction between Religion and civil government or the commonwealth which Locke is putting forward here is in opposition to the older, more orthodox idea of the commonwealth. I argued on the basis of textual evidence that Religion and the commonweal were two sides of the same coin, and that the civil government was not nonreligious in the modern sense but encompassed by Religion. Here, there is an opposition between them in terms of function, in terms of public and private, and, when placed more widely into the context of Locke's thought, in terms of ontology (body and soul). This seems to be qualitatively different from the kind of Religion about which Bunyan is writing, even though they both belong to the broad stream of Protestant theology.

In these documents, religion and nation have been frequently linked to the competition with other European nations over trade, reflecting the growing importance of plantations and colonies. In the seventeenth century, politics and economics, or political economy as it would appear, have not yet been conceptualised as distinct domains or discourses, but the mercantilist system which was developing if not actually named was to be the subject of critique by the Scottish Enlightenment thinkers of the eighteenth century—David Hume, Adam Smith, and James Steuart—who were arguably the founders and inventors of modern economic theory (Sakamoto & Tanaka, 2003).[8]

The word religion seems to appear in official rhetoric more frequently than in the earlier period, and this is probably due to an increasing problem about the meaning of religion in an age when different 'persuasions' interpreted Christian Truth in different ways. Retrospectively, this appears to us as the early beginnings of a process where church and state, or religion and political economy, are being prised apart and moving towards something like the modern essentialisation of two distinct spheres which today are represented widely as embedded in the nature of things. However, this is not meant to imply that anybody at the time was clear about this. The changes in usages have been caused by a number of factors. The most obvious factor from these readings is the debates over nonconformity and toleration, which increasingly gave rise to the notion that Protestantism and Catholicism are two different 'religions', and that the Dissenting sects also constitute different 'religions'. However, the pluralised word religions here means churches or sects or persuasions based on conflicting interpretations of Religion. And Religion is concerned with different interpretations of Christian Truth, not only in doctrinal matters but in terms of what we would call social order, since doctrine and concepts of governance and human relations were not really separated in people's minds, only slowly becoming so. Indeed, even the idea of a social order as distinct from a total encompassing cosmology of rank and degree is a modern essentialisation, implying a distinct entity 'society' that would only become formulated much later in the invention of sociology.

This pluralisation of 'religions' was being intensified by the arguments in which some parts of the nation had an interest. Yet, given that we are mainly reading the thoughts of the literate male elites, it seems likely that the vast majority of people in the country villages experienced little change in their day-to-day assumptions about the order of things. This might be challenged from the viewpoint of the agricultural revolution, the enclosures, and the early beginnings of an urban working class due to industrialisation. However, as Eric Wolf points out, the shift from mercantilism to capitalism and the visible beginnings of industrial classes as a major feature of society really occurred in the second half of the eighteenth century (Wolf, 1997 [1982]:266–69). It is open to debate who, in the much earlier period under review, that is to say, the late seventeenth and early eighteenth centuries, were actually included in the rhetoric of 'the nation', but the evidence from these documents is that it was the aristocracy and landed gentry, plus people with trading interests who could get patronage. The relationship between John Locke and his patron the Earl of Shaftesbury would be one indication.

In their introduction to volume 10, *1714–1783*, in the same series of *English Historical Documents* (1957), the historians D. B. Horn and Mary Ransome say that the enclosures, "which had occurred to some extent in preceding centuries...now became frequent by act of parliament and until all the available land had been enclosed" (1957:23). As a result of this process:

> The yeoman class, so long regarded as the backbone of the country,
> had virtually disappeared by 1800 and the pattern of English rural life
> had consequently altered. The typical village no longer contained
> representatives of every class from the lord of the manor to the
> pauper, but tended to social stratification. The lord of the manor
> remained at the top, the middle tier was occupied by a small ring of
> tenant-farmers, and the great bulk of the population of the village
> was composed of landless labourers whose condition for long
> was indistinguishable from that of the pauper. (23)

In particular, the yeomen lost the right to the common land, especially for pasturage and wood cutting. Most yeomen could not afford to buy their share in the enclosures and were forced to sell their rights and either work for a more-prosperous neighbour or move to the expanding industrial towns. This time scale gives us a view of the pace of changes in England, and suggests the degree to which the old order in broad outline withstood the incremental changes to which all traditional forms of life are subject, even though forces of change were clearly and powerfully at work.

Another source of change towards a modern concept of politics, which has not been much commented on in this chapter, was the development of the two-party system of Whigs and Tories since the late seventeenth century. Yet, according to the same editors, we do not get a picture of participatory democracy of the kind that North Americans may have been developing. They say that, during the eighteenth century:

> in most constituencies the result of a poll was a foregone conclu-
> sion and actual contests were few in comparison with unopposed
> returns. Sir Lewis Namier has calculated that only forty-eight
> constituencies finally went to the polls in the general election of 1761.
> In fact, Rousseau's jibe about the English people being free only

during a general election shows a misunderstanding of the functions of general elections in eighteenth century England. With the possible exception of that held in 1741, 'no government', Sir David Keir informs us, 'ever lost a general election, nor did any government, until the ill-success of that of Lord North in the American War caused its overthrow in 1782, ever fail to sway Parliament so long as it possessed the King's confidence'. (Horn & Ransome, 1957:9)

When governments were forced to resign, it was usually at exceptional times of failure in war, such as 1741 and 1782. This implies a system of patronage and a narrow electorate based on qualifications such as land ownership, rather than what we think of as a modern political system.

Even in the late eighteenth and early nineteenth centuries (Aspinall & Smith), there are clear signs that the issues of Dissent and nonconformity had not been resolved. It is true that in the selected extracts offered by Aspinall and Smith, editors (1959), in part VI of "Social and Religious Life," section B, "The Church and Nonconformity" (English Historical Documents, Vol. 11, 1783–1832), have several instances of the language of religion and politics. For example, in the debate on the Corporation Acts, 26 February 1828 (*Hansard's Parliamentary Debates*, new series, XVIII:676–781), and referring to the attempts to repeal the Test and Corporation Acts, Lord John Russell argued:

[T]he religious questions which had been the subject of the world's debate at the time of their enactment had given place to divisions purely political; that the dispute for power no longer lay between Catholic, Lutheran and Calvinist, but between the adherents of despotism, representative monarchy, and democracy; that he [Lord John Russell] could only defend the Constitution by rallying around it the victims of an extinct quarrel, and calling on men of different religious opinions to defend the same form of political government. (Aspinall & Smith, 1959:672)

Officially, Religion still meant Protestant Truth, but here we can surely see the view expressed that political theories are in the ascendancy. There were now multiple 'religions', albeit all variations on Christian Truth, and the growing power of Dissenters and trade and manufacturing interests, and the continuing expansion of colonialism and knowledge of other peoples, encouraged the widening gap between 'religion' and to what Lord John Russell here refers as "divisions purely political," implying that political parties or opinions are now conceptually separated from 'religions' as secular agencies.

Yet at the same time, the problem of nonconformism and the existence of the Test and Corporation Acts shows how much 'religion' was still entangled in 'politics', even if now conceptually distinct. This is indicated in the same section by advice given to Lord Hawkesbury, who had just been appointed chancellor of the duchy, 23 October 1786, by Francis Russell, who was employed in the office of the Duchy of Lancaster at the time of the debate in the House of Commons on the repeal of the Test and Corporation Acts:

> Under the several Acts of 25 Charles II, Ch. 2, and I George I, Ch. 13, Stat.2d, every person taking any kind of office or authority from the king is obliged to take the Holy Sacrament in a parish church on a Sunday, to be proved by the oaths of two witnesses and also the oaths of supremacy and allegiance either in one of the four courts at Westminster or at the Quarter Sessions of the Peace. The time for taking the sacrament is limited to three months after admission to office. That for taking the oath and subscribing the declaration is by 9 George II, c. 26 enlarged to six months. Lord Clarendon received the Sacrament at Watford and took the oaths at the Quarter Sessions for Hertfordshire. By a clause in the Act of 25 Charles II I observe that peers may take the oaths in parliament whilst sitting, and in the interval they may take them in Chancery. St. Martin's Church is the place where officers in general qualify for offices, and a person attends here with all the proper forms of certificates and stamps every Sunday. (Aspinall & Smith, 1959: 672)

We can get an insight into the struggle to define the correct relationship between 'religion' and 'politics' through the debates in the British House of Commons on the bill "To prevent persons in Holy Orders from sitting in the House," taken from Cobbett's *Parliamentary History* (XXXV:1402–20). The election in 1801 of the well-known radical agitator the Reverend John Horne Took for the borough of Old Sarum raised the question of the capacity of the clergy to be elected to Parliament. Sir Francis Burdett argued against the bill:

> He could see no fair reason why the clergy should be considered as more liable to sinister influence than any other order of persons.... The arguments on which the Bill was founded were the offspring of superstition, a superstition more gross and flagrant than the tenets of Popery itself. It was pretended that such a degree of sacredness attached to the sacerdotal character that it would be a profanation to meddle and interfere in lay matters. This was a doctrine which he had hoped had long since been exploded. There were a variety of cases in which the clergy took an active part in lay offices, infinitely more discordant to their sacerdotal character than parliamentary duties. (Aspinall & Smith, 1959:249)

Horne Took said:

> For a century and a half [that is, since the revolutionary government or interregnum of Cromwell] there has not been a single parlia-

ment in which some persons in holy orders did not sit.... No fears
or apprehensions were expressed of there being any danger of the
clergy rising en masse and rushing for a seat in the Parliament.
But the moment I show my face in the House, the signal alarm is
given, and my presence is supposed to endanger the Constitution. (Aspinall & Smith, 1959:249)

This indicates that the issue of whether or not the church, in the person of the
clergy, should be separated from the state, in the form of Parliament, was an
issue as late as the early nineteenth century in England.

9

Religion, State, and American Constitutionalism

The concept of private religion as essentially distinct from public politics, or the idea of religion as a voluntary organisation licensed by the state which itself has nothing essentially to do with religion, seems to have developed into a clear discourse in the late seventeenth century, at least insofar as it is represented in the English language.[1] I have already shown in chapter 1 how explicit was Locke's language in the distinction between religion and politics, one the concern of the inward soul and the after life of rewards and punishments in the other world; the other the concern of the magistrate and outward force for the protection of public order in this world. Another writer who developed a similar binary discourse was William Penn, the English Quaker who founded the state of Pennsylvania and wrote several early charters which influenced the eventual form of the U.S. Constitution and the Bill of Rights (see Soderlund, 1983; Hough, Vol. 2, 1872: 215–244).

William Penn was a wealthy man owning land in England and Ireland. However, defaults on rent payments by his tenants, combined with the expense of his work for the Quakers, which included missionary visits to Holland (where his mother came from) and Germany, and had led him to build up a considerable debt. He was probably looking to America as a financial investment, but this was conceived very much in terms of serving the Quaker cause (Clarke, 1955:340; Soderlund, 1983:19). His most pressing concern in England was the right of dissent and nonconformity, for which he had been a committed activist, suffering imprisonment on several occasions; and his most pressing interest in America was arguably the founding of a

Quaker colony. In the intense public debate about how Christians who were divided on the proper way to be related to Christ could share the same world without incessant violence, or without persecution by the church-state, there developed the idea that Religion is not a matter of state, and is essentially defined by individual conscience and by a church conceived as a voluntary association. In short, a critique of encompassing Religion got started. Religion came to be identified with the inner conscience of the individual, and with the idea of the church, or with churches, as voluntary organisations distinct from the state.

The origins for the ideological legitimation of this idea in the Bible are in my view not as clear as they may seem in retrospect. This is not precisely the same issue as the one with which Quentin Skinner is concerned in *The Foundations of Modern Political Thought*, in which he argues that it is in the work of Bodin that "we hear for the first time the authentic tones of the modern theorist of the State" (1978, 2:352). The emergence of a modern concept of the state is of course of fundamental importance in understanding the emergence of a modern, privatised concept of religion; but Skinner, as I argued in my first and fifth chapters, did not pay the same kind of attention to transformations in the category of religion as he did to those of the state. The issue I am raising here concerns the source of the ideological legitimacy of the claim that the essential meaning of 'religion' is to be located in a concept of a private faith divorced from power and organised as a merely voluntary association. Many scholars have claimed that the idea of 'religion' as belief in a spiritual reality separated from this mundane world was already inherent in the saying of Jesus reported in the Gospels "give unto Caesar the things that are Caesar's, and unto God the things that are God's." And this, with other similar passages, has also been used to justify the idea that the church is the 'religious' institution, which has struggled to be accommodated with earthly 'nonreligious' powers. On the other hand, there seems to be evidence that the Roman Christians of the fourth century did not read it this way. Christians were persecuted because they represented a threat to the Roman imperial state. Christianity had revolutionary implications for the survival of the Roman Empire under Constantine in the fourth century and required major ideological accommodation to Christian practice, which, in its turn, was greatly influenced and shaped by Roman practice (Freeman, 2003). It anyhow seems unlikely that Roman or Christian disciplines recognised a distinction between religion and the secular in the modern sense, not least because the Roman Emperor was himself simultaneously the equivalent of king and priest, a position or status adopted by the pope. If my argument in chapter 3 is accepted, then I suggest that it makes more sense to imagine Roman realities in terms of a relative distinct between sacred and profane than in terms of the modern essentialized religion-secular dichotomy, which I have argued is particular to modern ideology. Since the rhetoric of writers like Locke and Penn was designed to solve the problem of conflict within the seventeenth century church-state, or what the historian O'Gorman refers to as "the confessional state" in eighteenth-century England, then it seems difficult to grasp why that modern understanding should already have existed in the minds of the first Christians or in the dominant *imaginaire* of their Roman environment.[2]

I have suggested in chapter 5 that not even Luther or Calvin believed in a state in the modern sense as one which is essentially separate from Religion understood as Christian Truth. Nor could the Roman polity have been a state that was 'secular' in the modern sense. As William Bede Kristensen wrote about Greek and Roman kingship, "It is clear from certain ritual acts that in these nations not only was the king the high priest, but he was also conceived as a divine personage" (Kristensen, 2006:118).

We are not, therefore, talking about a situation in the fourth century in which it would have come naturally to anyone to think in terms of a distinction between religion (private 'faith' and church) and state (emperor or civil magistrate in principle neutral towards religion). It seems difficult to believe that the early Christians had a concept of individual privacy and civil tolerance of the kind that later emerged in seventeenth-century Europe. There were, of course, a range of different statuses and functions performed by different categories of actors and agents, and there were various cults that coexisted in various empires. But this does not mean that they fell into a 'religious' or a 'political' or 'secular' divide. The idea that the Romans of the fourth century— or the Jews of the first century—had 'religion' and 'religions' in the modern sense tends to look like a retrospective reading which is convenient for justifying present arrangements. And since present arrangements in which religion and politics are constitutionally separated seem in England to have been first *clearly* imagined in the context of seventeenth-century Dissent,[3] then it is understandable why such biblical passages might have come retrospectively to be read in such a way by Protestant thinkers.

Penn and Locke were developing a tradition of ideas inherited from Machiavelli and a number of French writers such as Jean Bodin; and this was happening in the context of significant expansions of world trade and colonialism. Penn, for example, was devoted to the cause of the separation of church and state in order to relieve the Quakers from persecution, and his interest in Pennsylvania was very much connected with his desire to found a Quaker utopia in a land free of ancient European oppressions. Such devotion led him to reconceive the meanings of 'religion' and 'politics' in ways that were similar to Locke and which doubtless were made possible by the struggles in France in the previous century.[4] Like Locke, Penn built the religion-politics dichotomy around ideas of inner and outer, soul and body, spirit and matter. The title of one of Penn's presentations on toleration (1680) is *The Great Question to be Considered by the King, and this approaching Parliament, briefly proposed, and modestly discussed: (to wit) How far Religion is concerned in Policy or Civil*

Government, and Policy in Religion? With an Essay rightly to distinguish these great interests, upon the Disquisition of which a sufficient Basis is proposed for the firm Settlement of these Nations, to the Most probable satisfaction of the Several Interests and Parties therein. By one who desires to give unto Caesar the things that are Caesar's, and to God the things that are God's. His appeal to the distinction between the things of Caesar and the things of God was the popular way of legitimating the separation of church and state alluded to before. It was the basis, for example, of the Anglican bishop Benjamin Hoadly's sermon before the king at the Royal Chapel at St. James's in 1717.[5]

This sermon (the sixth edition was published in 1718) is a clear argument for toleration and seems on the face of it to amount to a plea for the disestablishment of the church in which Hoadly was a bishop. The sermon is focused on an exegesis of Saint John 18:36, "Jesus answered, My Kingdom is not of this World." The sermon begins by drawing attention to the changing meaning of words, and the way words come over time to acquire meanings that were not the original intention of those who uttered them. He is particularly concerned with the changed meaning of the word 'religion', which he argues refers in the Gospels to the kingdom of Christ, to the salvation of the individual, to the individual conscience, and to rewards and punishments in a future life, none of which are concerned with the civil magistracy.

It is easy to criticise the apparent naïveté of Hoadly's argument that we can find the true and essential meaning of an English word like religion in the Gospels, since we know through the traditions of biblical criticism how difficult is the exegesis of the true and original meaning of the Gospels. On the other hand, the term 'religion' did not then have the definitional problem associated with it today: Hoadly would have assumed, like almost everyone else at that time, that 'religion' meant Christian Truth. This was not an etymological inquiry into the origin of the word 'religion', but an attempt to anchor the proper interpretation of Christian Truth in the original intended meaning of the Gospels. And what he meant by the changed meaning of the word was the changed conception of Christian Truth. The Truth as taught by Christ meant "in St. James's Days . . . Virtue and Integrity, as to ourselves, and Charity and Beneficence to others; before God, even to Father" (Hoadly, 1718:5). Religion, as he expounds it, refers to the realm of spirit, Truth; the "Affair of Religion" is found in "the Affairs of Conscience and Eternal Salvation" (11). It is also about rewards and punishments in a future life (14). This original understanding of the meaning of Religion (Christian Truth) has come, through a long process of degeneration, to falsely mean what he calls "External Religion," which is as different as day is from night. External Religion is not true religion, but "a punctual exactness in a Regard to particular Times, Places, Forms, and Modes" (5), presumably a reference to Catholic superstitious ritualism. This external religion varies according to "the various Humours of Men," by which he means local customs, a tacit recognition of relativism, that what counts as a "religious Man differs in every Country,"[6] just as do all other "Outward circumstances" (6).

In Hoadly's sermon, this inner and outer dichotomy has implications for the state. He contrasts temporal legislators (such as the king, to whom he is preaching) with Jesus Christ as the King of heaven, the sole law giver and judge of the things of the spirit, the legislator of the kingdom of Christ. This kingdom is not of this world:

> The *Laws* of this *Kingdom*, therefore, as *Christ* left them, have noth-
> ing of *this* World in their view; no Tendency, either to the Exalta-
> tion of *Some*, in worldly pomp and dignity, or to their absolute
> Dominion over the Faith and Religious conduct of *Others* of his
> Subjects; or to the erecting of any sort of *Temporal Kingdom*, under
> the Covert and Name of a *Spiritual* one. (Hoadly, 1718:18; original
> emphases)

The emphasis here is against the usurpation by worldly princes of author-
ity in matters pertaining to the kingdom of Christ; and when he says that Christ is the sole law giver and judge in matters of conscience and salvation, and that there is no one else who can claim to be his "human Authority," nor "Vicegerents" nor "Interpreters" (Hoadly, 1718:11), his main target may be the pope, rather than the king who is listening to him speak. If he is telling the king to stay out of the business of salvation, he is also telling the church to stay out of matters of temporal legislation. But the clear distinction between the kingdom of Christ and the legislators in this world is quite explicitly discussed, as when he points out that, while nobody has the right to claim absolute authority in the interpretation of the gospel, it *is* legitimate for worldly legislators who were not the original legislators to interpret and reinterpret laws because the conditions for law are different in this temporal world. So the king would presumably have understood the implications of the sermon, in its clear distinction between the inner and the outer, this world and the world to come. Hoadly is not therefore merely making a functional distinction between the civil and the ecclesiastical arms of the confessional state. He is making an essential difference between them, in terms of their ends, purposes, and means of legitimation. They essentially belong in different worlds.

In his *The Original and Institution of Civil Government, Discuss'd* (the second edition was published in London in 1710), and *The Measures of Submission to the Civil Magistrate Consider'd. In a Defence of the Doctrine. Deliver'd in a Sermon Preach'd before the Rt. Hon. the Lord-Mayor, Aldermen, and Citizens of London, Sept. 29, 1705* (1710), Hoadly again pursues a distinction between religion and the polity which is close to the kind being argued by Penn and Locke. For example, he directly attacks what he calls the "Patriarchal Scheme of Government," which implies Filmer, whom Locke critiqued in his *First Treatise*.

Taking this into account, what we can learn from Hoadly's sermon is that, in his attempt to undermine the hegemonic belief in the unity of church and state under the encompassing cloak of Religion (our Protestant Religion), he questioned the established or at least dominant meaning of words, and also tried to offer an alternative essential meaning by appeal to an 'original' and pure meaning, a meaning anchored in the words of Jesus in the Gospel of John. It should be noted, however, that he is giving a *sermon*, a sermon which argues that there has to be a clear distinction between the domains of religion and civil society, between Christ as King of the kingdom of heaven and the earthly king as king of a temporal kingdom. The irony of this arises because we today would regard this as having a political, as well as a religious, content, and it might as a consequence of that modern sensibility seem to amount to an overstraying of boundaries. At the time too it had a controversial content, yet the sermon was "Published by his Majesty's Special Command" and went through several editions. I read the sixth edition (1718), published only one year after the sermon was given, suggesting that it had a wide readership. We can infer from this that what we in retrospect see as the full implications of the distinction he was drawing—anticipating the modern separation of church and state in the way in which it became clarified many years later in the American Constitution of 1789—is really in the making rather than already made. It is a discourse gaining strength from an accumulation of instances, this one not from within a Dissenting church but from within the Anglican church itself. It will become apparent that this same point applies to the American public discourse which led to the Declaration of Independence and the Constitution: a good deal of the pamphlets circulating there were sermons.[7] The distinction between priests and politicians cannot be taken for granted because it was an ideology in the making.

Bernard Bailyn claims in *The Ideological Origins of the American Revolution* (1967) that Hoadly "was widely held to be one of the most notable figures in the history of political thought" in the colonies (37). This is another indication of the importance of the colonisation of America in the formation and clarification of this modern ideological construct. Locke, Penn, and Hoadly were among the most-cited and -quoted theorists in North America in the eighteenth century, and influenced the state charters, the bills of rights, and the various constitutions, all of which fed into the U.S. Constitution of 1789–1790.

Penn's *The Great Question to be Considered by the King*, published in 1680, thirty years earlier than Hoadly's sermon, produced the following remarkable and clear statement of the separation of church and state in a form which was close to that of Locke:

> Religion and Policy, or Christianity and Magistracy, are two distinct things, have two different ends, and may be fully prosecuted without respect one to the other; the one is for purifying, and cleaning the

soul, and fitting it for a future state; the other is for Maintenance
and Preserving of Civil Society, in order to the outward conveniency
and accommodation of men in this World. A Magistrate is a true and
real Magistrate, though not a Christian; as well as a man is a true
and real Christian, without being a Magistrate. (Penn, 1680:4)

In *The Great Question to be Considered by the King*, one can derive the
following oppositions:

religion	civil society
Inwardness	outwardness
otherworldly salvation	this-worldly governance
the private, individual soul,	the public realm of law
conscience	and magistrates

In *A Brief Account of the Rise and Progress of the People called Quakers* (1694),
Penn uses a series of inward-outward oppositions as a metaphor for the distinction between religion and politics, which can be schematised like this:

Inner conversion, regeneration, holiness	Outward schemes of doctrines, verbal creeds, new forms of worship (61)
the substantial, the necessary, the profitable part of the soul	religion, the superfluous, ceremonies, the formal part (61)
will of God's Spirit	studied matter (60)
inward and experimental knowledge of God	lifeless possessions (61)
Experiment	theory and speculation (63)
knowledge of the heart, the inward state	own imaginings, glosses, and commentaries on scripture (63)
extraordinary understanding in divine things/the light of Christ within	vanity of this world (63–65)

Given that Penn was questioning an entirely different and dominant assumption about Religion, these rhetorical oppositions surely have to be taken as
prescriptive rather than descriptive; they seek to persuade; they are forging the
ideas, constructing them, inaugurating a discourse on the inner and the outer
which still captivates us today. In short, the invention of religions and politics
is part of the same ideological transformation that invented the private inner
self of modernity.

The outwardness of the world seems to have three different meanings
here though.[8] On the one hand, it refers to outward actions, such as the

performance of ritual practices, the reciting of creeds, the formality of etiquette, and attachment to things that are mere objects and have no inner life,
as distinct from inner intentions. The clear implication is that the inner
things of the soul are closer to God and therefore more real and more authentic. This is a moral as well as an ontological distinction, in that it implies
that the outer actions and possessions are relatively valueless. It is derived
from the Protestant theological critique of Catholic and other forms of superstition, and a relative sundering apart of God and the world. Another meaning
of "outward" is the objectification of the world of solid matter, which he refers
to here as "studied matter," which may reflect an awareness of the development of science and the scientific conception of the empirical observation of
the material universe being developed by Galileo, Bacon, Descartes, Newton,
Locke, and many others. The world has been turned into an object, or a system of material processes, laid out in container time and space. And the third
meaning is the outer world in the sense of the public realm of civil government as opposed to the privacy of inner knowledge of spirit. To what extent
Penn was aware of these distinctions as he was writing is debatable. But we
know that he worked on a number of draft charters for the state of Pennsylvania which incorporated freedom of religion and conscience from an early
date (Soderlund, 1983).[9]

I suggest that it is the combination of these elements that gives us the
modern idea of what, in the mid-nineteenth century, came to be called the
secular world. The moral distinction here between the things of the spirit or
heart and the things of the world cannot only be understood as a relative
distinction between the sacred and the profane, for there is an incremental
shift of nuance here towards the modern dichotomy. For one thing, the
written constitutions and the rights that they made explicit which we would
see as definitive of secular modernity came to be understood as sacred. Thus,
while the world is relatively profane in relation to the things of the heart, there
are also relative sacralities within the world which is emerging as something in itself, a material world which is a self-sufficient domain of scientific rationality and causation that can be conceptually detached from that
idea of a divine teleology fundamental to earlier holistic ideas of the commonwealth. From this combination, many other 'secular' domains can develop, domains which in principle are independent of, and neutral towards,
'religion', such as economics and the Enlightenment theory of human nature
that it implies.

Given that dissent from the oppressive dominance of the church-state was
one of the prime motives for the establishment of colonies, then the idea of
such a separation would be well received by many settlers. Though some of the
earliest colonies instituted a new (Calvinist) church-state of their own, some
such as Pennsylvania were conceived in terms of dissent and freedom of

opinions from the beginning, albeit within a loosened framework of Christian commitment.

In England, the increasing demand for the separation of church and state was not the ideology of a new class in the Marxist sense, since the middling orders who supported many of the nonconformist churches were not themselves conscious of being a class, and as O'Gorman points out, English society was still dominated by the idea of degree and the value of deference, represented by "minor variations of speech, dress, and manners which are often too subtle and too varied to be conveyed in documentary evidence" (O'Gorman, 1997:115). An example of aristocratic dissent would be Lord Anthony Ashley Cooper, first Earl of Shaftesbury, Locke's patron, and a member of the king's Board of Trade and Plantations. Penn's father had been a navy admiral and friend of the King, and Pennsylvania was a gift to Penn offered partly as a repayment of the debt owed to his father. These are highly connected people. O'Gorman emphatically denies the existence of modern class consciousness in eighteenth-century England, and instead asserts an "integrated set of hierarchies, ascending and descending in minute gradations" (1997:115). This is one of the reasons that, in my view, we have to look to the dissenting, more egalitarian American colonies for the earliest and most unambiguous institutionalisation and constitutionalisation of the separation of religion and politics, and thus the radically changed meaning of the terms.

It is true and significant that Dissenters like the Quakers were explicitly in favour of egalitarianism in dress and manners, objected to hat etiquette and honorific language, and seem typical of the relationships among the religion of the heart, severe criticism of ritualism and hierarchy, trade, mobility in social and geographical senses, a more democratic concept of private property, and an emerging colonial world order.

The development of this kind of thinking in England and Scotland[10] was not inconsiderable and there were a number of influential writers in England and Scotland who criticised the establishment and the dominance of the church throughout the eighteenth century. As I will argue below, on the basis of important studies such as Bernard Bailyn's *The Ideological Origins of the American Revolution* (1967), some of these thinkers (and surely Penn and Hoadly were among them) had influence in the formulation of American thinking. But their degree of influence in eighteenth-century England could be exaggerated, and there is good reason to believe that it was the American Dissenters who first most effectively institutionalised this idea of modern politics as nonreligious in the sense of neutral towards, and separated from, religion, by making such separation and neutrality central to their state charters, bills of rights, and constitutions. England during the century of Enlightenment was still to a large extent a hierarchical and holistic society at the level of the dominant ideology, and the extent to which it had become a political state in the modern sense of 'nonreligious' or separated from religion is arguably less than might otherwise appear to be the case. O'Gorman weighs both sides of the equation. On the one hand, it could be said:

> England in the early eighteenth century was a confessional state, a state in which one official confession of faith, Anglicanism, was established by statute and enforced through the law—a faith, moreover, in theory accepted and practiced by the vast majority of the population. (O'Gorman, 1997:163)

The Test and Corporation Acts and the Licensing Act had maintained the church's dominance and established status. O'Gorman says that, for J. C. D. Clark, who takes a strongly revisionist stand, "the structural foundations of eighteenth century society were the monarchy and the aristocracy as well as the Church." The period was one of hierarchy, patriarchalism, and faith, rather than liberalism, individualism, and secularism. It should be thought of more as an age of monarchy and aristocracy, rather than one of reform, protest, and modernisation (O'Gorman, 1997:171). This revisionist picture of eighteenth-century England suggests that "the church was the dominant social force in the eighteenth century . . . . Anglicanism was much more than a 'political theology'; it was a pervasive social cement binding all orders of society" (1997:165). O'Gorman, quoting J. C. D. Clark, says: "The ideology of the confessional state thus legitimised social hierarchy, underpinned social relationships and inculcated humility, submission and obedience" (170).

On the other hand, the church may have appeared stronger than it really was. Various bits of legislation such as the Toleration Act and the repeal by the Whigs of the Occasional Conformity Act and the Schism Act had undermined the church's all-embracing position and introduced an element of voluntarism, religious pluralism, and apathy (O'Gorman, 1997:169). Commercial values had widely penetrated British society by the middle of the eighteenth century, intersecting with values from other sources, such as law and politics. A corporate theology of a graded hierarchy in which duties are assigned by birth gave way for many people to individual conscience and personal responsibility (1997:170). And though Parliament was still dominated by the figure of the king, the two-party system of Whigs and Tories, combined with state finance and the increase in trade and commerce, would surely have corresponded better to a trend towards the separation and privatisation of religion than to the continued dominance of the state church (172–73).

I am not trying to introduce a kind of teleological determinism here, as though certain developments were the inevitable unfolding of an internal Hegelian logic or divine purpose, or an evolution following irreversible laws of nature. I am merely suggesting that, from our retrospective standpoint, there was a transition between two analytically distinct paradigms, and that something new was emerging. This ambiguous picture points to a slower rate of transition between a dominant ethos of hierarchy and a relatively marginalised one of egalitarianism in England compared with the American states. It suggests that encompassing Religion—the confessional state—was still a reality in England, but that the separation of religion and politics as an idea was common currency among Dissenting groups but had not achieved anything like hegemony. The position of William Warburton, an Anglican bishop who was in favour of the monopoly of the church, gives us some insight into this halfway house. In his work *The Alliance between Church and State* (1766 [1748]), we find the idea of both their separation and also their interdependence, as implied by the title. It is interesting to find the expression "modern Politics" on the first page. The expression "their politic alliance," the older adjectival usage, can also be found in the preface, which is dedicated to Warburton's patron the Earl of Chesterfield. But here "modern Politics" sounds like the reified domain of contemporary rhetoric. Furthermore, Warburton distinguishes between the essence of church and state in modified Lockean terms: "The only subjects worth a wise Man's serious notice, are RELIGION and GOVERNMENT" (1766 [1748]:iii), he tells Chesterfield, and goes on to distinguish them: "the object of Religion being Truth...requires Liberty; and the object of Government, Peace...demands submission."

'Religion' has here been clearly identified with 'church'. This is surely a significant semantic shift. (But it is still the national church, and the king is still the head of both church and state.) However, Warburton argues that this separation requires an alliance between the two spheres such that the Church of England and the state are essentially distinct yet complementary, and provide a combination necessary for stability: "they seem naturally formed to counteract one another's operations" (Warburton, 1766 [1748]:iv). Their "Natures" (iv) and their "Agency" are different, but "there seems to be no more reason against their POLITIC ALLIANCE than we see there was against the *physical union* of the Soul and the Body" (iv). Here, Warburton makes two pieces of metaphysical speculation, what we could also describe as discursive formations or rhetorical tropes, mutually supportive by drawing an analogy between them, as has been noted in the cases of both Locke and Penn. He not only convinces us that Religion and government (or church and state) are things that have essentially different yet complementary natures, but he also virtually takes for granted the (by now) well-established discourse on the existence of two other essentially different but complementary things, the soul and the body. Church and state are distinct but complementary in a way analogous to soul and body. There is a whole library of rhetorical contestation here, for how can a nonmaterial entity such as the soul have a physical relationship, a great problem for Locke, Descartes, Spinoza, Kant, and the Scottish commonsense philosophers such as Thomas Reid, who were concerned about philosophical issues such as theory of perception and theory of knowledge. One only has to think of the different ways these supposed entities—a soulless body and a bodiless soul, brought into mutual relations in order to provide the other with what it lacks—have already been debated by Warburton's time by philosophers and theologians,[11] and this library of contestation has been compressed into an assumption and slipped neatly into his own text as an encapsulated strategy to support another essentialisation of imaginary entities: Religion and government or politics. He is therefore embedding his argument about church and state within a further dualism that could not have existed in the same senses in an earlier period, except in the minds of some rare individuals, but not at the official level of a bishop of a national religion which teaches the resurrection of the body and life everlasting.

The idea of secular (in the sense of nonreligious) scientific knowledge of a material world which is objective and external to the observer presupposes some idea of the observing subject who can stand back from the world and make factually true propositions about it. This idea of the possibility of objectivity was fundamental for Enlightenment concepts of the natural and social sciences. The system of binaries between spirit and matter, soul and body, supernatural and natural, turns the world into an object, or a system of objects, and us into master observers. It turns all other peoples and their visions of reality into objects subordinated to our master gaze and method. These self-confirming and serially replaceable metaphors of religion and politics, spirit and matter, soul and body, supernature and nature, have surely acted as foundational tropes in the rhetoric of modern ideology generally. Combined with colonial power, they have fed into the construction of 'other cultures' and underlie what Edward Said meant by Orientalism.

As already suggested, it was the North American colonies that brought these ideas about the essential difference between religion and politics into realisation first and most emphatically, and they were reexported from North America not only to other colonial societies but also back to England. And we have evidence that the separation of religion and politics has been exported from Western colonial powers such as Britain and America to different parts of the world as part of the logic of colonial control and global capitalism, as well as Enlightenment mastery (see, for example, various chapters in Fitzgerald, 2007).[12]

The full emergence of the modern idea of religion as the private exercise of a right granted by the state—a state that is defined by its separation from religion (and therefore as deserving to be characterised as nonreligious in the sense of a supposed neutrality towards religion)—is inseparable from the process leading to the final ratification of the U.S. Constitution in 1789. One way of bringing out the significance of this is to point out that the same process is also transforming the meaning of 'the state'.[13] And it is a process which also involves the gradual production of a distinctive modern meaning for the term politics.

It has been claimed that the secularity of the Constitution is synonymous with neutrality towards religion but *not* 'nonreligion'. One Web page called *Teaching about Religion and Worldview Diversity* has an article called "Untying a Terminology Tangle—Secular vs. Nonreligious" by Paul Geisert and Mynga Futrell. This article argues that, in the context of education the word 'secular' denotes a neutrality ideal, and is not synonymous with 'nonreligious'. The authors claim that to equate the term secular with nonreligious is "a serious semantic error":

> In U.S. public schools the educational enterprise must by law be *neutral* regarding religion—neutral among religions, and neutral between religion and nonreligion. In other words, it cannot favor one religion over another; nor can it privilege religion over nonreligion (or vice versa). The mandate that public schools, as government institutions, carry out a general evenhandedness concerning religion grows out of the Establishment Clause of the First Amendment to the United States Constitution, and a school system may be under further state constitutional constraints.

The authors are concerned that this ideal of neutrality, which they say is derived from the Constitution, "translates into educational policy and standard practice that make possible an academic milieu in which children of all the varied religious and nonreligious worldviews are able to participate in the educational program based on equal worth and mutual respect."

This idea that in U.S. law the term 'secular' means 'neutral' between religious and nonreligious world views, but is not itself 'nonreligious', seems itself to rest on a terminological muddle, not necessarily one created in the first place by these authors, and one which can only be understood through a historiographically contextualised approach.[14] If taken at face value, the argument seems to mean that, in addition to a religious and a nonreligious standpoint, there is a third one, which is itself neither religious nor nonreligious but neutral. But, semantically speaking, in what does this neutrality consist? If as a teacher one is neutral with regards to both religious and nonreligious world views, does this mean that one is not oneself located in any kind of world view? Can there be a position of neutrality which transcends both sides of the dichotomy, a position which the authors claim is the constitutionally correct one, and which is their own implied position?

I suggest that it would make more sense to claim that neutrality towards religion excludes *antireligion* rather than nonreligion. That is to say, if secularity is a form of neutrality towards religion, then it must logically itself be nonreligious, but not necessarily antireligious in the sense of being hostile towards religion. This would be true of the U.S. Constitution, for the Constitution takes the position (as we shall see below) that religion is a personal right. On the other hand, the Constitution also protects the state from religion. In this sense, it seems logically to follow that the Constitution represents itself as both neutral and also nonreligious.

This would also be consistent with the 'secularity' of some individuals who had significant influence on the way we have come to think about religion. As I argued above, John Locke and William Penn, though they did not use the term 'secular' (it had different and very specific meanings at the time), had influence on the making of constitutions in the United States and made a clear distinction between religion and politics. I do not deny that there may be inconsistency in their thinking. They were, after all, trying to think new thoughts. Goldie (1987:197–224) has claimed that Locke should be read as advocating a form of civil religion. For Goldie, the discourses on 'civil religion' have been powerful for centuries throughout Europe, but they have been ignored, at least by political theorists. He argues that for some commentators civil religion came to connote totalitarian obedience to the state. Some felt that it violated "what seemed the pre-eminent achievement of modern political sensibility, the secular separation of politics and religion" (Goldie, 1987:197):

> Perhaps the chief reason for the near invisibility of the concept of civil religion in studies of the mainstream Western political thought is the enormous intellectual investment that political science has in the notion of the disjunction between the civil and the religious. Secularism remains as much a boast as a fact. To discover the moment at which politics became 'autonomous' and 'rational' is a constant endeavour for a profession still deeply imbued with the Enlightenment presumption that the maturity of the species consists in its ability to conduct civil life without recourse to superstition. A modern civil religion can only be seen as backsliding into barbarism. The positivist mode in the history of political thought eagerly searches the era of human adolescence, and rewards philosophers for signs of 'science', the 'modern', the 'secular'. Machiavelli . . . and Hobbes are the pre-eminent bearers of this celebration of the struggle of science to emerge from the embrace of theology . . . . But consider instead the case of another canonical 'modern', James Harrington, the republican analyst of property and power in the mid-seventeenth century. (Goldie, 1987:198)

Goldie places Locke in this tradition. It should be obvious to the reader that Goldie's approach from the side of political theory meets quite well with my own approach. What I have been attempting in this book has been to show how positivism has became historically possible as an aspect of the dominant 'secular' or nonreligious discourse underpinned by various other binary oppositions. The development of this modern ideology has been served by projecting our own modern categories backwards in the reconstruction of our own

European past. In this book, I have been attempting to unpick this process and show how it constructs itself through the ritual reproduction of its own discursive formations. However, this critical approach in turn leads us to consider that, if the distinction between religion and secular politics is a rhetorical invention, and not in the nature of things as some academics and other public figures seem to believe, then it has also been a continual process of persuasion. Locke had to persuade himself as well as others and it would be likely that we would find ambiguity and different possibilities of interpretation in his philosophy. What his real intentions were with regard to 'civil religion' as against 'nonreligion' in relation to the state and politics, we can never know. The truth may be that he wavered between these positions. What can be said is that, in relation to the problem of dissent and toleration, he clearly did express an influential notion that the sphere of religion has to do with the soul and the possibility of a future life, and that it has nothing to do with law and order; while the sphere of the magistrate or civil society is concerned with law and order, and has nothing essentially to do with religion. The one is private and inward, the other is public and outward.

Locke, Penn, Hoadly, and others argued quite explicitly that these are distinct domains and have no necessary connection with each other. This must imply that they were separating religion and the state conceptually, in which case we are compelled to think of the state as nonreligious. This did not mean that they thought the state should be hostile towards religion, so their attitude does imply neutrality. More positively, these thinkers were favourably disposed towards what they understood by religion (which was some form of reasonable Christianity, and not a modern generic concept). But neutrality towards religion from a position that is explicitly defined in contrast to religion must in some sense be nonreligious.

If we jump forward from the late seventeenth to the mid-nineteenth century, when the word 'secular' began to be used to refer to an autonomous system of scientific materialism (see Cross, 1958:1236), we can see that it took both the form of neutrality towards religion and the form of hostility towards religion. Thus, for example, the anthropologist Edward Tylor, who was influential in founding the modern scientific study of religion, was an atheist; C. P. Tiele was a Protestant minister who nevertheless bracketed his belief and thus helped to construct a methodological agnosticism which can be described as neutrality towards religion. The evolutionary scientist and friend of Darwin T. H. Huxley, who actually coined the word agnostic, was ambiguously neutral and hostile towards religion. In this sense, I would suggest that 'secularity' insofar as it is defined as distinct from religion, is by implication unavoidably nonreligious, but that it can also be neutral, hostile, or sympathetic, depending on the context.

Can it really be maintained that the U.S. Constitution is neither religious nor nonreligious, but somehow in a category which transcends this categorical dichotomy? An indication of where we might look to unravel this perplexing notion is given on another part of the Web site mentioned earlier, probably written by a different author though this is not clear from the Web page itself. This author makes an interesting and valid point along the following lines:

A Religion/Nonreligion Border Zone

Deism is a life stance that was common in this country at one time (many of our nation's founders were Deists) but now is rather scarce. Deism seems to rest in a gray area between religious and nonreligious worldviews.

On the surface, eighteenth century Deism seems a religious worldview because the fundamental reasoning entails a transcendent deity (the Creator) who is apart from (above) his Creation. However, some scholars view Deists as having a nonreligious worldview. A dictionary may specify 'See *Skeptic*' or 'See *Atheist*' within the entry for Deist (believer in Deism). Which life understanding do Deists hold—a religious view, or a nonreligious one?

The dual perspective on Deists derives from the fact that, although they reason that laws governing nature do presuppose a supreme lawmaker or divinity, Deists firmly reject claims of supernatural revelation and generally follow an Atheistic life pattern. The fact that they regard the world's 'creation' as having been completed and do not believe any divinity is presently involved in the world or in any human affairs helps somewhat to clarify this enigma. (*Teaching About Religion: Worldview Diversity*, at http://www.teachingaboutreligion.org/WorldviewDiversity/nonreligious_worldview.htm)

I think the author is right in what she says here, that deism was ambiguous in relation to 'religion' and 'nonreligion' because it was transitional. Deism was part of the more fundamental process within which older meanings were sacrificed for the purposes of constructing a new paradigm. Deism was part of a significant and complex historical change in English-language meanings that occurred over several centuries beginning in the seventeenth century. This process of change was itself producing the very categories—religion and nonreligion—that are so problematic. The deism of the American founders referred to here, which is also the deism inherent in the language of the Declaration of Independence, is deeply contextualised within those changes. In particular, deism and the founding documents of the American republic reflect a transition from Religion, meaning Christian Truth, to religion, meaning a private right guaranteed by a nonreligious constitution. But there is no mention in the declaration of the terms 'religion', 'nonreligion', or the 'secular'. The one mention of God in the declaration is a deistic remnant of Christendom, and its use in the Declaration is in some ways analogous to the mummified but sacred remains of a revered ancestor who governed a different world out of which was born the present one. More fundamental in that document are such expressions "the Laws of Nature," "unalienable Rights," "Life, Liberty and the Pursuit of Happiness," "the consent of the governed," and "the right of Representation in the Legislature." By the time of the Constitution, the word 'God' has disappeared entirely.

I am not claiming that men like Locke and Penn were the definitive inventors of nonreligious politics since the idea might possibly have been anticipated in Machiavelli, Bodin, or Hobbes—though I argued above that an authority such as Quentin Skinner does not really clarify these issues, since he is mainly focused on changes in the meaning of the word 'state' to the exclusion of the changes in other related categories, such as religion. But until some historical moment coinciding with the scientific revolution in the early Enlightenment period, which was also a time when colonialism was well under way, there was arguably no concept in the English language either of 'a religion' or of 'the secular' in the sense of 'nonreligious' neutrality. Religion almost always has meant Christian Truth and civility, and was invariably contrasted with barbaric superstitions. Though there were a number of different sectarian interpretations about what Christian Truth meant, indicated especially by the Catholic-Protestant divide, but also within both sides of that division between different sects, few if any Europeans or Euro-Americans doubted that Religion referred to Christian Truth.

The change in concept proposed by writers such as Locke and Penn, and which became powerfully institutionalised in the Constitution one hundred years later, was revolutionary, and indicates a wider change of paradigm or world view. The idea of the nonreligious as the (Enlightenment) arena of the political and the rational can be easily inferred from the way that 'religion' (which as I said is not mentioned in the Declaration of Independence) became merely one of a number of rights in the Constitution. Furthermore, the English-language term secular, which does not appear in either document, was not used unambiguously until after around 1850 to refer to a 'nonreligious' realm, to atheistic materialism, or generally to an intellectual position or world view.

As far as I am aware, the word 'secular' is not used once either in the Declaration of Independence or in the U.S. Constitution. There is one mention of God in the Declaration:

> When in the Course of human events it becomes necessary for one people to dissolve the political bands which have connected them with another and to assume among the powers of the earth, the separate and equal station to which the Laws of Nature and of *Nature's God* entitle them, a decent respect to the opinions of mankind requires that they should declare the causes which impel them to the separation. (my italics)

There is no mention of God in the Constitution. 'Religion' and 'religious' are not used at all in the declaration, and used only once each in the Constitution. In both the First Amendment and Article VI, religion is defined as a private right, along with several others, and is simultaneously excluded from any definition of the state:

> Amendment I: "Congress shall make no law respecting an establishment of *religion*, or prohibiting the free exercise thereof; or abridging the freedom of speech, or of the press; or the right of the people peaceably to assemble, and to petition the Government for a redress of grievances." (my italics)

> Article VI: "The Senators and Representatives before mentioned, and the Members of the several State Legislatures, and all executive and judicial Officers, both of the United States and of the several States, shall be bound by Oath or Affirmation, to support this Constitution; but no *religious Test* shall ever be required as a Qualification to any Office or public Trust under the United States." (my italics)

Though it is true that sometimes in English-language discourses superstitions were referred to as 'religions' when talking about the beliefs and practices of non-European peoples—the Declaration of Independence does refer to "the merciless Indian Savages"—this was often an ironic usage, and only very slowly took on a surface covering of 'objectivity', a scientific gloss.

Thomas Jefferson, in *Notes on the State of Virginia* (1787), made a fundamental distinction between civil government and religion and imagined many religions in the world; there are "probably a thousand different systems of religion" of which "ours is but one of that thousand" (267). On the other hand, the indigenous Americans, Jefferson's own colonial others, to whom he referred as "Indians," "Aborigines," and "Savages," do not have either civil government or religion (150). They have "never submitted themselves to any laws, any coercive power, any shadow of government" (150).

Bernard Bailyn's seminal work on the ideological origins of the American Revolution (1967) not only helps us to analyse this process. It also gives many examples of why we still, in eighteenth-century America, could not assume that religion was already defined by its separation, and that the process was in action even as we read these documents. In other words, it is hazardous to assume and read back our modern distinctions into our descriptions of the processes that were producing them. For the Revolution, as Bailyn says, was a "transforming event" (1967:8), and it was surely an event that was transforming language. My own argument is that one of the most fundamental features of the American Revolution and its Enlightenment values and presuppositions was the transformation in the meanings of both 'religion' and 'state', and the Revolution is the single most important Anglophone[15] source for the institutionalisation of a modern sphere of 'politics'.

Much of Bailyn's historical research is based on his readings of the many pamphlets that circulated in America, which contained treatises on political theory, essays on history, sermons, correspondence, and poems (1967:v). He distinguishes five different sources for American revolutionary thought. One conspicuous source was the literature of classical Greece and Rome, especially the history of Rome and its republican ideals (25). Many of the authors of pamphlets and sermons attributed to Rome and its history the virtues that Americans wanted to embody, or thought they did embody, such as simplicity, patriotism, integrity, and love of justice and liberty (25). They compared these virtues with the corruption and the threat of tyranny that they perceived in colonial rule: "Britain...was to America what Caesar was to Rome" (26). Bailyn suggests that the actual knowledge that the pamphleteers had of the classical authors which they so frequently cited was small and selective, and that the main function of the classics was to provide form, respectability, and a vocabulary as a way of wrapping ideas and beliefs that had other sources (26).

The Enlightenment rationalism of writers such as Voltaire, Montesquieu, Locke, Rousseau, Grotius, and Pufendorf provided another important source of citations for many in the debates which led up to the Revolution. Benjamin Franklin, John Adams, and Jefferson, for example, all "cited the classic Enlightenment texts and fought for the legal recognition of natural rights and for the elimination of institutions and practices associated with the ancient regime" (Bailyn, 1967:26–27). They cited Enlightenment authors on the topics of natural rights, the social contract, the evils of clerical oppression, reform of criminal law, and principles of civil government. Yet here too, Bailyn tells us, the references to, and uses of, these Enlightenment authorities were frequently inaccurate.

A third source of popular citation was the tradition of English common law, especially seventeenth-century lawyers such as Sir Edward Coke, to whom citations are almost as frequent as those to Locke, Montesquieu, and Voltaire. Other frequently cited names in this connection were Francis Bacon and Sir Matthew Hale (Bailyn, 1967:30). In the later revolutionary years, Blackstone's *Commentaries*, along with those of Chief Justice Camden, were frequently cited. Bailyn comments that "English law—as authority, as legitimizing precedent, as embodied principle, and as the framework for historical understanding— stood side by side with Enlightenment rationalism in the minds of the Revolutionary generation" (1967:31).

A fourth source was the political and social theories of New England Puritanism and the ideas associated with covenant theology. Stemming from the leaders of the first settlements, these ideas had been transmitted by preachers and others in various forms throughout "almost the entire spectrum of American Protestantism" (Bailyn, 1967:32). (We can see here the tension between the use of the word political in the phrase "political and social theories" and the kind of theology they were actually disseminating; for the kind of polity that the descendants of Luther and Calvin advocated, as Bailyn himself acknowledges, was not one in which politics could be conceived in its modern sense, given that in the thinking of the Protestant founders, Religion encompassed all rules of living in the profane world. I pick up on this point again as I review Bailyn's analysis.) The important role of preachers as agents in the spreading, strengthening, and institutionalising of Lockean political theory has been emphasised also by Steven M. Dworetz in *The Unvarnished Doctrine* (1990:135 and passim).

The appeal of this covenantal theological tradition was, according to Bailyn, limited to "those who continued to understand the world, as the original Puritans had, in theological terms" (1967:32). Yet at the same time, it provided a cosmic narrative context within which the revolutionary impulse appeared thoroughly meaningful and glorious, in the idea that "the colonisation of British America had been an event designed by the hand of God to satisfy his ultimate aims" (32). It provided meaning, a teleology. It "stimulated confidence in the idea that America had a special place, as yet not fully revealed, in the architecture of God's intent" (33). It placed America in a special role and status in the unfolding of human destiny. (Again, we can see here how difficult it is to separate a major aspect of the revolutionary thrust from Religion understood as encompassing Christian Truth.)

Before identifying a fifth source, Bailyn comments on a contradiction among some of these sources. On the one hand, the common lawyers

> sought to establish right by appeal to precedent and to an unbroken tradition evolving from time immemorial, and they assumed ... that the accumulation of the ages, the burden of inherited custom, contained within it greater wisdom than any man or group of men could devise by the power of reason. (1967:33)

But this common-law tradition was therefore alien to the Enlightenment rationalists who wished to jettison the burden of custom and build human institutions on first principles, on the necessary deductions of human reason (36). And the covenant theologians believed that divine assistance was necessary, that politics should derive from divine purposes and should be concerned with redemption.

A fifth source, which Bailyn argues binds all the others together, lay in the radical thought of the English civil war and commonwealth, including works by Milton, Harrington, Henry Neville, and above all Algernon Sidney, whose *Discourses concerning Government* (1698) became a "textbook of revolution" in America (1967:35). From this seventeenth-century tradition came the group of eighteenth-century English and Scottish writers who "more than any other single group . . . shaped the mind of the American Revolutionary" (35). Bailyn mentions Richard Price, Joseph Priestley, John Cartwright, James Burgh, Catharine Macaulay, Bulstrode Whitelock, Gilbert Burnet, William Guthrie, James Ralph, and the exiled Huguenot Paul de Rapin-Thoyras. Most important according to Bailyn were John Trenchard and the Scotsman Thomas Gordon, whose weekly *Independent Whig* (some of which was published in book form in 1721) and *Cato's Letters* attacked and satirised the church and the establishment generally. Bailyn comments that the "writings of Trenchard and Gordon ranked with the Treatises of Locke as the most authoritative statement of the nature of political liberty and above Locke as an exposition of the social sources of the threats it faced" (1967:36). Another important writer for America was the liberal Anglican bishop Benjamin Hoadly, discussed earlier. Hoadly denied the sacerdotal powers of the church and held an extreme tolerance of dissent.

In England, these radical thinkers were a minority, and they were up against a complacent majority. Whereas mainstream English "purveyors of political thought spoke mainly with pride of the Constitutional and political achievements of Georgian England" (Bailyn, 37), these radical thinkers who so much influenced American revolutionary thought attacked the complacency by focusing on the dangers of corruption and the continual need for reform— adult suffrage, elimination of rotten boroughs, greater accountability, greater freedom of the press and the right to criticise government, withdrawal of government control over the practice of religion. These radicals distrusted the apparent stability of English politics under Walpole, believing that beneath the surface a system of corruption was in existence.

In this context, Bailyn makes an important comment on the difference between the radicalism in England and its reception in America which tends to support the contention in previous chapters that, despite the presence of a lively and public debate of these issues in England, focusing on such issues as corruption, the oppressive nature of the state church, and the lack of accountability in the government, it was in America that they found their truly congenial environment:

> [I]f these dark thoughts, in the England of Walpole and Gibbon,
> attained popularity in certain opposition, radical, and noncon-
> formist circles, they had relatively little political influence in the
> country at large. In the mainland colonies of North America, how-
> ever, they were immensely popular and influential. (1967:51)

What sounded like exaggeration in an English context sounded convincing to the colonists, and fed powerfully into the debates which, combined with profound historical events, led to the Declaration of Independence (1776) and the federal Constitution (1789–1790). The idea of a written constitution, which was very different from the English idea of a constitution, had precedents (as Bailyn explains) in the various charters, bills of rights, and state constitutions which had existed for a century or more. The charter of the Massachusetts Bay colony "had originated as commercial charters, concessions of powers by the Crown to enterprises willing to undertake the risks of exploration and settlement. These, in the colonial setting, had quickly changed in character" and become very much like a written constitution (1967:190). Similar things could be said about the Fundamental Orders of Connecticut of 1639, or the Crown Charters of New York, Maryland, and the Carolinas, which, "though anachronistic in their feudal terminology" nevertheless "provided for public institutions" that were expected to be permanent and unalterable. In particular, William Penn's constitution for Pennsylvania was a deliberate and conscious foundation for the protection of rights and the limits of government. The various charters he drew up established models for civil administration, elections, court procedures, the judiciary, and the duties and obligations of office holders (Bailyn, 1967:191; see also Soderlund, 1983).

In 1691, the General Assembly of New York published provisions for "Rights and Privileges of the Majesty's Subjects" which

> listed the rights of individuals in the form of a series of categorical prohibitions on government: the individual was to be free from unlawful arrest and imprisonment, arbitrary taxation, martial law, the support of standing armies in time of peace, feudal dues, and restrictions on freehold tenure; in addition, he was guaranteed due process of law, especially trial by jury, and, if Protestant, full liberty to 'enjoy his or their opinion, persuasions, [and] judgments in matters of conscience and religion throughout all this province'. (Bailyn, 1967:195)

The charters had often originally legitimated the power of vested interests of planters and colonisers from England, but by the revolutionary period were well established as protections against misuses of power. And "[e]verywhere in the colonies the charters were prized" as evidence of the rights of British subjects (Bailyn, 1967:192). Some people, such as those who subscribed to covenant theology, believed the charters had "an additional, transcendent sanction" (193). The charter was seen as a solemn covenant between the king and the ancestors who founded the colony, as a sacred proclamation and defence of rights and liberties (193). The idea of the individual state charters as written codifications of inviolable rights and liberties was already available and relevant, and by the time of the Constitutional Convention it was therefore logical for Americans to imagine a written constitution. For this reason, Bailyn describes these charters as "astonishingly modern," and he gives as an example the statement of the Fundamental Rights of West New Jersey (1693)—which presumably were derived from Penn's Laws, Concessions, and Agreements for the province of West New Jersey (1677)—that "no man nor number of men upon earth hath power or authority to rule over men's conscience in religious matters" (quoted in Bailyn, 1967:197).

Bailyn argues that, while on the one hand, the Americans wanted their rights to be guaranteed by English common law, custom, and Parliament, the very fact of their being far distant from any effective contact with the organs of that system meant that there was a tendency for the underlying principles to be emphasised and committed to writing:

> All of these codes and declarations—whatever the deliberate assumptions of their authors, and however archaic or modern-sounding their provisions—were ... efforts to abstract from the deep entanglements of English law and custom certain essentials ... by which liberty ... might be preserved .... [T]hese documents formed a continuous tradition in colonial American life, and drifted naturally into the thought of the Revolutionary generation. (1967:197)

The Constitution that evolved from these American traditions was a transformation of the meaning of 'constitution'. In 1776, in a reply to Tom Paine's *Common Sense*, Charles Inglis defined the traditional constitution, such as the constitution of England, as "that assemblage of laws, customs, and institutions which form the general system according to which the several powers of the state are distributed and their respective rights are secured to the different members of the community" (Bailyn, 1967:175). The radical change of conception in America arose from the new emphasis on the unalterable principles underlying the organic complexities of ancient constitutions. Whereas the English Parliament assumed the right to interpret, reinterpret, and alter the customary common law, understanding it as a living, pragmatic system of adjustment and readjustment, in the eyes of the American leaders any act of Parliament which seemed to them to be contrary to what they tended to abstract as the fundamental principles of the constitution—particularly equality, justice, and property—should be rejected as unconstitutional. For example, James Otis in *Rights of the British Colonies* (1776) said that if an act of Parliament violated natural laws "which are immutably true," it would thereby violate "eternal truth, equity and justice" (Otis, quoted in Bailyn, 1967:179). One might say that the process of American constitutionalism disembedded from a holistic or organic tradition a number of pristine and unalterable principles of Enlightenment rationality. I would suggest that a fundamental aspect of this process was the marginalisation of religion or 'faith' as a private right licensed by the nonreligious state. Here, two distinct domains are essentialised and transformed into the nature of things. Modern religious studies has further inscribed this rhetorical fiction by claiming to have knowledge of things that pertain to one half of the dichotomy, with insufficient attention to the massive historical shifts of meaning and power that have made this notion at all possible.

Bailyn quotes Samuel Adams in a 1768 series of letters on behalf of the Massachusetts House of Representatives that "the constitution is fixed; it is from thence that the supreme legislative as well as the supreme executive derives its authority," an idea that was incorporated into the Massachusetts Circular Letter of the same year. And in 1769, John Joachim Zubly distinguished legislatures from the constitution, declaring that the existing Parliament "derives its authority and power from the constitution, and not the constitution from Parliament" (quoted in Bailyn, 1967:181). In a Pennsylvania pamphlet of 1776 called *The Genuine Principles of the Ancient Saxon or English Constitution* "was stated the idea of the constitution as a '*set of fundamental rules* by which even the supreme power of the state shall be governed' and which the legislature is absolutely forbidden to alter" (Bailyn, 1967:184; emphasis in original). The pamphlet also contained ideas about how such a constitution should be instituted and conceived. It should be formed by a special convention of people's delegates; and the delegates, who have been entrusted with this responsibility to act on behalf of all the people, should be aware that the document is "for all eternity" (184). Such a constitution is based on eternal principles and proclaims rights which are "inherent in all people by virtue of their humanity" (185).

Bailyn argues that "there is in the proliferating discussion of constitutionalism a steadily increasing emphasis on the universal, inherent, indefeasible qualities of rights" (1967:186–87). Such rights, which are 'inalienable' and universal, are disembedded from the institutional context, whereby Parliament is conceived as sovereign and as such has the legitimate function of interpreting and changing the common law. The traditional view was that, for Britons, it was the common law as interpreted by Parliament that guaranteed rights. Judge Martin Howard, defending the traditional idea of rights, wrote against Stephen Hopkins's *Rights of the Colonies Examined* (1765) that "the common law carries within it and guarantees with special force the 'indefeasible' personal rights of men; for Britons it is the common law that makes these natural rights operative. But Parliament's power is no less a part of that same common law" (quoted in Bailyn, 1967:185). However, for the Americans, increasingly the emphasis shifted to the priority of abstract rights which are more fundamental than Parliament. We see here a fundamental reversal in the relationship between Parliament and the common law, on the one hand, and rights, on the other. The American revolutionaries stand the relationship on its head: instead of rights being guaranteed by Parliament and the common law, in which they are embedded, the authority of Parliament comes to be dependent on universal rights. Alexander Hamilton is quoted as writing in *The Farmer Refuted* in 1775 that "the sacred rights of mankind are not to be rummaged for among old parchments or musty records. They are written, as with a sunbeam, in the whole volume of human nature, by the hand of divinity itself" (quoted in Bailyn, 1967:188).

I take it that God, or 'divinity', is a transitional category here, whereby sacrality is shifted from lived tradition to abstract principles, from the organic commonwealth to the essentialising construction of the state. Legitimacy is disembedded from the institutionalisation of power in tradition, custom, legal precedent, and authority conceived as hereditary rights relative to status and context to inscription in natural reason, the self-evident, that which inalienably inheres in nature as a birthright independent of any particular circumstance of customary usage and place. The deistic God acts as a switch point that facilitates this major ideological reversal.

Bailyn shows that the meaning of 'sovereignty' was also transformed during this process. In England, the idea of absolute power shifted after 1688 onto Parliament understood as an aggregate body of the king, lords, and commons. This had been arrived at through the rejection of the absolute power of kings demanded by Charles I, and the rejection of the various radical proposals of the civil wars. It was this conception of Parliament as the sovereign power and as the legitimate maker of laws and guarantor of rights to which Americans looked. However, this increasingly came to be seen as oppressive to Americans because of the common experience of local provincial autonomy, combined with the sheer distance from the Parliament in England. Though England had a range of effective rights of government over the colonies, in day-to-day practice there were many areas of life where Americans governed themselves through courts and local assemblies, and they raised many taxes for themselves too: "The condition of British America by the end of the Seven years' War was therefore anomalous: extreme decentralization of authority within an empire presumably ruled by a single, absolute, undivided sovereign" (Bailyn, 1967:204).

When after 1763 renewed demands of Parliament were made, backed by renewed claims to the right to exercise sovereign power in America, the Americans felt that there was already a de facto sovereignty and self-government in the people. And the tradition of criticisms of English and Scottish radicals and Dissenters of the corruption of the English government, of the traditional constitution and common law, was well established in America. Americans already, by their distance from England, by their virtual autonomy in many areas of life, by the articulation of their rights and liberties in charters, bills of rights, and constitutions had grown defensive about the renewed interference of England after years of relative neglect. For this reason, Bailyn says near the beginning of his book:

> [T]he primary goal of the American Revolution . . . was not the overthrow or even the alteration of the existing social order but the preservation of political liberty threatened by the apparent corruption of the constitution, and the establishment in principle of the existing conditions of liberty. (1967:19)

More than this, the Americans had developed a collective image of themselves as the embodiment of freedom and dignity, and in that sense of being anomalous and even glorious in their destiny:

> What was essentially involved in the American Revolution was . . . the realization, the comprehension and fulfillment, of the inheritance of liberty of what was taken to be America's destiny in the context of world history. . . . Americans had come to think of themselves as in a special category, uniquely placed by history to capitalize on, to complete and fulfill, the promise of man's existence. (1967:19–20)

There are many aspects of this situation where the language tends towards the visionary and prophetic, and the American sense of liberty and destiny can sound soteriological and even apocalyptic. But can we use the modern distinction between 'religion' and 'politics' to describe this process? I suggest again that we are still observing the process whereby these ideas are being rhetorically constructed, at least in the English language. For example, Bailyn refers to the public discourse that emanated in pamphlet form from commemorative orations, "mainly of sermons delivered on election day in New England, together with a few of those preached on official thanksgiving and fast days" (1967:5). Are these religious or political? Clearly they are both, but then they are neither in the modern sense. There is no apparent sense of awkwardness about sermons being delivered on election day, nor about the celebration of public life and American identity through official thanksgiving and fast days. Bailyn says:

> [F]rom the mid-1760's on, celebrations of more secular anniversaries were added: the anniversary of the repeal of the Stamp Act, of the Boston Massacre, of the landing of the Pilgrims, and of an increasing number of fast and thanksgiving days marking *political rather than religious events*. (1967:6; my italics)

However, it is difficult to see what is meant by "more secular," or how these examples are political rather than religious. One can see that the repeal of the Stamp Act might in some regards be seen as relatively more *profane* than the landing of the Pilgrims, but surely these were becoming part of a sacred mythology. This is not to deny that demands for the separation of religion and politics were not by this time being clearly articulated by individuals, and were not already prefigured in some of the charters. However, these institutions of fast days, thanksgiving days, and election sermons indicate that our modern sensibility about the boundary between religion and politics was not yet clearly established as a dominant discourse, but was actually in the process of articulation.

Bailyn says that Andrew Eliot's election sermon of 1765, given before the assembled magistrates of Massachusetts, proclaimed that submission to tyranny is a crime (1967:6). Bailyn calls this "an act of political defiance." But it was a sermon. I am not arguing that 'sermon' meant 'religious' in the modern sense, in fact quite the opposite. For the modern sense would have this as a religious event being used (or misused) for political purposes. My point is that there does not seem to be anything strange for the magistrates to listen to a sermon on that topic, any more than for the king to listen to Hoadly's sermon on the distinction between the two jurisdictions in England in 1717. Again, John Carmichael, in his Artillery Company Sermon, *A Self-Defensive War Lawful* (1775; cited in Bailyn, 1967:7), in which he talks about the duties of Christian soldiers and "the Fervor of battlefield prayers," is doing no different from what thousands of preachers right up to the present may have done and said. The war against the British was surely both a religious and a political event, and thus in an important sense neither. It was a war, on the other hand, that constituted a profoundly important stage in the transformation of meanings and the founding of modern discourses on the distinction between religion and politics. If the Continental Congress could appoint a thanksgiving day; or if "an obscure Salem parson" could write "a paean to the promise of American life, and to devise an original blend of theological and constitutional principles" (7), then surely we can hold that the distinction between religion and politics is not yet fully applicable at this time, even though we are witnessing its advent through the establishment of an increasingly influential discourse.

It seems important to notice how these eternal values and verities, discerned by reason from the muddle of organic custom and the corruption of what they perceived as arbitrary power, became sacralised in the minds of the Americans. Sovereignty and rights reside in reason, and are accessible to all men (but not women, indigenous savages, or slaves). This is surely a profound aspect of the more general triumph of Enlightenment rationalism and the birth of modernity.

Bailyn emphasises the transforming effects of the Revolution and the processes leading up to it. Americans ceased to see themselves or to be seen as parochials, and became instead heroes of freedom, saints of the modern sacred:

> Their manners, their morals, their way of life, their physical, so-
> cial and political conditions were seen to vindicate eternal truths and
> to demonstrate, as ideas and words never could, the virtues of the
> heavenly city of the eighteenth century philosophers. (1967:160–61)

Jefferson referred to "the sacred fire of freedom and self-government" (Bailyn, 2002:25).

An important part of this transformation lay in the reshaping of words and concepts, the emergence of a new world of political thought from the implications of the beliefs they had adopted from radical England and put to use in their own revolutionary context. This transforming process was implicated in the writing and revising of state constitutions, in the drafting and ratifying of the federal Constitution, and in all the debates that these entailed. Bailyn comments:

> This critical probing of traditional concepts . . . became the basis for all further discussions of enlightened reform, in Europe as well as in America. The radicalism the Americans conveyed to the world in 1776 was a transformed as well as a transforming force. (1967:161)

Bailyn pursues some of these wider themes in the inaugural Caroline Robbins Lecture of 2001, *American Constitutionalism: Atlantic Dimensions* (2002), in which he is concerned with arguing for the widespread influence of the principles of American constitutionalism. He argues that "interest in American constitutionalism was intense throughout the Atlantic world in the Revolutionary years; and in the generations that followed it remained deeply embedded in the awareness of political leaders, publicists, and intellectuals" (2002:6–7).

People who were directly influenced by and admiring of the constitutions of America included Abbé Raynal; Talleyrand; the martyr of Brazil's aborted rebellion of 1789, Joaquim José da Silva Xavier; the Prussian Friedrich von Gentz; and Francisco de Miranda, who was involved in the Venezuelan Declaration of Independence. The U.S. Declaration of Independence and the state constitutions circulated in many translations all over Europe and inspired comment, debate, and admiration. Spanish-language newspapers carried translations of Jefferson's first inaugural address and commentaries in Caracas, Buenos Aires, Mexico City, and Santiago.

The influence also returned to England as a pizza effect, where English radicals of the 1790s, such as Cartwright, Cobbett, Hardy, Paine, Cooper, Hartley, Horne Tooke, Yorke, and Spence, made use of American constitutionalism, which "was drawn upon, was the inspiration for, and became the natural bridge to the populist, plebeian radicalism that lay behind the making of the English working class" (Bailyn, 2002:15–16). There was also an influence on the concept of the Declaration of the Rights of Man and of the Citizen, which was formulated by French revolutionaries and philosophers. Bailyn notes, "The structure of Virginia's Declaration of the Rights of Man and that of the French Assembly, and the sequence of provisions in the two documents, are remarkably similar" (2002:17).

The conditions in South America were, as a result of Spain's imperial rule, more complex and chaotic than those of North America:

> [T]he basic struggle everywhere—once the Spanish troops were defeated, was to bring together whatever elements of authority there were—mainly cities and provinces—into combinations that would agree to share a common authority. . . . enlightened aspirations were

rationalized and conceptualized with reference, in part to the classic texts of advanced European thought, in part to Hispanic traditions, and in large part to the widely circulating translations of North American constitutions. (Bailyn, 2002:21)

Bailyn concludes, "In the generations that have followed, that influence has remained pervasive—not merely in the design of specific constitutions but mainly and increasingly, as America's power has grown, in its embodiment of established western values" (25).

At one point in his lecture, Bailyn remarks, "awareness of provincial America, its successful revolution and constitutional creations . . . had quickly become part of the consciousness of officialdom and the clerisy in both cosmopolitan Europe and its colonial dependencies" (2002:11). My own suggestion is that constitutions modelled on, or influenced by, the American one, or indeed other versions which may have derived their structure and content from the American Constitution, became instrumental in the colonial context. There is a growing awareness of the ways in which the separation of 'religion' and 'politics' or secular ideology generally has been used by colonial powers to impose Western concepts of the state, along with other 'secular' Western concepts related to capitalism and imperial control (see Fitzgerald, 2007). For example, one of the essays in *Religion and the Secular*, by the Japanese historian Jun'ichi Isomae, analyses the way that Western demands of 'civility' were couched partly in terms of the formation of a modern nation-state and the possession of a modern constitution which guaranteed the separation of church and state, and the constitutional provision of freedom of religion. Traditional cultures that did not have such a modern form were considered barbaric or semi-barbaric. One of the purposes of this insistence on the possession of a modern constitution was no doubt to gain safe access—in the absence of direct colonisation—for 'Christian' (Euro-American) traders and capitalists. One of the significant points of Isomae's analysis concerns the public debates among the Japanese intellectual elite about the problems involved in translating the English-language term 'religion' into Japanese. Another point that emerges is that religion was conceived in terms of a privatised practice licensed by the state, and the secular state ideology of Shinto was invented and, since church and state were deemed to be separated, at one point became the structural equivalent of Japanese public secular morality. This equivalent ideology became the underpinning rationale for Japanese colonialism and imperialism, as the ideologies of secularism and capitalism were perceived as underpinning Western colonialism and imperialism (see also more details of the way that the postwar Japanese Constitution of 1946 was written during the American occupation in Mullins et al., 1993:75–134).

Such an analysis could be usefully pursued by scholars from any and every colonised or (as in the case of Japan) potentially colonised country: the problems of translation, and the way that Western-style constitutions and the separation of religion from politics were either used by the colonial powers to 'civilise' those countries or, alternatively, were adopted by freedom movements in their consolidation of national liberation and modernisation movements. The relevance of this for Muslim cultures seems obvious, but, as the case of Japan suggests, it goes far wider than Islam too.

I have argued that the idea of the sacred has never been confined to church matters, but that matters of state have for long been amenable to relative degrees of sacredness and profaneness. In the earlier context of encompassing Religion, the commonwealth conceived as a total organic order was sacralised, with special but not exclusive attention on the body of the king. In the transition to modern constitutional formulations of the state in which religion becomes essentialised and separated as a private right, the secular (nonreligious) constitution is itself a sacred document, and it legitimates sacred rights— including the right to freedom of religion.

Whether a document (or a time, space, or person) will be considered 'sacred' or not will depend partly on the degree to which a specific discourse can achieve wide and/or influential acceptance. It is perhaps possible that a memory or site or object can be 'sacred' to an individual, but such a usage carries no authority unless it gains significant recognition. It is surely arguable that things or persons who, within the context of one discourse, might be deemed 'secular' can still be regarded as sacred; Pauline Maier argues this about the Declaration of Independence in her book *American Scripture: Making the Declaration of Independence* (1998). This was a process that took time, because this document did not achieve instant fame, and the sacralisation process went along with the transformation of the leaders of the Revolution into giants or saints:

> In the course of recalling and recording the events of the Revolution, Americans of the 1820's remembered the revolutionaries as mighty fathers whose greatness threw into relief the ordinariness of their descendents [*sic*]. It wasn't the first time that Americans attributed superhuman characteristics to an earlier generation. New Englanders of the late seventeenth century had looked back at the Puritan founders of Massachusetts with a similar sense of awe. (Maier, 1998:178)

These feelings of awe were evoked in Americans in the early nineteenth century in various ways, for example, by the parading of revolutionary veterans (Maier, 1998:179). By 1864 only seven of these men and women survived, according to the Reverend Elias Brewster Hillard, who interviewed and photographed them for his book *The Last Men of the Revolution*, and he referred to them as those "venerable and now sacred men" (quoted in Maier, 1998:179).

When Lafayette visited the United States at the invitation of President James Monroe and Congress in 1824–1825, his secretary, who kept a diary of the event, noted that his visit generated souvenirs and also the exhibition of small revolutionary artefacts, "such as 'fragments of arms and projectiles', even 'military buttons' saved from the 1770s. All such 'monuments of the revolution' were preserved and revered" (quoted in Maier, 1998:179). Lafayette's secretary noted that "everything which recalls this glorious epoch is to them a precious relic, which they regard almost with religious reverence" and use to feed "the sacred fire of love of liberty" (179).

John Adams, who was descended from the Puritans, "compared the idolization of Washington and other revolutionaries to the canonization of saints and other 'corrupt' practices of a superstitious, hierarchical past" (quoted in Maier, 1998:186). Maier also has an interesting perspective on Jefferson. We saw earlier that Jefferson referred to "the sacred fire of freedom and self-government" (Bailyn, 2002:25). Maier shows that Jefferson, who on the one hand expressed disdain for "monkish ignorance and superstition" and who believed that the Catholic priests were bigots and responsible for the failure of the French Revolution, used "religious and often Catholic terms in describing America's revolutionaries and their heritage" (Maier, 1998:189). The children of the American enlightenment "spoke of relics and altars, of saints and canonizations" (190).

Upon Jefferson's death on 4 July 1826 (exactly fifty years after the publication of the declaration), he was depicted as a Christ-like figure of ascension, or a saint, like Washington, whose memory was canonised. They were venerated, their names were sanctified, their homes became shrines to which devotees made pilgrimages, people referred to the "altar of freedom" raised by the country's fathers, and the declaration was an "eternal monument" embodying the spirit of liberty (Maier, 1998:190).

Maier points out that "Jefferson played a particularly important role in rescuing the Declaration of Independence from its early obscurity and making it the defining event of a 'Heroic Age'" (Maier, 1998:180). He commissioned the artist John Trumbull to paint the signing of it. In 1824, he received copies of the new facsimile edition, sent to him under a resolution of Congress because of the evidence that republication gave "'of reverence for that instrument, and . . . view in it a pledge of adhesion to its principles and of a sacred determination to maintain and perpetuate them,' which he described as 'a holy purpose'" (quoted in Maier, 1998:186). This was the same Jefferson who (as Maier comments) "totally separated Church and State" in the constitution of Virginia: "Now, however, he applied the language of religion[16] not just to the Declaration, but to everyday objects associated with its creation. 'Small things may, perhaps, like the relics of saints, help to nourish our devotion to this holy bond of Union'" (186). For example, Jefferson proposed to give his desk to Joseph Coolidge, the husband of his granddaughter, and imagined that in another half century the desk might be "carried in the procession of our nation's birthday, as the relics of the saints are in those of the Church" (187):

[T]he sacralization of the Declaration of Independence after 1815
made it a powerful text to enlist on behalf of any cause that might
conceivably claim its authority. It could not, like the state bills of
rights, be used in court cases to strike down institutions and practices that violated its principles, but the Declaration's new found
status as a sacred document made it extremely useful for causes
attempting to seize the moral high ground in public debate. (Maier,
1998:187)

Maier says that the declaration has been cited by many groups that have
what in modern discourse might be called political goals: by those who wished
to demand equality and freedom from an oppressor; by workers against tyrannical factory owners; by women against the tyranny of men; by opponents
of slavery. Maier, using quotes from Abraham Lincoln, says he "idealized the
men who had participated in the Revolution: they were for him 'a forest of
giant oaks', 'pillars of the temple of liberty', 'a fortress of strength', 'iron men'"
(1998:202). The assertion of equality in the declaration became his "ancient
faith"; for him, it was "the father of all modern principles" (202). In time,
Lincoln's Gettysburg Address became an American sacred text itself (213).
Maier also points out that Britain had its own analogies, such as the Magna
Carta, which the historian F. W. Maitland is quoted as characterising as "a sa-
cred text, the nearest approach to an irrepealable fundamental statute that
England has ever had" (quoted in Maier, 1998:213). One might surely add
Adam Smith's *Wealth of Nations* as a sacred text for theorists of capitalism,
Darwin's *Origin of Species* as a sacred text for evolutionists, and Marx's *Capital*
and *Communist Manifesto* as sacred texts for socialists.

I cannot pursue the point much further here that the language of sacrality
has never been confined in the English language to 'religion' in the narrow,
modern sense of a privatised, nonpolitical faith in a future life or an unseen
world, but it has also been strongly connected to the values and aspirations of
the state, of government, of civil society, and of what has been constructed as
'the secular' in modernity. And this fact points to another aspect of the argument, which is that, while powerful institutions may claim control over the
meaning of words, and while under such hegemony some words may come to
appear to be essentially connected with a particular discourse or a particular
aspect of reality, countervailing forces and interests can redefine customary
usage. If the term 'religion' has changed in meaning so radically since the
seventeenth century, under the influence of new and powerful interests, then
'religion' has no essential meaning, a point made by J. Z. Smith (1998) though
from which we seem to draw different theoretical conclusions. I have argued
that we cannot use the term for descriptive and analytical purposes as though it
is neutral, and as though its meaning is ours for the choosing, because it is still
appropriated by powerful agencies and embedded in confused but widely

disseminated discourses which have largely unacknowledged ideological purposes. That these agencies and the discourses which they police invest the term with contradictory meanings deepens the problem. But then neither do those terms standing for domains from which religion is supposedly distinct, such as politics, law, and economics, have essential meanings; these have also been appropriated by powerful interests whose theoretical discourses render them apparently universal and yet highly ideological. I finish with this point because modern writers, mystified by an appearance of timeless reality in the meaning of words, have created an essentialised construct 'religion' separated from another essentialised construct 'the secular'. Or, rather than say "created," it would be more accurate to say that they have inherited a discourse that has a historical origin and that represents the emergence of specific interests and is institutionalised in powerful ways such as constitutions. Despite the well-established critical tradition in feminism and postcolonialism, many contemporary scholars across the humanities continue to reproduce discourses on religion as though it is a natural reality, or an unproblematic organising and descriptive category, not understanding that it is a field of discourse which has been rhetorically constructed.[17]

IO

Postscript on Civility and Barbarity in the Nineteenth and Twentieth Centuries

The ambiguities in the discourse on 'religion' in postrevolutionary America are notable in the published letter of 1786 of John Swanwick, *Considerations on an Act of the legislature of Virginia, entitled, An Act for the Establishment of Religious Freedom. By a Citizen of Philadelphia.* The letter is addressed "To the Reverend Clergy of all Christian denominations in the City of Philadelphia, and to the Public Friends of the respectable Society called Quakers, in this Metropolis." Swanwick's objections to the act are fundamentally that it is too extreme in its liberalism, and that it ought to make more provision for protecting and promoting the Christian faith. A strong indication of the development of a generic concept lies in his describing various non-Christian creeds as 'religions':

> By this act...a door is opened wide for the introduction of
> any tenets in religion, however degrading to Christianity...
> and the legislature of Virginia may be held and adminis-
> tered by men professedly atheists, Mahometans, or of any
> other creed, however unfriendly to liberty or the morals of a
> free country. (Swanwick, 1786:iii)

In contrast to Virginia, in Philadelphia Christianity is protected by its constitution "in which a pledge of security to the Christian faith hath been interwoven with its political sanctions" (iii).

Swanwick includes in his letter a copy of Virginia's Act for the Establishment of Religious Freedom (Swanwick, 1786:v–vi). It opens with various Enlightenment-inspired statements, such as the natural right of freedom of thought, and that nobody should be forced to pay taxes to subsidise a particular form of religion; and it clearly separates these rights from religious sanction and embeds them in nature and natural law: "our civil rights have no dependence on our religious opinions, any more than our opinions in physic[s] and geometry" (v). On the other hand, the civil magistrate should not be obliged "to intrude his powers into the field of opinion," since this "destroys all religious liberty" and would tend to result in the imposition on others of the "magistrates private opinions" (v).

It seems clear from this and other statements in the Virginia act that the civil magistrate and administration are defined as neutral towards religion, and that civil rights are grounded, not in religion, but in nature and natural rationality. Swanwick challenges this with various arguments. One of them is, "I know of no situation in which the mind can be said to be free, in the sense of this bill, unless it be that of a state of nature with the savages of the wilderness, if any such could be found, who had neither religion nor laws" (Swanwick, 1786:3/4). Here Swanwick is suggesting that even the Rousseau-esque savages in a state of nature are not completely free from religion and laws, though as indicated in other parts of his text, religion here means the same as superstition. This is a less extreme view than that espoused by Jefferson the next year in his *Notes on the State of Virginia* cited earlier. Swanwick also links the possibility of civil order on the existence of religion in an almost functionalist argument: "They who, in early times attempted to bring the wandering and scattered tribes of men from the woods, and to unite them in cities and communities, always found it necessary to begin with some institution of religion" (Swanwick, 1786:18). In this speculation, religion is useful, and has a function of binding and civilising people. This functionalist account of religion, even while it points to the necessity of religion for civility, implies throughout a distinction between politics and religion, as when he says, "Politicians may lay down what plans they please... but in truth it is... religion... which forms the strength and glory of a nation" (19).

And yet, while there is apparently a clearer Lockean distinction here between religion and the civil magistracy than we found 160 years earlier in Samuel Purchas; the apparent generic usage of the term is as ambiguous as it was with Purchas. For in Swanwick's mind, we come to realise, there is only one true religion, which is Christianity. It is really only Christianity that can perform this civilising function. He contrasts "the benevolence of our religion" with the "superstitions" (Swanwick, 1786:17) held by those not blessed with revelation. And he equates Christian Truth with peace and benevolence— civility—in contrast to the "false" religions: "Despotic governments have generally taken the firmest root among nations that were blinded by mahometan or pagan darkness, where the throne of violence has been supported by ignorance and false religion" (18).

The complete tolerance of Virginia will lead to "irreligion" or to "false religions" being practised to the detriment of the civil society. He compares the case of Virginia with those states whose constitutions show a preference for Protestant Religion, which is that "strong and elevated cement of social happiness" (Swanwick, 1786:26).

This letter gives us an insight into some of the usages of 'religion' that were common during the years leading up to the formation of the federal Constitution. It seems to me that we can find two discourses on religion and civil society and the state, and to some degree they are mixed up in Swanwick's letter. In one discourse, civil society is quite clearly marked out as neutral towards religion and having no place to interfere in the private right to practice one's religion. In this discourse, freedom of religion in principle increases the sphere of what can count as religion, and thus moves the category towards a more generic concept; here, even pagans and "mahometans" (and by implication Catholics) have religions. The other discourse is the much older one, in which Religion means Christian (Protestant) Truth upon which civil order depends, contrasted with superstition, falseness, despotism, and various other Orientalist tropes. Swanwick's letter makes clear that several state constitutions grant complete freedom of religion, and by doing so protect the civil government from religion, and also protect religion from interference by the magistrate. On the other hand, it indicates that behind this debate there is a strong Protestant Christian discourse that, while accepting a modified view of that distinction, still contrasts Christian Truth with superstitions and pagan darkness.

This value judgment about non-Christian forms of life as irrational barbarisms continued strongly into the nineteenth century in a different context, that of the British Empire. The relationship between nineteenth-century Protestant Christianity and the gospel of civility has been noticed by Brian Stanley in *The Bible and the Flag* (1990):

> There can be little dispute that, for most of the nineteenth century, British Christians believed that the missionary was called to propagate the imagined benefits of western civilization alongside the Christian message. It was assumed that the poor, benighted 'heathen' were in a condition of massive cultural deprivation, which the gospel alone could remedy. At present they were shockingly different from civilized Europeans; in years to come, when gospel power had done its work, those differences would be largely eliminated. (158)

Before the 1790s, there was little systematic missionising, at least from the British, except in North America and India. Though there was to some extent a missionising consciousness in both the Church of England and the Dissenters during the eighteenth century, it was with the evangelical revival that missions became more active. A precondition for the development at this time of a missionary consciousness was the weakening of the Calvinist concept of predestination among Baptists, along with the new denominations of Wesleyan and Calvinist Methodism, which Stanley expresses as "the weakening of the rationalistic hyper-Calvinism which had caused some mid-eighteenth century Dissenters to distrust the use of any human means of urging men and women to repent and believe" (Stanley, 1990:59).

Stanley says, "The missionary awakening in Britain is conventionally dated from the publication in 1792 of William Carey's *An Enquiry into the Obligations of Christians, to Use Means for the Conversion of the Heathens*" (1990:56). This had been influenced by the Baptist Andrew Fuller's *The Gospel Worthy of all Acceptation* (1785), which in turn applied "the moderate Calvinism of Jonathan Edwards" (59). Stanley stresses the importance of the piety of Jonathan Edwards and the Great Awakening in New England in the 1740s:

> The great majority of the pioneers of the British missionary movement shared Edwards' confidence that the propagation of the gospel throughout the globe in partnership with the earnest and united prayers of the church would usher in the last age of history. (60)

This was combined with the belief in the 1790s that the French Revolution "would result in the overthrow of the Roman Catholic church, which most Protestants identified with Antichrist" (61). However, he denies that the missionary awakening had much to do with the expansion of British imperial power: "British overseas interests merely shaped British missionary priorities: they cannot account for the birth of the missionary movement itself" (61).

Stanley gives examples of the relation between missionaries and cultural imperialism, and thus of the overlap between Christianity and the discourse of civility:

> The Congregationalist and Wesleyan missionaries who were present in some numbers in Melanesia and Polynesia from the 1820's onwards, found apparent conclusive evidence of the moral degradation of 'heathen' society. In many of the islands cannibalism, infanticide, human sacrifice and homosexual practice were endemic. The prevalent evangelical belief that God had given up non-Christian, idolatrous peoples to the consequences of their own depravity seemed amply confirmed. Satanic dominion had brought the islanders to the nadir of moral and cultural decline; the missionary task was to reverse the process. Moral elevation implied, not merely the elimination of blatantly inhumane practices, but also the inculcation of the virtues which these lower-middle class missionaries regarded as akin to godliness—industry, sobriety and decency. The missionaries created opportunities for the men of the islands to engage in honest manual labour, in the hope that this would cure their lamentable 'indolence'. They also attempted to persuade the islanders to abandon their traditional dwellings in favour of limestone block houses, built

and furnished on the model of the typical English artisan's cottage. (Stanley, 1990:158)

There seems to me to be an ambiguity in this and other passages in Stanley's book about whether he is merely describing the attitudes and thinking of the missionaries, or whether he himself accepts some of their claims about the practices of other peoples. This aside, Stanley says that they even tried to enforce this policy with sanctions, and he quotes from a missionary attached to the London Missionary Society (LMS) in the Society Islands in 1823:

> Today agreeable to a law the church established last church meeting I have with a book and pencil been to every house . . . and have noted down under the name of each member what has been done. . . . it is resolved that if they do not from this time forth begin to hurl such paganism in all its abominable shapes from our City such person shall not be a member of the church. The house must be plastered in and out, have doors and windows, bedrooms with doors and shutters, and a garden encircling the house. (quoted in Stanley, 1990:158)

Civilising the natives was also a matter of correct dress:

> Missionaries did regard Western clothing as a mark of civilization, and wrote home in shocked tones recounting the more striking instances of native immodesty in dress. But the strongest pressure to adopt full European dress came, not from the missionaries, but from the religious public in Britain and, significantly, from the islanders themselves. Western dress inevitably became a symbol of prestige and social advancement. (Stanley, 1990:159)

(Perhaps the perception of the islanders was the most accurate. They could see that Christian religion and its concern with civility was a matter of power and prestige.)

In the case of India, the Baptist missionaries were faced with an apparently more complex and sophisticated system. Typical barbarities here for Carey and his colleagues were *sati* and the caste system, which was invented by the devil "to enslave the souls of men" (Stanley, 1990:159). They had a negative view of the "Indian national character" (to use Stanley's phrase), which they thought was characterised by shameless avarice, servility, lying, and cheating. The sacred literature, such as the Ramayana, contained vile and destructive fables inspired by the devil (159). However, not everything was barbarous and contrary to the teaching of Christ and to Western canons of civility. The promulgation of the gospel did not necessarily require changes in "the names, the dress, the food, and the innocent usages of mankind, but to produce a moral and divine change in the hearts and conduct of men" (160).

The problem was to determine which customs were innocent, and which made the moral change impossible, indicating nevertheless the extent to which the discourses on civility and barbarity still overlapped with the discourses on Christianity and heathenism:

> Theoretical statements by missionary society secretaries or writers on mission tended to affirm the orthodox position that missions could be relied upon to transform heathen barbarism into Christian civilization.... The three society secretaries who testified to the parliamentary select committee on aborigines in 1836–37 were unanimous and unqualified in their confidence in 'the tendency and efficacy of Christianity to civilize mankind. ' A ringing statement by William Ellis of the LMS summed up the missionary consensus of the early and mid-nineteenth century: 'No man can become a Christian, in the true sense of the term, however savage he may have been before, without becoming a civilized man'. (Stanley, 1990:160)

Stanley identifies four main assumptions underlying missionary thinking:

> The first of these was the belief that the cultures which missionaries were penetrating were in no sense religiously neutral—rather they were under the control of the Evil One. 'Heathen' societies were the domain of Satan in all their aspects—not merely religion, but also economics, politics, public morals, the arts, and all that is embraced by the term 'culture'. (Stanley, 1990:161)

The second underlying assumption was

> the supposition that nineteenth century Britain constituted a model of Christian culture and society. Missionary magazines sometimes contained descriptions ... of what early Britain was thought to have been like before the coming of Christianity—primitive, barbarous and idolatrous. It was Christianity, and above all the national recognition of God and of the Word of God in the Protestant Reformation, which had made Britain what she was.... the culture of Victorian Britain was shaped by the Bible and by evangelical Protestantism to a degree which finds no parallel in any other period of British history (with the possible exception of the Cromwellian era). (Stanley, 1990:161)

The third assumption was

> the implicit faith in human progress which was one of the legacies of the Enlightenment to Christian thought. Evangelicals professed to believe that all people shared equally in the depravity of original sin, but they found it hard to resist the conclusion that centuries of

Christian influence within a society had held in check the human sinfulness that was given free rein in 'heathen' countries. Long before Darwin's theory of evolution, the thinkers of the Scottish Enlightenment had popularised a theory of social development which posited a progression from a primitive or hunting form of subsistence, via two subsequent stages of pastoral and agrarian forms of economy, to the highest or commercial stage of civilization. When integrated within a theological framework, this approach implied that 'heathen' societies remained frozen in an ice age of primitivism, which the warmth of the gospel light had long since thawed in Protestant Europe. (Stanley, 1990:162)

And the fourth assumption,

underpinning Christian faith in efforts to civilize the 'heathen' was quite simply the pragmatic one that such efforts could be shown to have worked. The most plausible evidence to this effect was provided by the rapid growth of the church in Sierra Leone ... [where] ... an African mirror image of respectable, middle class, English Christianity developed in the colony. ... It was sufficiently recognizable to provide visible proof that 'heathen savages' could be transformed into model Christian gentlemen. When Samuel Crowther, the Sierra Leone ex-slave who became the first black Anglican Bishop in Africa, stood in black frock coat before the British Christian public for the first time in 1851, the whole missionary enterprise ... seemed justified. (Stanley, 1990:162)

This passage clarifies the degree to which such matters as dress and manners were indicators of civility in the nineteenth and early twentieth centuries.[1] Stanley says that the assumption that the non-Christian world was under the rule of Satan survived intact mainly in theological circles:

The essence of the claim that other cultures were under the direct control of evil spiritual powers remained most plausible in Africa, where the late Victorian missionaries were still engaged in first-hand encounters with peoples they had no hesitation in describing as 'savages'. Societies marked by such features as domestic slavery, cannibalism, trial for witchcraft by ordeal, and the forcible burial of wives or servants in the graves of deceased chiefs, inevitably struck missionaries as depraved and cruel. (Stanley, 1990:162–63)

Stanley records that missionaries in the Congo were so shocked by some of the practices that they adopted the racist language of their secular contemporaries and denied the possibility that black people could ever be civilised. Karl Kumm is recorded to have said that the Sudan is "[t]he Land of Darkness. ... dark are the bodies of the people who live there, darker are their minds, and darker still their souls" (163). Other missionaries denied inherent racial inferiority but attributed the relative lack of intelligence which Kumm claimed to observe to the absence of civilisation, meaning Christianity.

However, missionaries "in the more sophisticated civilizations of Asia" were quicker to abandon the language of heathen and barbarian and to develop a new approach to the greater civility of Christianity. This was the world religion approach: there are positive aspects to 'the religions of the world' such as Hinduism, though they fall short of Christianity. Stanley cites F. D. Maurice's *The Religions of the World in Their Relations to Christianity* (1845), which argued that all religions contain some goodness and truth; and J. N. Farquhar's *The Crown of Hinduism* (1913), which found truth in Hinduism but claimed that only Christ could bring that system to the full realisation of its ethical potential. Stanley comments that such liberal and inclusive Christianity

> could fall prey to its own, more subtle brand of cultural imperialism. The fact that its values were more inclusive softens, but should not disguise, the reality that it too wished to fashion the non-European world in a particular Western image—the image of enlightened liberal optimism. (Stanley, 1990:165)

Missionaries had a range of positions on the issue of progress. For example, at one extreme were those conservative evangelicals "who had espoused a premillennial eschatology that removed the prospect of human progress beyond the parousia" (Stanley, 1990:166). Some liberal missionaries were optimistic about evolutionary progress and saw it in terms of "the blessings which western science and political values would impart to the waiting world" (166). Though they could feel respect for Asian cultures, they basically believed that everything would eventually give way for the better to the Christian civilisation of the West and its technological and evolutionary progress. Other missionaries were in the middle position, such as George Grenfell, who in 1901 expressed the opinion that genuine progress was not a matter of "steamships, telegraph, electric light, five editions of a paper in a single day" (167) but of moral and spiritual development. He did not mean that he was against material and technological progress, but that it was relatively less important.

Stanley goes on to discuss interestingly the impact of the First World War, the Nazi Holocaust, and the growing lack of confidence in Christian civility, especially from around the 1960s. He also looks at the realisation of many missionaries that Africa was "in many respects closer to the world of the Bible than were their own cultures" (Stanley, 1990:168). The extent to which Christian assumptions about the civilising mission of the West, for example, in the form of spreading democracy and teaching other peoples how to govern themselves, would be entirely relevant to the present discussion but must be postponed to another time. What this discussion of Stanley's research shows is that much of the rhetoric of Christian civility and rationality has not changed much through the centuries, despite the introduction of more recent tropes of racism, progress, and scientific rationality.

Another aspect of Christian thought which clearly survived in the minds of the missionaries, the idea that the fallen world is profane and in the grip of Satan, is not far distant from that of the Spanish lawyer/theologians of the sixteenth century and later (see chapter 4 of this volume), or of the Protestant vicar Samuel Purchas, who expressed similar views in the early seventeenth century (see chapter 7 of this volume). One important difference is that the idea that humankind is engaged in a progression through evolutionary stages only enters the picture in the eighteenth century with the Scottish Enlightenment. Another difference is that by the time of the nineteenth century, missionaries were living in a world increasingly dominated by capitalism and secularism. It was also a time when Euro-American power was, for the first time, clearly superior to other great empires, such as the Moguls in India or the Ch'ing dynasty in China (Stanley, 1990:51).

Stanley suggests ambiguity on the question of the relationship between missions and capitalism. On the one hand, the sheer extent of British imperial control suggested a divine providence that implied a commission from God to take the gospel to the world: "Christian belief in divine providence led by logical steps to the concept of Britain's imperial role as a sacred trust to be used in the interests of the gospel" (Stanley, 1990:68). If one combines this with his point that one of the underlying assumptions in the nineteenth century was that Britain, an industrialising capitalist economy, was a model of Christian culture and society, then it suggests that the missionaries, if not actually spreading the gospel of free markets, were at least not generally in opposition to that concept. By the late 1890s, the concept of the white man's burden was conceived as "a package of Christian civilization and liberal government in which Christianity itself was only one ingredient" (69). This concept was shared by imperial administrators and propagandists. American Protestants also shared a notion of national mission in propagating the gospel, and Josiah Strong, who was secretary of the Evangelical Alliance of the USA, believed that "America was called by providence to join Britain in spreading Christianity and Anglo-Saxon civilization throughout the globe" (69). Even the many individual missionaries who were not enthusiastic about the acquisition of colonies and imperial power, and who were critical of many aspects of imperial policy, still believed that the empire was a process which implied the hand of providence for the propagation of the gospel.

The role of commerce in this civilising process may have been ambiguous in the minds of many individual missionaries. Stanley quotes from David Livingstone's public address delivered in the Senate House of the University of Cambridge in 1857 as an example of the apparent relationship of missionary activity to the spread of commerce:

I beg to direct your attention to Africa;—I know that in a few years I
shall be cut off in that country, which is now open; do not let it be
shut again! I go back to Africa to make an open path for Commerce
and Christianity; do you carry out the work which I have begun. I
LEAVE IT TO YOU! (quoted in Stanley, 1990:70)

Isaac Schapera, in his introduction to Livingstone's *African Journals 1853–1856*,
explained Livingstone's rapturous reception back in imperial Britain primarily
by his geographical discoveries, which showed that Africa "was not a useless
desert but a land of incalculable commercial possibilities" (Schapera,
1963:xii).[2]

The relationship between the civilities of Protestant missionaries and
supposed barbarians is brought home well by Richard Gombrich in his social
history of Buddhism in Sri Lanka (Gombrich, 1988, especially chapter 7, 172–
197). This is all the more powerful for the ironic understatement of Gombrich's writing. There is no space to discuss this in any detail now, but to get
the flavour of Protestant British superiority in matters of civility, it is worth,
from the many possible examples, to quote the following at some length:

From the first they [the missionaries] courted encounters with the
Buddhists, and were merely infuriated by the refusal of monks to take
up the challenge. In 1823 it was written of a Methodist missionary:
"influenced by a desire to become intimately acquainted with the
superstitions of the natives, that he might be the better prepared to
expose their absurdity and sinfulness, Mr Clough took every oppor-
tunity of being present at their religious services, and endeavoured on
such occasions to engage the priests in conversations on religious
topics, in the hearing of their followers."

During a great religious festival outside Colombo, the local C of E
missionaries systematically destroyed their hitherto amicable relationship with the local Buddhist monks by turning up every night for
the whole week of the festival and distributing a specially printed
pamphlet on "the sin and folly of image-worship." ... The great
technical innovation of the missionaries ... was their use of the
printing press. ... From the start what was printed was more polemical than merely expository. With typical military metaphor, Go-
gerly, the manager of the Wesleyan Press, wrote in 1831, "At present
it is by means of the press our main attacks must be made upon this
wretched system. ... We must direct our efforts to pull down this
stronghold of Satan." ... For the first 50 years of this onslaught the
Buddhist response was eirenic. About 1835, to Christian horror, a
Buddhist priest wrote a tract saying that Christ had been incarnated
on earth after an existence in heaven (just like a Buddha), was virtuous and benevolent, and taught the truth in so far as he understood

it. Unlike many brahmins in India, Buddhist monks did not shun contact with Europeans, and two learned monks had even assisted with the first translation of the Bible into Sinhala.... Some monks allowed missionaries to use their preaching halls, and were puzzled when their reciprocal requests were refused. Writers in the 1850s remark on the lack of hostility to Christianity and on the monks' co-operative attitude in lending manuscripts from their libraries and explaining their contents. But this lack of opposition merely irritated the missionaries.

The most famous one, the Methodist Spence Hardy, when on his preaching rounds, usually spent the night at the village temples, where the monks treated him kindly. This he could only attribute to their "indolence, apathy and indifference in all matters concerning religion." Of monks' faces he wrote that "there is often an appearance about them of great vacancy, amounting almost to imbecility." ... He wrote in 1850, "It is almost impossible to move them, even to wrath." But on returning to Ceylon after an absence of 15 years, Hardy was delighted to note that the pernicious vice of tolerance was on the wane, that monks would no longer co-operate with missionaries, would no longer explain or lend their books, but had brought presses and were printing tracts.

"I have formed bright anticipations as to the future. There can be no doubt as to the result of the contest now carried on; for although it may be prolonged and severe, it must end in the total discomfiture of those who have risen against the Lord and his Christ, and in the renunciation of the atheist creed that now mars the happiness, and stays the enlightenment, of so many of the dwellers in Lanka." (Gombrich, 178–180)

I have not claimed in this book that a direct link can be established be-tween the intentions of missionaries and the priorities of capitalism, but it seems difficult to resist the view that the two distinct discourses noted in the debate in which Swanwick was engaged continued throughout the nineteenth and into the twentieth century. Both of these discourses, often mixed together, have at least facilitated a rationale for Western imperialism and a justification for colonial rule. One discourse has been on Religion as Christian Truth and civility in opposition to superstitions as barbarous irrationalities; the other has been on 'religion' in relation to the secular state and civil society conceived as neutral or indifferent towards religion. While a generic concept of 'religions' is present in both discourses, from Purchas in the early seventeenth century to Swanwick, Jefferson, and William Carey in the late eighteenth, it is a highly ambiguous term which often oscillates with 'superstitions' and 'heathen idolatry'. The degree to which these two analytically separable discourses and their historically embedded meanings are reproduced, consciously or unconsciously, in contemporary scholarship and wider rhetoric has led me to argue in this book that the proper study of 'religion' is the category itself in its discursive relation ship to 'state', 'politics', 'secular', 'sacred', 'profane', 'civility', and 'barbarity'.

Notes

1. The argument here is an elaboration of my previous book *The Ideology of Religious Studies* (2000), and is closely connected to a recent publication of twelve papers in *Religion and the Secular: Historical and Colonial Formations* (Fitzgerald, 2007). Much of the argument behind both of these publications is that the study of religion is largely uncritical of its wider tacit role in the legitimation of positivistic forms of social science, of its promotion and legitimation of a truncated and distorted discourse on 'religion' and 'religions', and of its ideological connection with colonialism and Anglo-American triumphalism.

2. I have critically discussed other aspects of Michel Despland's work in "Playing Language Games and Performing Rituals: Religious Studies as Ideological State Apparatus" (Fitzgerald, 2003a).

3. See Ivan Strenski's representation of my own and others' work (1998:118), where he accuses me of being a part of an "inbred clique" of writers whose work is "alternatively an exercise in naiveté, bad faith, or ignorant mischief, or indeed, all of the above." This approach to public debate would not be worth mentioning were it not for the fact that Strenski is one of the two editors of the journal *Religion* in which, like so many of my colleagues, I myself have published papers.

4. This was the topic of my own Ph.D. thesis, "Philosophical Issues in Agnosticism since Hume and Kant," King's College, London, 1983.

5. This is not to say that they invented the idea, but that however they derived it (perhaps from Machiavelli, Bodin, or Hobbes), they formulated it in such a way and at such a time that the idea grew to have historical significance. It married with the emergence of a concept of material nature favoured by the mechanical or corpuscular theory, with the radical distinction

between mind and extended matter, and with an increasingly reified separation between natural reason and supernatural faith.

6. I am using the French term *imaginaire* because it has different nuances to the English word 'imagination' (see the useful discussion by Collins, 1998:72–89). *Imaginaire* is linked to other related terms in critical history and sociology, such as 'ideology' in Marxist and Althusserian usage, and Durkheim's, Hubert's, and Mauss's 'représentation'. A collective act of the imagination is not 'imaginary' in the sense that it is 'unreal', for it constructs what a collectivity experiences as reality, is embedded in dominant discourses that totalize a world order, legitimates power, and has a significant degree of stability over historical time.

7. The expression Christian Faith could be used; however, I use the term Truth to emphasise the point that what lay outside of Christian faith was not knowledge in the modern sense of the binary opposition between faith and knowledge, since all *scientia* was encompassed and legitimated by Christian authority. The opposite of faith was superstition, which was irrational and barbarous.

8. A similar ambiguity can be found in Andrew Brown, *Church and Society in England, 1000–1500* (Basingstoke & New York: Palgrave Macmillan, 2003); see, for example, "The Social Dimension of Religion," 15.

9. I am using 'secular' as a noun ('the secular') in this formulation. It could also be expressed as the religion-secular society dichotomy. But 'secular' in the expression 'the religion-secular dichotomy' includes a range of discourses such as those on secular society, secular politics, secular science, and the secular academy which are all explicitly or implicitly separated from a different and distinct domain called 'religion', and therefore themselves tacitly non-religious.

10. See, for instance, his characterisation of "the manifestly silly or even barbaric forms" of ancient Egyptian polytheism as compared with the pure religion of monotheism; C. P. Tiele, *The Egyptian Religion*, available at http://www.revelation37.freeserve.co.uk/contents/ter.htm.

11. I have been considerably influenced by Louis Dumont's thinking, and while my own general position does not concur with his in every respect, I believe his variety of structuralism, developed in a comparative context in *Homo Hierarchicus* and *Essays on Individualism*, is much more interesting and powerful than has been given proper credit by some of his critics. Dumont is in the tradition of Durkheim and Mauss.

12. It will be obvious from my article that I was indebted to many other writers who had gone before me; but the impulse to write it came out of my own duties as a lecturer to teach Hinduism in a college of higher education where many of my students were training to be teachers, and the problems of conceptualisation of Hinduism which I encountered as a result. Since my argument was taken seriously at the time by several much better informed Indologists and anthropologists, that the debate out of which the article grew has been completely ignored by the chair of the Association of Religious Education Inspectors, Advisors and Consultants in the UK makes one wonder what the point of writing and publishing academic articles is.

13. God, by the way, is male gendered, as in most traditional Christian theologies.

14. See Tayob (2007:189), whose quote from Imam Hassan al-Banna conveys the same encompassing idea of Islam opposed to the idea of 'religion' as a mere private

faith separated from a secular state. Tayob describes Imam Hassan al-Banna as "one of the most influential leaders of contemporary Islam."

15. Ellen Knickermeyer's reportage appeared in similar forms in the *Washington Post* and in the "News Analysis" section of the *Japan Times* (1 September 2006).

16. The confusion of English-language terminology which our educators are busily involved in institutionalising in the school system can similarly be found reproduced in the English-language translation of the draft Iraq Constitution, available at http://news.bbc.co.uk/1/shared/bsp/hi/pdfs/24_08_05_constit.pdf#search=%22Iraq%20constitution%22.

17. The idea of 'civil religion', as developed by Bellah (1970:168–89), for example, could be read as recognition of this point. Bellah has to argue for the legitimacy of interpreting the stories of the founding of the colonies, the escape from persecution, the Revolution, as the myths of the civil religion; the Declaration of Independence and the Constitution as 'religious' documents or scriptures; and Washington as "the divinely appointed Moses" (1970:176). However, in Bellah's writing, it sometimes isn't clear if the idea of 'religion' in 'civil religion' is an analytical category by which to pursue an enquiry, or the object of enquiry itself. What he in effect does is to extend the sphere of 'religion' into 'the secular', to the extent that it becomes difficult to know what stands outside religion. The more that is included in religion, then the less is included in nonreligion or the secular, in which case the distinction becomes increasingly uninformative, irrelevant, and contradictory. Why not then adopt an idea of encompassing religion, in which Religion means Christian Truth, and there is no discrete, separated domain called 'the secular' in the sense of nonreligious? This immediately forces on us the contradictory paradigms both derived from our Christian history and present in our discourses, the idea of privatised religions being predominant.

18. See chapter 3 for an attempt to analytically separate the modern religion-secular binary from the sacred-profane with which it has been arguably confused.

19. It is of course possible that he is doing a kind of reverse essentialisation, by constructing 'Islam' in a way that is the complementary opposite of what he sees as a dominating and dogmatic secularism that wishes to marginalise and subordinate 'minorities'.

CHAPTER 2

1. See the arguments by Nancy Lindisfarne which connect critical and feminist practice and interdisciplinarity with the view from below in "Starting from Below: Fieldwork, Gender and Imperialism Now," the Richards Lecture, sponsored by the Centre for Cross-Culture Research on Women and Gender, Queen Elizabeth House, University of Oxford, 22 May 2002.

2. This concept continues in the modern British legislature: "The phrase 'Crown in Parliament' is used to describe the British legislature, which consists of the Sovereign, the House of Lords and the House of Commons." See http://www.royal.gov.uk/output/page4691.asp.

3. Christian Faith is equally valid, but I use Truth here because its opposite was, and for some still is, irrational superstition and therefore falseness. The idea that faith is in opposition to scientific knowledge is a modern one, whereas Christian Truth or

Faith encompassed knowledge. This profound change in the meaning of faith needs to be marked.

4. Yet it is instructive to note that the philosopher Mary Midgley has written a persuasive book entitled *Evolution as a Religion*, which might be thought to turn the tables on Dawkins and others who follow a similar set of assumptions and require some response. Some of Midgley's criticisms of Dawkins have been discussed in another critique by McGrath 2005:41–42 and 98–99.

5. Undoubtedly, there have been individual missionaries who have been anti-capitalist and anti-imperialist, and writers such as Brian Stanley have questioned the generalisation that missionaries supported capitalism. Stanley has also showed that historical evidence does not directly equate imperialism and capitalism in *The Bible and the Flag: Protestant Missions and British Imperialism in the Nineteenth and Twentieth Centuries* (Leicester: Apollos, 1990). My argument, however, is about what has been made conceivable by changes in the concept of 'religion', and in the accompanying changes in other categories. It is not so much a matter of individual intention as what implications different ideas about faith can have for a wider configuration of representations.

6. I am aware that some writings as early as the 1620s could arguably be said to have started separating issues such as production, consumption, trade, and exchange from morals, and thus to have begun the process of imagining a relatively independent economic domain much earlier. However, I question the extent to which this development could be thought of as a nonreligious, properly modern domain.

7. The historian John Bossy, in his persuasive article "Some Elementary Forms of Durkheim" (1982), said (and I gloss) that to attribute to the people we study the thing though they did not have the word is an invitation to misdescription.

8. Published before 1539, according to Williams (1967).

9. By 'Western', I refer to any scholar of whatever origin who is thinking, writing, and representing the world in European, and particularly English-language, categories.

10. Lincoln uses the term "quasi-religious" to characterise nationalism, viz., "the nation can acquire a quasi-religious aura of its own, becoming the moral, spiritual, and ritual community that calls forth the highest devotion of its members, imbuing their lives with meaning and purpose" (63). On the other hand, he uses the term "the religious nation" (65) mainly in distinction to the "secular state," though there may also be an implicit distinction with the minimalist secular nation in which religion has been rolled back and relatively marginalised. At any rate, whereas nations can be the object of religious devotion, the religious nation is one that has a different religion from nationalism, quite possibly a religion that would categorise worship of the nation as irreligious. I have discussed other examples of such tortuous attempts to preserve the validity of ideologically loaded categories as though they are neutral analytical ones in *The Ideology of Religious Studies* (2000).

11. He has four elaborate models on pages 66, 69, 70, and 72, which are designed to incorporate as many 'religious phenomena' as possible in a comprehensive, universalising scheme.

12. This is why Weber (1963:1) left the definitional problem till the end of his treatise; but the category is somehow pervasively present throughout. His assumption seems to have been that we know what we mean but we cannot know how to define it until we have exhaustively discussed as many of its known instances as possible.

CHAPTER 3

1. I am aware that I have slipped into the equation of religion with the term ritual. This is justified by common historiographical and anthropological usage. Whereas ritual is usually treated as symbolic activity associated with religion and the sacred, instrumental rational action is defined purely by a practical means-end relationship and is therefore secular or profane. In fact, these assumptions also need to be criticised.

2. Though see below in this chapter a discussion of the historian Phythian-Adams's distinction between the ritual and secular halves of the year, in a paper which acknowledges the influence of structural functional anthropology.

3. Durkheim has had an influence on this formulation. However, I am deliberately not bringing Durkheim into the picture here because his theory of religion, and his characterisation of the sacred-profane dichotomy, is complex and in some ways confused. For example, at some points, he talks as though the sacred and the profane are absolutely distinguished, and at other times as though they are merely relative in relation to context. This mars his otherwise fruitful approach.

4. There is a further nuance of 'profane' which is contrary to the sacred and the religious. This is important and I discuss it below.

5. I have given many examples of this in my book *The Ideology of Religious Studies* (2000), and more follow here.

6. McCutcheon (2001:63–64 and 181) has useful critical points to make about the terminology of 'the sacred', and it is my hope that my own approach here and in subsequent chapters will contribute some resolution of the issues he identifies.

7. This would explain resistance to the deconstruction of religion as a category by oppressed or subaltern peoples whose own language has no equivalent. A good example would be the Pueblo peoples of America (Wenger, 2005). The paradox is that, in order to protect their own traditions such as dance performances from obliteration by the state and by the dominant English-language categories, the Pueblo peoples have strategically claimed that their traditions are 'religious' and therefore ought to be protected by the rights guaranteed by the U.S. Constitution. Ironically,

> their use of the language of religious freedom introduced new elements of individualism that slightly changed Pueblo norms of ceremonial participation. In this way, Pueblo leaders' adaptation of the category of religion contributed to a subtle shift in the very tradition they were defending.
> (Wenger, 2005:4–5)

8. Some historians, perhaps many, would dispute this view, and I have in later chapters tended to follow the view that a society dominated by hierarchy, degree, and deference continued to dominate in England through the eighteenth and well into the nineteenth century, and that 'class' became a viable concept in the nineteenth century.

9. See future chapters for more on the commonweal or commonwealth.

10. I have walked through many neighbourhoods in Tokyo and Nagoya and been struck by a common composition. In a haphazard and indeed organic network of narrow streets you can find a mixture of small family houses; small blocks of flats which are little more than single rooms with bath and kitchen for single workers; occasionally a very large and expensive house (land prices in Nagoya and especially

Tokyo are high) belonging to a local politician or corporation (or perhaps even *yakusa*) boss; workshops of many different kinds such as engineering and machine main- tenance, electronic-engineering, or more traditional crafts such as carpentry or tatami- mat weaving; small family-run shops of various kinds; *izakaya* or small bar-restaurants; twenty-four-hour convenience stores; area distribution centres for, say, Honda motor- cycles, or automobile or builders' supplies; or *takkyūbin* (express home delivery ser- vices) which are organized by nationwide companies through a wide network of such local centres. Neighbourhood identities are strong, and indeed celebrate many local public festivals and parades organized by local committees. These have the effect of counteracting the tendency, so common in Western cities, of separate and essential- izing class identities and instead tend to strengthen local integrated hierarchies of social inclusion. Crime is very low, and there are hardly ever signs of public disorder. Not far away there may well be larger tenement blocks, wider streets, and larger stores. But even the newer tenement blocks tend to copy the pattern and characteristics set by the older communities.

11. There is an issue here, alluded to above, of whether 'class' and class interest is the best term, given its association with the much later nineteenth-century Marxist analysis; and also whether private property was sanctified in this era in the same sense of private property later argued by Locke, whose intention was to redefine many of these categories. But for my present purposes, I do not intend to pursue that issue further here.

12. It would be truer to say that these processes *constituted* what we reify as the Enlightenment.

13. Steven J. Sutcliffe (ed.), *Religion: Empirical Studies* (2004).

14. The interest of the city-country distinction may lie in its connections with the ancient distinction between, on the one hand, the city, civility, and Christianity, and, on the other hand, the country and paganism (*paganus*). However, Phythian-Adams does not explore this particular association (see chapter 4 in this book on civility and barbarity).

15. Readers may claim that no one seriously believes that religions are 'things'. On the contrary, in academic as much as non-academic discourse, religions are talked about as things, countables, and comparables, and even animated with lives of their own.

16. San Ildefonso Pueblo to the Secretary of the Interior, 16 January 1924, reel 9, John Collier Papers, Manuscripts Division, Sterling Library, Yale University, New Haven, Connecticut.

17. There is no entry in the index, and I cannot find a mention within the text.

18. I have discussed these issues in depth in my on-line discussion paper in ejcjs (*Electronic Journal of Contemporary Japanese Studies*), which is a critique of the con- struction of Japanese religion in the English language by Reader and others. See my paper and replies at www.japanesestudies.org.uk/discussionpapers/Fitzgerald.html.

CHAPTER 4

1. It should also be noted that one of the criteria of civility among nations, ac- cording to Euro-America, was the formation of a modern nation-state defined in terms of having a constitution that distinguished between religion and politics, church and

state. The Japanese Meiji Constitution of 1890 and the later Constitution of 1946 (which was written by the U.S. military) reflect this demand. But there is a serious theoretical issue about what constitutes 'religion' in Japan.

2. Jones refers to 'men' throughout as, by the way, do some women scholars of the early 1970s (see, for example, Hodgen, 1971), indicating that feminist critique had not yet bitten deeply into authorial consciousness.

3. Such a generalisation is only that. My own children are half Japanese and bilingual, and their mother and many of my friends clearly do not feel like that. But many cultures arguably have versions of prejudice against what the Japanese colloquially refer to as *gaijin*, or outside people. Historically, the Japanese also have their own internal barbarians, today usually referred to as the problem of *burakumin*, equivalent in some respects to the untouchables in India, 'pagans' within Christian Europe, and 'blacks' or more politely 'ethnic minorities' in contemporary Britain.

4. In a speech last year at the University of Regensburg, Pope Benedict XVI quoted a fourteenth-century Byzantine emperor, Manuel II Paleologus, "Show me just what Muhammad brought that was new and there you will find things only evil and inhuman, such as his command to spread by the sword the faith he preached." He went on to say that violent conversion to Islam was contrary to reason and thus "contrary to God's nature." Reported at http://ww4report.com/node/2480; see the full text at http://d.hatena.ne.jp/sumita-m/20060917/1158471763.

CHAPTER 5

1. It needs to be repeated that such a statement is not intended to marginalize the importance of non-Anglophone history. The consequences of what are known generically as the French enlightenment and revolution are not only as important in the articulation of modern categories generally, but were closely linked historically to the events in America. The same kind of thing can be said about the German and Scottish enlightenments. I have given my methodological justifications for confining this study to Anglophone history.

2. Skinner's own use of words such as religion, religions, secular, politics, and political seems uncritical and confusing in some sections of the same work.

3. J. Z. Smith makes a similar point in "Religion, Religions, Religious," and also connects the ordinary language usages that are still current with the sense of the Latin *religio* as "the careful performance of ritual obligations" (1998:269). See also the *OED* for such a meaning.

4. Bossy (1982) has written interestingly about the homologies between the biblical kin of the patriarchs and of Jesus and his family, the importance of kinship relations in the fifteenth century, and the post-Reformation changes in the way the holy family became more constricted.

CHAPTER 6

The work discussed in this chapter has also been summarised by Tomoko Masuzawa in *The Invention of World Religions* (Chicago & London: University of Chicago Press, 2005), 51–52, 56–57.

1. Thompson provides rich insights into the ambivalent role of Methodism in particular (see especially ch. 11, "The Transforming Power of the Cross," 385–440) in both promoting a 'religion' identified with equality in the next world and thus legitimating the status quo in this, and yet also swinging into a this-worldly, radical, often millenarian struggle for rights which bordered on the revolutionary and which was much influenced by Jacobinism and by writers as diverse as Tom Paine and William Blake.

2. It also suggests a different concept of the relation between soul and body. As with church and state, religion and politics, the soul and the body are fused together. We do not have here a Cartesian dualism, a dualism which the doctrine of bodily resurrection logically denies.

CHAPTER 7

1. See J. Z. Smith, "Religion, Religions, Religious" (1998).

2. This is the Stuart Charles VI of Scotland, who was also Charles I of England.

3. This is probably, approximately, modern Iraq, ironically and tragically now turned into hell.

4. Purchas only seems to use 'society' either in the sense of a specific example of human relationships (when, for example, a person enjoys the society of another or of a specific group) or in the sense of a company like the East India Company. It is not an abstract reified entity in Purchas. Probably 'company' is also shifting its nuance, from something like "we are a company of adventurers" who enjoy each other's companionship to a company in the formal and reified sense.

5. But there is no dominant discourse on 'political economy' in Adam Smith's eighteenth-century Scottish Enlightenment sense yet, and the idea of a separate theorised domain of economics is at least two centuries in the future.

6. J. Z. Smith says, " 'Religion' is an anthropological not a theological category" (1998:269). This does not seem to me to be true; it is both theological and anthropological. The anthropological discourses attempt to shed the theology much later, though how successful or convincing this has been is debatable.

7. There is a misnumbering in the original, there being two pages 242, plus 241.

CHAPTER 8

1. How 'nation' should be understood is problematic, and presumably it cannot be thought of as a modern nation yet (Gellner, 1983; Anderson, 1991; Hobsbawm, 1990). But patriotism is certainly on the agenda, and had been in the 16th century, perhaps only at this stage for an elite class centred on the sovereign.

2. I discuss Locke and especially Penn in more detail in the chapter on American constitutionalism.

3. I would prefer not to use the expression 'premodern' because it carries a nuance of 'backward' or 'undeveloped'. The only sense in which I would say that the seventeenth century was relatively undeveloped was technologically. I cannot see that the modern world has clearly improved in terms of moral sensibility or intellectual sophistication.

4. See Peter Lasslett's (1988) introduction to his edition of Locke's *Two Treatises of 1690* where he says of Sir Robert Filmer that he was "the author whose works had become the official exposition of the Royal and Tory view of the basis of governmental power" (32). Sommerville, in his introduction to Filmer's *Patriarcha*, for which he gives a publication date of 1680 (though it was presumably written earlier), says in his introduction that "it is difficult to understand Locke unless we understand Filmer, for Locke's Two Treatises were...a polemical refutation of Filmer's case. The first treatise is a detailed response to Sir Robert's arguments...He (Filmer) is arguably at his most interesting, and challenging, when he attacks democratic theory, and the notion that government rests on a contract between ruler and subject" (introduction, xxiv).

5. See Locke's *Two Treatises of Government: In the Former, The False Principles and Foundation of Sir Robert Filmer, And His Followers, are Detected and Overthrown. The Latter is an Essay concerning The True Original, Extent, and End of Civil-Government* (1689–1690).

6. I am grateful to the librarians at Friends House in Euston Road, London, for supplying me with the (unpublished) historical evidence for this and the historically various names that have been used.

7. This is not a general criticism of Keeble's useful notes. Also, Bunyan uses 'spirit' several times; but his various usages do not have the modern, generic nuance of 'spiritual' and 'spirituality' which we read back into earlier expression.

8. However, Douglas Dowd, in *Capitalism and Its Economics* (2000), 14–16, partially defends Smith from the aspects of capitalist economics that rendered it amoral like a natural process, and attributes the later development more to Ricardo and Bentham (2000:31–40).

CHAPTER 9

1. The importance of Scotland in this process deserves more attention than I have been able to give it here. The role of the Stuart kings, as kings both of Scotland and England, and the attempts of James VI in the early seventeenth century to impose on the Scottish Presbyterian church the episcopacy of England, may have raised the issue of church and state relations in a different but significant context, which I cannot explore here.

2. The entries for 'Secular Games' in the 1773 and 1815 editions of the *Encyclopaedia Britannica* indicate that these included everything that modern ideology would describe as 'religion' and 'religious'. Even by that late date, coterminous with what we have hypostasized as the Enlightenment, the editors of the Encyclopaedia found no reason to comment on any surprising change of meaning in 'secular'.

3. In *The Foundations of Modern Political Thought* (1978), Quentin Skinner has shown that the foundations for the modern idea of the state as an abstract entity distinct from the traditional commonwealth were laid in the sixteenth century, especially by French humanists in the context of "the Huguenot Revolution" (for example, volume 2, chapters 7, 8, 9). The idea of a distinct discipline of political theory of a modern kind also developed in England, no doubt under Italian and French influence. While I would not, and have no need to, contest Skinner's formidable learning or doubt his conclusions, my argument is that a modern concept of 'politics' could only

become clearly articulated when a modern concept of 'religion' also developed. The relationships between categories such as religion, church, secular, sacred, profane, and state were presumably all in a process of transition in the Huguenot wars, and my argument is that these need to be theorised simultaneously as far as possible if the meaning of any one of them is to be conveyed.

4. Again, developments in Scotland may turn out to have been crucial, at least later in the eighteenth century, and quite possibly ahead of England. John Simpson (in Barron, Edwards, and Storey [eds.] 1993:45–61) has indicated the later though important influence of Scottish Enlightenment writers such as Hutcheson, Hume, Thomas Reid, and John Millar on the Philadelphia Quaker James Wilson who in turn had a significant influence on the framing of the 1790 constitution.

5. See also Hoadly, *The Original and Institution of Civil Government Discussed* (1710), and *The Measures of Submission to the Civil Magistrates Consider'd* (1710).

6. There is no indication that, by "differs in every Country," Hoadly is referring to the vast range of non-Christian as well as Christian cultures that would be implied in contemporary discourse. He is referring to the different practices of Christians in different Christian countries, and his main target as a Protestant is the pope and Catholicism, which was typically characterised by Protestants as concerned with outward rituals and superstitions rather than with the inner truth of the heart.

7. A point made by Dworetz, *The Unvarnished Doctrine: Locke, Liberalism, and the American Revolution* (1990).

8. At least two of these meanings are found in Hoadly's sermon, viz., the external/outward as punctual exactness and a concern with the correct performance of rituals; and the temporal world as concerning human legislators.

9. This should not be exaggerated by our retrospectively projected assumptions about generic religion and religions. Religion still meant Christian Truth. According to Hough, the 1701 charter of government "secured liberty of conscience and worship, and all persons professing to believe in Jesus Christ might be chosen to serve the government in any capacity", and this charter "continued to be the organic law of the Province down to the American Revolution" (Hough, Vol. 2, 1872:216). Even as late as the 1838 revised state constitution belief in God and a future life were still required, though by this time it was not necessary to believe in the divine inspiration of the Bible.

10. I have not done justice to the early contribution of Scotland to the development of Dissent. Garry Wills, *Inventing America: Jefferson's Declaration of Independence* (New York: Vintage, 1979), has argued that the Scottish Enlightenment thinkers had more influence than Locke on Jefferson and the other leaders of the American Revolution.

11. For one thing, it complicates the doctrine of the resurrection of the body. These issues are far from dead. The professor in the history and philosophy of religion at King's College, London, in the 1970s when I was a student there, H. D. Lewis, was engaged in published debates with fellow philosophers of religion about the possibility of continued identity after death of a self conceived as a mental substance, and the problems of conceiving of an afterlife through the reconstitution of decayed bodies.

12. But more systematic research on this profoundly important aspect of colonial and postcolonial processes seems inevitable.

13. This is the aspect of the process on which Quentin Skinner has focused in his authoritative *The Foundations of Modern Political Thought* (1978).

14. This equation of 'secular' with 'neutral' rather than 'nonreligious' has also been made in an entirely different context by the distinguished historian of religion Michel Despland. In an article concerned with the establishment of the science of religion in France in the period 1830–1848, Despland contends:

> As Baubérot puts it, the July Monarchy is the best illustration of the first threshold of secularization: the State is secular in that it is neutral, i.e., it does not favour any one religion; but it is religious in that it believes in the social benefits of religion in general and favours the religions to which the citizens adhere. (Despland, 1998:34)

Despland is citing Jean Baubérot, *Vers un nouveau pacte laïque?* (1990). It is not clear what he means when he says that the state is secular, neutral, and also religious. There is the additional question of in what sense the French term *laïque* translates into the English word 'secular', which itself is historically ambiguous in meaning, and which at that time in history did not mean 'neutral' but usually referred to a status of priests.

15. I stress Anglophone, because I do not want to suggest that the Francophone or any other historical context is not as or perhaps even more important.

16. Though what her argument surely shows is that there is no "language of religion" as essentially distinct from that of 'politics'.

17. Michael Cahn refers to the "tendency of rhetoric to constitute itself as the agent of a pre-existent nature" and its art as lying in strategies whereby "rhetoric constitutes itself as a discipline and simultaneously makes us forget the rhetorical conditions of its disciplinary existence" (Cahn, 1993:79–80).

CHAPTER 10

1. It seems likely that they still are. See Fowler (2007) on recent media reportage of Afghan women wearing the burqua, for example.

2. Terence Ranger's paper to the Oxford Christian Mission Society (Ranger, 2005) reviews some of the contributions to (and disagreements about) a continuing debate among historians and anthropologists, such as J. D. Y. Peel (2000), John Comaroff and Jean Comaroff (1991 & 1997), and Elizabeth Elbourne (2002), concerning the relationship between Christian missions and capitalism, which there is no space here to review. I am grateful to Terence Ranger for sending me a copy of his paper and giving me permission to cite it. Ranger has not read this book.

Bibliography

Ackroyd, Peter, 1998. *The Life of Thomas More.* London: Chatto & Windus.

Ainsworth, Robert, 1740. *Thesaurus Linguae Latinae Compendiarus.* London.

al-Banna, Imam Hassan, 1978. *Message of the Teachings.* Trans. H. M. Najm. Durban: MYM Publications. (Originally published Islamic Party Publications [USA], 1977.)

Ambedkar, B. R., 1982 [1936]. *Annihilation of Caste.* Jalandhar: Bheem Patrika Publications.

Anderson, Benedict, 1991. *Imagined Communities: Reflections on the Origin and Spread of Nationalism.* London: Verso.

Asad, Talal, 1993. *Genealogies of Religion: Discipline and Reasons of Power in Christianity and Islam.* Baltimore, Md., & London: Johns Hopkins University Press.

Asad, Talal, 2003. *Formations of the Secular: Christianity, Islam, Modernity.* Stanford, Calif.: Stanford University Press.

Aspinall, A., & Anthony E. Smith (eds.). 1959. *English Historical Documents,* vol. 11, *1783–1832.* London & New York: Routledge.

Bailyn, Bernard, 1965. *Pamphlets of the American Revolution.* Cambridge, Mass.: Harvard University Press.

Bailyn, Bernard, 1967. *The Ideological Origins of the American Revolution.* Cambridge, Mass.: Harvard University Press.

Bailyn, Bernard, 2002. *American Constitutionalism: Atlantic Dimensions.* Caroline Robbins Lecture of 2001. London: Institute of United States Studies, University of London.

Balagangadhara, S. N., 1994. *"The Heathen in His Blindness": Asia, the West, and the Dynamic of Religion.* Leiden: E. J. Brill.

Bal, M., 2003. "Visual Essentialism and the Object of Visual Culture," *Journal of Visual Culture* 1, no. 2: 5–32.

Bari, Muhammad Abdul, 2006. "Islam, Social Enrichment and Social Justice", *The Edge*, [Magazine of the Economic and Social Research Council (ESRC)], 22 (July) http://www.esrcsocietytoday.ac.uk/ESRCInfoCentre/about/CI/CP/the_edge/issue22/.

Baumgarten, Martin, 1704 [1507]. "The Travels of Martin Baumgarten, a Nobleman of Germany, through Egypt, Arabia, Palestine and Syria, with the Author's Life done out of Latin", in A. Churchill & J. Churchill (eds.), *A Collection of Voyages and Travels*. London.

Baylor, Michael G. (ed.), 1991. *The Radical Reformation*. Cambridge: Cambridge University Press.

Bellah, Robert, 1991 [1970]. *Beyond Belief: Essays on Religion in a Post-Traditional World*. Berkeley and Los Angeles: University of California Press.

Berger, Peter, 1973. *The Social Reality of Religion*. Harmondsworth, UK: Penguin.

Biller, Peter, 1985. "Words and the Medieval Notion 'Religion'." *Journal of Ecclesiastical History* 36:351–69.

Bloch, Maurice, 1992. *Prey into Hunter: The Politics of Religious Experience* Cambridge: Cambridge University Press.

Bloom, Harold, 1994. *The Western Canon: The Books and Schools of All Ages*. New York: Harcourt Brace.

Blume, Anna, 2007. "Dialectics of Conversion: Las Casas and Maya Colonial and Post-colonial *Congregación*." In Timothy Fitzgerald (ed.), *Religion and the Secular: Historical and Colonial Formations*. London: Equinox.

Bossy, John, 1982. "Some Elementary Forms of Durkheim," *Past and Present* 95:3–18.

Bossy, John, 1985. *Christianity in the West, 1400–1700*. Oxford: Oxford University Press.

Breckenridge, Carol A., & Peter Van der Veer (eds.), 1993. *Orientalism and the Postcolonial Predicament: Perspectives on South Asia*. Philadelphia: University of Pennsylvania Press.

Browning, Andrew (ed.), 1953. *English Historical Documents*, vol. 8, *1660—1714*. London & New York: Routledge.

Bunyan, John, 1984 [1678, 1684]. *The Pilgrim's Progress*, ed. N. H. Keeble. Oxford: Oxford University Press.

Cahn, Michael, 1993. "The Rhetoric of Rhetoric: Six Tropes of Disciplinary Self-Constitution." In R. H. Roberts & J. M. M. Good (eds.), *The Recovery of Rhetoric: Persuasive Discourse and Disciplinarity in the Human Sciences*. Charlottesville & London: University of Virginia Press, 79–80.

Cannadine, David, 2001. *Ornamentalism: How the British Saw Their Empire*. Oxford: Oxford University Press.

Carrette, J., & R. King. 2004. *Selling Spirituality: The Silent Takeover of Religion*. London: Routledge.

Catholic Encyclopedia. Available at http://www.newadvent.org/cathen/01498a.htm.

Cavanaugh, William T., 1995. "'A Fire Strong Enough to Consume the House': The Wars of Religion and the Rise of the State," *Modern Theology* 11:397–420.

Cavanaugh, William T., 2007. "Colonialism and the Myth of Religious Violence." In Timothy Fitzgerald (ed.), *Religion and the Secular: Historical and Colonial Formations*. London: Equinox.

Chappell, V. C. (ed.), 1968. *Hume: A Collection of Critical Essays*. London & Basingstoke: Macmillan.

Chidester, David, 1996. *Savage Systems: Colonialism and Comparative Religion in Southern Africa.* Charlottesville: University of Virginia Press.

Chidester, David, 2007. "Imperial Inventions of Religion in Colonial Southern Africa." In Timothy Fitzgerald (ed.), *Religion and the Secular: Historical and Colonial Formations.* London: Equinox.

Chillingworth, William, 1638. *The Religion of Protestants: A Safe Way to Salvation; or, An Answer to a Book entitled Mercy and Truth, Or, Charity Maintain'd by Catholiques, which pretends to prove the Contrary.* Oxford.

Churchill, A., & J. Churchill (eds.), 1704. *A Collection of Voyages and Travels.* London.

Clark, P., & P. Slack (eds.), 1972. *Crisis and Order in English Towns 1500–1700: Essays in Urban History.* London: Routledge and Kegan Paul.

Clarke, Sir George, 1955. *The Later Stuarts 1660–1714,* 2nd ed. Oxford: Clarendon.

Columbia Encyclopedia, 2004, 6th ed. New York: Columbia University Press.

Collins, Steven, 1998. *Nirvana and Other Buddhist Felicities,* Cambridge: Cambridge University Press.

Comaroff, John, & Jean Comaroff, 1991 & 1997. *Of Revelation and Revolution,* 2 vols. Chicago: University of Chicago Press.

Cooper, G., 1988. "North American Traditional Religion." In S. R. Sutherland et al. (eds.), *The World's Religions.* London: Routledge.

Cooper, Michael, 1974. *Rodrigues the Interpreter: An Early Jesuit in Japan and China.* New York & Tokyo: Weatherhill.

Cox, James, 1995. "Ancestors, The Sacred and God: Reflections on the Meaning of the Sacred in Zimbabwean Death Rituals", *Religion,* 25, 339–55.

Cox, James, 2006. *A Guide to the Phenomenology of Religion: Key Figures, Formative Influences and Subsequent Debates.* London & New York: Continuum.

Cox, James, 2007. "The Alaskan Native Claims Settlement Act in the Context of the Colonization of the Indigenous People of Alaska." In Timothy Fitzgerald (ed.), *Religion and the Secular: Historical and Colonial Formations.* London: Equinox.

Cross, F. L., 1958. *Dictionary of the Christian Church.* Oxford: Oxford University Press.

Dawkins, Richard, 2006. *The God Delusion,* London: Bantam Press.

Despland, Michel, 1998. "Sciences of Religion in France during the July Monarchy [1830–1848]." In Arie L. Molendijk & Peter Pels (eds.), *Religion in the Making: The Emergence of the Sciences of Religion.* Leiden: Brill.

Despland, Michel, & Gérard Vallée (eds.), 1992. *Religion in History: The Word, the Idea, the Reality; La Religion dans l'histoire: Le Mot, l'idée, la réalité.* Waterloo, Canada: Wilfrid Laurier University Press.

Dowd, Douglas, 2000. *Capitalism and Its Economics: A Critical History.* London & Sterling: Pluto.

Dubuisson, Daniel, 1998. *L'Occident et la religion: mythes, science et idéologie.* Brussels: Editions Complexe. Trans. Sayers, William, 2003, as *The Western Construction of Religion: Myths, Knowledge and Ideology.* Baltimore, Md.: Johns Hopkins University Press.

Duke, Lynne, 2006. "Rebuilding the Cultural Base: The Voice of Kenya Practises the 'Aesthetics of Resistance' in His Mother Tongue", *Guardian Weekly,* October 6–12, 30.

Dumont, Louis, 1980. *Homo Hierarchicus: The Caste System and its Implications [Complete Revised Edition]*. Chicago & London: University of Chicago Press

Dumont, Louis, 1986. *Essays on Individualism*. Chicago & London: University of Chicago Press.

Dunn, John, 1969. "The Politics of Locke in England and America in the 18th Century." In John Yolton (ed.), *John Locke: Problems and Perspectives*. Cambridge: Cambridge University Press.

Durkheim, Emile, 2001. *The Elementary Forms of the Religious Life*, trans. Carol Cosman, ed. Mark S. Cladis. Oxford: Oxford University Press.

Dworetz, Steven M., 1990. *The Unvarnished Doctrine: Locke, Liberalism, and the American Revolution*. Durham, N.C., & London: Duke University Press.

Elbourne, Elizabeth, 2002. *Blood Ground: Colonialism, Missions, and the Contest for Christianity, 1799–1853*. Montreal: McGill-Queen's University Press.

Encyclopaedia Britannica, 1773. Edinburgh.

Encyclopaedia Britannica, 1815. Edinburgh.

Filmer, Sir Robert, 1991 [1680?]. *Patriarcha and Other Writings*, ed. Johann P. Sommerville. Cambridge: Cambridge University Press.

Fitzgerald, Timothy, 1999. "Hinduism and the World Religion Fallacy", *Religion* 20:101–118.

Fitzgerald, Timothy, 2000. *The Ideology of Religious Studies*. New York & Oxford: Oxford University Press.

Fitzgerald, Timothy, 2003a. "Playing Language Games and Performing Rituals: Religious Studies as Ideological State Apparatus," *Method & Theory in the Study of Religion* 15, no. 3.

Fitzgerald, Timothy, 2003b. " 'Religion' and 'the Secular' in Japan: Problems in History, Social Anthropology and the Study of Religion," Paper No. 3, *Electronic Journal of Contemporary Japanese Studies*. http://www.japanesestudies.org.uk/discussionpapers/Fitzgerald.html

Fitzgerald, Timothy, 2006. "Bruce Lincoln's Theses on Method: Antitheses," *Method & Theory in the Study of Religion* 18, no. 4:392–423.

Fitzgerald, Timothy, ed., 2007. *Religion and the Secular: Historical and Colonial Formations*. London: Equinox.

Flood, Gavin, 1999. *Beyond Phenomenology: Rethinking the Study of Religion*. London & New York: Cassell.

Forrester, Duncan B., 1963. "Luther and Calvin." In Leo Strauss & Joseph Cropsey (eds.), *History of Political Philosophy*. Chicago: Rand McNally/University of Chicago Press, 277–313.

Fowler, Corinne, 2007. "Journalists in Feminist Clothing: Men and Women Reporting Afghan Women during Operation Enduring Freedom, 2001," *Journal of International Feminist and Women's Studies* (Spring).

Freeman, Charles. 2003. *The Closing of the Western Mind: The Rise of Faith and the Fall of Reason*. London: Pimlico.

Gatens, Moira, 1997. "Corporeal Representation in/and the Body Politic." In Kate Conboy, Nadina Medina, & Sarah Stanbury (eds.), *Writing on the Body: Female Embodiment and Feminist Theory*. New York: Columbia University Press.

Geertz, Armin, 2004. "Religion and Community in Indigenous Contexts." In Steven Sutcliffe (ed.), *Religion: Empirical Studies*. Aldershot: Ashgate.

Geisert, Paul and Futrell, Mynga, 2002. "Untying a Terminology Tangle—Secular vs. Nonreligious", *Teaching about Religion and Worldview Diversity* http://www.teachingaboutreligion.org/WhitePapers/untying_tangle.htm

Gellner, Ernest, 1983. *Nations and Nationalism*. Ithaca, N.Y.: Cornell University Press.

Goldie, Mark, 1987. "The Civil Religion of James Harrington." In Anthony Pagden (ed.), *The Languages of Political Theory in Early Modern Europe*. Cambridge: Cambridge University Press.

Gombrich, Richard, 1988. *Theravada Buddhism: A Social History from Ancient Benares to Modern Colombo*. London & New York: Routledge.

Greenfeld, Liah, 1992. *Nationalism: Five Roads to Modernity*. Cambridge, Mass., & London: Harvard University Press.

Gwatkin, H. M., 1908. "Religious Toleration in England." In *Cambridge Modern History*, vol. V. Cambridge: Cambridge University Press, 324–37.

Gwatkin, H. M., 1917. *Church and State to the Death of Queen Anne*. London: Longmans, Green.

Hakluyt, Richard, 1809. *Hakluyt's Collection of Early Voyages, Traffiques, and Discoveries of the English Nation: A New Edition, with Additions*. 5 vols. London. This is a republication of Hakluyt's 1599 *The Principal Navigations, Voyages, Traffiques, and Discoveries of the English Nation, Made by Sea or Overland to the Remote and Farthest Distant Quarters of the Earth, at any Time within the Compasse of These 1600 Yeres: Divided into Three Severall Volumes, according to the Positions of the Regions, Whereunto They Were Directed*. 3 vols. London.

Hansen H. B., & Michael Twaddle (eds.), 2002. *Christian Missionaries and the State in the Third World*. Oxford: James Curry/Athens: University of Ohio Press.

Harrison, Peter, 1990. *Religion and the Religions in the English Enlightenment*. Cambridge: Cambridge University Press.

Hartz, Louis, 1955. *The Liberal Tradition in America*. New York: Harcourt, Brace and World.

Hervieu-Léger, Danièle, 2000. *Religion as a Chain of Memory*, trans. S. Lee. Oxford: Polity.

Hill, Christopher, 1972. *The World Turned Upside Down: Radical Ideas during the English Revolution*. Harmondsworth: Penguin.

Hill, Christopher, 1980. *The Century of Revolution*, 2nd ed. London & New York: Routledge.

Hoadly, Benjamin, 1710. *The Measures of Submission to the Civil Magistrate Consider'd. In a Defence of the Doctrine. Deliver'd in a Sermon Preach'd before the Rt. Hon. the Lord-Mayor, Aldermen, and Citizens of London, Sept. 29, 1705*. London.

Hoadly, Benjamin, 1710. *The original and Institution of Civil Government Discuss'd, viz. I. An Examination of the Patriarchal Scheme of Government. II. A Defence of Mr. Hooker's Judgment, Etc, against the objections of several later Writers*. London, 2nd ed.

Hoadly, Benjamin, 1718. *A Sermon Preach'd before the King, at the Royal Chapel at St. James's, on Sunday March 31, 1717*, 6th ed. London.

Hobsbawm, E. J., 1990. *Nations and Nationalism since 1780: Programme, Myth, Reality.* Cambridge: Cambridge University Press, 1990.

Hodgen, Margaret, 1971. *Early Anthropology in the Sixteenth and Seventeenth Centuries.* Philadelphia: University of Pennsylvania Press.

Hookyas, R., 1972. *Religion and the Rise of Modern Science.* Edinburgh & London: Scottish Academic Press.

Horn, D. B., & Mary Ransome (eds.), 1957. *English Historical Documents,* vol. 10, *1714–1783.* London: Eyre & Spottiswoode.

Hough, Franklin B. (ed.), 1872. *American Constitutions: Comprising the Constitution of Each State in the Union, and the United States, with the Declaration of Independence and Articles of Confederation,* 2 vols. Albany, N.Y.: Weed, Parsons.

Hume, David, 1957 [1757, 1777]. *The Natural History of Religion,* ed. H. E. Root. Stanford, Calif.: Stanford University Press.

I'Anson, John, & Alison Jasper, 2006. "New Lines of Flight? Negotiating Religions and Cultures in Gendered Educational Spaces," *Discourse* 5, no. 2 (Spring):81.

Inden, Ronald, 1990. *Imagining India.* Oxford: Blackwell.

Isomae, Jun'ichi, 2000. "Kindai nihon ni okeru 'shūkyō' gainen no keisei katei," *Nihon joshi daigaku sōgō kenkyūjō nyūsu* 8 (March):20–25 [The formative process of the category 'shūkyō' in modern Japan, *Japan Women's University Research Institute Newsletter*].

Isomae, Jun'ichi, 2007. "State Shinto, Westernization, and the Concept of Religion in Japan." In Timothy Fitzgerald (ed.), *Religion and the Secular: Historical and Colonial Formations.* London: Equinox.

Jefferson, Thomas, 1787. *Notes on the State of Virginia.* Microfiche, National Library of Scotland. Edinburgh.

Jensen, Merrill (ed.), 1955. *English Historical Documents,* vol. 9, *American Colonial Documents to 1776.* London: Eyre and Spottiswoode.

Johnson, Chalmers, 1995. *Japan: Who Governs? The Rise of the Developmental State.* London: Norton.

Jones, W. R., 1971. "The Image of the Barbarian in Medieval Europe." In Anthony Pagden (ed.), *Facing Each Other: The World's Perception of Europe and Europe's Perception of the World.* Aldershot: Ashgate Variorum (originally published in *Comparative Studies in Society and History* 13:376–407).

King, Richard, 1999. *Orientalism and Religion: Postcolonial Theory, India, and the 'Mystic East'.* London & New York: Routledge.

Kinney, A. F. (ed.), 1975. *Homily on Obedience* (1559), in *Elizabethan Backgrounds: Historical Documents of the Age of Elizabeth,* vol. 1. Hamden, Conn.: Archon.

Kirby, Ethyn Williams, 1935. "The Quakers' Efforts to Secure Civil and Religious Liberty, 1660–1696," *Journal of Modern History* 7:401–21.

Kramnick, Isaac (ed.), 1987. *James Madison, Alexander Hamilton and John Jay: The Federalist Papers.* Harmondsworth: Penguin.

Kristensen, William Brede, 2006. "The Meaning of Religion: Lectures in the Phenomenology of Religion." In Ivan Strenski (ed.), *Thinking about Religion: A Reader.* Cambridge: Blackwell, 115–19.

Kuchta, David, 2002. *The Three-Piece Suit and Modern Masculinity: England, 1550–1850.* Berkeley: University of California Press.

Lincoln, Bruce, 1996. "Theses on Method," *Method & Theory in the Study of Religion* 8, no. 3:225–27.

Lincoln, Bruce, 2003. *Holy Terrors: Thinking about Religion after September 11*. Chicago: University of Chicago Press.

Lindisfarne, Nancy, 2002. "Starting from Below: Fieldwork, Gender and Imperialism," Audrey Richards Lecture for 2002, *Critique of Anthropology* 22, no. 4:403–23.

Lloyd, C. (ed.) 1825. *Formularies of Faith Put Forth by Authority during the Reign of Henry VIII*. Oxford: Clarendon. [Containing: "Preface of the Editor"; "Preface of King Henry VIII"; Articles About Religion (1536)"; The Institution of a Christian Man (1537)"; "A Necessary Doctrine and Erudition for any Christian Man (1543)"]

Lloyd, Genevieve, 1990. "Augustine & Aquinas." In Ann Loades (ed.), *Feminist Theology: A Reader*. London: SPCK.

Locke, John, 1689. *A Letter concerning Toleration*, 2nd ed. London.

Locke, John, 1988 [1690]. *Two Treatises of Government*. In Peter Laslett (ed.), *Cambridge Texts in the History of Political Thought*. Cambridge: Cambridge University Press.

Logan, F. D., 1968. *Excommunication and the Secular Arm in Medieval England: A Study in Legal Procedure from the 13th to the 16th Century*. Toronto: Pontifical Institute of Medieval Studies.

Longley P., and Kronenberg, S. (eds.), 1973. *Photopak 3: Discovering Religion in Festivals*. Guildford and London: Lutterworth Educational.

Macfie, A. L. (ed.), *Orientalism: A Reader*. Edinburgh: Edinburgh University Press.

Macpherson, C. B., 1962. *The Political Theory of Possessive Individualism*. Oxford: Oxford University Press.

Maier, Pauline, 1998. *American Scripture: Making the Declaration of Independence*. New York: Knopf.

Masuzawa, Tomoko, 2005. *The Invention of World Religions*. Chicago & London: University of Chicago Press.

Mayer, T. F. (ed.), 1989. *Thomas Starkey, A Dialogue between Pole and Lupset*. Camden Fourth Series, Vol. 37. London: Offices of the Royal Historical Society, University College, London.

McCoy, Richard C., 2002. *Alterations of State: Sacred Kingship in the English Reformation*. New York: Columbia University Press.

McCutcheon, Russell T., 1997. *Manufacturing Religion: The Discourse on Sui Generis Religion and the Politics of Nostalgia*. New York & Oxford: Oxford University Press.

McCutcheon, Russell T., 2001. *Critics Not Caretakers: Redescribing the Public Study of Religion*. New York: State University of New York Press.

McFie, A. L., 2000. *Orientalism: A Reader*. Edinburgh: Edinburgh University Press.

McGrath, Alister, 2005. *Dawkins' God: Genes, Memes, and the Meaning of Life*. Oxford: Blackwell.

Midgley, Mary, 2002 [1985]. *Evolution as a Religion*. London & New York: Routledge.

Miller, Joyce, 2006. "Lets Talk about Religion and Keep Teaching It," *The Edge* [Magazine of the Economic and Social Research Council (ESRC)], 22 (July) http://www.esrcsocietytoday.ac.uk/ESRCInfoCentre/about/CI/CP/the_edge/issue22/.

Mizuta, Hiroshi, 2003. "Adam Smith in Japan." In Tatsuya Sakamoto & Hideo Tanaka (eds.), *The Rise of Political Economy in the Scottish Enlightenment*. London & New York: Routledge.

Molendijk, Arie L., & Peter Pels (eds.), 1998. *Religion in the Making: The Emergence of the Sciences of Religion*. Leiden: Brill.

Muller, Max, 1893 [1870]. *Introduction to the Science of Religion*. London: Longmans, Green.

Mullins, Mark, Susumu Shimazono, & Paul L. Swanson (eds.), 1993. *Religion and Society in Modern Japan*. Berkeley, Calif.: Asian Humanities Press.

Nicolson, Colin, 2001. *The "Infamas Govener": Francis Bernard and the Origins of the American Revolution*. Boston: Northeastern University Press.

Noxon, James, 1968. "Hume's Agnosticism." In V. C. Chappell (ed.), *Hume: A Collection of Critical Essays*. London & Basingstoke: Macmillan, 361–83.

O'Gorman, Frank, 1997. *The Long Eighteenth Century: British Political and Social History 1688–1832*. London: Arnold.

Pagden, Anthony, 1982. *The Fall of Natural Man: The American Indian and the Origins of Comparative Ethnology*. Cambridge: Cambridge University Press.

Pagden, Anthony, 1995. *Lords of All the World: Ideologies of Empire in Spain, Britain and France, c. 1500–1800*. New Haven, Conn., & London: Yale University Press.

Pagden, Anthony (ed.), 1987. *The Languages of Political Theory in Early Modern Europe*. Cambridge: Cambridge University Press.

Pangle, Thomas L., 1988. *The Spirit of Modern Republicanism: The Moral Vision of the American Founders and the Philosophy of Locke*. Chicago: University of Chicago Press.

Parry, J. H., 1940. *The Spanish Theory of Empire in the Sixteenth Century*. Cambridge: Cambridge University Press.

Peel, J. D. Y., 2000. *Religious Encounter and the Making of the Yoruba*. Bloomington: Indiana University Press.

Penn, William, 1680. *The Great Question to be Considered by the King, and this approaching Parliament, briefly proposed, and modestly discussed: (to wit) How far Religion is concerned in Policy or Civil Government, and Policy in Religion? With an Essay rightly to distinguish these great interests, upon the Disquisition of which a sufficient Basis is proposed for the firm Settlement of these Nations, to the Most probable satisfaction of the Several Interests and Parties therein. By one who desires to give unto Caesar the things that are Caesar's, and to God the things that are God's*. Microfiche found in National Library of Scotland, Edinburgh.

Penn, William, 1694. *A Brief Account of the Rise and Progress of the People called Quakers in which their fundamental Principles, Doctrines, Worship, Ministry and Discipline are Plainly Declared to Prevent the Mistakes and Perversions that Ignorance and Prejudice may make to abuse the Credulous . . .* London.

Peterson, Derek, & Darren Walhof (eds.), 2002. *The Invention of Religion: Rethinking Belief in Politics and History*. New Brunswick, N.J.: Rutgers University Press.

Phythian-Adams, Charles, 1972. "Ceremony and the Citizen: The Communal Year at Coventry 1450–1550." In Peter Clark & Paul Slack (eds.), *Crisis and Order in English Towns 1500–1700: Essays in Urban History*. London: Routledge and Kegan Paul, 57–85.

Plattner, Stuart (ed.), 1989. *Economic Anthropology*. Stanford, Calif.: Stanford University Press.

Pocock, J. G. A., 1972. "Virtue and Commerce in the 18th Century," *Journal of Interdisciplinary History* 3 (Summer):119–34.

Pocock, J. G. A., 1975. *The Machiavellian Moment*. Princeton, N.J.: Princeton University Press.

Pope Benedict XVI, "*Faith, Reason* and the University: *Memories* and Reflections"; speech given at the University of Regensburg in Germany on Friday, September 15, 2006. The full text is available at: http://d.hatena.ne.jp/sumita-m/20060917/1158471763.

Purchas, Samuel, 1625. *Hakluytus Posthumus or Purchas his Pilgrimes, contayning a History of the World in Sea Voyages and Lande Travells, by Englishmen and others,* 4 vols. London.

Purchas, Samuel, 1626 [1613]. *Purchas, His Pilgrimage; or, Relations of the World and the Religions Observed in All Ages.* London.

Ranger, T. O., 1988. "African Traditional Religion", in S. R. Sutherland et al. (eds.), *The World's Religions.* London: Routledge.

Ranger, Terence, 2005. "Christian Missions, Capitalism and Empire: The State of the Debate," paper presented at the Oxford Christian Mission Society, 21 June.

Richards, Glyn, 1999. "Religion and Religions", in C. Lamb and Dan Cohn-Sherbok (eds.), *The Future of Religion: Postmodern Perspectives:Essays in Honour of Ninian Smart.* London: Middlesex University Press, 16–25.

Riddle, J. A., & T. K. Arnold, 1847. *A Copious and Critical English-Latin Lexicon.* London.

Roberts, R., & J. M. M. Good (eds.), 1993. *The Recovery of Rhetoric: Persuasive Discourse and Disciplinarity in the Human Sciences.* Charlottesville & London: University of Virginia Press.

Roe, Sir Thomas, 1704. "Embassador from his majestie King James the First of England, to Ichan Guire, the Mighty Emperor of India, Commonly call'd the Great Mogul. Containing an Account of his Voyage to that Country, and his Observations there." In A. Churchill & J. Churchill (eds.), *A Collection of Voyages and Travels.* London, 757–813.

Said, Edward, 1991 [1978]. *Orientalism: Western Conceptions of the Orient.* London: Penguin.

Sakamoto, Tatsuya, & Hideo Tanaka (eds.), 2003. *The Rise of Political Economy in the Scottish Enlightenment.* London & New York: Routledge.

Schapera, Isaac (ed.), 1963. "Introduction" to David Livingstone, *African Journals 1853–1856,* 2 vols. London: Chatto & Windus.

Searle-Chatterjee, Mary, 2000. "'World Religions' and 'Ethnic Groups': Do These Paradigms Lend Themselves to the Cause of Hindu Nationalism?" *Ethnic and Racial Studies* 23, no. 3:497–515.

Segal, Robert, 1994. "Hume's *Natural History of Religion* and the Beginning of the Social Scientific Study of Religion", *Religion* 24, no. 3:225–34.

Simpson, D. P., 1977. *Cassell's New Latin-English English-Latin Dictionary,* 5th ed. London: Cassell.

Simpson, John, 1993. "James Wilson and the Making of Constitutions", in Thomas J. Barron, Owen Dudley Edwards, & Patricia J. Storey (eds.), *Constitutions and National Identity.* Edinburgh: Quadriga, 45–61.

Skinner, Q., 1978. *The Foundations of Modern Political Thought*, vol. 2, *The Age of Reformation*. Cambridge: Cambridge University Press.

Smith, Adam, 1993 [1776]. *An Inquiry into the Nature and Causes of the Wealth of Nations*, ed. Kathryn Sutherland. Oxford: Oxford University Press.

Smith, J. Z., 1982. *Imagining Religion: From Babylon to Jonestown*. Chicago: University of Chicago Press.

Smith, J. Z., 1998. "Religion, Religions, Religious." In Mark C. Taylor (ed.), *Critical Terms for Religious Studies*. Chicago: University of Chicago Press, 269–84.

Smith, W. C., 1978 [1962]. *The Meaning and End of Religion: A Revolutionary Approach to the Great Religious Traditions*. London: SPCK.

Soderlund, Jean R. (ed.), 1983. *William Penn and the Founding of Pennsylvania: A Documentary History*. Philadelphia: University of Pennsylvania Press.

Southern, R. W., 1970. *Western Society and the Church in the Middle Ages*. Harmondsworth: Penguin.

Stanley, Brian, 1990. *The Bible and the Flag: Protestant Missions and British Imperialism in the Nineteenth and Twentieth Centuries*. Leicester: Apollos.

Starkey, Thomas, 1989 [1539?]. "A Dialogue between Pole and Lupset." In T. F. Mayer (ed.), *Camden Fourth Series*, vol. 37. London: Offices of the Royal Historical Society, University College.

Strauss, Leo, & Cropsey, Joseph (eds.), 1963. *History of Political Philosophy*. Chicago: Rand McNally/University of Chicago Press.

Strenski, Ivan, 1998. "On 'Religion' and Its Despisers", in Thomas A. Idinopulos and Brian C. Wilson (eds.), *What Is Religion? Origins, Definitions, and Explanations*. Leiden: E. J. Brill, 113–132.

Sutcliffe, Steven J. (ed.), 2004. *Religion: Empirical Studies*. Aldershot: Ashgate.

Swanson, R. N., 1989. *Church and Society in Late Medieval England*. Cambridge: Blackwell.

Swanwick, John, 1786. *Considerations on an Act of the legislature of Virginia, entitled, An Act for the Establishment of Religious Freedom. By a Citizen of Philadelphia.* Philadelphia.

Tanner, J. R., 1962 [1928]. *English Constitutional Conflicts of the Seventeenth Century*. Cambridge: Cambridge University Press.

Tawney, R. H., 1962 [1926]. *Religion and the Rise of Capitalism*. Gloucester, Mass.: Peter Smith.

Tayob, Abdulkader Ismail, 2007. "Religion in Modern Islamic Thought and Practice." In T. Fitzgerald (ed.), *Religion and the Secular: Historical and Colonial Formations*. London: Equinox.

Taylor, Mark C., 1995. "Rhizonic Fields of Interstanding", *Tekhnema* 2:24–36.

Taylor, Mark C., 1998. *Critical Terms for Religious Studies*. Chicago: University of Chicago Press.

Thompson, E. P., 1991 [1968]. *History of the English Working Class*. Harmondsworth: Penguin.

Tiele, C. P., 1890. "The Egyptian Religion," available at http://www.revelation37.freeserve.co.uk/contents/ter.htm.

Tiele, C. P., 1897. *Elements of the Science of Religion*, part I: *Morphological*, part II: *Ontological*. Edinburgh: Blackwood.

Tillyard, E. M. W., 1998 [1943]. *The Elizabethan World Picture*. London: Pimlico.

Turner, Mary, 2002. "The Colonial State, Religion and the Control of Labour in Jamaica." In H. B. Hansen & Michael Twaddle (eds.), *Christian Missionaries and the State in the Third World*. Oxford: James Curry/Athens: University of Ohio Press, 17–29.

Tyndale, William, 1967 [1848]. "The Parable of the Wicked Mammon." In H. Walter (ed.), *Parker Society*, 100–103, reprinted in C. H. Williams (ed.), *English Historical Documents*, vol. 5. London: Eyre and Spottiswoode, 292–93.

Warburton, W., Lord Bishop of Gloucester, 1766 [1748]. *The Alliance between Church and State; or, the Necessity and Equity of an Established Religion and a Test Law Demonstrated in Three Books*, 4th ed. London.

Weber, Max, 1963 [English translation by Ephraim Fischoff based on 4th edition of 1956; originally published in German in 1922], *The Sociology of Religion*, Boston: Beacon Press

Wenger, Tisa, 2005. " 'We Are Guaranteed Freedom': Pueblo Indians and the Category of Religion in the 1920's", *History of Religions* 45, no. 2:89–113.

Whitehead, A. N., 1979. *Process and Reality*. New York: Free Press.

Williams, C. H. (ed.), 1967. *English Historical Documents*, vol. 5, 1485–1558. London: Eyre and Spottiswoode.

Wills, Garry, 1979. *Inventing America: Jefferson's Declaration of Independence*. New York: Vintage

Wilson, Bryan, 1990. "New Images of Christian Community." In John McManners (ed.), *The Oxford History of Christianity*. Oxford & New York: Oxford University Press.

Wolf, Eric R., 1997 [1982]. *Europe and the People without History*. Berkeley & London: University of California Press.

Zavos, John, 2000. *The Emergence of Hindu Nationalism in India*. New Delhi: Oxford University Press.

Zavos, John, 2007. "Understanding Politics through Performance in Colonial and Postcolonial India." In T. Fitzgerald (ed.), *Religion and the Secular: Historical and Colonial Formations*. London: Equinox, 135–152.

Zeeveld, W. G., 1948. *Foundations of Tudor Policy*. Cambridge, Mass.: Harvard University Press.

Index